The Journal Book

The Journal Book

Edited by
TOBY FULWILER

BOYNTON/COOK PUBLISHERS
HEINEMANN
PORTSMOUTH, NH

BOYNTON/COOK PUBLISHERS
A Division of
HEINEMANN EDUCATIONAL BOOKS, INC.
361 Hanover Street
Portsmouth, NH 03801
Offices and agents throughout the world

90 91 6 5 4

Library of Congress Cataloging-in-Publication Data

The Journal book.

    1. English language—Rhetoric—Study and teaching.
2. English language—Composition and exercises—Study and teaching. 3. Diaries—Authorship—Study and teaching. 4. Interdisciplinary approach in education.
1. Fulwiler, Toby, 1942-
PE1404.J67 1987   808'.042'07   87-9415
ISBN 0-86709-175-4

Printed in the United States of America

Acknowledgments

Fulwiler, Megan. "Still Writing and Learning, Grade Ten." *Language Arts*, Vol. 63, No. 8, December, 1986. Reprinted by permission of Megan Fulwiler and the National Council of Teachers of English.
Fulwiler, Toby. "Writing and Learning, Grade Three." *Language Arts*, Vol. 62, No. 1, January, 1985. Reprinted by permission of Toby Fulwiler and the National Council of Teachers of English.
Medway, Peter. Excerpts from *Finding a Language*. Published by Writers and Readers Cooperative in association with Chameleon Books. © 1980 by Peter Medway and reprinted by his permission.
Stillman, Peter. "Of Myself, for Myself." From *Writing Your Way*. © 1984 by Boynton/Cook Publishers, Inc.

Foreword

KEN MACRORIE

Some years ago there was a school—I believe it was in Canada—called Knowplace. My first reaction to the name was that it was brilliant: it suggested that traditional schools aren't places where students come to know. My second reaction was that the pun in the name was black humor: most schools are *no* places, where *no* rather than *yes* is the operative word.

In a way, I feel that Toby Fulwiler's *The Journal Book* belongs over there in that ambiguous realm where Knowplace existed. Toby gave this book a modest name—indubitably accurate. Every article in it discusses journal keeping. But as several contributors say, when they found how journal keeping could set students thinking, they made it the central mode of learning in their classes. And it worked.

As a title, *The Journal Book* doesn't hint at the glorious revolution that would occur in schools and universities if all students would write journals of the kind described in this book.

You'll think that I'm talking from No-mind, just bragging up a book because I'm writing a foreword to it. I'll show what I mean by the *thinking* that students have done in their journals. Here are two journal entries as examples:

A 13-year-old British boy responding to a passage read from The Teachings of Don Juan *by Carlos Castaneda:*
...Some parts could be true but the parts I think are not true are: Meeting the spirits in the mountains, going through the door and coming out somewhere else. But if the things are true why don't scientists go looking for them. And if it is all true it proves that the so called red Indian isn't so primitive after all. Do you agree with me? And also there could be a lot to learn from them. And if all the other primitive people know things like this it could open up a whole science or range of studies. And I think that I might want to look into what the man's saying a little bit more. Although I think it can't be true I have got a feeling it could be true. Do you think so?

A fifth-grade American boy's journal entry about experiencing the divorce of his parents:
My mom and dad care about me. They don't live together but they do in my heart.

I won't go on citing examples, but such thinking and feeling entries are presented in the book from classes in English, mathematics, French, sociology, political science, physics, economic geography, and many others. The writers of its chapters look at school journals in new forms like dialogue journals and old ones like learning logs, the latter like those written by Darwin or Lewis and Clark or Admiral Byrd, only now by students in school.

In this book journals are seen in every situation and from every angle, as if mounted on a slow turntable under a spotlight. The conclusion of most of the teachers and students using them is that they get people thinking, they help them test their own experience against the ideas of many others—the authorities they're studying, their teachers, their fellow students. As they become more and more engaged, they often write more clearly, and their journal entries display fewer mistakes in spelling, punctuation, and grammar, although the teachers have taken pains to let them know at the very beginning that they will not be graded on these mechanics of writing. For the majority of these students, journals are *yes* places.

The payoffs from using journals in classrooms are here shown to be astounding. Students learn from making mistakes and half-forming ideas. They learn to think, not by doing exercises in a faddish "critical thinking" textbook, but by working their way through real questions, with real interest and real intent.

What is at the heart of this activity? What is its secret? Journals can become precious, sanctifying every word, gesture, and possession of the writers just because they are theirs, while failing to universalize them.

But more often journals move through the personal to thought that affects many readers. What's in them that gives us the expectation that here in these pages we are likely to encounter honesty and secrets close to the bone that are sweeter or more terrifying than we find in other writing?

Who makes up that contract to tell truths that so many journal keepers sign? Why do journals do their work so well in school? I think because schools and universities are weighted down, made dull by, that heavy rock—"Right! Now you've got what was in my mind. I'll give you an 'A'." But when two or more persons are finding out what's in the other's mind, then a new spirit arises, both questing and reciprocal. And that's what happens in a classroom where everyone, including the teacher, is keeping a journal and revealing parts of it. Often journals give us the privilege of dealing with each other's truths, with our gropings and mistakes; our mislaid plans and insights. A journal is like a cave. What will we find there? It's not like a textbook, with the questions at the end of each chapter and the teacher up in front of the room tomorrow to tell us we didn't find the right answers, but that she has them for us, and there isn't time right now to discuss them.

The book shows in rich detail that journals are valuable in school in all their manifestations—dialogue journals, think books or learning logs, and diaries—because they counter the tendency of school to freeze the mind, to incapacitate it from ranging and connecting as is its physiological wont. School is a place too often unfriendly to students' wants and wonts. We all know that, and yet many teachers haven't yet handed their students this tool for drilling, sewing, and welding called *journal*.

Why not introduce this mind and feeling opener into the school experience? A glance back at the second journal entry quoted above will tell you. Journals are dangerous. Like any other corkscrew, a journal is apt to open bottles containing habit-forming liquids that once swallowed will bring into being Temperance Societies that scream, "Journals read by teachers are an invasion of personal privacy!" "Journals encourage self worship that threatens the authority of God." I'm not exaggerating. Some of today's teachers are stopped from assigning journal writing to students because of such complaints from concerned parents and organizations.

To write in school something other than a digest or précis of what an authority has said is to take on god-like powers oneself. For a teacher and student to commit their whole person (as Jana Staton puts it in an article in this book) to a continuing dialogue on paper with each other is to enter into an intimate and wonderfully disturbing relationship.

How to convince frightened parents, school board members, and trustees that a journal's power for generating disturbance is to be celebrated rather than censored? How to convince them that student journals should be bound in leather rather than burned by book-banners? Perhaps a class or school newsletter that prints and circulates journal excerpts that will appeal to older folks? That would be a chancy move. These days most of us teachers know that reading is a transaction between the reader's experience and a text, and that no two readings can be exactly the same. And so we would have to expect that a few parents would find one student's journal entry scandalous, unpatriotic, or rebellious, when the rest of the readers might find it noble, sprightly, or even Hallmarkish.

But after reading *The Journal Book* I think you'll find the stakes are too high to surrender in this battle. Mostly, and unwittingly, society has set up schools as places in which bodies and minds are to be controlled—places where young people will be safe from both physical violence and the sweet violence that is thinking.

The Journal Book offers suggestions for avoiding the charge of intruding on students' private personal lives. It demonstrates how students may learn to write and write to learn in ways that constitute *thinking* in the most productive sense of that word.

The book asks us all to open ourselves to persons who have opened themselves on the pages of their journals. To suggest that people should keep journals is to suggest that even their quickest thoughts and feelings caught in mid-flight might be valuable to them and to others. It is the kind of suggestion that belongs in the ceremony of democracy.

Contents

The Journal Book

Introduction

In the academic world, journal writing starts off on the other side of the tracks. It is exactly the kind of prose teachers have learned to associate with haste, sloth, incompetence, immaturity, and maybe even anti-establishment radicalism—a certain irreverence manifested in gamey language. Academic prose is supposed to be clear, conventional, organized, assertive, and objective. (Never mind that academic prose is seldom that; it is supposed to be.) There has been little use for prose which is meandering, colloquial, loosely-structured, often speculative, and highly personal. So, while teachers with formal academic training may find it difficult to request and read the informal language of journals, they may find it even harder to give such language legitimacy by identifying criteria against which to evaluate it.

However, recent research and scholarship suggest that the informal language of journals is too important to ignore. Leading language scholars, including Vygotsky (1962), Moffett (1968, 1982), Britton (1970, 1975), Emig (1971, 1977), Elbow (1973, 1982), Shaughnessy (1977), and Berthoff (1983), have argued, variously but persuasively, that human beings find meaning in the world by exploring it through language—through their own easy talky language, not the language of textbook and teacher. Such language explorations may be oral as well as written, and are often expressed in language characterized as quite personal and colloquial.

Good examples of such language use can be found almost everywhere, daily, in lunchroom conversation, telephone talk, informal letters, private diaries and personal journals. The skillful educator makes use of such language for learning wherever she finds it—and the journal is one of the handiest places. Such journals have become recognized useful pedagogical tools in other disciplines—not just English—where critical independent thought, speculation, or exploration is important.

Journals Across the Disciplines

As a result of the increased scholarly attention to informal writing which began in the late 1960s, journals have been looked on with increasing favor in an ever wider variety of educational settings. Traditionally journals have been used in English and language arts classes—

especially composition and creative writing—to help writers experiment
with language and document their progress. They have also been widely
used in programs which have internship or independent study components, such as nursing, education, and counseling, to help learners keep
track of their professional growth while they are on their own. Journals
—or something like them called logs or notebooks—have also been long
associated with the professional fieldwork of observational sciences such
as biology, anthropology, and sociology, and increasingly undergraduates studying these fields are being asked to employ similar documents.

Characteristics

Whenever journals have been assigned, in the humanities or the
sciences, elementary school or college, there are certain characteristics
that good ones have in common, characteristics which separate them
from more formal prose assignments and make them especially fun to
both write and read.

But what, exactly, are *good* journals? An indirect answer to this
question is given by the forty or so teachers who have written chapters
for this book; while their answers are not identical, a remarkable
consistency emerges as these authors describe why they assign journals,
what they look for when they read them, and what students get from
them.

After talking to these and other teachers who use journals across a
spectrum of grades and disciplines, I have found a core of common
features which characterize good journals. The following list of such
features is based on my own experience and the various testimonies of
other teachers. The list is suggestive rather than formulaic, but it should
prove a good place to start.

Language Features: The language of journals will look a lot like
speech written down (Britton, 1975). As such, it will have the qualities
we often associate with conversational language, among which the
following should be noted.

1. *Colloquial diction:* the word choice will often be informal, characterized by short, simple words, contractions, abbreviations, and
   whatever other language shortcuts will serve to show the writer
   his or her thoughts with a minimum of exertion and a maximum
   of speed.
2. *First Person pronouns:* in many ways each journal entry is a
   matter of personal reflection on this or that issue—what the
   writer thinks as opposed to what someone else may think. Consequently the frequent use of "I" marks both the speaker's position and concern.
3. *Informal punctuation:* whatever gets the job done is most likely
   to be used; expect more dashes than semicolons in journal entries;
   more underlining than quotation marks or footnotes.
4. *Rhythms of everyday speech:* journals are dialogical in nature,
   often documenting a running debate between a writer and one of
   his or her several selves; in such a conversation there is simply no
   point in writing in formal or pretentious prose.

5. *Experimentation:* this category leaves room for the unpredictable, for whatever form, style, voice, or persona a journal writer wants to try on for a while.

Cognitive Activities: It would be impossible to list here all the possible mental modes likely to be found in journal entries, as there would be virtually no limits to what a writer could try out. However, it is worth listing a few of those which serve an especially useful function to critical thinkers—those creatures so often praised in the literature of liberal education. Good journals will have liberal amounts of the following modes:

1. *Observations:* writers see something of interest and attempt to capture it in language. This activity is primary to scientists, who must witness in order to test. as well as to literary scholars, who must read in order to interpret.
2. *Questions:* writers use journals to formulate and record questions: personal doubts, academic queries, questions of fact, administration, and theory. It is more important, here, that there be questions than that yet there be answers.
3. *Speculation:* writers wonder aloud, on paper, about the meaning of events, issues, facts, readings, patterns, interpretations, problems, and solutions. The journal is the place to try out without fear of penalty; the evidence of the attempt is the value here.
4. *Self-awareness:* writers becoming conscious of who they are, what they stand for, how and why they differ from others.
5. *Digression:* writers departing as they write from what they intend to say, sometimes to think of personal matters and sometimes to connect apparently disparate pieces of thought.
6. *Synthesis:* writers putting together ideas, finding relationships, connecting one course or topic with another.
7. *Revision:* writers looking back at prior entries, realizing they have changed their minds, and using the journal to update and record their later thoughts. Ann E. Berthoff recommends this as a systematic practice and calls such endeavors "double-entry notebooks" (1978).
8. *Information:* Does the journal contain evidence that reading has been done, lectures listened to, facts and theories understood? Journals that read like class notebooks will be dull, but journals should give evidence that attention is being paid to course materials.

Formal Features: Certain formal features also indicate quality in journals. Consider the following:

1. *Frequent entries:* the more often a journal is written in the greater the chance to catch one's thoughts.
2. *Long entries:* the more writing one does at a single sitting the greater the chance of developing a thought or finding a new one.
3. *Self-sponsored entries:* how often a student writer intitiates writing without teacher prompts.
4. *Chronology of entries:* the key to journals is the location of each entry in a particular time; good journals have systematic and complete chronological documentation.

Teachers considering assigning journals as a major portion of a student's work will find these lists of qualities useful when reading for even general impressions of student learning. Some of these qualities—observation, synthesis, and natural speech rhythm, for example—may well characterize good essay writing as well as good journals; other features are quite opposite the usual criteria for more formal writing—colloquial diction, experimentation, and digression, for example. These latter, more unorthodox features are the ones most likely to cause problems with the journal's respectability.

About This Book

As the chapters of this book will attest, teachers in many fields and grade levels have discovered the considerable value of assigning journals to improve student learning. In planning this book I had once thought to include chapters representing every field of study. As I began to solicit chapters for the book, however, that plan didn't work out: some teachers in the same fields were doing wonderfully different things while, at the same time, teachers in different disciplines were often doing similar things. And so on. In the end, I took the best chapters I could get and let the disciplinary spread fall where it might. As a result you will find a whole section on English journals (both literature and composition), three chapters written about philosophy, two each about physics and music, but none in some disciplines you might expect—psychology, anthropology, or biology.

The same uneven representation is true of grade levels as well: because I teach college English and work primarily with college teachers, I was able to solicit more chapters from that grade level than any other. There are, however, enough examples from elementary, middle, and high school to suggest rich possibilities there as well. My suggestion to readers who don't find their discipline or grade level represented is to read with broad translations in mind; you may find a very adaptable practice for using journals presented by a teacher far from your own field or level of study.

• • • • • •

In recent years questions have been raised about the ethics of using journals in classroom settings. Some of the concerns are related to students' right to privacy; other concerns seem more focused on the manner in which journals promote self-examination and the questioning of traditional values. To address these concerns, the Commission on Composition of the National Council of Teachers of English (NCTE, November 1986) prepared a statement on the use of journals for educational purposes. The complete text follows:

Guidelines for Using Journals in School Settings*

Approved by the NCTE Commission
on Composition, November 28, 1986

Student Journals

In recent years teachers in elementary and secondary schools as well as in college have been asking students to keep personal notebooks most commonly called journals, but sometimes called logs, daybooks, think-books, and even diaries. These informal notebooks serve a range of educational purposes, from practice in self-expression to figuring out problems in science classes. Some teachers encourage students to write about whatever they want, while other teachers carefully specify topics. In most cases, students are encouraged to express honestly their personal opinions, take some risks with their thought, and write in their own natural voices.

Because journals give students great freedom to express their thoughts and feelings, students often write about things more private and intimate than teachers are comfortable with—things that more properly belong in personal diaries than in school journals. The problem for teachers is how to encourage students to write personally and frankly about subjects they care about without, at the same time, invading their private lives.

This document will outline some of the assumptions behind journal assignments and suggest guidelines to help teachers avoid the problems of privacy which journals occasionally present.

Assumptions About Language and Learning

Students are asked to keep journals for strong pedagogical reasons, based generally on the following assumptions about the connections between thought and language:

1. When people *articulate connections* between new information and what they already know, they learn and understand that new information better (Bruner, 1966).
2. When people *think* and figure things out, they do so in symbol systems commonly called languages, most often verbal, but also mathematical, musical, visual, and so on (Vygotsky, 1962).
3. When people *learn* things, they use all of the language modes to do so—reading, writing, speaking, and listening; each mode helps people learn in a unique way (Emig, 1977).
4. When people *write* about new information and ideas—in addition to reading, talking, and listening—they learn and understand them better (Britton, 1975).

*This document was drafted by Toby Fulwiler with considerable help from members of the NCTE Commission on Composition, including Glenda Bissex, Lynn Galbraith, Ron Goba, Audrey Roth, Charles Schuster, Marilyn Sternglass, and Tilly Warnock.

5. When people *care* about what they write and see connections to their own lives, they both learn and write better (Moffett, 1968).

Writing to Learn in Journals

Teachers assign journals—and logs and thinkbooks and daybooks—for a variety of specific and practical reasons, including the following: (1) to help students find personal connections to the material they are studying in class and textbook, (2) to provide a place for students to think about, learn, and understand course material, (3) to collect observations, responses, and data, and (4) to allow students to practice their writing before handing it in to be graded.

In general, teachers in all subject areas, from history and literature to psychology and biology, have found that when students write about course readings, lectures, discussions, and research materials they understand better what they know, don't know, want to know—and how it all relates to them. In elementary classes, as well as in high school and college, when students study science, math, and reading, they log what they are learning about science, math, and reading in their journals. Teachers commonly ask students to read aloud voluntarily from their journals to help start class discussions or clarify for each other points of confusion or differing interpretation. In short, journals are active, methodical records of student thought and opinion during a given term, meant to help students prepare for class discussions, study for examinations, and write critical papers.

In addition, English and language arts teachers commonly assign journals to help students learn to write formal assignments. Here student writers keep journals for many of the same reasons as professional writers: to find and explore topics; to clarify, modify, and extend those topics; to try out different writing styles; to sharpen their powers of observation; to practice fluency; and in general to become more aware of themselves as writers.

In most instances, teachers consider journals to be the students' territory, a place in which students can experiment and try out ideas without being corrected or criticized for doing so. Consequently, while most teachers periodically collect and read journals, they neither correct them for spelling nor grade them for ideas. Instead, they respond personally and positively to selected entries, usually in soft erasable pencil. Sometimes teachers simply respond positively to selected entries; at other times they ask questions or make suggestions in response to student questions; in many cases the journals provide a place where a non-threatening dialogue between teacher and student is possible.

Journals are useful tools for both students and teachers. They can help students prepare for class discussion, study for examinations, understand reading assignments, and write formal papers. In the following section are some of the guidelines for assigning journals which teachers have found helpful in the past.

Guidelines for Assigning Journals

1. Explain that journals are neither "diaries" nor "class notebooks," but borrow features from each: like the diary, journals are written in the first person about issues the writer cares about; like the class notebook, journals are concerned with the content of a particular course.
2. Ask students to buy looseleaf notebooks. This way students can hand in to you only that which pertains directly to your class, keeping more intimate entries private.
3. Suggest that students divide their journals in several sections, one for your course, one for another course, another for private entries. When you collect the journal, you need only collect that which pertains to your own course.
4. Ask students to do short journal writes in class; write with them; and share your writing with the class. Since you don't grade journals, the fact that you write too gives the assignment more value.
5. Every time you ask students to write in class, do something active and deliberate with what they have written: have volunteers read whole entries aloud; have everyone read one sentence to the whole class; have neighbors share one passage with each other, etc. (In each case, students who do not like what they have written should have the right to pass.) Sharing the writing like this also gives credibility to a non-graded assignment.
6. Count but do not grade student journals. While it's important not to qualitatively evaluate specific journal entries—for here students must be allowed to take risks—good journals should count in some quantitative way: a certain number of points, a *plus* added to a grade, as an in-class resource for taking tests.
7. Do not write back to every entry; it will burn you out. Instead, skim-read journals and write responses to entries that especially concern you.
8. At the end of the term ask students to put in (a) page numbers, (b) a title for each entry, (c) a table of contents, and (d) an evaluative conclusion. This synthesizing activity asks journal writers to treat these documents seriously and to review what they have written over a whole term of study.

Of all writing assignments, journals may be the most idiosyncratic and variable. Consequently, good reasons exist to ignore any of these suggestions, depending on teacher purpose, subject area, grade level, or classroom context. However, these suggestions will help many teachers use journals positively and efficiently in most school settings.

References

Britton, J. et al. (1975). *The development of writing abilities, 11-18.* London: Macmillan Education.
Bruner, J.S. (1966). *Towards a theory of instruction.* Cambridge, MA: The Belknap Press of Harvard University.

Emig, J. (1977, May). Writing as a mode of learning. *CCC, 28,* 122-128.
Moffett, J. (1968). *Teaching the universe of discourse.* Boston: Houghton Mifflin.
Vygotsky, L. (1962). *Thought and language.* Cambridge, MA: MIT Press.

Part I

The Language of Speculation

When people write about something they learn it better. That, in a nutshell, is the idea behind asking students to keep journals. While some of us who assign these personal notebooks might argue about what they should be called—logs, learning logs, daybooks, thinkbooks, dialectical notebooks, field notebooks, diaries, whatever—we would not disagree about their purpose and value: writing helps our students learn things better and these notebooks provide a place in which to write informally yet systematically in order to seek, discover, speculate, and figure things out.

This first section contains eight chapters which explore the ideas that support the practice of journal writing:

In Chapter 1, "Dialectical Notebooks and the Audit of Meaning," Ann E. Berthoff argues that the fundamental use of language is to make meaning and that double-entry journals are one of the best places in which to plan for this to happen.

In Chapter 2, "Desert Island Discourse," Peter Elbow and Jennifer Clarke raise questions about the oft-repeated advice for writers to keep their audiences always in mind. There are important times, Elbow and Clarke argue, when writers need to forget about their audience and pay attention to other matters.

In Chapter 3, "Not in Utopia: Reflections on Journal Writing," Geoffrey Summerfield takes us through the published journals of a variety of writers, including Amelia Earhart, Francis Kilvert, and W.H. Auden, to make the case that all writing, including that done in private journals, is essentially a social activity.

In Chapter 4, "Writing to Learn," Pat D'Arcy introduces the idea of writing as an activity which promotes reflection by looking at the journal writing of several English fourteen-year-olds. She concludes her chapter with observations on the use of journals by a group of Wiltshire science teachers.

In Chapter 5, "The Power of Responding in Dialogue Journals," Jana Staton outlines the role of the journal in promoting student-teacher and student-student interaction in the classroom. While this chapter focuses on the journals of elementary children, the translations of this idea to other grade levels are readily apparent.

In Chapter 6, "Logs for Learning: Writing in One English School," Peter Medway, who worked with James Britton and Nancy Martin on the Schools Council Project in the early 1970's, describes the way in which informal writing promotes what he calls "real education" with average students of high school age.

In Chapter 7, "Of Myself, for Myself," from his student text, *Writing Your Way*, professional writer Peter Stillman shares pieces of his own journal as well as those of nineteenth-century explorers to suggest that journals "can and probably should include anything at all that seems likely *to you* at the moment."

In Chapter 8, "A Brief History of Journal Keeping," Sharyn Lowenstein traces the origins of private writing back to the pillow books of ancient Japan and follows their emergence as travel diaries in the European Renaissance and spiritual diaries in Colonial America. She concludes with a look at the personal journals which have flourished throughout the twentieth century.

1.

Dialectical Notebooks and the Audit of Meaning

ANN E. BERTHOFF

I would claim that anybody concerned with working out ideas could, should, must be—willy-nilly—a writer, because writing provides the readiest means of carrying out what I.A. Richards calls an *audit of meaning*.[1] Writing as a way of knowing lets us represent ideas so that we can return to them and assess them.

Keeping a journal is the best habit any writer can have; indeed, most real writers probably couldn't function without their notebooks, whatever form they take or however they are kept. Notebooks can serve as cradles, which is the way Henry James characterized his jottings—scraps of conversations, speculations about one image or another, sketches of characters, plot ideas, etc.; notebooks can serve as shorthand records or as detailed accounts. Of what? Of observations—and observations of observations; recollections, remembrances, things to be remembered—memoranda; things to be returned to—*nota benes;* things to be looked up—ascertainable facts; notions to be puzzled over. Keeping a notebook is a way of keeping track of the development of ideas, as well as of their inception and origin, of monitoring a work in progress: What work? A writer's work is getting "it" down and the essential thing to realize is that "it" is an opinion, an observation, a recording, a formulation, a representation—there are no facts, "raw data" *given* to us. Thinking begins with perception: *all knowledge is mediated.*

Journals, diaries, monthlies, annuals, daybooks, almanacs, calendars, chronicles: we could say that these all constitute a class by reason of the fact that they all either record events chronologically or are organized as daily, monthly, or annual reports. It gets interesting when we begin to differentiate these kinds of records and representations, noting to what degree and in what respects they are public or private; speculative or factual; closer to history than to story. It gets very interesting, indeed, when we begin examining in what sense they are all fictions, in the sense that all representation is constructed. Records of all sorts provide the means of orienting ourselves in time. Orientation: Where do we start from? What directions are we to follow? What is a point of departure? Thinking about journals can bring us to the heart of current critical theory—and if we are to learn to use them to teach writing, we will need to be somewhat theoretical. It is the nexus of theory and practice which gives us method, and without freshly apprehended and considered method, pedagogy is enslaved to whatever implicit method comes with whatever practice we take up. Journals can be just as deadly as any other heuristic, if we don't think about what we are doing with them.

I will describe here a special kind of journal which I call a dialectical notebook. I like to remind myself (and others) that dialectic and dialogue are closely related; that thinking is a dialogue we have with ourselves; that dialectic is an audit of meaning—a continuing effort to review the meanings we are making in order to see further what they mean. The means we have of doing that are—meanings. The dialectical notebook keeps all our meanings handy. Here is how it works: the dialectical notebook is a double-entry journal with the two pages facing one another in dialogue. On one side are observations, sketches, noted impressions, passages copied out, jottings on reading or other responses; on the facing page are notes on these notes, responses to these responses —in current jargon, "meta-comment." The first thing the dialectical notebook can teach us is toleration of those necessary circularities. Everything about language, everything in composing, involves us in them: thinking about thinking; arranging our techniques for arranging; interpreting our interpretations.

For positivists—and therefore for most rhetoricians—these circularities are dizzying. They are abjured as *self*-consciousness. "Why tell people what they are doing when they are doing it normally, naturally? Why intervene with theory when they are creating without it?" The short answer is that *knowing how* to make meaning in one instance is facilitated by *knowing that* we have done so in other circumstances. Consciousness of consciousness makes that knowledge apprehendable.

All acts of symbolization take place in a social world framed by language; hence the importance of dialogue, pedagogically. We can't get under the net to reach "reality" directly . All knowledge is mediated: all knowledge is therefore partial. Making meaning is not very much like learning to ride a bicycle; nor is it "instinctual." Human beings are language animals: we are not controlled, limited, by a repertory of instincts. Language gives us the power of memory and envisagement, thus freeing us from the momentary, the eternal present of the beasts, and recreating us as historical creatures. The essential principle for a philosophy of rhetoric is what C.S. Peirce called Triadicity: interpreting interpretations is entailed in the way the mind works; interpretation is not added on the sign but is itself a constituent element of the sign.[2]

In an essay in *The Making of Meaning*, I explain this concept of mediation as follows:

> Let me suggest how we might keep in mind the nature of meaning as a means, a way to remember that meaning is dynamic and dialectical, that it depends on context and perspective, the setting and the angle. The model I'm thinking of is a triangle, but of a radically different sort from the familiar "triangle of discourse," which looks like this:

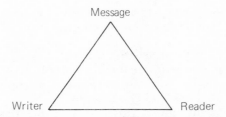

Sometimes, *speaker/reality/audience* are at the three points, with language or text occupying the field enclosed. In this model there is no way of telling the relationship of message to either its sources or to the speaker or the form in which it is expressed. As we know, "messages" are continually sent in the real world without being understood, but there is nothing in this model to explain why, or what we, as teachers of reading and writing, might do about failures of "communication."

The triangle I'm suggesting as a model helps on that score; it looks like this:

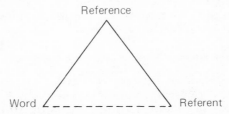

This diagram represents the "sign," the "meaning relationship." What the word stands for—the referent—is known is terms of reference. The dotted line stands for the fact that there is no immediate, direct relationship between words and things (including other words); we interpret the word or symbol by means of the idea it represents to us. It takes an idea to find an idea. We know reality in terms of our ideas of reality. This curious triangle with the dotted line can help us remember that what we know, we know by means of mediating form. The triangle represents mediation, the interdependence of interpreter (what he already knows), the symbol (image or word), and the import or significance it has. Ironically, by not being quite a triangle, this triangle represents the triadicity of meaning relationships. It can help us keep in mind that we must include the beholder, the interpreter, in our account of texts; that texts require contexts and that contexts depend on perspective.[3]

The dialectical notebook serves many purposes, both in the general sense of helping to develop habits of mind and in the practical sense of helping with academic work. I will list these, commenting briefly, before discussing procedures and actual academic uses of the notebook.

1. Looking and looking again.

Learning to look carefully, to see what you're looking at, is perennially acclaimed as the essential skill for both artist and scientist, to say nothing of its being crucial for maturity in psychological terms. Looking is the *sine qua non* of inquiry; looking again is the method of inquiry.

The willingness to entertain further questions, to return to assumptions, to re-assess what has been given or asserted is entailed in learning to think.

Ezra Pound first recounted the story of Agassiz and the fish—how the great naturalist sent a novice scientist back to look again—and again and again—at the specimen.[4] Paulo Freire freshly captures just what it is to teach oneself to look and look again:

> One focus of my efforts (in understanding the role of thinking about thinking)...is turning myself into a tramp of the obvious ....In playing the part of this vagrant, I have been learning how important the obvious becomes as the object of our critical reflection, and by looking deeply into it, I have discovered that the obvious is not always as obvious as it appears.[5]

Exercises in looking and looking again should properly include both the most careful observation of a natural object and what Freire calls "problematizing the existential situation." Such study becomes, then, a model for close reading: reading the Book of Nature has long provided the prolegomenon to critical inquiry, and if we add reading the environment we have two very powerful models for composing.

2. Fostering fluency: gush vs. dialectic

All writers dream of fluency, of having the words come, of not having to struggle towards accurate expression and substantial representation. But fluency can, of course, be gush: a competent writer—typically, say, the National Honor Society Freshman, miffed at not being exempted from English 101—is capable of running off at the mouth precisely because he is capable of combining syntactical elements without really worrying about what weight they might bear. (Sentence combining is more likely to foster this kind of "competence" than it is to teach ways and means of subordination.) Fluency is something other than gush when the dialectic of feedback and feedforward is operating; how to get the dialectic going is the challenge.

"Free writing" can be very useful, but it is not always the best option for "getting started." The dialectical notebook can encourage list making and the development of a lexicon; it can accommodate phrases and fragmentary formulations—sketches which are not in the form of statements. What I have called "generating chaos" allows the writer to make use of looking again and thinking about what has been thought and is thus more likely to encourage a dialectical sort of fluency. Without this preparation, "free writing" is as likely as not to produce quantities of stuff, without necessarily producing points of departure. Once the dialectic of *feedback* and *feedforward* is in operation, the writer has a very powerful resource to call upon, namely the heuristic power of language itself. The tendency of words is to cluster, to form syntactic units. This tendency of words towards syntax is the *discursive* power of language: syntax brings thought along with it as it *runs along*. This is the kind of fluency the dialectical notebook can foster.

3. Tolerating ambiguity

Learning the uses of chaos prepares the writer for tolerating ambiguity. I.A. Richards once remarked that "ambiguities are the very hinges of all thought"[6]—but they can't so function if they aren't recognized. The dialectical notebook offers the means of identifying ambiguities, of addressing them, of unsnarling contradictions and resolving paradoxes. The novice writer, if she does spot an ambiguity, may well decide that the best strategy is to disguise it by stretching words illegitimately, covertly. She may eliminate it by suppressing the element that has created it. Tolerating ambiguities, looking at them again as symptoms of faulty logic or of inadequate definition or as symptoms of unsorted plenitude is probably the best way of learning the strategies of argument. The dialectical notebook allows the writer to keep things tentative, to forestall "closure," in the jargon of psycholinguistics. The most important benefit is learning to make revision not a stage but a dimension of composing.[7] One of the hardest things about revision is how to keep from focusing too narrowly too soon. The dialectical notebook lets writers practice keeping the options open; it can toughen the resolve to change direction, to follow in new directions, if that's the way things seem to be going. The high cost of thesis statements and outlines and of the much vaunted "process" model of Prewriting, Writing, Rewriting is that they tend to cut down on the options, to hinder writers from learning to take risks by looking again at the meanings that are emerging.

4. Coming to terms with allatonceness

In composing, everything happens at once or it doesn't happen at all: we say and mean; we express and represent; we find words and words help us discover our meanings. If students can come to terms with this allatonceness, the problems and snarls which bedevil writing will more easily come under control. If teachers learn to come to terms with allatonceness, they will, in the process, revolutionize their practice. The chief virtue of the dialectical notebook is that it helps writers convert the allatonceness of composing from a formidable anxiety-producer to a resource for the making of meaning. Keeping a dialectical notebook is a way of making writing a mode of learning and a way of knowing, because its dialectical/dialogic form corresponds to the character of the inner dialogue which is thinking. In making meaning, complexity comes first: the dialectical notebook lets us begin with complexity—with looking again, with the chaos and ambiguity which are its consequence.

Because the dialectical notebook can serve as a medium for lecture notes and reading notes, as well as for notes towards the generation and development of ideas for assigned papers, it can help develop a sense of the interdependence of reading and writing, listening and speaking. All critical uses of language require the same habits of efficient apprehension, thoughtful expectation, and accurate representation. Thus, developing a skill in any one of them can help strengthen capacities in the others. The chief academic value of the dialectical notebook is that it helps a student to become a good reader, thereby learning to be a good writer. By helping students to take notes on their notes, it helps them learn to interpret their interpretations deliberately and cogently; it fosters the habit of questioning which is, of course, at the heart of inquiry and argumentation.

What writers need to learn is how to formulate questions which have heuristic value. They won't find out how from handbooks, rhetorics, or guides which generally urge students to *be clear;* to *think* of their audience; to *go over* their writing and *take out* unnecessary words and *put in* transitional phrases. Exhortation is not instruction. (Books which in one chapter mouth the slogan "Show, don't tell" are notably weak when it comes to showing how to do anything connected with actual writing.) Learning to question is not a matter of learning to convert Study Questions to ready-made thesis statements. The important challenge is to invent one's own study questions. One teacher who has been experimenting with dialectical notebooks in a rather traditional Freshman English course featuring the study of literature reported to me recently that the first thing to happen was that her students began asking if they could make up their own topics for the weekly paper. That seems to me symptomatic of an engagement with texts that is not entirely common these days. Inventing topics, recognizing points of departure, choosing perspectives—all of that flows from learning to question. Questioning is *problem-posing* and it engages the mind more radically than *problem-solving,* as generally conceived. Anything we can do to foster a student's capacity to pose questions in substantial terms will be helping to develop the inquiry procedures which are essential to all academic writing.

The logic most appropriate to inquiry is what C.S. Peirce called *abduction.* It is a matter of moving sideways, as it were—developing analogies, drawing inferences, hypothesizing, putting claims to the test, thereby making clear the conditions under which a statement might be said to be true, of laying bare assumptions and defining presuppositions. The best way to develop skill in abductive reasoning is to practice formulating "iffy" questions. For one thing, it keeps the *what* of the statement in dynamic dialectic with the *how.* To explain that changes in language are by no means all superficial—"just semantics"—I ask students to consider this question when they are working on their meta-comment: "How does it change my meaning if I put it *this* way?" A comparison, then, of two ways of saying allows for the exercise of choice and sets up a direction.

Inquiry proceeds with drawing out implications of the way the problem has been posed, a process Peirce called *ampliative inference.* The guiding question is "Does it follow, then, that X is a cause of/a source of/an analogue of/an instance of/etc. of Y?" Practice with double entries makes the task of handling further questions a way to foster fluency in writing.

The next phase is to represent inferences which have been drawn, to come to cases. In so doing, a writer learns to differentiate necessary and probable inferences and to see how they both differ from unwarranted claims. The best way I know to control this process is by developing opposite, borderline, and model cases.[8] It helps to organize an argument instead of putting off that problem until all the "examples" have been gathered. The absurd conception of research which informs the Term Paper only institutionalizes an irrational procedure of Gathering Data First. It is one more example of the positivist penchant for beginning with the allegedly particular and putting off generalization; whereas in the composing process dialectically conceived, there is no question of a linear progression.[9] The dialectical notebook develops the habit of moving continually from the general to the specific and back to the general, the movement of thought which Vygotsky saw as the essential characteristic of concept formation.

The topics of classical rhetoric—irrationally selected and only time-honored—are transmogrified, when students practice composing dialectically.[10] They become not slots to be filled or hoops to be aimed for but instruments of thought. We are no longer assigning a Compare-Contrast Paper, worrying about how it's related to Narrative and Description. We no longer save Definition for English 102. The interdependence of rhetorical modes, the dialectic of the "topics," is a discovery which can set students and teachers alike on the way to a pedagogy of knowing.

I have been claiming that the dialectical notebook is useful for students as they learn the procedures of critical inquiry, which is, in my view, neither psychologically nor logically antithetical to "creative" endeavor. The more we can see in common between science and poetry, the easier it will be, then, to value the peculiar strengths of each, as forms of knowledge. Those learning to write can learn a great deal from seeing how the scientist's work is related to the poet's and how what the historian does is close to both. As thinkers and formers, interpreters and creators—as composers and writers—they are all naming the world, bringing ideas to bear on what they are naming and imagining and hypothesizing and transforming.

The motive force that drives this process of interpreting interpretation in order to make meaning is analogy—or metaphor, if we name it in rhetorical terms. Analogy and metaphor are forms of comparison in which likeness is apprehended as being *in relation to, in terms of, with regard to:* these little connectors are emblematic of Triadicity. They remind us of the semiotic principle that just as we see or apprehend likeness only if we have a scale or context, so in all our judgments, we must know by some means. Analogy provides the chief and readiest means of knowing, of making meaning. J. Robert Oppenheimer's observation that analogy is an "indispensable instrument" for both exploration and analysis in science is a useful reminder that science is not to be reduced to measurement any more than writing is to outlining. And Walker Percy's disquisition in "Metaphor as Mistake" should dispel forever the notion that metaphor is cake frosting, something you add to your writing.[11]

Analogy is an idea we can think with; it is, in I.A. Richards' phrase, a "speculative instrument."[12] The habit of keeping a dialectical notebook makes the powerful instrument of analogy available to writers as a way of looking and looking again; of generating names and oppositions which create ambiguities which can serve as the hinges of thought. Analogies insist on being interpreted; no sooner do we create them than they yield further questions. Practice in double-entry journals is practice in analogizing and thus in critical and creative thought.

Notes

[1]I.A. Richards, *How to Read a Page* (1942; rprt., Boston: Beacon Press, 1958), p. 240.

[2]In *The Making of Meaning: Metaphors, Models and Maxims for Writing Teachers* (Upper Montclair, NJ: Boynton/Cook, 1981), I have set forth the philosophical principles which I find essential for the development of what Paulo Freire calls a "pedagogy of knowing." See especially: "Forming Concepts and Conceptualizing Form"; "A Curious Triangle and the Double-Entry Notebook: or, How Theory Can Help Us Teach Reading and Writing"; "The Intelligent Eye and the Thinking Hand." In the comment introducing the four sections of *Reclaiming the Imagination: Philosophical Perspectives for Writers and Teachers of Writing* (Upper Montclair, NJ: Boynton/Cook, 1984), I have suggested how the arguments and speculations of the artists, scientists, and philosophers whose work I have gathered in this anthology can help us develop a philosophy of rhetoric. The sections are "Perception and the Apprehension of Form," "Language and the Making of Meaning," "Interpretation and the Making of Meaning," and "Artists at Work."

[3]Pp. 33-34. See also my essay, "Is Teaching Still Possible?", *College English*, 46 (1984), 743-755.

[4]*The ABC of Reading* (1934; rprt., New York: New Directions, 1960), p. 17.

[5]*The Politics of Education* (South Hadley, MA: Bergin & Garvey, 1985), p. 171.

[6]*How to Read a Page*, p. 24.

[7]I have tried to make this case in "Recognition, Representation, and Revision," *Journal of Basic Writing*, 3 (Fall-Winter, 1981), 19-32; reprinted in *Rhetoric and Composition*, ed. Richard L. Graves (Upper Montclair, NJ: Boynton/Cook, 1984), pp.27-37.

[8]For explanations and demonstration, see John Wilson, *Thinking with Concepts* (Cambridge: Cambridge University Press, 1963). It is very important to note that the sequence in which Wilson presents the cases—model, borderline, and opposite—is precisely the reverse of the one which is logically appropriate to the composing process: it is far easier to say what a concept is *not* than it is to define it at the start; that only encourages lexical definition, which cannot do the work of concept formation.

[9]In *Forming/Thinking/Writing: The Composing Imagination* (1978; Upper Montclair, NJ: Boynton/Cook, 1982), I have tried in all the exercises to keep the dialectic going. Only if complexity is recognized and accommodated from the first will there be a chance for writing to be a mode of learning.

[10]As Knoblauch and Brannon have pointed out, the topics we find perennially in the table of contents of each year's "rhetorics" represent only a fraction of, say, Aristotle's original list. See Chapter Two, *Rhetorical Traditions and the Teaching of Writing* (Upper Montclair, NJ: Boynton/Cook, 1984).

[11]Both Walker Percy's essay and Oppenheimer's "Analogy in Science" are reprinted in *Reclaiming the Imagination*.

[12]The idea of mediating ideas is recurrent in all of Richards' work, but see especially *Speculative Instruments* (NY: Harcourt, 1955).

2.

Desert Island Discourse:
The Benefits of Ignoring Audience

PETER ELBOW and JENNIFER CLARKE

In the face of a seeming consensus of advice to writers—"Think about your audience while you write"—someone needs to celebrate *ignoring* your audience as you write. We'll try.

It's not that writers should *never* think about their audience. It's a question of when. An audience is a field of force. The closer we come—the more we think about these readers—the stronger the pull they exert on the contents of our minds. The practical question, then, is always whether a particular audience functions as a helpful field of force or one that confuses or inhibits us.

Some audiences, for example, are inviting or enabling. When we think about them as we write, we think of more and better things to say—and what we think of somehow arrives naturally shaped and coherently structured: just right for those readers. It's like talking to the perfect listener. Such audiences are helpful to keep in mind right from the start.

There are even occasions when it helps to keep a *threatening* audience in mind right from the start. We've been putting off writing that letter to that person who intimidates us. If we finally sit down and write right *to* them—walk right up to them as it were and look them in the eye—we may manage to stand up to the threat or grasp the nettle and thereby find just what we need to write.

Sometimes, however, audience awareness blocks writing altogether. Here is a student telling what happens when she tries to follow the traditional advice:

You know _____ (author of a text) tells us to pay attention to the audience that will be reading our papers, and I gave that a try. I ended up without putting a word on the paper until I decided the hell with _____; I'm going to write to who I damn well want to; otherwise I can hardly write at all.

The effect of audience awareness is usually somewhere between those extremes: it disrupts writing and thinking but does not completely block it. For example when students have to write to someone they find intimidating (and of course they often experience teachers as intimidating), they often start thinking wholly defensively. As they write down each thought or sentence they think of nothing else but how the intended reader will criticize or object to it. So they try to qualify or

19

soften what they've just written—or write out some answer to a possible objection. Their writing becomes tangled. Sometimes they get so tied in knots that they cannot even figure out what they *want* to say. We may not realize how often audience awareness has this effect on our students when we don't see the writing processes behind their papers: we just see texts which are either tangled or empty.

Another example. When students (or any of us) have to write to readers with whom they have an awkward relationship (and of course students often have an awkward relationship with teachers), they often start beating around the bush and feeling shy or scared; or start to write in a stilted, overly careful style or voice. (Think about the cute, too-clever style of many memos we get in our departmental mailboxes—because of the awkward selfconsciousness academics experience when writing to other academics.) Or when students are asked to write to readers they have not met or can not imagine (such as "the general reader" or "the educated public"), they often have nothing to say except clichés that they know they don't even quite believe.

When we realize that an audience is somehow confusing or in-hibiting us, the solution is fairly obvious. We need to ignore that audience altogether during the *early* stages of writing by directing our words only to our selves or to no one in particular—or even to the "wrong" audience, that is, to an *inviting* audience of trusted friends or allies. This strategy often dissipates the confusion; the clenched, defen-sive discourse starts to run clear.

This strategy of putting audience out of mind has of course been a traditional practice of writers down through the years: using private journals for early explorations of language or thinking. But many writing teachers seem to think that students can get along without the private writing that real writers find so crucial—or even that students will *benefit* from keeping their audience in mind for the whole time. Things often don't work out that way—as the case study below will illustrate.

After we have managed to write a draft or copious exploratory material to work out our own thinking—perhaps finding the right voice—*then* we need to follow the traditional rhetorical advice: think about readers and figure out any adjustments that are needed to suit our words and thoughts to them. For a particular audience it may even turn out that we need to *disguise* our point of view. But it's hard to disguise something while engaged in trying to figure it out. As writers, then, we need to learn *when* to think about audience and when to put audience out of mind.

An Illustrative Case: Joe

Joe grew up with two languages. Other than that, his writing problem might seem at first to be so common that it's not worth analyzing. But if we engage the issues his writing brings up, we will find ourselves forced to question some common assumptions.

Clarke was well engaged in a case study of Joe and found herself trying to demonstrate that Joe's tangled writing came from interference by a second language. (Her own children—for a long time after their return to the U.K. from seven years in France—had thought in French and translated their thoughts into English when forced to write.)

Joe was born and had his early schooling in the U.S., then moved with his family to Sicily for a number of years, and then took the last few years of high school back in Brooklyn before becoming a freshman at SUNY Stony Brook. Joe's vocabulary was quite sophisticated right from the start and he was clearly engaged in expressing interesting thoughts. But the way he put words together sometimes defied a reader's attempts to put sense into them. Clarke began to formulate the hypothesis that Joe's problems must come from thinking in Italian and then making, as he wrote, a literal translation into English. She began to translate some of Joe's sentences into Italian, and though she recognized the occasional Italian construction, she soon saw that the basis of the problem lay elsewhere.

When Joe's required journal came in for the first time, there were no contorted sentences two lines long but containing no verb; in their place were short, usually grammatically flawless sentences. Clarke was delighted and sure that her help and corrections on his papers had at long last taken effect. Wrong. When the next paper came in, it was as bad, if not worse than its predecessors.

At the next conference, when questioned tactfully why there was such a difference between journal and papers, Joe said, "Ah! The papers are for you as a teacher, but the journal is mainly for me. It's me speaking to me and you are only being allowed to overhear." Clarke explained that she had really enjoyed his journal writing and asked whether he could possibly write like that in his papers. Joe was horrified at the idea. In his opinion, his journal language was too simple and colloquial, not formal enough. Again, Clarke said that his journal language seemed perfectly fine to her and asked if he wouldn't like to try it. But Joe was adamant; journal language did not belong in a paper and he was not about to put it there. It was a stalemate. At mid-semester his essays were still not passing. Here is a paragraph from Joe's revised essay about Julius Lester's "On Being a Boy":

> As he becomes an adolescent, he achieves formal, and abstract thoughts. He must prove himself no longer with his male peers, but to females. At this age, every boy goes through the mental conflict of having to prove oneself to girls. One's ego becomes aware, and one must satisfy what adolescence brings about at this time, that is, the feeling that a girl is a figurehead of oneself, a girl proves that a boy has it "made," lives a normal life, is happy, and content. Although it is not easy to prove oneself, many problems arise. One of them is, putting the ego at risk, which may take place, for example, when a boy may ask a girl out, but she refuses him, thus causing a depressed ego in the youngster where he tends to gain a negative aspect of adolesence.

Joe was upset at this failure and came in to see how to put things right. Clarke moved through the paper paragraph by paragraph and asked Joe to tell her what he was trying to say. But he could not even *speak* his intended meaning. She then asked him to take out his journal and to write one paragraph as if it were a journal entry. The result was a little like magic:

> Whenever a boy has to deal with girls, his ego is at risk. The reason is that he must prove to himself that he is able to deal with them. If he gets turned down by girls, he feels that he has failed and becomes unsure of himself and consequently he reaches a state of depression. To him, girls represent everything since they create an image of the male success of having a girl; they show that he has a way of becoming successful and is capable of achieving success.

Joe was speaking to Joe and the teacher was "only being allowed to overhear."

Of course a reader might object that Joe's problem is not one of audience awareness but "register": a mistaken view of the kind of language teachers or authorities are looking for. But consider that Joe's discourse remained clogged even when Clarke asked him to speak his thoughts informally: the register problem had been removed but audience awareness remained. A reader might also wonder whether it was nothing but common shyness which kept him from being able to speak his meaning informally. (Joe could be considered somewhat shy.) But what else *is* shyness than the very phenomenon we are writing about here: interference in discourse because of audience awareness?

Consider also what Joe wrote at the *end* of the semester when he had a chance to re-revise his mid-semester essay. At this point he surely understood—through hard experience—that his teacher didn't like his "mistakenly formal register." Yet despite some improvement, his late semester revising still leaves much of the same tangle:

> As he becomes an adolescent, he achieves formal and abstract thoughts. He must prove himself no longer with his male peers, but to females. At this age, every boy goes through the mental conflict of having to prove himself to girls. Whenever a boy has to deal with girls, his ego is at risk. The reason is that he must prove to himself that he is able to deal with them. If he gets turned down by girls, he feels that he has failed and becomes unsure of himself and consequently he reaches a state of depression. To him girls represent everything, since they create an image of the male success of having a girl, they show thay he has a way of becoming successful and is capable of achieving success.

A reader might object further that Joe's problem is not really audience awareness but is simply the common tangle students (and the rest of us) often produce when we *revise*—and that his journal writing is better simply because it is *un*revised. But this objection fails too if we compare two unrevised pieces Joe produced towards the end of the semester—one for his teacher and the other only for himself in his journal. First, here is an in-class unrevised essay which is to be handed in to the teacher. When Joe refrains from revising but writes for the audience, his language still has much of that clogged quality:

> One reason why I would substain the prohibition of smoke in a public area is that, smoke is hazardous to health. Many medical reports have proven that smoke causes cancer. I am not surprised,

since the presence of tar in a cigarette, is known to us all. Besides cancer, emphisema has been a major disease that has been asked for a lot of attention. Research and analysis have been stimulated in the past years to fight against these diseases, although positive results have been achieved, nothing has been found to stop and avoid them. This causes a problem in our society. We are living in a period where time means money, where a problem can disrupt someone's laid out plans.

The journal entry, on the other hand—also unrevised and produced at about the same time—offers some very different writing:

My morning seemed as when an agitated sea takes total control of a small ship and drags her along with it.

• • •

I went out with my friends, we went to see a movie, but something inside of me tells me that it's not the same with them any more. The friendship is still there on the outside, but I don't know, it's a feeling that I have inside of me that I can't explain, there just seems to be a gap.

It is significant that Clarke started out trying to show that his problem had to do with second language interference but was compelled by her evidence (before learning of Elbow's explorations of ignoring audience) to conclude that audience awareness was a much greater problem. There are many students like Joe, who suffer from a tendency to write a stiff, tangled prose when they think about readers—especially about readers who will judge their writing. As teachers we are continually tempted to try to cure their disturbing syntax by teaching them this or that technique of syntax—thereby making them think all the more about us as they write—when the main cause of their disturbing syntax is too *much* awareness of us as they write.

A Weak Claim and a Strong One

We are actually making two claims here. The weaker one is probably uncontroversial: that ignoring our audience may lead to poor or ineffective writing at first, yet lead to *better* writing in the end than we could have produced if we'd kept readers in mind from the start. That is, if we are writing about a topic in which we are not expert or in which our thinking is still evolving, and if we put aside any attempt to write for our audience, we are likely to produce exploratory writing that is a mess—inconsistent or disorganized or perhaps even incomprehensible to anyone else. Yet by doing this exploratory "swamp work" in conditions of safety, we can often coax our thinking through a process of new discovery and development. In this way we can end up with something better than we could have produced if we'd tried to write all along to our audience. Without privacy and safety, we can't do the exploratory new thinking our topic requires. In short, ignoring audience can lead to "worse" drafts but better revisions.*

Notice the conflict between two principle pieties of composition theory: think about audience as you write; use writing for *making* meaning, not just transmitting meaning you've already worked out. It's often difficult to work out new meaning while worrying about audience.

The stronger claim is that ignoring audience can lead *immediately* to better writing. We take Joe as a case in point because his writing for a teacher audience was such a tangle and his unrevised writing for himself was so much better. But we would also point to students very different from Joe—students whose writing for teachers is in a way fairly skilled or competent, yet nevertheless seriously weakened by audience awareness. That is, much seemingly competent yet depressingly mediocre writing shows the writer thinking too much about how the audience will receive her words; acting too much like a salesman trained to look the customer in the eye and think at all times about the characteristics of the "target audience." There is something too staged or planned or self-aware about the voice in writing. We see the same quality in much second-rate newspaper or magazine business writing. "Good student writing" in the awful sense of the term. (Writing produced this way reminds us of the ineffective actor whose consciousness of self distracts us—she makes us too aware of her own awareness of us.) When we read such prose we wish the writer would stop thinking about us—would stop trying to "adjust" or "fit" what she is saying to our frame of reference: "Damn it, put all your attention on what you are saying," we want to say, "and forget about us and how we are reacting."

When, on the other hand, we examine really good student or professional writing we can often see that its goodness comes from the writer's finally getting so wrapped up in her meaning and her language that she forgets all about audience needs—she finally "breaks through." It is characteristic of much truly good writing to be, as it were, on fire with its meaning: consciousness of readers is burned away; involvement in subject determines all. Such writing is analogous to the performance of the actor who has managed to stop thinking about the audience watching her. The writer is not leaking attention away from her meaning or her language into awareness of the audience.

The arresting power in a good deal of writing by small children comes from their obliviousness to audience. As readers, we are somehow sucked into a more-than-usual connection with the meaning itself because of the child's gift for more-than-usual concentration on what she is saying. In short we can feel some pieces of children's writing as very "writer-based"—yet it's precisely that quality which makes it powerful for us as readers. After all, why should we settle for a writer entering

*Because we are professionals and adults we often write in the role of expert: we can get away without having to figure out what we think or engaging in new thinking; and we can speak with some confidence even to difficult audiences. Think how seldom students write from this position. And think how much richer *our* writing would be if we defined ourselves *in*experts still exploring our thinking.

our point of view, if we can have the more powerful experience of being sucked *out of* our point of view and into *her* world? This is just the experience that children sometimes give because they are so expert at total absorption in what they are writing.

What most readers value in really excellent writing isn't prose that is right for readers but prose that is right for thinking, right for language, or right for the subject being written about. If in addition it is clear and well suited to readers, we appreciate that—indeed we feel insulted if the writer did not somehow try to make her writing *available* to us before delivering it. But if it succeeds at being really true to language and thinking and "things," we are willing to put up with much difficulty as readers. Here is Paul Goodman on this issue:

(M)uch serious writing, perhaps most, is written for no particular audience; and much fiction and poetry for none at all. Nevertheless, the writer is always under an obligation to make it "clear"... But "clear" does not mean easily comprehensible. Consider Mallarmé, an exceedingly clear and logical writer, but who cannot sacrifice the conciseness, texture, and immediacy of his style just to be easily understood by readers, so you have to figure it out like a puzzle. My opinion is that, in most cases, the writer is not thinking of a reader at all; he makes it "clear" as a contract with *language*. (1972, pp. 163-164)

The effects of audience awareness on *voice* is particularly striking— if paradoxical. Even though we often develop our voice by finally "speaking up" to an audience or "speaking out" to others—and even though much dead student writing comes from their not really treating their writing as a communication with real readers—nevertheless the opposite effect is also common: we often do not really develop a strong, authentic voice in our writing till we find important occasions for *ignoring* audience—saying, in effect, "To hell with whether they like it or not. I'm saying this the way *I* want to say it." Ignoring audience may permit an overly self-conscious, mannered, or cute voice finally to run clear. Joe's voice was never strong or clear except in his journal writing.

Admittedly, the voice that emerges when students ignore audience is sometimes odd or idiosyncratic in some way, but usually it is stronger. (Indeed, teachers sometimes complain of student writing as "reader-based" when the problem is simply the idiosyncrasy—and sometimes in fact the *power*—of the voice. They would value this odd but resonant voice if they found it in a well-known author. (See "Real Voice"in Elbow, 1981.) We cannot usually *trust* a voice unless it is unaware of us and our needs and speaks out in its own terms. John Ashbery said it bluntly: "Very often people don't listen to you when you speak to them. It's only when you talk to yourself that they pick up their ears." (Lehman, 1984)

Our celebration of ignoring audience could be given the most damning criticism possible these days and called *romantic:* a plea for just warbling one's woodnotes wild. But our position also contains the austere *classic* truth too that writers must almost invariably *revise* with conscious awareness of audience. Thus even though Joe will be better off and have less revising to do if he learns to start out writing privately and reflectively in his journal rather than writing "an essay for his teacher," nevertheless nothing will spare him from revising—from having to learn how to recognize which passages to keep, which to throw away, and how to make the transformations and additions that are needed. Revising is a hard skill; it requires audience awareness and other sophisticated rhetorical skills; many students produce strong and interesting freewriting but end up with revisions that are dull or even confusing and poorly structured. It's not surprising that the NAEP tests show that roughly half of the high school students tested make their writing *worse* when they revise it. The fact remains, however, that students have a better chance of ending up with strong revisions if they have better ingredients to start with.

Writer-Based and Reader-Based Prose

In effect, our weak claim is an argument for inviting writer-based prose in the early stages of certain writing projects—for the sake of producing better reader-based prose in the end. That is, writers often figure out their meaning better and fit words to readers better if they start out ignoring readers altogether.

Linda Flower (1979) gave currency to the terms "writer-based" and "reader-based" prose. Because people are so quick to see her article only as a story about what's wrong with writer-based prose, they miss the substantial degree to which she was celebrating it: to produce discourse without awareness of readers is, she maintains, a writer's natural response to the cognitive overload caused by trying simultaneously to worry about readers and work out new thinking. Writer-based prose is developmentally enabling.

But our stronger claim is that writer-based prose can be *better* than reader-based prose—even for readers. That is, the terms "writer-based" and "reader-based" finally break down. Does *writer-based* mean:

1. That the writer was wrapped up in her own point of view and ignored readers as she wrote?
2. Or that her text doesn't work for readers?

The two conditions are not the same. And does *reader-based* mean:

3. That the writer was attending to readers as she wrote?
4. Or that her text works for readers?

Again, there is a big difference between these two conditions. If we want a model of the writing process that does justice to the complexity of what actually happens in both writers and readers,we need terms for the four conditions marked above. For sometimes a writer produces something good for readers without awareness of them; sometimes something terrible for readers with lots of awareness of them.

Two Models of Cognitive Development

Some of the current emphasis on audience awareness probably derives from a model of cognitive development that needs to be questioned. According to this model, reader-based prose is "more mature" than writer-based prose: if you direct your words to readers or keep your audience in mind as you write, you are operating at a higher level of psychological development than if you ignore readers or don't direct your words to readers. Flower relates writer-based prose to the inability to "decenter" which is characteristic of Piaget's early stages of development, and she relates reader-based prose to later more mature stages of development.

On the one hand, of course, this view must be right. Children do decenter as they develop. As they mature they get better at suiting their discourses to the needs of listeners—particularly to listeners very different from themselves. Especially, they get better at doing so *consciously*—thinking *awarely* about how things appear to people with different viewpoints. Thus much unskilled writing is unclear or awkward *because* the writer was doing what it is so easy to do—unthinkingly taking her own frame of reference for granted and not attending to the needs of an audience that might have a different frame of reference. And, of course, this failure is more common in younger, immature, "egocentric" students (and also more common in writing than in speaking since we have no audience present when we write).

But on the other hand, we need a contrary model that affirms what is also obvious once we reflect on it, namely that the ability to *turn off* audience awareness—especially when it confuses thinking or blocks discourse—is also a "higher" skill: the ability to use language in "the desert island mode"—an ability that tends to require learning, growth, and psychological development. Children—and even adults who have not learned the art of quiet, thoughtful, inner reflection (an art we like to associate with the fruits of higher education)—are often unable to get much cognitive action going in their heads unless there are other people present to have action *with*. They are dependent on live audience and the social dimension to get their discourse rolling or to get their thinking off the ground.

For in contrast to a roughly Piagetian model of cognitive development that says we start out as private, egocentric little monads and grow up to be public and social, it is important to invoke the opposite model (which has links with L.S. Vygotsky and George Herbert Mead) that says we *start out* social and plugged into others: only gradually through growth and development do we learn to "unplug" to any significant degree and learn to function in a more private and differentiated fashion.

Where the Piagetian (individual psychology) model calls our attention to the need to learn to enter into viewpoints other than our own, the Vygotskian (social psychology) model helps us notice something just as obvious once we attend to it: the need to learn to produce good thinking and discourse *while alone*. A rich and enfolded mental life is something that people achieve only gradually and with practice. We see this need in all those students who experience themselves as having nothing to say when asked to freewrite or to write in a journal. They can dutifully "reply" to a question or a topic, but they cannot seem to *initiate* or *sustain* a train of thought on their own. Because so many adolescent students have this difficulty, many teachers chime in and agree: "Adolescents have nothing to write about. They are too young. They haven't had significant experience." In truth adolescents don't lack experience or material, no matter how sheltered their lives, but they *do* lack practice and help: reflective writing in the desert island mode is a learned cognitive process. ("All the unhappiness of men arises from one single fact, that they cannot stay quietly in their own chamber." Pascal, *Pensée* no. 139.) It's a mistake to think of private writing (journal writing and freewriting) as merely "easy"—merely a relief from trying to write right. It's also hard. Many students cannot use private writing productively because they haven't developed the cognitive skill of desert island mentation. (There are exercises and strategies which help: Ira Progoff's "Intensive Journal" process, Sondra Perl's "Composing Guidelines," or Elbow's "Loop Writing" and "Open-Ended Writing" processes.)

The Piagetian and Vygotskian developmental models (language-begins-as-private vs. language-begins-as-social) gives us two different lenses through which to look at a common weakness in student writing: the tendency to leave so much unexplained and undeveloped. Using the Piagetian model, as Flower does, one can specify the problem as a weakness in audience orientation. The writer has immaturely taken too much for granted and unthinkingly assumed that her limited explanations carry as much meaning for readers as they do for herself. The cure or treatment is for the writer to think more about readers.

Through the Vygotskian lens, however, the problem and the "immaturity" look altogether different. Yes, the writing isn't particularly clear or satisfying for readers, but this alternative diagnosis tells us not to analyze everything in terms of readers. It suggests a failure of the private desert island dimension: the writer's explanation is too thin because she didn't work out her train of thought fully enough *for herself.* That is, the writer displays a weakness in the ability to engage in that reflective discourse with herself that is so central to any mastery of the writing process. The suggested cure or treatment is not to think more about readers but more to think more for herself—more practice in exploratory writing to discover or generate her *own* thoughts on the issue.

Perhaps the current emphasis on audience awareness is particularly strong now because it is fueled by *both* psychological models. From one side, the Piagetians say, in effect, "The egocentric little critters, we've got to *socialize* 'em!" Ergo: "Think about audience when you write!" From the other side, the Vygotskians say, in effect, "No wonder they're having trouble writing. They've been bamboozled by the Piagetian heresy. They think they're solitary individuals with private selves. We've got to make 'em realize they're just congeries of voices which derive from their discourse community. (And while we're at it, let's hook them up with a better class of discourse community.)" Ergo: "Think about audience when you write!" To advocate *ignoring audience* is to risk being caught in crossfire between opposing armies.

Some Vygotskians will object that what looks like private, solitary mental work is not really private or solitary: since language and thinking start out social and usually continue social, *discourse is always and inherently social.* According to this view, even on the desert island, we are talking *to* voices and *through* voices which we have internalized through our social history. Ken Bruffee (1984) likes to quote Frost on this point: "Men work together,.../Whether they work together or apart." ("The Tuft of Flowers")

But though we need this social perspective and the Frost dictum as a corrective to the one-dimensionality of the contrary Piagetian perspective, it would be a mistake to embrace it as the sole truth—to flop over into the arms of the opposite one-dimensionality. To call *all* language "social" and *all* work "together" is to undermine clear thinking and lose a necessary distinction. We need the distinction between *public discourse* which is intended for the eyes or ears of others (which we must therefore try to suit to them), and *private discourse* which is intended for ourselves (which we are therefore free to suit only to ourselves—or even to no one at all). Even *if* all discourse derives from a social matrix, (which we question, below) and even *if* private or solitary discourse always has a social dimension, there are still compelling theoretical and practical needs to distinguish between public and private discourse and cognition.

As teachers, particularly, we need models and terminology to talk about that crucial cognitive capacity which we try to impart to all our students but which we fail to impart to so many—the capacity to engage in extended and productive thinking that doesn't depend on audience prompts or social stimuli. It's sad to see students abandon an issue which sparks their interest just because they don't find other people who are interested in talking about it: they haven't learned to talk reflectively to *themselves* about it. Desert island discourse can do its job well yet *not* fit the needs of others: when it is good, it's good because it fits the needs of self or language or thinking.*

Discourse as Communication and Discourse as Poesis or Play

There are dangers in borrowing psychological models too glibly. We are liable to overlook our own and our students' experience—in this case the common experience of finding it helpful sometimes to put

---

*Some readers might further object that "private" or "solitary" writing does not really ignore audience but rather directs itself to the "audience of *self.*" But this is an unhelpful locution—an unhelpful way to use the word "audience"—since the word usually specifies people *other* than the self. The main thing that most people experience when they "write only for the audience of self" is relief at *not* thinking about audience. To talk about "addressing discourse to the audience of self" is to talk about *refraining* from doing all the things that audience-awareness advocates say we should do: refraining from "keeping our audience in mind while we write," refraining from trying to "decenter," allowing ourselves to be "egocentric." Surely we should save the paradoxical phrase "audience of self" for those striking situations when we somehow *do* experience ourselves as split or double: when we definitely feel ourselves watching or listening *to* ourselves. Usually we do not.

audience out of mind as we write. We can't avoid having—or at least implying—a psychological or developmental model for writing, but we'd better make sure it's complex, paradoxical, or spiral—or better yet, be deft enough to use *two* models or *contrary* lenses. (Jerome Bruner [1973, 1979] stresses development as complex movement in an upward reiterative spiral—not simple movement in one direction.)

On the one hand, it is characteristic of the youngest children to direct their discourse to an audience. They learn discourse *because* they have an audience; without an audience they remain mute (like "the wild child"). Language is social from the start. But it is also characteristic of the youngest child to use language in a *nonsocial* way. Children use language not only because people talk to them but also because they have such a strong propensity to *play* and to *build*—often in a non-social or non-audience-oriented fashion. Thus although one paradigm for discourse is social communication, another is private exploration or solitary play. Babies and toddlers characteristically babble in an exploratory and reflective way—to themselves and not to an audience—often even with no one else near. This archetypally private use of discourse is strikingly illustrated when we see a pair of toddlers playing next to one another—each busily talking in parallel but not at all trying to communicate with the other.

Therefore, when we choose paradigms for discourse, we should think not only about children using words to communicate, but also about children building sandcastles or drawing pictures. Of course sculptures and pictures are different from words; yet one of our main uses of words is to build structures and pictures—not send messages. Though children characteristically show their castles or pictures to others, they just as characteristically trample the castle or crumple the picture before anyone else can see it. Children seem to show a natural satisfaction in the making and the unmaking: both are important parts of the process of discourse as poesis.*

As children get older the developmental story remains complex or spiral. On the one hand, babies start out with a natural gift for using language in a social and communicative fashion, yet as they mature they must continually learn to relate their discourse better to an audience—to decenter better. And yet on the other hand, babies also start out with a natural gift for using language in a *private*, exploratory, and playful way, yet as they mature they must continually learn to master this solitary, desert island, "poesis" mode better. Thus we mustn't think of language only as communication—nor allow communication to claim dominance as the earliest or most "mature" form of discourse. Language is inherently communicative (and without communication we don't develop language), yet it is just as inherently the stringing together of

---

*Consider a striking piece of behavior at the other end of the life cycle: Brahms staggering from his deathbed to his study to rip up a dozen or more unpublished string quartets that he was unsatisfied with. How was he relating to audience? Was he worrying too much about audience? Or not giving a damn about the very people who, he knew well, yearned for the work he was destroying? It's not easy to say.

exploratory discourse for the self—or the creation of objects (play, poesis, making) for their own sake.*

About the important "poesis" function of language, we need not discount (as Berkenkotter [1983] does) the striking testimony of so many witnesses who think and care most about language: professional poets, writers, and philosophers. Many of them maintain that their most serious work is *making*, not *communicating*, and that their commitment is to language, reality, logic, experience—not to readers. Only in their willingness to cut loose from the demands or needs of readers, they insist, can they produce their most valuable work. Here is William Stafford on this matter:

> I don't want to overstate this...but...my impulse is to say I don't think of an audience at all. When I'm working, the satisfactions in the process of writing are my satisfactions in dealing with the language, in being surprised by phrasings that occur to me, in finding that this miraculous kind of convergent focus begins to happen. That's my satisfaction, and to think about an audience would be a distraction. I try to keep from thinking about an audience.

Donald Murray says, "My sense of audience is so strong that I have to suppress my conscious awareness of audience to hear *what the text demands.*" (Berkenkotter [1983]—my emphasis.)

Some writers describe their writing activity as more like "getting something right" or even "solving a problem" for its own sake than like communicating with readers or addressing an audience. It's interesting to see how poets come together with philosophers on this point, even with mathematicians: all are emphasizing the "poetic" function of language in its literal sense—"Poesis" as "making." Doing mathematics or logic would seem to be a limiting case at one end of the spectrum of discourse uses: to solve an equation or work out a piece of symbolic logic might seem the opposite of communicating with readers or addressing an audience. Yet to make that statement would be to fall again into a one-sided position. Sometimes our mathematics *is* for an audience, sometimes it is not. The central point in this essay is that we cannot answer audience questions in an *a priori* fashion based on the "nature" of cognition or language or discourse: only in terms of the different *uses* and *purposes* to which humans put cognition or language or discourse on different occasions. If most people have a restricted repertoire of uses for writing—if most people only use writing to send messages to readers—that's no argument for restricting the *definition* of writing: it's

---

*James Britton (1975, 1982) makes a powerful argument that the "making" or "poetic" function of language grows out of the expressive function. Expressive language is often for the sake of communication with an audience, but just as often it is even more for the sake of the speaker—working something out for herself.

Note also that "writing to learn"—which Writing Across the Curriculum programs are discovering to be so important—tends to be writing for the self or even for no one at all, rather than for an outside reader: you throw away the writing (often unread) and keep the neural/synaptic changes it has engendered.

an argument for helping people expand their repertoire.

The value of learning to ignore audience while writing, then, is the value of learning to cultivate the private dimension: the value of writing to make meaning to oneself, not just to others. This involves learning to free oneself (to some extent, anyway) from the enormous power exerted by society and others: to unhook oneself from external prompts and social stimuli. We've grown accustomed to theorists and writing teachers puritanically stressing the *problems* of writing: the tendency while writing to neglect the needs of audience because we usually write in solitude. But let's also *celebrate* this same feature of writing as one of its glories: writing *invites* solitude, the inward turn of mind, and the dialogue with self. Though writing is deeply social and though we must also practice enhancing the social dimension of writing, writing is also the mode of discourse best suited to helping us develop the reflective and private dimension of our mental lives.

References

Berkenkotter, C., & Murray, D. (1980, May). Decisions and revisions: The planning strategies of a published writer and the response of being a rat—or being protocoled. *CCC 34.2.*

Britton, J. (1975). *The development of writing abilities, 11-18.* London: Macmillan Education.

————— . (1982). Writing to learn and learning to write, and Spectator role and the beginnings of writing. In G. Pradl (Ed.), *Prospect and retrospect: Selected essays of James Britton.* Upper Montclair, NJ: Boynton/Cook.

Bruffee, K.A. (1984, November). Collaborative learning and the conversation of mankind, *CE 46.7.*

Bruner, J. (1973). In J. Anglin (Ed.), *Beyond the information given: Studies in the psychology of knowing.* New York: W.W. Norton.

————— . (1979). *On knowing: Essays for the left hand.* Cambridge: Harvard University Press.

Cicotello, D.M. (1983). The Art of writing: An interview with William Stafford. *CCC, 34,* 173-179.

Elbow, P. (1981). *Writing with power.* New York: Oxford University Press.

Flower, L. (1979, September). Writer-based prose: A cognitive basis for problems in writing. *CE, 41.*

Goodman, P. (1972). The literary process. In *Speaking and language: Defense of poetry.* New York: Random House.

Perl, S. Composing guidelines. Distributed by New York City Writing Project.

Progoff, I. (1975). *At a journal workshop.* New York: Dialogue House.

Vygotsky, L. (1962). In E. Haufman (Ed. & Trans.), *Thought and language.* Cambridge: MIT Press.

3.

Not in Utopia:
Reflections on Journal-Writing

GEOFFREY SUMMERFIELD

"Not in Utopia,—subterraneous fields,—
Or some secreted island, Heaven knows where!
But in the very world which is the world
Of all of us—the place where, in the end,
We find happiness, or not at all!

Wordsworth, *The Prelude*, Book 10

Let me plunge straight in and argue that every utterance, every text, embodies, enacts, or realizes a social act, a movement toward an other. If that is so, then where does it "leave" the journal? What, if any, are the social dimensions of the journal? Is it a deviant form, a regression into "talking to oneself"? A manifestation of solipsism?

Picture yourself scribbling away in your journal: Who, other than your own reflexive "other" self, is your audience? Surely it must be someone else, however dimly or remotely apprehended? Someone sufficient to your needs: after all, when lonely people talk of their needs, they speak of wanting someone—not to listen to—but to talk to.

Every text exists in a rich and subtle network of social relationships, actual or fictional: every text is implicitly a reconstruction or a realization of one or more "societies." Without such societies, no text would ever be written. This is not to deny that there are special cases: think, for instance, of Seamus Heaney's marvelous account of Wordsworth composing, and of Heaney's use of Gottfried Benn's term, "a first voice"— "the voice of the poet talking to himself—or to nobody" (*Preoccupations*, p. 70). As Heaney remarks, in Wordsworth's case we "are presented with a version of composition as listening, as a wise passiveness, a surrender to energies that spring within the centre of the mind, not composition as an active pursuit by the mind's circumference of something already at the centre" (p. 63). But Wordsworth was also acutely aware of the fact of audience and recognized his need to himself create the taste whereby he would be appreciated.*

*Heaney quotes as epigraph for his book a passage from W.B. Yeats' "Samhain: 1905," which is very much to my present purpose: "If I had written to convince others I would have asked myself, not 'Is that exactly what I think and feel?' but 'How would that strike so-and-so? How will they think and feel when they have read it?' and all would be oratorical and insincere...."

33

Our words on the page always arrive at a moment or a point where they are felt to reach out to an absent other; and that other is apprehended inescapably as a possible or actual audience, a responsive eye and ear. What, then, is our social posture, our stance, when we pen a journal entry? Is it a turning away? A whispered "This is not ready for the world. The world is not ready for this. For the time being, this is for myself alone"?

Surely we all need on occasion to turn our back to the world— "Shut, shut the door, good John"—and become as near autochthonous as may be; and to hold at arm's length the flux and pressure of pragmatic participation-in-society, the stress of unpredictable contingencies. In a word, spectators. Even as we write of our most recent almost current lives (turning an event into an experience) we distance it by representing it; and the act of representing is itself inherently ideational, and simultaneously recuperative.

But to place such delicate movements of mind within the schemata, the plannings, of a composition course is a potentially deformative act. Even if managed with delicacy and tact, it may be construed as a blurring of crucial boundaries—those lines that separate the public from the private.

A text for the self alone, a private text, is inherently unguarded: and it is characterized by many of the lexicogrammatical features that Vygotsky (1962) recognized as typifying inner speech. Because it not only derives from but also removes itself from actual society, withdrawing, escaping, it is free to take all sorts of liberties; it is elliptical, it predicates without specifying a subject, and so on. And when a journal voice approximates closely to a transcript of inner speech, then it is very likely that even the writer herself, turned reader at a later time, will have difficulty in teasing out all those decontextualized fragments. So we are reminded that "private" derives from the same root as "deprived." For such reason, and others, I believe that any defensible composition course must be predicated fairly and squarely on a simple but inalienable premise: that writing is a social act, albeit displaced.

What place, then, can we find for the journal? When we ask students to keep journals, are we thereby seducing them into a regressive use of langauge? And if we rationalize, "Ah, but their journals are intended for other eyes," then are we not saying, "Look: just take this pot of paint and this brush, and put stripes on the beast. See? It's not a leopard after all—it's a tiger"?

Let's recognize that a journal that is initiated, required, and overseen by someone other than the writer is no longer *sui generis* a journal, as we generally understand it: It is, in fact, possibly something better—a displaced serial conversation; the drafting of a possible meeting of minds; the premeditation or blueprint of a social act; a representation to be presented, shared. But, if this is possibly so, then its *raison d'être*, its point, will lie not so much inherently in itself, as in the uses to which it is to be put, its aftermath.

Let me, then, enforce a distinction that strikes me as illuminating: it was discovered by the sociolinguist, Michael Halliday (1975), when he was making an exhaustive record of the speech-acts of a child between the ages of 9 and 18 months. Halliday discovered that all of the child's utterances fell into a basic contrastive binary set of functions: the pragmatic and the mathetic. Pragmatic utterances are those whereby the child participates in family life in order to satisfy his desires; they are interactions with others, many of which make demands of others; Halliday labels them "intrusive": the child intrudes into the life of others. Conversely, mathetic utterances have no practical outcome: they are utterances of the speaker-as-observer; they make no demands of anyone else; they are a commentary, and often simply a naming. Halliday observed here the spectator's use of language for learning through representation. Eventually, as the child abandoned its proto-language and took on the language of its adult society, the two functions began to overlap and blur: with the acquisition of the lexicogrammatical system, the child became capable of doing two things at once with language, both the interpersonal and the ideational things.

Approaching this from a markedly different angle, Keats, in his "Ode on a Grecian Urn," argued that all we can ever know on earth, and all we need to know, is what we know as participants and what we know as spectators; his shorthand for what these two frames of mind construe is "Beauty" and "Truth." And each is incomplete, or insufficient, even lopsided without the other.

When we read the "great" journals, it seems to me that we are irresistibly led to the conclusion that both functions—the pragmatic and the mathetic—are present; but that the primary one, the one that claims most time and space, is the mathetic, the ideational. And that, underlying all this ideational work, are the longer-term participatory, interpersonal, social purposes. In other words, that we withdraw for the long-term purpose of re-entering. The ideational work, the reflecting, the speculating, is done so that at some later moment its fruits will be available for the interpersonal work that we inevitably return to, unless we are irreversible hermits. Put it in a nutshell: journals start life as intrapersonal but are directed to long-term interpersonal desires.*

Trollope (1980) offers an interesting case. In middle age he pulled out a trunk that contained his juvenilia: he skimmed through the manuscripts and concluded that they were rubbish; but he also admitted that it was in those pages that writing had become for him "second nature."

He realized that before he could present any text to a readership, he had needed to get all those private inchoate and jejune texts under his belt; he had served his apprenticeship as a closet-writer; and thereby evolved into a writer.

Conversely, there are those who insist on publishing their journals. But what do such revealed texts reveal? One thinks of Anaïs Nin or May

*Writers themselves can be deluded about this, and deceive both themselves and others. Valéry made many public statements about his indifference/ antipathy to publishing his notebooks; but in a letter to a friend he said that he considered his notebooks to be his major work. When he did publish selections, he observed that "there are times when one has to give way to the preposterous desires of lovers of the spontaneous and ideas in the rough."

Sarton; what do they offer a reader beyond a rather precious self-regard, a self-conscious displaying of self, an implicit invitation to value wood-shavings as Chippendale? The best Valéry journals—and it's probably more than a coincidence—were, with few exceptions, published posthumously: their peculiar integrity is vouchsafed by our recognition that the writer had no intention of publishing such a self-revealing, self-serving text—self-serving in the sense of "serving to offer a way to realize, constitute, the inner life of the speculating, surmising, contemplating mind." What distinguishes the great journals is the evidence of an unusually responsive and idiosyncratic mind, innocent of any designs on the reader.

These are easily distinguished from those that offer interesting "cases," odd, deviant, pathological, or whatever. The main interest of such texts is in what they unwittingly reveal or betray. Charles Altamont Doyle's Journal* is an example of this plight; Coleridge's *Notebooks* often so; whereas Richard Doyle's journal*, written during his fifteenth year, is a marvelously sane and disarming revelation of a precocious, unspoilt genius exploring the world-to-be-known. Let us, however briefly, consider a great journal, the work of a man at the height of his mature powers.

Francis Kilvert's (1960) journal, severely pruned by William Plomer, runs from January 1870 to March '79, and extends to 1300 pages. Here is God's plenty: fragments of social history, folklore, rural manners and customs, the seasons, day and night, and, above all, hundreds of stories, mostly from the lips of old people. But when one puts oneself in the place of the writer, and asks, "Why is all this to be written down?" the text becomes mysterious, since it was never intended for publication (and contained, indeed, sporadic confessions of a problematic sexual interest in girls of tender years). Mysterious, that is, for anyone who has *not* experienced that radical anamnestic urge to resist the Heraclitean flux, to resist time. Writing was clearly, for Kilvert, the most effective way of counteracting the attritions of time.

His text seems to have served two main intentions or needs: to record the minutiae of rural life in a quiet backward backwater, and to offer a place for moral and spiritual evaluations of the lives of all the various types and classes of people that he came to know in the course of his pastoral duties. Certainly, there is no trace of any pragmatic intent, unless one can interpret his reflections on his own weaknesses and failings as a parson as in some sense a way of trying to do a better job. But very little of his writing is about himself: his eye always seems to have been drawn to forms of life outside himself, and, more distinctive, he never seemed to fail to respond, to be aroused, enlivened, interested.

At this point it would be temptingly easy to see Kilvert, in all his textual plenitude, as one blessed with what William James characterized as "a responsive sensibility"; but this, albeit true, misses the mark: it fails to see the journal-keeping as not merely retroactive, but also

The Doyle Diary, ed. Michael Baker, Paddington Press, 1978; Dick Doyle's *Journal of 1840*, 1885; see *Richard Doyle and His Family*, Victoria and Albert Museum, 1983.

formative. There is a clue to this in James Agee: "I keep talking so much about it simply because I am respectful of experience in general and of any experience whatever, and because it turns out that going through, remembering, and trying to tell of anything is of itself...interesting and important to me...I am interested in the actual and in telling of it." (1960, p. 220). Implicit in Agee's work is some sense of the generative effect of the act of recording, not merely in terms of what has already been known, experienced, and recorded, but also in terms of what the future may hold: the relationship between observing and writing is not a one-way traffic: the more acutely and passionately one observes, the more there is that feels worth recording, yes; but conversely the more one becomes committed to such writing, the more active—as a consequence —one's observings become. Commitment to such recording generated the very acts that are generally construed as being prior to writing; but those acts also follow from writing. The world that is verbalized is more interesting potentially than the world that remains unverbalized.

In a nutshell, it was in part because Kilvert was so persistent a journal-keeper that he could wake up each morning with a positive expectation of what the coming day would offer. "Wednesday, 16 March, 1870...Below Tybella a bird singing unseen reminded me how the words of a good man live after he is silent and out of sight. 'He being dead yet speaketh.'" His own words are his best epitaph: he died tragically of peritonitis, not yet forty and newly married. The evidence of Kilvert's journal is also clear in this sense: he was an intensely social/ sociable man: his journal was not the work of someone looking for something to fill solitudes; one may claim, indeed, that his journal-writing was a social act, even though his writing was revealed to others only after his death.

If, then, a journal of integrity is free of that glance we cast to confirm that someone is "listening," then it follows that if we are asking our students to "use" a form or medium that is similar to the journal, it must nevertheless be recognized as crucially different. Even if we fail to find another name for it, our students need to know that in our courses their "journals" are, willy-nilly, directly or indirectly "speaking" to others, are ways of preparing for conversation, are fragments of work in progress, accountable and answerable—part of a tribal enterprise. In such a tribe, we talk to ourselves primarily in order to talk more effectively to others; the alternative is to end up talking only to ourselves.

If we intend to enable student-writers to produce texts—guided or assisted doings—with a developing recognition and control of options and possibilities, moving toward some effective repertoire expansion, then the "journal" has a part to play, as a semi-private workshop in which the various possibilites of textuality can be explored so as to build a belief in the worthwhileness of making texts; not only that, but also build belief in that which the text is to mediate. I suspect that the second of those beliefs is in fact prior, that the proposition "I cannot write/ cannot think of anything to write" is a veiled way of saying, "There is nothing in my life that I believe to be significant enough to write about." And any acount of significance must acknowledge that the creation/recognition of significance is first a social act. In such matters we are, it seems, still trying to pull our feet out of the swamps of romanticism, trying to free ourselves of the perverse creepers of rampant individualism. Every learner needs a society, a little world, a community; and our teaching must work carefully to generate such sodalities. The privileged Oxbridge tradition has always tacitly recognized this, resting its pedagogical orthodoxy firmly in the tutorial, a society, a microcosm, of two or three. For fourteen years I was fortunate to work within that system, as adopted and modified by the University of York; it is, needless to say, economically labor-intensive, and goes hand-in-glove with an extremely rigorous process of selection; but its benefits are considerable, if only in terms of allowing for a continuing conversation between teacher and taught. Currently, my classes at Queens College, where I teach composition as an adjunct, number around 25, and we meet for 2½ hours a week. Despite three office-hours meetings in a 15-week semester, I find it difficult to understand how my students do their thinking; my solution—better than mere guesswork—is to require two texts: a text and a meta-text, a text and a commentary on it. In their commentaries, students can raise the questions that they need to have answered, forcing me to be accountable to them. The result is a kind of displaced conversation, with this advantage: that I don't do all the talking. Better still, in writing such commentary, students become aware of the conduct of their own minds—not emotionally self-conscious, but more mentally articulate, more mathetic.

When students think aloud on paper about their performative acts as writers, revealing the inner ebb and flow, the fluctuations of confidence, certainty, tentativeness, and so on, they are in effect writing a history—a "natural history"—of their own minds.* When they look back and read such reflections, they are again reminded that they do indeed have minds; any such reminder is to be welcomed at a time when young people could be excused for concluding that they are only bodies, to be jogged, stretched, exercised, reduced, pampered, decorated, or whatever the latest consuming fad happens to be.

Over the last three years, deriving much from the work of Denys Harding, Jimmy Britton, Michael Halliday and others, my wife and I have evolved a composition agenda that rests on the fundamental binary of participant and spectator, of pragmatic and mathetic.* We have discovered that almost universally our students have done virtually all of their previous writing in the spectator role: e.g. book reviews, in which the reviewer is *outside* the experience of reading. We offer them many and varied occasions for writing not only from outside, so to speak, but also from *inside*, creating texts that read as transcripts of participant utterance. The results continue to be extremely encouraging in a variety of ways: students not only generate a repertoire of texts ranging from an extreme parataxis to complex hypotaxis, but are alerted to the distinctive strengths and limitations of texts that "come from" the detachment of

*The classic case of such a "natural history" was produced by Paul Valéry, who, in Auden's words, "made it his daily habit to rise before dawn and spend two or three hours studying the interior maneuvers of his freshly awoken mind"—"Un Homme d'Esprit," in *Forewords and Afterwords*.
*See our *Texts and Contexts*, Random House, 1986.

the spectator role and, conversely, the inwardness of the participant role.
Let us offer an example: consider the following text:

140 m.p.h. now. Wonderful time. Temp. 52. The heater from
cockpit warms the cabin too.
Bill says radio is cuckoo. He is calling now.
There is so much to write. I wonder whether ol' diary will hold
out.
I see clouds coming. They lie on the horizon like a long shore
line.... There is nothing to see but churned mist, very white in the
afternoon sun. I can't see an end to it. 3600 ft. temp. 52, 45 degrees
outside. I have et a orange...[*sic*]
It is about 10. I write without light. Readable?...
The exhaust sends out glowing meteors.
How marvellous is a machine and the mind that made it. I am
thoroughly occidental in this worship.
Bill sits up alone. Every muscle and nerve alert. Many hours to go.
Marvellous also. I've driven all day and all night and know what
staying alert means.
Slim and I exchange places for a while. All the dragons and sea
serpents and monstrosities are silhouetted against the dawn...

How would you begin to typify that text? Which features would you
isolate in order to characterize it? What desires or needs does it seem
likely to fulfill?

You will probably agree that it is performing at least two of the
tasks of a journal—both recording and commenting, both representing
and evaluating it. It is both pragmatic—part of a segment of work,
synpraxis—and also mathetic or reflective. But as it stands, it offers few
if any contextual clues such as would appear quite intentionally to be
"putting the reader in the picture." On the other hand, although it is
clearly mediating, as all text is, it offers the reader a powerful illusion of
*im*mediacy, of presence. We, the readers, can enjoy the illusion of
reading over the shoulder of the writer. It is also a concurrent text: it
unfolds in time, moves in step with the situations that it represents. No
part of the text can anticipate what the next part can be: the parataxis is
inescapable.*

Let me now put you in the picture: that was a short extract from the
journal or log-book kept by Amelia Earhart (1929) during her first
transatlantic flight in June 1928. She was neither pilot or mechanic, but
she had an important role, keeping a comprehensive moment-by-
moment record of a pioneering flight, the outcome of which was
extremely uncertain. Without her record much of the benefit of the
venture would have been lost to amnesia. But her text clearly serves
another purpose, which is to "tell the world" how it felt.

*The most extraordinary example of paratactic "groping" or tentativeness
in concurrent journal writing may well be the final entry in Jules Renard's
Journal, which had so powerful an effect on Samuel Beckett that he kept
repeating it to himself, over and over: clearly a crucial moment in the
evolution of Beckett's own prose.

It was Earhart's distinctive privilege and responsibility to occupy both roles, serving as both participant and spectator: her writerly instincts served her well; her candidly disingenuous journal captures the intentness, the uncertainties, the bravura of that flight as no coolly distanced spectator's discourse could hope to. As she scribbled each word, she could not know what she would have to write next; she was writing, as she was flying, almost by the seat of her pants. Later, in the early weeks of a blazing fame, she could sit back and construct her more measured, contextualized, hypotactic account of that which had happened, that which was no longer happening:*

An even more remarkable case is offered by Admiral Byrd's journal of his solitary sojourn through a South Pole winter, when he was on the verge of dying from carbon monoxide poisoning; it is a text that quivers on the edge of total breakdown, and yet the very act of writing it (with its implicit belief in the continuing feasibility of talking to someone else) contributed to Byrd's survival. His account of how he came to decide *not* to print his journal verbatim is one of the best discussions I know of some of the crucial choices facing a writer tip-toeing delicately between the private and the public, the immediate and the mediated, the "raw" and the "cooked," the non-contextualized and the contextualized, the participant and the spectator.

It is on the strength of such considerations as these that I rest my belief that there is considerable learning mileage for student-writers in both the reading and the writing of the journals. On one condition: that the withdrawal to the relative privacy of the solitary act of journal-writing is always construed as complete only when the writer and her text (at least in selected part) have re-entered "the very world which is the world of all of us."

*i.e. her book, *20 Hours, 40 Minutes.*

References

Agee, J., & Evans, W. (1960). *Let us now praise famous men.* New York: Ballantine.

Auden, W.H. "Un Homme d'Esprit" [Paul Valéry]. In *Forewords and afterwords.* London: Faber & Faber.

Britton, J. (1982). *Prospect and retrospect: Selected essays of James Britton.* Upper Montclair, NJ: Boynton/Cook.

Doyle, C.A. (1978). *The Doyle diary.* London: Paddington Press.

Earhart, A. (1929). *20 hours, 40 minutes.* New York: G.P. Putnam.

Halliday, M.A.K. (1975). *Learning how to mean.* London: L'Arnold.

Harding, D.W. (1937). The role of the onlooker. *Scrutiny, 6.*

Heaney, S. (1980). *Preoccupations.* London: Faber & Faber.

Kilvert, F. (1960). In W. Plomer (Ed.), *Kilvert's diary.* London: Cayse.

Trollope, A. (1980). *An autobiography.* London: Oxford University Press.

Vygotsky, L. (1962). In E. Haufman (Ed. and Trans.), *Thought and language.* Cambridge: MIT Press.

4.

Writing to Learn*

PAT D'ARCY

Donald Murray tells us that when writers think of writing, they think of a blank page—and everything that went before the blank page—all the experience on which the writer is drawing in order to shape fresh meaning. When teachers think of writing I wonder what comes into their minds. A pile of papers waiting to be marked? Their own pen moving across students' writing, editing, annotating, questioning—and finally, grading? A display of pupils' work on the classroom wall? Perhaps heads bent over desks as a class work in silence....

My guess is that the "writing" teachers think about is rarely their own. Whatever the pictures that form inside their heads, they will involve pupils' writing and teachers responding.

This is not to say that all teachers approach pupils' writing in the same way. Indeed, the expectations which they bring to writing assignments can vary widely and in their turn affect the views that students form about the nature of writing as an activity—who it is for and what its uses are.

Many teachers of primary, secondary and even older students seem to regard the correct handling of the *medium* of written language as a top priority. They look *at* the words on the page rather than *through* the words to the meaning. Thus they become conscientious proofreaders of their pupils' writing, indicating where words are misspelled, punctuation marks omitted, paragraphs ignored. For these teachers "writing" is predominantly a code. In such classes pupils come to form an impression of themselves as good at writing if they are accurate encoders and failed writers if their spelling is shaky and their punctuation spasmodic.

Another very common way to approach writing, as a teacher faced with that pile of papers all waiting for their grades, is to think of it as a collection of finished pieces or products which she is going to evaluate for her pupils to let them know how successfully (or unsuccessfully) they have included the information that the teacher is looking for. In these classes pupils come to think of writing as "evidence" that has to be

*I am indebted to the classroom practice of the teachers in Wiltshire with whom I have the opportunity to work—namely, in this paper, Margaret Jensen, who teaches English superbly well at Hardenville Comprehensive School, Chippenham; and Lorraine Canard, one of the best science teachers I know, at Headlands Comprehensive School, Swindon.

produced for an evaluator who will then judge it for better or worse, according to how it matches up to pre-determined expectations.

Over the last decade or so, a small but steadily growing group of teachers in Britain and in the States, dissatisfied with the limitations of both these approaches to writing in school, have sought alternatives that would enable more students to make a better use of this particular mode of language *to think for themselves.*

Back in the mid-seventies, I was one of those teachers searching for strategies that would encourage the teenagers that I taught to take a much more positive hold on their own writing instead of approaching it with the kind of caution they might give to a mad dog. I stopped being an immediate editor of the writing they handed in; I also stopped instant evaluation. Grades went but comments grew longer. I made a conscious effort to analyze instead of assessing, asking myself what clues could be picked up from the page in front of me as to what had been happening inside that writer's head.

I came to realize that waiting at the finishing post, stopwatch in hand, was of little help to my student writers. What they really needed was some help along the way, constructive suggestions as to how they might develop the meanings they were seeking to evolve so that they learned more *through* the writing as they went along.

This led me, as it has led others, to some major changes in my classroom practice. I began to give my students longer stretches of time to work on any piece of writing which they undertook so that new meanings and clearer perceptions had a much better chance to evolve. I spent more time talking to them while the writing was underway—and even more importantly encouraging them to talk to me about the directions they saw the writing taking or the problems they were encountering as they struggled for clarity. I also came more and more to encourage my students to use journal writing as a kind of running commentary on their other work—a way of thinking onto paper which didn't require any particular form or shape, thus freeing the writer to express whatever feelings she chose, to recollect information piecemeal and jot it down, to confess confusion without guilt, to ask questions.

In searching for a form of writing that would serve students as *a mode of learning,* I discovered paradoxically that the formlessness of journals enabled the students' own voices to be heard in their writing—perhaps by them for the first time as well as by their teacher. Listen to 14-year-old Sarah, who clearly feels free to let her thoughts run on about the opening sequence of scenes in *Romeo and Juliet*:

> Well, Shakespeare certainly didn't believe in letting the audience catch their breath did he? No sooner does one exciting scene end than another one starts! We have now been introduced to Romeo and Juliet (for a moment I thought they'd gone home!) and they have been introduced to each other.
>
> Both of these characters seem different—but you know what they say "Opposites attract." Juliet is a level headed, loving and VERY beautiful girl—she seems to have a wise head on a young pair of shoulders. Perhaps its all the good advice she gets from her nurse!

Talking of the Nurse, although she makes some rather crude remarks about how Juliet will lose her balance when she gets older, I think that she has a good heart and as we will find out, J seems to have confidence in her.

I can't help feeling rather sorry for poor Paris. What with some fellow sweeping his would-be bride off her feet, I can't help feeling he might be getting left out. Perhaps he should team up with Rosaline?!

It's amazing how Romeo flits from one beautiful girl to another —although by the time we reach Act 2 Sc. 2 it is obvious that Juliet IS rather special—I mean, would you go into a graden where you would be likely to get killed if you were discovered? Mrs. J. said that he was in the second most dangerous place he could be in— yes, I suppose he could have strolled into the house—'Oh, hi there Lord and Lady Capulet, I've come to see Juliet!'

Juliet says to Romeo that if he disowns his name she will disown hers and will be only too pleased to marry him. Crikey! Altogether they must have only spoken for about five or ten minutes in all— and he hasn't even asked her. Even so, I think it's really sweet and romantic—but I can't imagine any of the boys in 4.1 turning up at any of the girls' houses in 4.1 in the night can you Mrs. J.?

I would have thought that Lord and Lady Capulet would have heard Romeo clambering up the creepers at the side of the house without much success! And surely the Nurse would have heard him? Still, I suppose that would have cut the play short!

From the same class of 14-year-olds, here is Neil letting his thoughts circle round the play so far, identifying issues which puzzle him and others which please.

I think that it is a bit odd that Romeo and Juliet are in each others arms and saying that their lives are not worth living without each other after they had only met each other for the first time a few minutes ago.

After Romeo is discovered gatecrashing Capulet's party why is he not thrown out immediately? Instead he is allowed to stay and chat up Capulet's only daughter. What happens to Paris who was supposed to be introduced to Juliet? Surely Lady Capulet whose idea it was in the first place would make more of an effort.

I can't help thinking that if there was no Tybalt the relations between the Montague and Capulet families would be a good deal better. Also Tybalt's powers of perception must be truly brilliant to recognize a Montague underneath a mask just by his voice. Also another great disappearance—what happened to Rosaline? Did she find true love elsewhere? Up until Act 2 Scene 2 the Nurse was the most prominent character. The nurse is a very good character to have around as she tends to throw a little more light on the more complicated situations.

I think that the more prologues the better, it is a very good idea to have one at the start of each act.

Going on to Act 2 now, I think Benvolio and Mercutio seem a
little bit too concerned for Romeo's safety than is normal. I mean
do they follow Romeo around all day trying to persuade him not to
see Juliet? Would it not have been easier and a lot less dangerous
for Romeo and Juliet to meet on neutral ground?

I am surprised that the nurse did not suggest a more sensible and
safe wedding. How can Romeo and Juliet possibly lead a normal
married life. They will be lucky if they set eyes on each other once
a day let alone speak to each other.

Surely the answer to their problems would be to elope together.
This seems the only thing that will keep them together now as
Romeo has just killed Tybalt and got himself banished from
Verona.

Just as the student writer is freed in the journal or the log to catch
thoughts as they come—for as long or as little time as it takes*—so the
teacher-reader is freed from the need to evaluate and is thus able to
respond not to form and structure but to feelings, questions, hesitations.
Here is just one example of a teacher's response to an entry from one of
his advanced level English students. Unlike in a finished paper the
student's comments are fairly brief. Nevertheless, they offer the teacher
plenty that he can reply to.

Although I have continued to discuss 1984 I am finding that I can't
think of anything to say about it, why, I don't know! There is one
point which I could make though, and this is that I have noticed,
by writing the last essay on 'How does the Party seek to remain in
Power?' that I referred mainly to "Goldstein's book" to obtain
information. By writing the information down I sorted the points
out clearly in my head, and where I previously said that I did not
understand Goldstein's book, now I find that I do.

Teacher's reply:

Interesting. Does this suggest that a time in each lesson ought to
be allotted to recording the thoughts so that they stick? Is this a
limitation on the value of discussion alone? Are you setting up a
justification for the "boring" Goldstein's book?

Conversations like this can easily get started. In my experience
journals often seem to demand this kind of response. Freed from the
duties of the conscientious proofreader, the teacher has time to talk back
to the student on paper, a dialogue which is often appreciated and in its
turn responded to by the journal writer.

This point among others is taken up in the two following entries
from a science class of twelve-year-olds. Their teacher had asked them to
write a final journal entry for her at the end of the school year to let her
know how they had found this "new" way of writing helpful:

*Journal writing doesn't have set time limits; it offers students an oppor-
tunity to think on paper for however long it takes to find a first formulation. This may amount to, "Let's all journal write for five minutes, then
share..." At home the time taken is entirely up to the student, of course.

Rachel

I find that writing things down helps me to associate with the teacher in the way that I want to. I can express my feelings much better writing them down than saying them out loud. I can ask questions about the subjects which I haven't quite cottoned onto and to ask the teacher that same question face to face could mean embarrassment in front of my friends. I once wrote down that Mrs. C. told us that the test was easy and I thought it the same sort of tricky test. In the margin Mrs C. put "Sneaky." This humoured me and I think that the teachers find it an easier way themselves of communicating with pupils. But I also find that I can take the answers to my questions in, much easier then the ones in my school book.

Claire

I think that the journals are a way of closer communication to a teacher. I think that when you write a journal you can go on thinking of loads of ideas which just shows how much you do or don't know and I think this is useful as in class you sit down and get on with your work. You don't stop to think of questions, you just ignore them but if you keep your thoughts in your head later on you will forget what they are and they could have been useful. You can see where you have gone wrong. Journals are like another science lesson but privately.

I don't think the name we choose for "process focused" writing matters—journals, learning logs, think books, neuron notes—as long as the students come to understand that (just like "product focused" writing) it can serve a *range* of purposes for them.

Recently a small group of Wiltshire science teachers tried to identify some of these purposes and came up with the following list:

- They enable pupils to collect ideas and information together before they embark on a continuous piece of writing.
- They can help pupils to "re-discover" the information that they have already taken in.
- They can help pupils to come up with their own questions about what they still need to find out.
- They allow pupils to express their feelings about the work they have been doing with honesty to the teacher.
- They make two kinds of internal conversation possible: a conversation that the writer carries on with herself; and a conversation that the writer can have with the teacher without the rest of the class hearing.
- They can provide a pupil and her teacher with a personal map of the progress she is making. They can be a valuable source of information for any detailed profiling scheme.
- Journal/log writing does not demand a special writing style; the pupil/learner/writer is free to think onto paper as the words come. For this reason journals often carry a strong sense of the writer's voice in a way that more formal, transactional or product-oriented writing does not.

As with any classroom activity, some students catch on to how journals can help them with their learning more quickly than others. One mystified seventeen-year-old who had never before been asked to "think as she went along" added a footnote to her first journal entry which read "I can't make head or tail of it. . ." Her teacher responded by referring specifically to comments that she had made about the test they were studying and demonstrating to her how her own uncertainties led on to further points for discussion.

If you haven't used journals with a particular group before, their introduction always requires patience—as well as good humor and a willingness to respond. Feedback into the class of entries which raises interesting questions or areas of confusion will help to indicate how we can all use writing to help us through patches when learning is difficult—or to freewheel when the going is easy. The teacher who was reading *Romeo and Juliet* with her 14-year-olds for the first time invited them to discuss in class issues that were raised in their journals, following her perusal of what they had written.

For me, these two major changes in the way teachers can approach writing intermesh: a willingness to reflect about the learning that's going on through the journal pages often provides the stimulus for a willingness to redraft and reshape product oriented work. Journals provide that space essential for rehearsal and reflection, finding out what you know, discovering new thoughts, fresh perceptions, dealing with feelings, asking questions. They help to point the way very often for the writer, give her confidence as a learner to find a path instead of wallowing in uncertainty. At my last school, shortly after I arrived, I received this request from the Head of the history department: as Head of English, would I please make sure that all fifth-year students were taught how to write "the essay" as their external History examinations required essays to be written.

I tried to point out without sounding too defensive or dismissive that I didn't believe in this platonic all-purpose essay form, which, if taught, would somehow sort out of its own accord confusions of meaning. Writing which has something interesting to say and which expresses ideas or conveys information coherently, has achieved that clarity because the writer has spent a considerable amount of time grappling with meaning, shaping, re-shaping, coming at it from different angles, finding out orally and on the page through the act of formulation and reformulation what it is, finally, she has to say.

In classrooms if they are lucky, students will sometimes find teachers who are willing to accompany them on that journey towards a clear meaning—willing to listen to their questions and to come up with helpful suggestions when the going is difficult. These teachers probably also keep journals themselves because they have rediscovered the power that writing has to help us all to learn.

5.

The Power of Responding in Dialogue Journals*

JANA STATON

Dialogue journals bring into writing the power of dialogue, of living conversation. Dialogue journals are a responsive form of writing in which the student and teacher carry on a conversation over time, sharing ideas, feelings, and concerns in writing.

Because this entire volume is about journals, and their use in developing students' minds and selves, I don't need to stress the value to students of being able to write down thoughts freely and openly in a journal. What needs to be stressed and clarified is the importance of written, interpersonal dialogue as one means for introducing children, particularly in elementary school, to the open, expressive, thoughtful uses of writing as a mode of knowing oneself and knowing the world.

The mutual responsiveness of a written conversation is different from *replying*. We reply to questions; we respond to persons. A brief reply to a student's text is not a response to that student. A response involves an implicit commitment of self, an engagement with the other. Dialogue journals involve this kind of response by the teacher, and eventually by the student as well—first by an act of "listening" to the student's person/voice as it comes through the page itself and then by making a commitment of self in written response. Figure 1 (Reed, 1982) shows what a typical handwritten dialogue journal page looks like.

Dialogue journals consist of the written interactions *and* the minds of the student and teacher. The access to the teacher's mind, and to an interactive, personalized *response* makes the dialogue journals work. In *Middlemarch*, Mary Ann Evans (George Eliot) expressed as well as anyone could the power of entering into a responsive dialogue with another:

> O, the comfort, the inexpressible comfort of feeling safe with a person, neither having to weigh thoughts nor measure words, but pouring them right out just as they are, chaff and grain alike; certain that a faithful hand will take and sift them, keep what is worth keeping and then with the breath of kindness, blow the rest away.

*I would like to express my special appreciation to Roger Shuy for his thoughtful comments and encouragement on drafts of this chapter.

...Yes I like studing on the heart
It will help me when I'm a docter.
        Thank you for saying that.
I saw both of the films
but when I saw them
the second time I enjoyed
them even more. The second
film is funny.

                        May 12, Monday
    I agree with you! Seeing the
films the second time does make
them even more interesting!
    Good! When you get to be a
Doctor I will come to see you
when I am not feeling well!
What kind of a Doctor would
you like to become?

    I don't know yet. Maybe
a regular doctor that
fixes broken pieces of
the human body. What are
they called. We merely
finshed our hot water heat
but we didn't.

                        Tue. May 13
    A General Practitioner is
a doctor who takes care of most
ordinary sickness and simple
breaks. A doctor who only deals
with setting broken bones is
an orthopedic doctor.
    Your solar water heater should

Figure 1

This sense of feeling safe enough to pour out ideas and thoughts is what dialogue journals create for students. In this chapter, I'll present some of what I have learned from classroom teachers about the use of dialogue journals in elementary schools. Much of this comes from research on the dialogue journals of one classroom teacher, Leslee Reed, which I conducted with colleagues Roger Shuy and Joy Kreeft Peyton (Staton, Shuy, Peyton, and Reed, in press).

Dialogue Journals: What Are They?

A dialogue journal contains a genuine conversation, written rather than spoken, a means by which individual students at any age can carry on a private discussion with their teacher. The interactive format of equal turns on the same topics is quite different from the traditional student personal journals, in which a teacher may sometimes make some kind of marginal comment on a student's entry, but only days or weeks after the student wrote it. The distinguishing characteristics of dialogue journals are their *interactive, functional* nature, and the creation of mutually interesting topics. Such dialogues occur on a daily or regular basis throughout the school year, extending the conversation across time for purposes of communication, self-understanding, negotiation of the classroom relationship, and problem-solving. In the elementary school classroom, this simple, teacher-developed practice also involves meaningful, functional reading and writing as a single whole, just as speaking and listening are a seamless whole in oral discourse.

Picture an ordinary classroom, in which second grade students have conversations like this every day with their teacher Marley Casagrande, a Fairfax County, Virginia teacher:

Kelly: I like to read. Evry' time I woth a skery movy I have a drem.
Teacher: Scary movies give me bad dreams, too, Kelly. Maybe we shouldn't watch them. What good books have you read?
Kelly: The little red hen and Dick and Jane. I have problims some times well I have this problim it is I am not very god on my writeing.
Teacher: I think you *are* a good writer. Keep on trying your best. I like *The Little Red Hen,* too, Kelly. Keep on writing!
Kelly: Oh kay. Do you have a problem. if you do I will help you. and what are you going to be for Halloween
Teacher: I am going to be a farmer. I will wear overalls and a straw hat. Everybody has problems, Kelly. Some problems are big and some are small. One of my small problems is that I can't stop eating chocolate when I see it!

[several weeks later, new topics have emerged]

Kelly: are you going to have a terky on thanksgiving
Teacher: Yes, I am going to have a turkey with stuffing, sweet potatoes, green beans, salad, and pumpkin pie with whipped cream! What are you going to have?

Kelly: turkey to. Do you want a dog. I do. you could play with it. and do
  you want a cat.
Teacher: I used to have a cat, Kelly, and I really loved it. But it got very
  sick when it was old. Now I have two children and I don't have time
  to take care of a dog. I think a dog might get lonely left alone all
  day at home, don't you.
Kelly: No. Are you going to see your grandmom for thanksgiving

Kelly is in a program for students who are at least one grade below
expected reading level. Notice the responsiveness of this student to her
teacher as an audience, and her obvious comprehension of the teacher's
writing.

At sixth grade, the content of the conversations may differ, but the
interaction and the involvement of student and teacher in these conversations are the same (Staton et al., 1982):

Sue: Bryan's mother came she's a prosicutor. Everybody one the other
  team today said we cheated but we didn't. We played fair and
  square. Wow, Gorilla Adventure is incredibly interesting. I hope to
  get the rest of his books for my birthday. Also I've waited a hundred
  years to read my own great brain books, which I also like Shoot.
  Mrs. Windsor left while I was putting on my paperclips. She just
  took it. oops I didn't loose it. Oh dummy me!
Mrs. Reed: Of course you aren't a dummy! Everyone loses things—unless
  they do nothing! Mrs. Windsor will be back. She is extremely
  interested in our reading habits. Did you see the blurb on the door
  about an author who writes much like Fitzgerald? (Author of Great
  Brain books.)

Especially for the second language learner, the written dialogues
allow students to put their thoughts down quickly without worrying
about correctness, and to begin exploring a new world with the assistance of their teacher.

September 26, 1980
Michael: Mrs. Reed equator is a North, East, West, South, right?
  Mrs. Reed we doing math is How many right, how many wrong?
  Mrs. Reed, you know, I'm live in Burmese. The Burma school is no
  good. You know why? At the Burma school is no free lunch. At the
  America school is good free lunch and the games is funny games. At
  the Burma school is no games. Only is you can fight so I don't like
  the Burma school. The America school is "you very good student
  and you can skip to the 6 grate or 5 grate anything!" So I like a-am-
  America school. Where are you come from? How old are you Mrs.
  Reed? You know Mrs. Reed, here is all is good friend.

Mrs. Reed: The equator goes east and west around the middle of the globe.

In the math test you have 19 correct (right) and only 1 wrong. That is very good.

I'm glad you are at Alexandria Avenue school. You study and work hard so you will be very smart. It is good to learn to play games to get exercise. To grow well everyone needs to eat a good lunch. Your mind works better if you have eaten the right food.

I was born in Idaho. It is in the United States.

I am very old! Yes! Everyone is glad to be your friend so we do not hit or fight.

[Kreeft et al., 1985]

Dialogue Journals as a Teacher-Developed Practice

Until recently, the concept of a dialogue belonged entirely to oral interaction. In fact, no one had any idea that a dialogue with genuine two-way responding could occur naturally in writing, and particularly not with elementary school students. Even though Moffett (1968) had provided a strong theoretical base for writing as dialogic, school practice kept all writing in monologue form. It took an experienced sixth grade teacher in Los Angeles, Leslee Reed, to teach us that written dialogue could be just as powerful and functional as the spoken.

About 1964, Leslee Reed began asking her sixth grade students to respond to her in writing each day about what had happened to them, what they had learned or had trouble learning. Students began really communicating with this teacher who was willing to listen, asking questions, complaining about homework, promising to do better, predicting football games, giving their opinions about lessons and books, and often asking for help or advice with interpersonal problems. She asked her students to write in their free time, when they really had something to say.

She quickly found that the time she spent in responding (about an hour for sixth grade; less for primary students) was not only enjoyable, but that in the same hour she could do most of her lesson planning for the next day. This daily written feedback also led to the elimination of many busy-work assignments which didn't have much meaning for the students or for her.

Typically, in elementary school classes students write during the school day and the teacher responds at night, returning the dialogue journals the next morning. The small bound journals are passed back and forth for each new response. The students are encouraged to comment on any topics or concerns they have. The privacy of each dialogue is an essential element; students want assurance that other students will not have access to their personal conversation. Thus, unlike some other kinds of journal use, student comments are not read to the class by either teacher or student.

Rather than making the dialogue journal an assigned task, teachers have found that it works best if students have their journals available during the entire day, so that they can write whenever an idea or concern pops into mind. This makes for brief entries; the goal is to carry on a discussion about some important topic over several days, adding to it as new thoughts or events occur. With elementary students, a good rule of thumb is to write about as much as the students write, and to discuss the students' topics first before bringing up new ones.

The teacher's greater competence in responding and elaborating on each student's topic is essential to making this journal a dialogue and to encouraging the continual expansion of ideas: teachers who have tried to develop student-student dialogues in writing at elementary levels report that these seldom result in continued topics and usually are not maintained for very long.

At the secondary level, Nancie Atwell has adapted the dialogue journal concept into a process for discussing literature with her junior high students, by first writing back and forth in a letter format to her students on a weekly or semi-weekly basis and gradually having them begin dialoguing with each other (Atwell, 1984).

Functional, Interactive Communication

It's important to understand that dialogue journal communication is real student-teacher communication, not a writing "assignment." Although many writing skills are practiced in the daily entries, the dialogue journal is not a method of teaching specific writing skills. Instead, the students write about their lives and concerns in order to be understood and often to change something, and the teacher responds to students, not to their writing, for the same reasons.

Studies of the dialogue texts have shown that because they are an interactive conversation in writing with a real audience even the youngest students use the full range of language functions common in oral discourse. Examples of the functional nature of the dialogue journal can be seen in these examples:

REQUESTING INFORMATION:

Joan: But what is a whole number? my mother and sister and brother could not find out.

PROMISING:

Gordon: I like math better because I'm trying harder. And I'm going to try and bring in more extra creddit work.

GIVING DIRECTIONS:

Willie: Please don't forget to bring a book to school on drawing different letters.

OFFERING:

John: for the party I can get my grandma to bake a cake. In the shape of a mogen daivid or a Xmas tree. She is a very good cook.

The Dialogue as a Reading Event

Communication in dialogue journals is clearly very different from asking children to "keep" a personal journal which the teacher checks now and then, and may or may not ever really read. The dialogue journal replicates in written language the interactive nature of first language acquisition—for every brief entry the student writes, there is a literate, interesting response (cf. Shuy, in press; Staton, in Kreeft *et al.*, 1985). So we might as easily call dialogue journal writing, dialogue journal *reading*. And it is the quality of the response, in an informal conversational style, that creates endless opportunities for learning.

Figure 2 shows my favorite example of the dialogue journal as a reading text. The student is a seven-year-old who is profoundly deaf. She attends Kendall Demonstration Elementary School on the Gallaudet College Campus. In this page from her journal, she has just finished telling Jean Slobodzian, her teacher, a story about something that happened and says, "Now it's your turn to tell me a story about Paddington." What she gets back is a wonderful short story about how her teacher actually met Paddington Bear (cf. Puthoff, Searls, Slobodzian, and Staton, 1986; Staton, 1985).

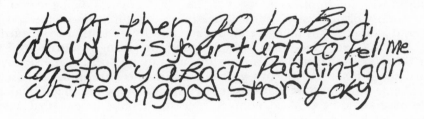

to PJ then go to Bed.
(NOW it is your turn to tell me
an story about Paddington
write an good story oky)

  —you really did not write a story. It
was more of a "news report".

  Anyway — About Paddington... I really
love him. I learned about Paddington in
1979 when I was flying back from
Australia. A girl got on the plane,
holding a stuffed animal under her arm.
It was a bear and he had on a blue
coat, yellow hat and a tag around his
neck that said:

  Please look
  after this
  bear. Thank you

  It was a Paddington bear!

Figure 2

In effect, this teacher and student together are constructing a reading text each day that is of personal interest to the student. Even those students whose own entries are minimal race to get their journals every morning, to read the teacher's responses, and their one-sentence replies show that they have understood the teacher's writing.

Analysis of the dialogue journals as a reading text shows that: (1) the teacher's writing is usually much more complex syntactically and more varied in function and more mature in propositional reasoning than is the basal reading text for that grade level, yet students understand the message and respond appropriately (Shuy, 1986); (2) the teacher in responding can progressively increase the complexity of his or her response, staying just ahead of the student. This creates a text which is continually challenging in terms of comprehension and inferencing (Staton, 1986).

The Power of Responding

The dialogue journal is designed to create interactions in which two minds can unite to bring about new understanding, new ideas, new possibilities. In a dialogue, the student and teacher are equal participants, with the right to comment on the other's entry. A dialogue means continuity of discussion, until the meaning of a topic has been worked out; dialogue means unpredictability and novelty—it cannot be scripted.

In the sixth grade class of Leslee Reed, the dialogue journal topics include books that students are reading, a traumatic spelling bee victory, and the death of a student's grandmother in the Philippines. In each dialogue, students have that sense of feeling safe enough so that thoughts do not have to be weighed, nor words measured, but can be poured right out, "chaff and grain alike."

Here is a private discussion between the class "tough guy" and Leslee Reed about the book she is reading to her class. The teacher in her response is careful not to focus attention on Gordon's feelings, but suggests which other books might give him the same experience.

March 27, 1980

Gordon: Boy, the green knowe is really exciting. Mrs. Old Know is really in shock. I feel sorry for her. I really do feel sorry for Hano. It was really sad I felt like crying. But I would of been really emberrased. So I just held it in.

Mrs. Reed: The Stranger at Green Knowe was an unusual book. Ping is in some other Greene Knowe stories. You may want to read them.

Jenny, a very bright student, finds that winning the school spelling bee causes her classmates to say she won unfairly. In her dialogue with the teacher, she finds a friend who can understand her agony.

3/6/81

Jenny: I wish that I didn't win the Spelling Bee. I know I should be happy about winning but I feel worse than I ever did. I don't care if

I cry too much or what but I have to anyway. I feel very much as if the whole world is against me. Even what I thought were my best of friends. The people I trusted now hate me. Why can't they understand?

Mar. 6

Mrs. Reed: It is difficult to understand—and I understand and share your weird feelings! Do cry if you feel like it! You are human, your feelings are hurt and you are not at fault. It is very disturbing. It is most difficult to be a good loser. The act of destroying the winner makes a poor loser feel better. Being a winner always puts you in the position of being a target for anyone who feels insecure or inferior.

Jenny: I am feeling much better about the Spelling Bee. Now I can easily forget all the bad things about it and remember the good things about it.

[Kreeft, et al, 1985]

Ricardo is late to class and then writes this in his journal:

Fri. April 3, 1981

Ricardo: My grandmother died at the first. Thats why I havent been concentrating. Simon and I are going bowling and have fun.

Mrs. Reed: I am sorry about your grandmother. Did she live here? I'm glad you told me—now I understand. So glad you made it to school today! I was afraid you were absent!

Tues, April 7, 1981

Ricardo: Ya! me to I am sorry about my grandmother dying I miss her....I'm sorry that I didn't learn anything because I was worried of my mother.

Mrs. Reed: I'm sure your mother and dad are sad, too. They will enjoy seeing their families in the Philippines but they are sad that your grandmother is dead. Is your mother very upset?... When someone we love dies, we do cry and feel very bad. That is natural. I did, when my mother died. You can help your mother by understanding that it is good for her to cry and to show her feelings.

These short excerpts can't adequately convey the continuous quality of this mutual response. Day after day the teacher is there to listen and reflect back.

What strikes me about these written conversations is the mutual elaboration of mind as two persons become engaged in thinking on the same topic, an elaboration which the use of a private written mode encourages. Vygotsky (1978) first pointed out that writing and speaking differ in their relationship to our inner thoughts; he believed that writing was more directly connected to internalized thought than speech, because of the other-directed, socially unconstrained nature of spoken utterances. In written dialogues, the closeness of the writing to one's thoughts is retained. There is time for the student and teacher to elaborate on and spin out the web of meaning which an event or experience holds, and to negotiate that meaning together.

I cannot stress enough that the dialogue journal works only if the teacher is committed and fully engaged, for it is the *teacher's* responses which create the motivation and provide the models of thought and reflection, of unpredictability and honesty which students need. The characteristics of good written responses in the dialogue journals are the same as those we use to maintain and deepen a conversation with a good friend: acknowledge and say something interesting about the other person's topics before bringing up your own; add new, relevant information; be honest and avoid quick, glib comments. Our research has shown that teachers who are willing to elaborate and make thier own writing interesting, quickly draw students into making more elaborative responses. In marked contrast, teachers who ask students many questions in order to make them write more tend to cause students to change the subject or not respond at all. (See Appendix for a brief guide to starting dialogue journal use.)

Communicating with Students Who Need It Most

Regular journals often don't work for the children who dislike writing or who just aren't ready to write "for themselves" without the support of someone answering back. In contrast, dialogue journals are used enthusiastically by both native English speakers and ESL students from kindergarten through college, *if* their teachers are initially committed and enthusiastic about their role in the dialogue. Typically, 80 to 90 percent of any class are consistent and motivated users, with boys equally if not more enthusiastic than girls.

In particular the dialogue journals can be an effective means of written communication for the very students who disliked reading and writing most, and this can be a good starting point for teachers who aren't sure they could manage a whole class.

Imagine for a moment that you are Eduardo, a bright, sensitive 11-year-old boy from a Hispanic home who has been in American schools for six years. At first you were afraid of failing at school, and so you started fights and disturbances in the classroom, which led to being kicked out and sent to the playground a lot. By the start of sixth grade, you are barely able to read at the first grade level, and have few writing skills. You don't even know your times tables. You are going to be sent to a special education class with the label "educationally handicapped." In the meantime, you are parked in Mrs. Reed's class, and are given a dialogue journal along with all the other students. By the tenth day, you have started communicating with this teacher in writing despite your fears and dislike of school, as these entries show:

September, 1978

[10th entry]
Eduardo: Mes. Reed, I cant do it. I ges can't do it. I em a dime. my cetres

tel me the dime and all my famele tel me the dime. my mom tel me I have a good mind. Mes Reed I want to lorn efi dont I no I lurin sumer on reed and on spell mor

Mrs. Reed: Good! If you want to learn you will. I will be there to help you—but I cannot learn for you.

7 × 8 = 56, what is 8 × 7? _____

6 × 9 = 54, what is 9 × 6? _____

Eduardo: Mes Reed I now more fracens and mor timstebol and to reed mor and rid mor I like thes day

Mrs. Reed: You must read more and write more every day. I will make you some math cards to study at home.

Eduardo: I dont want to lurn I genh my mind I het school I want to be a dime.

Mrs. Reed: You can be what you want to be. If you can read and write and do math you'll be better at whatever you decide to be.

Eduardo: Mes Reed I now Im a dume and I want to be a dume I dont want to lurn nothen good by

Mrs. Reed: I care! You have a million dollar brain! Someday when you are driving a big fancy car you'll be glad you worked. You are not dumb.

Eduardo: Then you Mes. Reed. It you cares and my mom dus cares to and one of my sestrs cares too.

This dialogue between Eduardo and Mrs. Reed was the beginning of a year-long conversation about his fears and hopes. Eduardo was not sent to a special education class. By the end of the year he was almost at grade level in reading and he no longer thought he was a "dime" (dummy).

[March, 1979]

Eduardo: I hade a good day I can do berer in every thing and I can. Mrs. Reed I hope I can gate my gurnal and I will rite more and raed more in Math and the class and I had a good reces and a good lunch. I play far and I had a good day and I I got ever bory out in socco and a soco ges ones thay got me out and we wan all the games and we play and I had a good day and in Math I got 100 and Mer Nicholsen he was happ and I had a fantatic day Mes Reed I we be good and I love all the world.

For Eduardo, communication with the teacher in this private mode was the key to finding his way out of failure and isolation and into the social world of others.

Starting Out with Dialogue

By providing functional written responses to children's own writing and to the ideas children have, dialogue journals are simply restoring to education and to literacy the essence of language in its natural form. Language and thought itself are both fundamentally dialogical in their very nature, and are acquired through conversational interaction. The dialogue journal functions like conversational interaction to provide support for young students who are just beginning to write.

As children move from drawing into print by adding labels and letters to their drawings, the teacher's response to the drawing/writing message gives the child affirmation that the message is understood and models new strategies for talking about the topics which are most important at the moment. Lynn Murray, a kindergarten teacher in Fairfax County, Virginia, has found that dialogue journals work much better for her students than having them keep a monologue journal. She reports that just adding simple responses to early drawing/writing encourages children to move beyond the "I like—" stage of writing and that they soon begin to incorporate her words into their messages.

First grade children have no trouble entering into a dialogue in writing; in fact, the dialogue is much easier (and more interesting) than having to start out writing whole sentences and paragraphs. In this first grade exchange provided by Selma Horowitz of Los Angeles, her responses validate the meaning the child has constructed, and very naturally extend the dialogue by sharing experiences, asking a question.

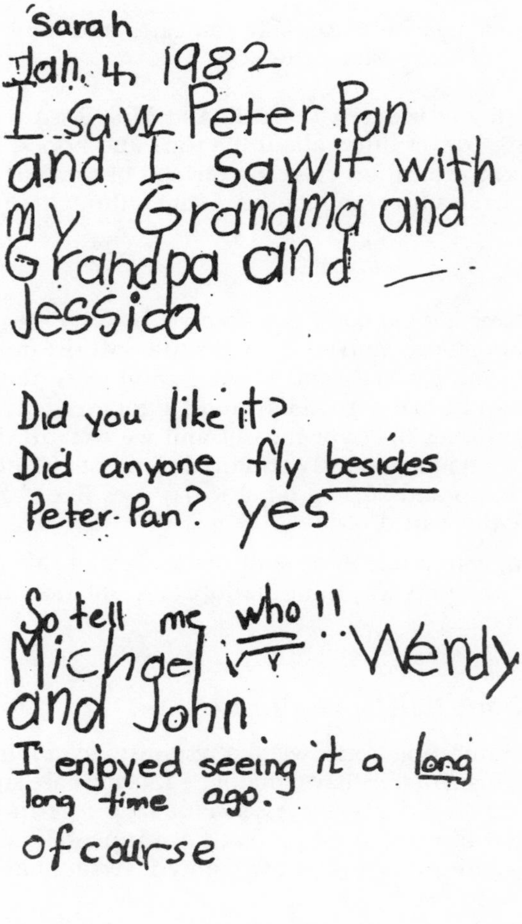
Sarah
Jan. 4, 1982
I saw Peter Pan
and I saw it with
my Grandma and
Grandpa and
Jessica

Did you like it?
Did anyone fly besides
Peter Pan? yes

So tell me who!!
Michael Wendy
and John
I enjoyed seeing it a long
long time ago.
of course

Figure 3

Even in first grade the teacher is clearly getting a thoughtful response to her entries, as when she says that she saw Peter Pan "a long time ago," and Sarah replies, "Of course."

The basic premise of the dialogue journals as a means of literacy acquisition is that literate discourse is not *inherently* meaningful or important but becomes so through the social interactions in which it is embedded. Literacy in this broader, socially oriented view is acquired most effectively when attached to one's own life experience, social context and goals. The same principles should guide literacy acquisition as guide oral, first language acquisition: written language use must be natural and necessary to get things done, and it must be an important mode of social interaction with valued other persons.

The Joy of Responding

I have stressed the power of the dialogue to engage the students and teacher in genuine communication. But there is also joy in responding and in getting a response each day, as these comments, taken from interviews with a class of sixth grade students and their teacher, Leslee Reed, make clear.

Martin: If I have a question, and I feel embarrassed to ask her personally, I write her in the [dialogue] journal. It's easier...You can just write it and she'll answer back. Before I didn't write that much about myself but now I do.

Claudia: When you write just three sentences, it seems like you don't explain anything, and you don't have anything fun to read. It doesn't fit.

Jenny: When we are writing in journals, she doesn't act like a teacher. She doesn't insist on her thing, she just answers my questions and tells me what she thinks. But she doesn't say you shouldn't think like that, like some people.

Laetitia: It helped me to learn English better, because I say something that doesn't make sense, and sometimes she writes me the same but with different words and I understand and so next time I put it right.

The teacher has her own perspective on the mutuality and understanding that develop in the dialogue:

Like everyone else, I am exhausted by the end of the day, but when I sit down to do my journals, I get exhilarated....I get greatly amused at some of the comments the children make. The feedback is so good for me and I really do look forward to it. I can be just dog tired, but as soon as I get involved in my journals, I'm no longer weary.

I think the journals...help us to develop a comprehension, too, that is deeper. We work on comprehension in reading and math and everything else, but I think this is a comprehension perhaps on an emotional level, of values, of moral rights and wrongs, of sensitivity to other people. I would like for everyone to see the love that goes into the journals, not just on my part, but on the children's part too: the love, the respect, the mutuality of goals, the feelings that we develop for each other.

I think that the value of the dialogue journals for students, like any genuine dialogue in speaking or writing, is fairly obvious from these comments—developing understanding and rapport; using written language in a functional, lively way; participating with the teacher in thinking together (Staton, 1984).

But there is also tremendous value for teachers in this activity, which does take up precious time. There is real joy and renewal for teachers as well when they become involved in genuine dialogues with their students.

I am struck continually by the isolation, the loneliness of teaching; we often deny this fact, but in our unguarded moments we will admit that spending all day with 30 live wire children can leave us feeling very alone. The dialogue journal is one way to alter this isolation, and as such, it represents one essential human truth: we become and remain human not through the acquisition of factual knowledge or skills but through participation in social communities which respond to us as persons. The process of socialization itself must be a community of persons, responding to the person-ness of each other. The quality of our responses to each other is central to our students' survival, and our own.

Carl Rogers has said that when we are truly heard by another, we are released from our loneliness, we have become human beings again. (1980, p. 10). I also use dialogue journals with teachers in the classes I teach, for the same reasons that they are used in classrooms with younger children—to reach out to others, to turn the keys of their cells, and release them through dialogue so that together we can begin learning. Then I notice that as a teacher I too am released from my cell.

• • •

Examples in this article came from the dialogue journals of students and teachers who have given their personal consent for these excerpts to be shared with others, in order to explain the concept and use of dialogue journals. Written parental consent was also given. Student names and personal or identifying information have been changed or omitted.

The examples in the text which are cited by teacher's name have not been published elsewhere and are from the following sources: dialogue journals written by Leslee Reed and her students, part of the data base collected by Staton for the NIE study (Staton, Shuy, Kreeft, & Reed, 1982); from Marley Casagrande, Fairfax County Public Schools, 1985-86 school year; and from Selma Horowitz, K-1 teacher, Los Angeles Public Schools, 1982-83 school year.

Appendix

BRIEF GUIDE FOR GETTING STARTED IN USING DIALOGUE JOURNALS
WITH ELEMENTARY STUDENTS

Introducing the Idea

- Discuss the natural need to communicate and understand each other in the classroom; use the analogy of phone conversations in which each person gets a turn. DO NOT talk about the dialogue as a way to "improve your writing."
- Discuss the importance of privacy: each dialogue journal belongs to the two writers, to be shared only with consent.
- Brainstorm some possible topics and functions for writing the first day or two. Functions might include evaluating lessons, describing playground activities, giving opinions, requesting help, suggesting class activities, complaining or expressing feelings.
- Stress that entries can vary in length, but set a minimum (such as "two lines" of writing, or "three sentences") for those days when there just isn't much to write about.
- Students should write first each day, to reinforce their ownership and personal responsibility for coming up with topics.
- Don't worry about the content of the first entries—what matters is getting students into the routine of writing and expecting your response.

Management

- You can start gradually, with a few students who seem ready or with one group at a time, to gain experience in responding to children's entries before doing it with a whole class.
- Provide a journal for each student, preferably one with a cover which can be decorated.
- Set aside a brief time in the morning for students to read your responses and write back. Often this can be done in the period before the class formally begins. At first you may also need to set aside a 5-10 minute period later in the day for a new entry. Later, older students can use independent work time and transition times.
- Create a special place where students can leave their journals for you when they are finished for the day.
- Use positive reinforcement strategies to encourage regular entries, expressing your own interest in what they are writing and providing "extra" time during recess for those who "forget." Do make clear that this kind of daily communication is a requirement, even though the writing is not graded.

- It takes one or two months for most students to "get going" and much longer for a few. Teachers also find they need almost a year to feel completely comfortable with this new kind of communication. Give yourself and your students time.
- A few students are not going to like a dialogue with you, and will do only the minimum—that is their choice. Just as the dialogue journal won't work for every teacher, it won't work for every student.

Guidelines for Teacher Responses

Responding is the most enjoyable part of the process. Teacher responses should encourage and stimulate a continued dialogue when important topics come up. Some suggestions:

- acknowledge the students' topics and encourage them to elaborate on their interests;
- affirm and support each student: the private dialogue is a great place for compliments about appearance, behavior;
- add new, relevant information about topics, so that *your* response is interesting to read;
- don't write (much) more than the students do;
- avoid glib comments like "good idea" or "very interesting." These cut off rather than promote dialogue;
- ask very few questions. The goal is to get students to ask *you* questions, and make your writing so interesting that they will want to know more.

For more practitioner-oriented information on using dialogue journals with elementary students, see:

It's Your Turn Now!: Dialogue Journal Use with Hearing-Impaired Students. (Handbook) 1986. C. Puthoff, S. Searls, J. Slobodzian, and J. Staton. Gallaudet Pre-College Outreach Program, Washington, D.C. 20002

DIALOGUE, the Newsletter About Dialogue Journals. Center for Applied Linguistics, 1118 22nd Street, N.W. Washington, D.C. 20037. (3 issues a year.)

Elementary Writing Guide Update. Elementary Language Arts Program, Office of Curriculum Services, Fairfax County Public Schools, Annandale, Va. 22003.

References

Atwell, N. (1984). Writing and reading literature from the inside out. *Language Arts, 61*, 3, 240-252.

———. In press, in this volume. Building a dining room table: Dialogue journals about reading.

Cazden, C. (1983). Adult assistance to language development: Scaffolds, models, and direct instruction. In R.P. Parker & F. Davis (Eds.), *Developing literacy:*

Young children's use of language. (pp. 3-18). Newark, DE: International Reading Association.

Eliot, G. (Mary Ann Evans) (1874). *Middlemarch*. London: Blackwood and Sons.

Kreeft, J.R., Shuy, R.W., Staton, J., Reed, L., & Morroy, R. (1985). Dialogue writing: Analysis of student-teacher interactive writing in the learning of English as a second language. Final report to the National Institute of Education, NIE-G-83-0030/. Washington, DC: Center for Applied Linguistics. (ERIC ED 252-097).

_____ . (1984, February). Dialogue writing: Bridge from talk to essay writing. *Language Arts, 61*, 2, 141-150.

Lehr, F. (1985, October). ERIC/RCS Report: Instructional scaffolding. *Language Arts, 62*, 6, 667-672.

Moffett, J. (1968). *Teaching the universe of discourse.* Boston: Houghton Mifflin.

Murray, L. (1985). Secret messages: Dialogue journals as a reading event in kindergarten. *Dialogue, III*, 1. Washington, DC: Center for Applied Linguistics.

Puthoff, C., Searls, S., Slobodzian, J., & Staton, J. (1986). *It's your turn now!: A handbook for using dialogue journals with hearing-impaired students.* Washington, DC: Gallaudet Pre-College Outreach Program.

Rogers, C. (1980). *A way of being.* Boston: Houghton Mifflin.

Shuy, R. (1986). Dialogue journals and reading comprehension. *Dialogue, II*, 1. 1-2.

_____ . In press. The oral language basis of dialogue journal writing. In J. Staton, et al. *Dialogue journal communication: Classroom, linguistic, social and cognitive views.* Norwood, NJ: Ablex.

Staton, J. (1980, May). Writing and counseling: Using a dialogue journal. *Language Arts, 57*, 5, 514-518.

_____ . (1984). Thinking together: Language interaction in children's reasoning. In C. Thaiss & C. Suhor (Eds.), *Speaking and writing, K-12* (pp. 144-187), Champaign, IL: NCTE.

_____ . (1985). Using dialogue journals for developing thinking, reading, and writing with hearing-impaired students. *Volta Review, 87*, 5, 127-154.

_____ . (1986). The teacher as a reading text. *Greater Washington Reading Council Journal, XI.*

_____ . Shuy, R., Peyton, J.K., & Reed, L. In press. *Dialogue journal communication: Classroom, linguistic, social and cognitive views.* Norwood, NJ: Ablex.

Vygotsky, L. (1978). In M. Cole, V. John-Steiner, S. Scribner, & E. Souberman (Eds. and Trans.), *Mind in society: The development of higher psychological processes.* Cambridge: Harvard University Press.

6.

Logs for Learning:
Writing in One English School

PETER MEDWAY

In examining the use of writing in the other subjects we need to draw on English teachers' experience, interpreting it, however, from the point of view of a primary concern with understanding rather than with language. The procedure must be to specify the sort of educational needs which writing might fulfill and to discover the conditions and contexts which would enable it to perform those functions.

To begin with a basic question. When students are learning about a new area of knowledge, what is the point of their writing anything? It has been the normal school practice for any new piece of learning to be accompanied by writing, and yet a typical adult who has become interested in a subject and is engaged in finding out more about it, outside the context of formal educational study, will not automatically turn to writing as an essential aid; many people simply read books from the library and derive knowledge adequate to their purposes from that activity alone; or they seek out others with the same interest and talk to them.

Here is a piece of school writing

Los Angeles has a population of seven million, the city is divided into 47 townships. It is about six times bigger than greater London. There is one car for every two people so there is a terrific traffic problem, there is 450 miles of motor way some with ten lanes going the same way. Just out side Los Angeles is hollywood where every actor wants to go and become a star. Los Angeles's main industries is aircraft. They also make all their own materials for the wheels, metals etc. In Los Angeles the buses only work in the morning and evening rush hours, because so many people have cars. It is the home of the Great Lockheed Company, Santa Barbara just out side Los Angeles. The climate is hot all year round, it only rains about two weeks a year, so it attracts a lot of visitors in winter. But the sky is not blue because of all the exhaust fumes caused by all the cars, there is a continuous haze over the city, the Americans call it smog.

Paul, a 12-year-old boy, wrote this in the second half of a geography lesson. During the first part the teacher had talked, in an interesting way, about Los Angeles, using the blackboard to jot down a few facts and names, and then had asked the class to write their account of Los Angeles. Most teachers will recognize the writing that resulted as a familiar type, and the procedure as a common and accepted one.

The statements in Paul's account are more or less true. The teacher would have been justified in thinking that something of what he had said had got over. But it is worth noting also that the facts are not presented in a coherent order: three sentences (the first two are divided by a comma) about the size, two (punctuated as one) about cars, one about Hollywood; then two about the aircraft industry, another relating to cars, and a further one about the aircraft industry—but to recognize it as such you need to know that Lockheed makes aircraft, for we are not told this; climate; then a final point relating climate to cars.

To many of us, this way of organizing our lessons, with this sort of provision for a writing task in Part 2, comes as second nature and we do not think very hard or often about the educational theory the practice expresses. But if we were pressed, our justification would probably be in these terms:

- Having to write it down forces the students to go over the information again in their heads; this second exposure will help them to remember it, and there may also be something about the physical business of writing that aids the memory—the fact associated with the particular pattern on the page, perhaps.
- The student also has to get the knowledge organized into some sort of shape in order to write it down.
- It provides a convenient way for the teacher to monitor what has been learned.

This seems like a reasonable case.

It is a feature, however, of writing that arises out of this kind of educational context that it does not notably show evidence of any particular intelligence or qualities of mind which the writer may possess: one student's work is very like another's. It is as if, when what is required is the taking in of information, there is little to be intelligent about. The justification for this sort of rehearsal of a set of facts would be that it is simply a means of taking possession of them and that this part of the process does not call for intelligent thought.

It is certainly true that intelligence and skill come into the process at the point when knowledge is mobilized in new contexts; it is also noteworthy that most teaching does little to develop that ability. But perhaps there are also more intelligent and less intelligent ways of receiving the knowledge in the first place. Perhaps the use you make of knowledge later depends partly on what you do with it when you first encounter it.

Anecdotal evidence may give us a way in. We all know good talkers who not only can express themselves well but who also have things to say on a wide variety of issues and are worth listening to for the interpretations they put on almost anything that comes up. One way of characterizing their ability is to say that they are exceptionally able to make use of the knowledge they have acquired from different sources in the course of their living—knowledge from direct experience, from reading, from school, from conversation and from the media. Whatever the topic is, they can find something relevant which will throw light on it or make it look different, and the pieces of illuminating knowledge or thinking may come from the most disparate origins. They have efficient retrieval systems, cross-indexed under a very large number of headings.

When I look for what is different about the way such people operate, my impression is that they are special in the way they deal with new knowledge. Watching television, for instance, they tend to comment on the information as it arrives, rather than to receive it in silence—drawing comparisons, expressing surprise, speculating on implications, formulating hypotheses—provided there is someone else in the room, that is. If a second person arrives on the scene only halfway through, or afterwards, the viewer will produce the commentary then, in an instantly turned-on flow, as if the information has already somehow been composed into a near-verbal mode ready for utterance. Thus the processes that appear to be characteristic of these individuals' eventual *use* of information in contexts that arise, also typify their initial *reception* of it. New knowledge is immediately related to other experience.

These efficient "natural learners" also seem, to a greater extent than the rest of us, to have general views. They exhibit not only a rich fund of particular knowledge and ideas but also an integrated overall outlook towards whole aspects of reality, in such a way that one feels they have come, perhaps not explicitly, to some large conclusions about the world, which gives a distinctive color to all their attitudes. It is as if the habit of asking the "so what?" question about everything has led to the continual consideration of larger and larger issues and the synthesizing and integration of broad areas of experience. This process, which occurs spontaneously in some people, could possibly be promoted in school in far more people. Perhaps writing could help; perhaps it could carry the function of questioning and connection-making in relation to new knowledge, and of synthesizing and integrating knowledge over wide areas.

We know that an active and questioning reception of new information can occur naturally in talk. But it also happens in writing; there are letters and diaries which are full of a very obvious processing of whatever has recently impinged on the sensibility. Why can it not occur naturally in school writing? Or perhaps the question is better asked negatively in the first place: What at present is stopping it happening?

The categories for classifying writing which were developed by the Schools Council Writing Research are a useful tool here.* They enable us to locate a piece of writing on a grid according to two dimensions, in relation to other pieces of writing. One beauty of such grids is that they suggest types which have not been found but could theoretically exist; then we can, if we wish, set about bringing them into existence. Two dimensions of classification were developed in detail, those of Function and Audience. The functions of writing, in this sense, are not simply the

*Britton J. et al., *The development of writing abilities 11-18*, Macmillan, 1975.

purposes for which it is in fact used but are socially recognized types of writing associated with types of purposes.

If we apply this model to Paul's piece on Los Angeles, it appears to fall into the informative function. It looks like the type of writing you get when a writer is concerned to make available to a reader a set of facts about a topic. Paul imitates what informative writers—probably text-book writers—do. But a peculiar feature of Paul's writing soon becomes apparent. A type of writing which has been developed to perform a particular function—informing—is being used not for that function but for a quite different one: for it is no part of the student's intention here to inform anyone of anything. No one's ignorance is to be alleviated by Paul's account. So far from that being the case, the person who will read it—the teacher—is the one in the whole world who is least in need of being given this information, since he was the immediate source of it. If the point of the writing was to aid the grasping of the information and to provide the teacher with evidence of understanding, the question suggests itself, Why not use a form specifically adapted to those purposes instead of one which was intended for completely different ones?

The conventional answer is that requiring students to write as if they were informing others is actually the best way to help them to make sense of the knowledge. But the writing that results, while it may aid factual recall, manifestly does not do much for those processes of questioning and making connections that I indicated might be essential if the information is later to be usable. Here there is little scope for anything but facts, or indeed for the facts in more or less the form they were given in. Moreover, this use of writing is not even an adequate means of testing since, while it reveals that certain facts have been recollected, it does not show what misunderstandings and delusions lie around and just outside the area specifically dealt with.

It is unlikely, after all, that Paul was seeking to provide the teacher with *true* information about the state of his knowledge—gaps and all: the unspoken aim in this game is to satisfy the teacher that you know it, whether you actually do or not. Well below the surface and at a level where few teachers would be conscious of it, the assumption behind this practice is that students will not willingly seek to improve their knowledge, so that devices have to be found to force them into it and to show up the gaps they will naturally try to conceal. Clearly, such procedures will be unlikely to produce learning to compare with that of the motivated and spontaneous "natural learners" we referred to earlier.

The second dimension of classification in the Writing Research model is Sense of Audience: the way a message is written will vary according to the type of recipient it is intended for. In this respect too we find a pretense operating in the Los Angeles and similar pieces. The writer in no way acknowledges the actual relationship obtaining between himself and his reader, the teacher. Instead, he adopts certain outward characteristics of a writer whose work was destined for a general readership. Paul pretends to be addressing an audience who will not in fact read his work; and he pretends to be someone other than who he is, in that he plays the role of the fully informed expert in a position to teach others about Los Angeles. Manifestly, there is little scope in such a contrived performance for him to express any of his own tentative thoughts, reactions and puzzlements.

Not surprisingly, most students do not do well with this type of writing. Keeping up the pretense of writing for an imaginary audience for an imaginary purpose in an imaginary persona presents unnecessary additional problems to a student faced with mastering a new body of knowledge. Younger students' experience of using language, almost all of it, has been of communication between particular, known people. So the task the child is faced with must feel something like talking in an empty room, to nobody—and under observation from a one-way mirror.

Some students are able to manage something even under these constrained circumstances, and even to enjoy the game, pleasurably anticipating the teacher's reaction to their pretend public communication. But it is worth noting that such success comes not from the students' achieving the implicit requirements of the talk but from their discovery of a successful way round it, in finding a real and personal addressee to hold in mind while writing rather than in developing an adequate concept of a public audience.

An alternative is possible: to see writing as an option we can take up for a variety of purposes, and to specify the type of writing which will best achieve the needs of the moment. We can control the process, rather than simply submit to its irrational demands.

One can work out in general terms the requirements for a type of writing which would give learners the opportunity to do something for themselves with the knowledge they were being presented with. Such writing would depend on a context in which students were taken seriously as learners with some stake in the business of learning; its form would not be dictated by the need to test them. The writers would have to be able to be themselves, and to talk in a natural way to whoever really was to be the reader. Any pretense should be conscious role-playing deliberately assumed. Above all, the child should be able to feel at ease with the form of the writing and the relationship it expressed. Coming out with thoughts and ideas of your own entails the risk of making a fool of yourself, as does admitting difficulty and ignorance; the student must therefore feel confident that the teacher will read as a sympathetic helper and not as a judge and marker.

When writing like this ceases to be a mere theoretical possibility and begins to occur in our students' exercise books as a result of changes in our practice, its appearance can first be disturbing. Its informality and lack of clear structure, and the way that personal responses, emotions and even humor get mixed up with the information, upset our ideas of what school learning should look like. But learning never was—except in psychology books and education lectures—the precise, white-coated, cleanly cognitive affair we would half like it to be. We have learned to think of our students' observation of the internal structure of the dogfish as the real substance of their dealings with it, and to dimiss their feelings of nausea or excitement at cutting into the flesh and smelling its smell as mere "noise." Yet the intellectual apprehension of a reality does not come on its own. The learner is a whole person and responds with all of a person's faculties and sensitivities. The intellectual grasp may actually be keenest when the other, non-cognitive sorts of attention are most aroused. Even if cognitive understanding is the outcome we are ultimately concerned to promote, we nevertheless need, in the early stages at least, to be hospitable to the entire response. This comes in one global form and not as a collection of separable expressions, and if we attempt to exclude the "irrelevant" aspects we will almost certainly kill off the part we want as well.

We have considered one piece written in response to new knowledge. Here is another:

China is a large overcrowded country in Eastern Asia that inhabits a ¼ of the population in less than ⅛ of the area but this country is not like you may think it may be but it is one of the most organized states in the world. All that everybody thinks about is "We are doing it for the People's Republic just like Chairman Mao says." It may in one way be a backward country but in many others it is the most industrialist country in the world. Everything done is done in a simple way. If a rock has to be moved a man in a red monkey suit will say, "You two move it" and they will not get a lorry or a tractor but sling a piece of rope round it, put a piece of wood through, pick it up and take it to where is should be. No problem of a fuel crisis, all that's needed to keep these going is a handful of rice a day. That's how things work in this most happy and honorable of countries. A little man in a red suit with a yellow face seems to be everywhere telling you what to do, where to go, how to get there like a mini information bureau. All those people believe in an ideal, work for an ideal and live for an ideal, a better land, a better home, the chance of a better race, the fair and promised land, the essence of all communism, all good communism at least. This is a land where selfishness is a dirty word. Nobody must think of China just like a poor man's Russia.

This recalls those qualities of the "natural learner" and good talker which I spoke of earlier. The information (in this case from a film shown in the lesson) is immediately seized on and ascribed a significance; the student (Tony, aged 15) wastes no time in putting the new knowledge to a use of his own, which is to arrive at a rapid judgment of China. What he is saying here is, this is what China represents for me. The specific bits of information act as evidence for his general implicit assertion that China is such-and-such a sort of place. The general idea provides Tony with the criteria for what to include and what to miss out, and what weight to give to each part. This is not to say that the piece is highly organized, but it is effective and economical in the same way as the speech of a person with a clear point of view.

I am not suggesting that this piece represents a satisfactory *final* outcome of a piece of learning: merely that it makes a hopeful starting point. At least we can feel confident that the information recorded here has been securely "learned" and will stay with Tony for some time. The fact that he is now thinking about the topic and has arrived at a provisional interpretation means that it will be easy to get him to consider further evidence and other interpretations; he will have a stake in looking seriously at them since they will affect the construction he has made.

This piece is not simply and objectively about China; rather, it is about "China and me." In this it is like "English Writing." We often find when we open up the writing channels and enable students to say whatever they feel a need to say about a new topic that what they need to say turns out to be not only observations on the, as it were, "internal" details of the topic but reactions to encountering the topic as a whole. It seems there is a need for students to answer for themselves questions like: "How do I place me-doing-this in my total idea of myself? What do I make of the experience of being here and engaged in this activity?" Until one sees this happening in the writing one may not realize there is a need for it; we expect students immediately to become absorbed in a new topic, whereas in fact there sometimes needs to be a definite stage in which they get into a relationship with it.

There has to be an explanation why Tony wrote this way about China and Paul wrote the other way about Los Angeles. There are several differences in the two situations. Tony actually was in an English lesson, not a geography lesson: the film had been hired for a course on China but it was decided to show it in addition to an English group. So different expectations about the type and function of writing were operating. Secondly, Tony wrote this off his own bat, without being asked. The group was not instructed to write about the film but Tony decided to because he felt he had something to say. So he was not in the position of being told to say something and having to cook up something to say, which leads so commonly to the type of writing which the Writing Research informally dubbed "random information retrieval." Lastly, although the writing is not ostensibly addressed to anyone in particular, it is probably relevant that he and I got on exceptionally well and he could feel sure that I would enjoy his effort.

We tend to expect writing to be "special" in a way that we don't expect of talk. If a child makes an observation in talk we are satisfied if it is useful and helpful. Is there not a place for a sort of writing which claims to do no more that a spoken comment may and can be accepted simply as a small but probably useful formulation? The other pieces I am going on to quote should be looked at from that point of view: that is, they show not what surprising things can be achieved but simply what that writing looks and smells like which assists the everyday function of thinking and talking on paper, with a supportive audience in mind, about new knowledge and ideas.

It is helpful to think of this writing in terms of another of the Writing Research Function categories, not the informative but the expressive. Most of our everyday talk is in this function. Although "expressive" suggests that we use it to display our feelings, which we do, we also give information, tell stories and do many other things: it is an unspecialized and mixed use of language which comes easily to us in relaxed communicative situations and which we naturally resort to when we need to "think aloud." Its educational relevance in view of the requirements we have noted for our sought-after language for learning will be quite clear.

Tony's China piece occurred without being planned for by the teacher. In the humanities department I worked in, we deliberately set about creating a writing channel which students could use in an informal and relaxed way, and the idea of log books suggested itself. The way we explained the log book to students was that it was *at minimum* a record of what they had been doing, useful to us because there was often a variety of activities going on in the group, including ephemeral ones like discussion and film-viewing which would not otherwise get recorded; but beyond that it could, if the students wished, be a space in which they could think aloud on paper and write to their teacher in any way they chose. The teachers would write back and a correspondence could develop.

When we first introduced logs, such was the strength of traditional expectations about school writing that it was hard to get students to accept that they could actually write to their teachers directly and not just in the guise of addressing some imaginary public. Thus in the early days of a school year (14 October) Carl (13), writing to me (he knew very well there was to be no other reader), put (my italics)

> *Mr Medway* was wrong when he said that I had been watching Ice Station Zebra. I'd been watching a million dollar brain. This morning I have been writing my thoughts on two topics. The first one was what would happen if oil went up to £2.50 a gallon and the second was what would happen if oil went down to 50p a gallon. If any should come true I would prefer the first one, would you *who ever is going to read this?*

By 13 January his log book was fulfilling more of the role we had intended. In this entry he refers to a passage from *The Teachings of Don Juan* by Carlos Castaneda:

> The thing that you read to us on Monday, I thought it was very interesting but somehow I don't think it could be true. Some parts could be true but the parts I think are not true are: Meeting the spirits in the mountains, going through the door and coming out somewhere else. But if the things are true why don't scientists go looking for them. And if it is all true it proves that the so called red Indian isn't so primitive after all. Do you agree with me? And also there could be a lot to learn from them. And if all the other primitive peoples know things like this it could open up a whole new science or range of studies. And I think that I might want to look into what the man's saying a little bit more. Although I think it can't be true I have got a feeling it could be true. Do you think so?

It is useful, to claim nothing more, that students should be able to note down questions, uncertainties and possibilities as they reflect in an unpressured and unhurried way (there's the difference from classroom talk) on the new experience they have been exposed to. It enables the teacher to know which lines could be pursued to most advantage with particular students, but it also helps the students if they consciously identify points of interest or concern: they are opening files which can be taken up and worked on in the future. We could have said about our "good talkers" that they have files already building up on many topics and are constantly prepared to open new ones.

What emerged as probably the prime function of the log books was the making of an overall response. They were not normally used as vehicles for going systematically over the detail of the topic. The writing of Joanne (13) was a good example. On one occasion I had given her an extract to read about an anthropologist who was accepted by an Amazonian tribe only after a long period in which he was regarded as an animal; the piece describes many features of this experience and of the Indians' way of life, attitudes to dreams, special interest in pottery and so on, most of which Joanne does not pick up, choosing instead to use the evidence of the extract towards conclusions of her own:

Anthropologist in the Xingu

> It is a very fascinating story, and I think he is lucky to be able to tell it. They could easily not have accepted him, and left him to die. It was very exciting for him I expect. I would like to be him, the Waura tribe are very interesting. The Waura tribe know a lot about medicines and stuff which we don't. We are ruled by machines, they do everything for us. But the Waura are opposite to us, they have to get their own food. And make everything which they use. They don't use money, so they don't fight over it. They seem to enjoy life a lot without machines, they eat all different things as well. If you stayed there for a very long time you might not want to go back to civilization. I think it would be good if people went there to live for a year, they would appreciate life better. And might even find it fun. The Waura tribe must be clever to keep alive. Because if most of us went and tried to live like them, not many people would keep alive.

Between the native expressive of the young writer and the disciplined communication of developed informative discourse lies a wider range of intermediate possibilities than is generally recognized. It is therefore quite possible for students to preserve their sense of their own voice and of their personal involvement with their subject matter as they gradually take on more demanding forms.

The final section of this article will be about how one student made himself into a learner, and how writing helped.

Neil came into the fourth year, at the age of fourteen, without previously having been thought very highly of: "pretty average grades. I wasn't doing so well in fact. Nowt special." Nor did he see any reason to question this valuation: "I never expected to get a top grade." During the first few weeks nothing happened to disturb his feelings about education.

> The first five weeks in that humanities, I thought, oh well, how boring this is. I remember starting the project, me and Ivor Bell, just copying out things about the Second World War, one of the worst projects I've ever...I was getting nowhere with that, even though I thought I was in a way, 'cause I'd got a lot of work on it, but it was just copying directly out of books.

It was only after he had got mildly into trouble for skiving out of lessons that I seriously intervened. I suggested he try our unit on China. He did, and from then on things were different.

That's it. As if just overnight. When I got on that China project, that's what did it. Everything seemed to work for me then. I kept thinking, well, I've achieved something. I'm really interested.

When he had just started on China, I commented in my records: "All his work so far is recording of facts, answering of worksheet questions. Nothing open-ended or reflective or imaginative." That was dated 11/8/75. By the 15th, however, I am writing "Great comments in log on the experience of reading *Red Star over China* by Edgar Snow and how he goes back to study difficult bits again. Model of right sort of motivation." Then: "12/3/75 Terrific series of questions he asked me in the log. Really what the log is for."

This is the log entry referred to:

11/28/75

Today I was wondering what China might be like when Mao's reign comes to an end, whether the new communist leader will be as good as Mao (even though I dont think China could have another leader as good as Mao). Who do you think will be the new leader after Mao?

(Here he leaves a space for my answer, and after each of the questions that follow.)

I think it ought to be one of Mao's close friends who has followed Mao through all battles and things like the Long March, somebody who is very loyal to Mao, somebody who has honoured and served Mao even through hardships, somebody who could follow Mao's way of ruling China. One question I'd like to know, is whether Taiwan (Formosa) is an island run by the Communists or the Nationalists?

Could you tell me some other Communist countries apart from these I know (if there is any more) Poland (I think), Russia, East Germany.

I would like to know them because I want to see where Communism has spread to. A few weeks ago I heard that Communism could happen in Italy. I heard about it on the telly, I think it was on a programme called "TONIGHT" but I forgot to watch it. I wish I would of saw it because it seemed an interesting program. Was Russia the first Communist country?

If so what year did Communism start in Russia?

Anyway is there a chance of China being overtaken by Nationalism?

Or are the majority of people aware tht China doesn't want another Nationalist government?

I understand China has now got NUCLEAR POWER and Japan has too. Japanese produced many good cars, bikes, etc. But rarely do I hear of Chinese cars, bikes, etc., but many plastic stuff from Hong Kong. Is China as rich as Japan nowadays?

Japan to me seems a lot more technological and up to date (than China)—is it?

The Chinese aren't a very sporting country, but one thing I know is that China have a soccer team and they soon could be official F.I.F.A. members.

I began to write in the best answers I could, found his spaces too cramped so took a fresh page, got carried away and wrote three pages.

Normally the teacher asks the questions, to be answered orally or in writing. Yet who is the one who is supposed to be wanting to know? It was good to see a student reversing the procedure and using it for his own purposes. (Later, it happened that I did ask questions for him to answer in writing, but the spirit of this transaction was very different from the usual routine.) This writing, it seemed to me, was not only instrumentally seeking information; at the same time it was expressively making a personal relationship with the topic. The writing derived from and also served to confirm Neil's commitment to the work and his sense that this was his own enterprise. Further entries from his log seem to show the same function being performed.

6/28/76

Watched a good program last night on telly. It was the WORLD ABOUT US series which featured a documentary on the ASMAT of N. Guinea. It showed how they lived and the brilliant carvings they did. The carvings were done on trees made into poles with stories on it carved in.

These people were headhunters but law recently forbids any more heads to be taken. So the spirits are disburbed now, say the ASMAT. The ASMAT are average in numbers but are declining. White missionaries teach the ASMAT "civilized" ways of the white living, but the ASMAT don't like this, as many fights still occur over things like cutting down a tree which belongs to somebody else. The tree isn't on his land, it's just one tree in the vast jungle. The missionaries teach the ASMAT to be Christians and are trying to get them as quickly as possible into the civilized world, so they aren't destroyed by the impatient oil seekers and foresters. The ASMAT now have jobs and are paid 5p a week and buy tobacco and stuff from this money. The carvings are in museums but the people that made them most likely will cease to exist with their old customs and traditions which are now slowly disappearing with the new life the ASMAT are being put into. They come to face pollution and other things in the new world but in their own land they never had any problems such as this. They followed the life of their ancestors and would most likely have carried on for another century or so living the life which didn't destroy them. Now it seems only a matter of *short* time that the old life of the ASMAT will disappear for good.

9/10/76

Today an important factor in Chinese history, Mao Tse-tung the great leader of China had finally deceased at 83. All sorts of questions are now aroused on the future of this vast country. Started reading a book on Anthropology called THE TRIBE THAT HIDES FROM MAN.

9/23/76

On Tuesday night I watched a good program on telly. It was called THE WATER MARGIN. Its an interesting story set in 13th century China. Today doing some writing about the book I read "The Cowards." After "The Cowards" is finished off I think I'll write some notes from Fanshen, as I read through it. Then I can get on with the primitives after this is completed, because doing them both at the same time is a bit confusing, as I cannot concentrate going halfway through one book and then starting half of another book without finishing the first book. I'll answer the questions on Fanshen you gave me. The questions are a good thing, they can get me thinking about what I've read from the book. The primitives is a bit harder, I think, because the same things are happening to most of the primitive tribes today and so nothing much different is learned between what's happening to destroy the tribes in different areas of the world. I started this "topic" as just a general interest in habits and ways of living and traditions that generate in these tribes, and suddenly I've noticed they are rapidly disappearing from the world, like an extinct animal! I'm a bit lost for ways of thinking of the right things to put in a topic like this.

10/5/76

Finished my English this week on the argument between council and public over old sheds. I was supposed to be a reporter, but my excitement and long tale has involved me in the action and in the end it has turned out to be a bit like a story. Not intentionally though.

10/23/76

Read a bit more of Fanshen. Altogether read nearly 450 pages of this historical book. The author certainly put in some hard work in compiling this book.

2/14/77

Been reading a great book called "The Borstal Boy" by Brendan Behan. It is a true account of Behan's early life. When he was 16 he was caught in possession with detonators, wiring, timing devices etc. used for making bombs. Being an Irishman born in Dublin he

worked for the I.R.A. Anyway this book tells of how he was caught
in Liverpool and put in jail and finally taken to Borstal.

2/15/77

Started reading a book called "The Trial" by Franz Kafka. It's a
hard book to understand because of the words in it. It is a very slow
moving story. There isn't a great deal of interest in it. But I want to
read it because he gets arrested without knowing the exact reason
for arrest. He keeps asking why he is arrested but hasn't found out
yet. I am on p43 and he doesn't know yet. He just attends this place
like a court.
It is a very "sinister" book.

For Neil "doing a project" consisted largely of reading; and as the
reading went along he made notes from time to time (e.g. on certain
chapters of *Fashen*, though he read the whole book), and wrote regularly
in the log book. He was learning much more than could be conveyed in
those two forms of writing, so it seemed important that towards the end
he should do some writing which could enable him to look at what he
had read in a broad way, and to provide evidence for the assessors of the
extent of his knowledge and thinking. We agreed between us that the
best way might be for him to write answers to some very broad questions
I would put to him. Thus on China I wrote down five or six questions,
which he answered in the space of many pages. (One of them in fact was
not a question but a suggestion that he write in the role of Mao Tse-
tung looking back over his life and assessing his own achievements.)
This form seemed to allow him to display his thinking to good effect; it
appeared to be well fitted to the stage of development he was at as a
writer. The answers, as compared with the log book entries, are moving
towards the "well structured essay," deploy much more information and
are more sustained, but are still "personal" in the dual sense that they
present "how I am thinking about this" rather than a detached argument which could stand on its own, and appear to express a relationship
with a particular reader rather than an unknown public.

Neil's writing seems to me to convey with particular immediacy
what real education looks and feels like.

7.

"Of Myself, for Myself"

PETER STILLMAN

> I imagine that the notebook is about other people. But of course it is not.
>
> Joan Didion

(9/8/81)
Hiked up the trail at dawn today to pick the last of the blackberries for breakfast. A fawn stood suddenly in the track. We looked at each other for a moment; then she vanished. Poof. Gone. I love the way deer disappear.

Heard last night about someone with a tumor as big as a grapefruit. Ella N. told about it—some cousin in Ohio. Always tumors are described as being grapefruit-size. Wouldn't it be odd to hear about a grapefruit the size of a tumor?

Three crows are sitting in my poplar tree. I have the uncomfortable feeling they're talking about me.

(10/1/81)
Raining. Shining roads. Pimpling puddles. Mud. Mud. Mud. Rain-shining puddle-pimpled, muddy roads; splash-bang potholes; star-soaking, moon-bruising rain. We-sure-need-the-rain kind of rain.

A "shunpike," I heard on the radio last night, is an area term for someone who avoids straight highways (pikes) in favor of winding lanes. What a fine little word.

Would love to see again *The Mummy's Curse*, the movie that scared me silly when I was a kid. Mummy walked with locked knees, right arm sticking out stiff as a 4 × 4. Killed most of the people in the movie with it but couldn't move more than maybe a half-mile an hour. Was it Lon Chaney who played the part? Impossible to recognize under all that bandaging. Ancient Egyptians must have emptied whole drugstores wrapping up a mummy. Here he comes, shuffling out of his tomb, arm out like the gate on a tollbooth. Glog! Another dead archaeologist, never a gurgle. Little kids hiding under movie seats screaming, popcorn boxes flying all over the place: "Lemme know when he's gone, Louie!"

(3/20/82)
Saw printed on a waiter's t-shirt: "'Now that we've seen each other,' said the unicorn, 'I'll believe in you if you believe in me.'
Lewis Carroll"

(easy scene to imagine:...The little girl looked at the unicorn without alarm but with considerable interest. Its eyes, she noted, were blue. The way the sun touched them made it look as if tiny golden clouds floated across them.

The unicorn was chewing slowly and with much dignity, its lower jaw slurring from side to side in the manner that some very old people chew. It continued to look down at the little girl, who had grass-brown hair. "Good afternoon," it said.

"You talked with your mouth full," she answered.)

Can you think of any reasons why the writer of this stuff bothered to put it on paper? It doesn't resemble the kind of writing we can classify as essay or report, poem or news article. It jumps around, offering the reader only a string of unconnected bits that might or might not be pieces of something else. It almost seems, doesn't it, that these odd little whatever-they-are's were never meant to be printed in a book for others to read? That the writing is so wrapped up in the writer and so unfinished that our reading almost amounts to snooping?

These are, of course, journal entries, mine; they're being used here partly as proof that journals aren't necessarily meant to be read by others, and also to persuade you that a journal can and probably should include anything at all that seems likely *to you* at the moment. Maybe, too, these sample entries will demonstrate that (a) even if, as I've heard a hundred young writers say, "Nothing happened today," you can still find something worth jotting in your journal; and (b) a journal comes as close as any writing can to reflecting the private and often wacky ways our minds dart and meander just under the smooth surface we let the rest of the world see. Also (and very importantly), a journal is the perfect place to store what may eventually turn into more public forms of writing. The deer in the path, for example, became this:

> An owl lives in the hemlock tree.
> Last year it did the same.
> Still heaven-hung's the mousing hawk,
> Its shadow grown quite tame.
>
> Fall waits like drying shutters propped
> Against a leaning sky,
> Scant challenge for the rhymer
> To catch and versify.
>
> Yet twenty crumpled pages past
> My berrying at dawn
> I've failed to trap in poetry
> A foolish, frightened fawn.

It shouldn't be difficult to see in these entries a half-dozen other possibilities that could find expression in any number of ways.

Journals are usually *chronological*—kept in order of time and dated—but they don't have to be records of the often-boring details of this day or that. A journal should, in fact, be a clear proof that being you isn't boring, even on those days when we shrug and say, "Nothing happened." Too many journals I've looked at seem meant to establish just the opposite, beginning each entry with such exciting stuff as "Got up. Took a shower. Had breakfast. Caught the bus for school." Etc. Even a goldfish would have more interesting matters to note. The routine things in life—the experiences nearly everyone has from day to day—*are* boring and furthermore have nothing to do with the unique individual who lives inside the person going robot-like through the same morning routine as millions of others. The truth is that scarcely a moment goes by in your life that doesn't hold something worth jotting down; and although a journal needn't be a daily matter, no day is ever empty of material.

Henry David Thoreau, this country's most quoted journal-keeper, described his journals as being "of myself, for myself." What he meant, I think, is that a journal is a fine way to capture life as each of us sees, understands, and reacts to it. Better to do that than just to live life out, never noting the particulars that together make each of us who we are and very different from the rest. He also meant that a journal has for its audience the *self*—and this can be the most sensitive and important audience most of us will ever know.

"Of myself, for myself." There's a pleasant ring of privacy and freedom about those words. Nowhere in them is there a hint that a person's journal should satisfy any requirements beyond his own. Even if you're required to keep a journal—and I'm requesting it—your journal should remain *yours;* you shouldn't be keeping it to satisfy someone else. If a fragment floats to the surface and draws you into ten pages of frantic scribbling, fine; don't worry about spelling, organization, neatness; just get it down. Only one concern bouncing around in your head? That was sometimes a day's worth of journal-keeping for Thoreau, as well as for a student of mine who recorded on a particular day only this: "Today my stupid rabbit died." Nothing is too silly, painful, crazy-sounding, angry, sentimental, corny, trivial, or important to go into a journal—not if at the moment it is *of yourself* and *for yourself.* Just one rule applies: Don't write phony or puffed-up stuff. If you can't sound like you in your journal, where else can you?

(One ticklish point: Put terribly confidential stuff in a journal and you'll probably spend part of every day worried sick that someone will get hold of it. This isn't an empty fear; even the most trustworthy people have a touch of the snoop in them. I can recall a couple of upsetting, embarrassing situations growing out of parents' reading through journals and discovering things that shocked them. You must be the judge of what goes into your journal and what doesn't.)

So far this talk about journal-keeping has been kind of vague. By attempting to avoid telling you exactly what to put in a journal and how you should keep it, I've left you with mostly generalized comments. When students asked, "What am I supposed to keep in a journal?" it rarely helped when I told them, "Anything that seems to belong there," or "Whatever ideas and experiences seem worthwhile." This often led to pages of neatly dated entries that began, "Got out of bed. Took a shower, etc." Saying that a journal can include *anything* led students to space-fill with strings of *nothing,* and looking back, I can't blame them. Listing subjects to write about didn't work either. Such a list was originally planned for this unit but ended up in the wastebasket because it sounded like a bunch of composition topics, and that's exactly what a journal *isn't* for. What should be helpful and interesting is a list of possible journal *functions:*

- A journal can be a place for putting incidents and events that, although they're small, provide examples of larger concerns we believe to be important. Here's such an entry from the journal of Ralph Waldo Emerson, 19th century scholar and writer:

(1862)
I like people who can do things. When Edward and I struggled in vain to drag our big calf into the barn, the Irish girl put her finger into the calf's mouth, and led her in directly.

This is from a student's journal:

(2/1/80)
How I hate the cold. Hearing the morning ski report reminds me every day how much I dread winter. Harry Duffy on the radio makes being wet and freezing sound like fun, but his cheerful report only makes me feel colder.

- Think of your journal as being a net for catching shining particles from the day:

(4/12/81)
When I watch water pour forth from the lip of the pitcher pump in the kitchen, I'm as fascinated as Isaac Newton must have been when Nature whispered in his dozing ear, "This is how it works—this is how the whole thing works." Sometimes I stand there and pump just to watch the water come sparkling out.
(3/28/82)
I paused at my chores tonight when a flock of Canada geese flew over. I couldn't see them until they moved across the moon. Then they were gone again, trailing behind them their wild, anxious *cree-onk*-ing yodel.

- Historians use the journals of ordinary people like you and me to find out about the past. This doesn't mean that journal-keepers try to record *history.* It's enough that a journal be one person's view of how life is. Here are samples of two journals, both from an earlier time. Neither reads like a history book, but both let us discover parts of the past. The first records the events of one day in the Adirondack Mountains in 1851; the second covers three days in central Africa. It was written in 1827.

A.

(Tuesday 16th)
It is difficult to describe the sensation one feels in camping out for the first time. You lie down upon a bed of hemlock boughs which is soft & fragrant as a bed of roses—above the dark blue sky glittering with stars—at your feet a roasting fire, which blazes & crackles & throws up the merry sparks—the very sight of which warms your heart towards the whole world & softens into nothing the little troubles & vexations of life & the old enmities which have so long hung about our hearts are gradually dispelled by the cheerful blaze & soon forgotten. And as the fire burns higher & brighter & the hot ashes fall in great heaps—you form (in imagination) of them queer, fantastic shapes of men or huge Castles & then do the dear old castles in the air rise, and you build them still higher—& dream of bright, happy days—till, like all day dreams, unfulfilled, a softening influence creeps over you—a strange forgetfulness—a drawing of your blanket closer & then—

The fish that had been saved over the night were frozen so cold had been the air. After a hearty breakfast off of them we betook ourselves again to the river. Our success was "ravishing". For at least an hour we continued to draw out with our lines trout the largest & most beautiful we had ever seen. One in particular which the heavier body succeeded in landing—weighed over three pounds & according to the guide's statement—the largest he had seen that year but unfortunately from clumsy handling—he broke the hook from the snell & escaped. About 10 o'clk, our lines having become entangled in stumps, at the bottom, we were obliged to make such a stirring up of the waters that the fish became frightened & left & we followed their example. The lighter bodys line in particular had a great partiality for stumps & addicted itself to the same exclusively. We dined this day on *patridge & trout*—schgqpt!!! (an expression of delight. Don't your mouth water?) At 1 O'clock along came the expected wagon from Holmes', bearing the *boat* of the aforesaid Mr. Williams who did not arrive at the time appointed. Couch & Tim also came to join *us*—the boat, they were carrying in to Louis Lake. After a short consultation as to the best place for running deer, we concluded to shanty at Mason Lake three miles below Louis. We arrived here about sun-down & built ourselves a shanty of hemlock boughs in the woods. We built a roaring fire, cooked some pork—into which & the bread and butter we dove extensively & then went to sleep.

> *Journal of a Hunting Excursion to Lewis Lake, 1851.* Adirondack Museum, 1961.

B.

(9th)
At six in the morning, having got everything in readiness, left Zulamee. Both men and beasts seemed much invigorated with the rest they had enjoyed, and at two in the afternoon reached Gundumowah, a small but neat Fellata village. The chief sent me a little milk.

(10th)

Early in the morning started for Sansanee. The country traversed was thickly wooded, and the path lay for three hours through a large bush, which, having recently been visited by a horde of elephants, the prints of whose feet were very perceptible, rendered travelling extremely unpleasant, and even dangerous. Reached Sansanee at one at noon. The site on which the town is built not being long cleared, none of the houses were quite finished. On our arrival, the chief had an open shed, occupied by fifteen calves, cleaned out for our reception. In the evening, putting the goods in the centre, I ordered the men to lie around them, whilst I placed myself near the most valuable articles. Not deeming them sufficiently secure, my sleep was rather disturbed; and awaking about ten o'clock, I found my camel had strayed from outside the hut, and being unwilling to arouse my drowsy companions, went myself in search of him. On my return, to my infinite surprise and alarm, discovered Pascoe had decamped, taking with him a valuable gun, two pistols, a cutlass, six sovereigns, nineteen dollars, ten large and ten small knives, and several other articles, which he had contrived to take from the boxes in which they had been placed. To deceive me, the artful old villain had put a pillow into a sack, which he had laid along on his own mat. On the discovery, I immediately made an alarm, and sent to the chief for twelve horsemen to go in pursuit of him.

(11th)

About three o'clock in the afternoon, as I was standing in my shed, I perceived a party of horsemen coming towards me in full gallop. On coming within a few yards of me, they suddenly checked their horses, and flourishing their spears over their heads, exclaimed, "Nasarah, acqui de moogoo!" (Christian, we have the rogue!) They informed me that a little before daybreak in the morning they heard the report of a gun, and going towards the place whence the sound seemed to proceed, saw Pascoe perched on the top of a high tree, and the stolen goods lying at the root of it. They threatened to shoot him with their poisoned arrows unless he immediately came down. This had the desired effect. He hastily descended, and delivered himself into their hands. One of the soldiers took the trembling scoundrel behind him on his horse, when the whole party immediately clapped spurs to their horses, and made all the haste they could to the village. I asked Pascoe what could have induced him to leave me in so disgraceful a manner. He replied that his countrymen (the Gooburites) were at war with the Fellatas, who would cut off his head on arriving at Soccatoo. The chief coming up at the instant, cried out, "A blessing, a blessing; you have taken the thief, let me take off his head!" This was Pascoe's third offence; and I ordered him to be heavily ironed and pinioned in the town dungeon.

Journal of the Second Expedition into the Interior of Africa from the Bight of Benin to Soccatoo, by Hugh Clapperton. Frank Cass Co, Ltd., 1966 (London). Orig. published 1829 by John Murray.

- You probably haven't given any thought yet to what you'll want to leave to others when you die. Yet you're not too young to begin compiling the finest possible gift for unborn generations of your family. People inherit money, spend it, and it's gone; people who inherit journals treasure them always. Although a journal should be filled with *now*, it's really meant for forever. My great-grandfather was a faithful journal-keeper and lived a life filled with adventures. By the time he was an old man, his journals filled boxes. Then, the same week he died, my great-grandmother burned every one of them. No one ever figured out why. It still upsets me to think about it. How would you feel about such a loss?

- Journals are for storing stuff that's amusing:

(4/11/80)
Learned in science today that the vitamin was discovered by Casimir Funk. I think we should have a Casimir Funk Day every year.

(7/16/81)
Volunteer fire department report last month listed "two grass fires, one ambulance call, and one skunk removal."

(5/3/81)
Bing told me about an 81-year-old woman who used to go to revival meetings at church: "When she let out a whoop and jumped over three pews, you could tell the spirit had hit her."

(3/10/82)
Bobby can't stand the kid next door. He was splitting firewood the other day and the boy started taunting him. "Got so doggone mad I hit myself on the head with the go-devil. Swung her back and caught the doggone clothesline. Back she come and whacked me right on the skull." (A go-devil head weighs 8 pounds. The blow should've killed him.)
  "That made me so mad I did it again."
  "You mean *twice?*" I said.
  "Yup. Don't go tellin' anybody, but yeah, twice in a row."

- A journal's a good place to put resolutions too. You know what happens to most resolutions: we conveniently forget them. But put them in a journal and, like it or not, they don't go away. On paper, lying before you every time you page through your journal, a resolution seems much more like a contract between you and yourself than a half-remembered intention.

- Journals provide a way for people to talk to themselves on paper. There are times, though, when we don't want to "talk"—when filling the blank spaces with words seems a terrible effort. At times like these—and all journal-keepers experience them—the journal becomes a symbol of the self-discipline that all writers, you included, need. May Sarton, a poet and novelist, wrote this one day: "I have not felt like writing in this journal. It lies in wait each morning, and I long to put it off." (Notice that she wrote just the same.) Why should we write when we don't feel like writing? Not for practice. Not to prove that we're not lazy. And certainly not just to keep our journal entries neatly up to date. We should write because there's always something to discover, and the privacy of a journal provides the best place for finding out.

* * *

If you don't already keep a journal, start one today. Don't go out and buy one of those expensive things that looks like a hardcover book but is filled with blank pages. They don't lie flat and they're hard to write in. Start with a spiral or tablet-type notebook, and fill it with dreads and dreams and the deaths of rabbits. Keep it faithfully and don't stuff it full of showers and breakfasts, and when in ten years I offer you a thousand dollars for your stack of notebooks, you'll tell me to go jump in the lake.

At the same time, pick up a smaller notebook too, the kind you can fit in your pocket. It's for catching those small, sharp particulars that vanish almost as readily as they appear. It may take as little as 12 to 15 seconds to scribble enough of an impression so that your note will make sense that night or the next day. The pocket scribbler isn't meant to be filled with complete scenes, finished poems, or polished lines; it's for trapping fragments, whether they occur somewhere in the *outside* world: "Charlie says his brother hates his shadow"; or from somewhere *inside:* "My father's hands get angry before the rest of him." I can't say what of you belongs in such a scribbler, but something does, and daily.

A quite different function of a journal is connected directly with school. This kind of record is commonly called a "learning log," and according to most people who have kept them they're extremely useful. While the learning log isn't meant for capturing the random, unconnected fragments of life that only you experience, it *is* intended to be personal, to house only your thoughts and experiences. Nor is it meant to be graded. A learning log is a means for communicating with yourself and your teachers how you're responding to and understanding something you're studying.

It's not unusual for a teacher to meet with 150 students a day. Sometimes you can forget that, especially when the going gets rough—when you miss an important point under discussion or begin to hate a subject (or a teacher) because...well, just because. Few teachers think of students only as so many faceless lumps of humanity sitting in assigned seats. But it gets very difficult to deal with everyone on a person-to-person basis, to sense when a student is falling behind or losing interest. Sadly, this is when most students tend to clam up, and when that happens, even the most conscientious teacher can overlook those who most need to communicate with him. That's where the learning log comes in (although it's definitely not limited to times when there's a problem). It doesn't take more than five minutes to jot down in such a log your responses to a particular lesson or subject. Putting down what you think you've learned (or didn't) that day, whether it's in science or English or history, is an excellent way to make it stick, or to clarify a problem.

Class notes won't accomplish the same thing. Notes are usually taken without much thought; they're seldom summaries of anything; most of the time they're attempts to catch what the teacher has just said before she says something else. Here's what a class note usually looks like:

Sonnet—14 lines. Iambic pentameter = each line 10 stresses, 5 iambs = 1 weak stress + 1 strong stress, example = *today, about, beware.* Shakespeare used iambic pentameter. Sample line ="Shall I compare thee to a summer's day?" Shakespeare's sonnets = 14 lines, 3 4-line stanzas and 2 lines at end with rhyming couplet.

Here's what a learning log entry, jotted down sometime after class, might look like:

Today Miss Nelson talked about the sonnet form of poetry. I don't really like poetry that much, especialy when it's not modern. It seems harder to understand than prose, and most of the stuff we study in class is pretty old. I also wonder whether when Shakespeare wrote he expected teachers to pull his poems apart and make lessons out of them. The sonnet we studied today, for example. We never even got to the meaning of it—instead we learned about iambic pentameter, which is how many syllables fit in a line and where the accents are supposed to fall. I paid attention but I don't understand it. Does it have anything to do with rhyme? I'm afraid we'll have a quiz on it tomorrow. If we do I'm sunk. I realized something worrying about this, though. I read Sonnet 18 (Shakespeare numbered them) about 4 times and I began to know what it said. It's about someone so beautiful that there's nothing on earth to compare her with. I think I could put it in my own words. If the quiz is about what the poem means I'll be okay.

Or it might come out this way:

After class I read another poem, not Shakespeare, and I think it's in iambic pentameter. It was Robert Frost's "Mending Wall." It would be a good idea to use some poems like this that we know and have discussed to point out things like iambic pentameter. It's harder to learn about something when the wording of a poem is difficult too. Anyhow, I'd like to find out whether I'm right about Frost and iambic pentameter.

You can see how looking over such entries might benefit Miss Nelson. And you can also see how such a device might be helpful to you. Suppose a teacher read over your learning log once or twice a week and jotted responses to your comments and questions. What positive effects might this have on learning? In what class(es) in addition to English might such a log be useful to you? to the teacher? Are there advantages to one-to-one avenues of communication between student and teacher? Would a learning log make it easier for you to comment on matters that trouble you? excite you? Discuss these questions. Their answers could put you on to something that'll work for you not only now but for as long as you're a student.

* * *

The idea of a group journal may seem at odds with the rest of this chapter, but a journal in which more than one person enters a thought or experience can eventually become a treasure trove, especially if its contributors are family members. Such a journal, when it's left in some prominent place, begs to be read and written in. Now that you're acquiring the writing habit, why not urge it on others in the family too? The more I think about it, the more I wish that my family had made use of such an idea. It makes sense that if family members had a closer notion about how others in the same home felt and thought, people might avoid stepping on each other's toes so much. And that what might be awkward to say aloud might find its way into a family journal and please another. And that writing together could form a good, strong bond among the people we care about most.

Why don't you buy an inexpensive notebook, find a pen to go with it, write prominently on its cover something like "This is the _____ family journal, Volume One. Please put in it whatever is on your mind as you walk by. And don't walk off with the pen." Leave it in plain sight and make the first entry. Then watch what happens. (To avoid making what happens a disaster, don't use it as a gripe book. Its purpose is for sharing, communicating, not bellyaching or jotting down nastinesses you're afraid to utter aloud.)

8.

A Brief History of
Journal Keeping

SHARYN LOWENSTEIN

Introduction

Investigating the history of personal journal writing is akin to tracing the development of self-consciousness. Journal keeping dates from at least 56 AD, when, in China, journals were both written and then archived as historical documents. Since that time, journal keeping has continued in wide-ranging cultures by those in all socio-economic classes and life circumstances. Even a brief historical survey of the journal can be instructive, revealing the extreme flexibility of the form, a variety of practices, and interesting, complex relationships between the journal and the journal keeper.

Private, autobiographical writing does not come until the Renaissance, when individuality becomes important. Weintraub (1978) reports that in classical Greek culture, one individual, the self, was seen as replaceable—indeed, mothers were told to become pregnant when sons died. What mattered most was the polis, the family and the family honor, the ideal of the rational person. Early journals, then, tend toward more public writing and contain communal material. Such examples include Roman household account journals called "Commentari"; and even cave paintings; the Bayeaux Tapestry, a community journal commemorating the Norman Conquest; and, on teepees of the Plains Indians, a pictorial record of the winter count.[1] Over time, the journal expands to include private content: the confessional, the self-exploratory and the therapeutic. Throughout its history journal keeping will shift back and forth over the public and private domains, with some journal keepers staying on one or the other end of this continuum, and some journal keepers incorporating both. Today, for example, one entry might contain a wine tasting notation, a runner's vital statistics, a calorie count, a weather forecast, as well as an agonized description of a love affair and an analysis of a particularly vivid dream.

Japanese Journal Writing

Just one of the diary types in tenth-century Japan was the pillow book, so named because it was placed in the bed chamber or perhaps in drawers of wooden pillows. Written primarily by the Heian court ladies, these records incorporated both factual accounts as well as dreams, other fantasies, and poetry. One example is the pillow book of Sei Shonagon, lady-in-waiting to Empress Sadako. This journal of periodic, non-daily writing, spanning ten years, was probably initiated as private notes—of lists, character descriptions, and stories about upper-class Heian life, such as the following:

> When the Empress moved into the house of the Senior Steward, Narimasa, the east gate of his courtyard had been made into a four-pillared structure, and it was here that her Majesty's palanquin entered. The carriages in which I and the other ladies-in-waiting were travelling arrived at the north gate. As there was no one in the guard-house, we decided to enter just as we were, without troubling to tidy ourselves; many of the women had let their hair become disordered during the journey, but they did not bother to rearrange it...(Morris, 1977)

After being discovered, Shonagon's pillow book became more literary and self-conscious.

Plutschow (1973) notes that in Japan the diary has long been understood and respected as a way of recording history. Within this tradition is the travel diary, categorized by Japanese critics as a separate genre from the other diary forms then used, and totally or partially comprised of poetry.

From the tenth to the seventeenth century the act of traveling was spurred both by the changing religious practices and the break-up of traditional rule—resulting in loss of familiar structures and a quest for a new life. Travel was undertaken by priests, officials, and the military, partly to improve their poetry, which was used in prayers and oracles, and understood as a dialogue between human beings and gods. In fact, scribes so frequently wrote officials' diaries that the latter were also separately classified, as the diaries of accompaniment. Excursions to places cited in famous poems were thought to give religious power. Once at the destination, the traveler might compose a poem by incorporating a line from the original, and such practices functioned as ancestor worship. Another and lengthier form of travel occurred when a master died: his disciple might journey to and write poetry in places familiar to the master, perhaps for the purpose of continuing the deceased's life.

Such travel can be interpreted as a return to time past to increase awareness of an ancient world and its values. Further, the mere passage of time as one traveled allowed the journal keeper to experience the transience of life, and, as if to emphasize this, many journeys took place in autumn. Because travel was deliberately undertaken by older people, it may have been viewed as a path toward death. Finally, travel was a way to discover basic laws of Buddha and transcend time.

The following passage from the Kaido-ki travel diary, which shifts from narrative to poetry and back again, illustrates this search for basic laws:

> Thinking about my journey, the mountains and the rivers I crossed—Was it a dream or reality? Was it yesterday? Was it today? If one thinks of the present as the past, one feels old. If one thinks of the past as if it were present, one's mind is young. The passage of time from past to present is [only] in one's mind. Though they

say that death is merely like a past dream, I feel sad indeed. After yesterday has passed, it became today's dream. Leaving this place today, today will become yesterday somewhere tomorrow. The passage of time and age is a passage from one dream into another like this mountain path which yesterday and today passes from one cloud into another.

Tomorrow and again
Yesterday
I marvel at the clouds
Of tomorrow and of yesterday
As I cross today
The pass of Mt. Utsu [Reality][2]

I stayed at Togoe no Shuku and rested my feet.

In the Japanese travel diary we can see that art plays an important role; objective truth and poetry are interwoven with no attempt to distinguish between them. In fact, one of the earliest travel diaries was written by Kino Tsurayuki, a man using a woman's voice, perhaps to recognize his deceased daughter. In the Japanese travel diary a public audience is intended, not only evidenced by the inclusion of poetry, but also through the use of several modes of writing to provide variety, the frequent presence of a prologue and epilogue, narration in the third person, and the copying of most of the well-known diaries into scrolls, rolled and unrolled according to prescription.

Other Travel Diaries and Their Variants

In contrast to the earlier Japanese travel diary, the western travel diary is a narrative emphasizing the factual, what the diarist has done or seen, and during the 1500's-1700's in Europe, often written by privileged young men taking continental tours. Francis Bacon (1958), in his essay "Of Travel," actually instructed these men on writing travel diaries, encouraging observation of, "...the courts of princess...the courts of justice...the churches and monasteries...the walks and fortifications of cities and towns; and so the havens and disputations, and lectures..." (pp. 113-114) In sixteenth- and seventeenth-century Europe travel diaries, some published in their diary form, supplied much of the existing information about distant places. These diaries functioned as map supplements to places no one else had explored.

Henry Fielding's *Journal to Lisbon* (Fothergill, 1974) provided an interesting example of a travel diary clearly meant for publication:

Can I say then I had no fear?
Indeed, I cannot, reader, I was afraid for
thee, thou shouldst have been deprived of that
pleasure thou art now enjoying...

While in Europe there was a strong travel diary tradition by the seventeenth century, the American travel diary writing had only just begun, because the first explorations had been made by Europeans. Besides explorers, hundreds of pioneers also kept journals, often sent to others later making the journey. A special type of travel diary, the war diary, appeared with the French and Indian Wars (1689-1763), the American Revolution (1775-1783) and the Louisiana Purchase (1803). Soldiers, physicians in the army, and civilians kept diaries, and, at least during the American Revolution, American prisoners of war also kept them despite punishment if they were found. One such example was in the diary of Charles Herbert, captured at 19 by the British during the American Revolution. Herbert commented on the conditions at Old Mill prison this way:

> We have trouble enough here, without hearing bad news, for it is enough to break the heart of a stone to see so many strong, hearty men, almost starved to death through want of provisions...often the cooks, after they have picked over our cabbage, will cut some of the but-ends of the stalks and throw them over the gate into the yard, and I have often seen, after a rain, when the mud would be over shoes, as these stumps were thrown over the gate, the men running from all parts of the yard...and nearly trample one another under feet to get a piece...(Kagel, 1979, p. 115)

It was not uncommon for the diary writing to decrease or cease altogether with furlough or the war's end. However, Baxter (1976) notes at least one example, in John Joseph Henry, who described his experience in the American Revolution 36 years later!

American Spiritual Diaries

The spiritual or confessional diary focuses on the writer's relationship to God and the degree of straying from religious teachings. In general, the spiritual or confessional diary shows more self-preoccupation than the travel diary. The early spiritual diary is often quite stylized in its presentation, emphasizes the quest for an ideal relationship to the church and to God, and is sometimes used as a means to teach the entire community.

Spiritual diaries of the sixteenth, seventeenth, and eighteenth centuries were born out of the dissent of the new religious groups, the Puritans, Quakers, Methodists, Calvinists. This precedent, a diary born out of crisis, a diarist's struggle to control what may seem out of control, was, as noted above, one of the reasons for the Japanese travel diary, and is still one of the most important motives today for both initiating and maintaining the personal diary.

In his diary, kept from 1653-56, Michael Wigglesworth (Morgan, 1973), an American Puritan, displays his sins and chastises himself for inadequate piety. Like other Puritan diarists, Wigglesworth uses a highly confessional, meditative, non-narrative style, and concentrates on self-doubt and isolation:

> Peevishness vain thoughts and especially pride still prevails in me.
> I cannot think one good thought. I cannot do any thing for god
> but presently pride gets hould of me: but I feel a need of christ's
> blood to wash me from the sins of my best dutys and from all that
> deadness of heart, and want of spirit for god this day.

The journal also centered on his coming of age, assuming more responsibility, and overcoming sexual anxieties. At this point, perhaps because the tensions have been reasonably resolved, the journal writing decreased, like many of the war diaries.

The Puritan confessional diary type, itself, was, in fact, a critical literary form of the religion, and had its own established conventions. John Beadle, in The Journal or Diary of a Thankful Christian (Haller, 1957), a handbook for diary writing published in 1656, advised Puritans to record all confirmed prayer answers and blessings of God, and to describe the

> Times we have lived in, what Minister we have lived under, what
> Callings we were of, what Wealth was bestowed on us, what places
> of Authority and Command were committed to us. (p. 97)

The Puritan diary incorporated the current collective events which were evaluated through their parallel to the Old Testament. The Puritans used the diary material to educate the community, and included diary selections in the "lean-to" or the biographical narrative of the funeral sermon. Most significantly, the Puritans used the diary to examine their feelings to ascertain whether they were worthy of salvation, a thought which daily preoccupied them. According to Puritan belief salvation was pre-determined and only for the elect, but by watching carefully, by writing and then examining one's acts in enormous detail, the Puritans believed they could interpret their fate. (It is interesting to note here that while these soul-searching confessional diaries were publicly used to communicate with the entire community, the Puritans also wrote business/secular journals, which they didn't publish.)

Another religious group keeping diaries at this same time was the Society of Friends, or Quakers. In general, their journal material contained accounts of the first to speak at the meetings or services, missionary journeys and the difficulties they imposed, the call to the Quaker ministry, and conversions. The journals—seen as fostering group cohesion—were sometimes published posthumously with group approval. Quaker founder George Fox published a revised journal, which later served as a model.

Quaker diaries were not as extensive as those of the Puritans, possibly a consequence of the greater opportunity for Quaker interaction at their meetings and the freedom from constantly evaluating chances for salvation. With the Quaker emphasis on waiting and contemplation, the final opinion on what might be divine truth, and not the fluctuations of day-to-day thought about that truth, the Quakers' journals tended to reflect a more unified perspective, sometimes even making them difficult to distinguish from straight autobiography. An excerpt from the diary of

John Woolman (Moulton, 1971) illustrates this more removed and coherent viewpoint:

> The 13th Day, 2nd month, 1757...I woke in the night and my meditations as I lay were on the goodness and mercy of the Lord...It was yet dark and no appearance of day nor moonshine, and as I opened my eyes I saw a light in my chamber at the apparent distance of five feet, about nine inches diameter, of a clear, easy brightness and near the center of the most radiant. As I lay still without any surprise looking upon it, words were spoken to my inward ear which filled my whole inward man. They were not the effect of thought nor any conclusion in relation to the appearance, but as the language of the Holy One spoken in my mind. The words were, "Certain Evidence of Divine Truth," and were again repeated exactly in the same manner, whereupon the light disappeared... (p. 58)

In the mid-1800's Transcendentalists kept journals as tools for communicating with the divine, understood to be a part of each person. These rather lengthy—some, thousands of pages—journals were exchanged and included comments about each other's entries.

Members of the Mormon Church (Church of Jesus Christ of Latter-day Saints) have also kept and continue to keep diaries. Founded in 1830, the religion is conceived of as a restoration of communication with God. Several principles of Mormonism actually encourage journal keeping:[4] for example, Mormons believe eternal progression, or spiritual and intellectual growth, occurs in each individual and is accountable for his/her actions; keeping a journal is a valuable aid in evaluating individual development. Mormons believe God's intervention in an individual's life is a possibility for all people. By reviewing past journal entries the journal keeper can recognize and become increasingly aware of God's influence. Mormons view life as eternal, with earthly existence preceded and followed by other life forms. This last belief promotes a feeling of continuity and interconnectedness with ancestors and future generations. Leaving a journal describing one's spiritual difficulties is understood as a way to guide posterity.

The Personal Journal

Evolving much later, but derived from and a combination of the other diary types, is the personal diary. This type emphasizes the self, often in relationship to other people, events, ideas, and religions. Although a single entry may stress only one of the aspects above, taken as a whole the personal diary helps the diarist facilitate and appreciate individual growth and unique qualities. While there is debate about when the first personal diary was written, there is little doubt that Samuel Pepys' was one of the earliest developed ones. (He himself discredited the quality of prior personal journal writing.)

Pepys (Latham and Matthews, 1970) wrote the major portion of his diary from 1660-1669, from his twenty-sixth to his thirty-sixth years. As a high civil official, he was able to gather local and overseas news events for his diary, in the process cultivating the acquaintance of all potential informants, even those he disliked. He was systematic and organized and intended his diary work "to make good" and "to set right." Pepys' self-examination parallels that of the spiritual journal keepers (which, indeed, is not surprising since he was raised in a Puritan household, although at the time covered in the diary he was not practicing). Pepys' diary, like that of the Puritans, also stressed group values, such as his belief that with less time devoted to his extramarital affairs, he would prosper financially.

Among the hallmarks of Pepys' diary are optimism, concise character sketches, love of gossip and enjoyment of small detail. Such detail, sometimes embedded in the context of more serious thought, is evident in the selection below:

> And so home, and with the painters till 10 at night, and so this night I was rid of them and all other work, and my house was made ready against tomorrow being Christmas day. This day the Princess Royal died... (p. 115)

While Pepys' diaries were in shorthand code, presumably to decrease accessibility to others, he intended, ultimately, that they be public documents, leaving the manuscripts in his library, which he eventually bequeathed to his alma mater. (Of interest is that Pepys edited his entries from rough drafts as much as two weeks old.)

In the next century comes another personal diary sub-type, the French Journal Intime. This highly intense, self-preoccupied, confessional, passionate writing came at the time of the French Revolution, a questioning of old values, even the existing literary forms, and relationships with government and between sexes.

One example, novelist George Sand's *Journal Intime* (Howe, 1977), was begun in 1834, apparently as letters to her lover, Alfred de Musset. The entries sometimes address him directly or speak about him in the third person. The journal addresses a range of audiences, as two sections below suggest:

> ...but this miserable masculine vanity! From the moment I began to confess, how you treated me! You wanted to strike me, you threatened to proclaim to the world that I was a c _____ . Yet if I had not lied to you at that time...your insane rage would have killed you... (p. 32)

> But to whom is all this raging addressed? To you, walls of my room, echoing my sobs! To you, grave and silent portraits! To you, terrifying skull, full of poison surer than any that kills the body! Or is it to thee, deaf and dumb Christ?.... (p. 34)

By the nineteenth century in both Europe and the US, so many personal journals are being published that few major diarists can be sure of remaining unpublished. At this point, conversation is being recorded in the journal, and well-known people are cited. Diaries for recollection, not unknown in the eighteenth century, are now more frequent, reflective of a more romantic age in which nostalgia was obviously acceptable and even exalted.

In this century there are millions of journals being written, some producing powerful results: For example, in *A Life Of One's Own*, Marion Milner (1936) vividly described her diary experiment, begun in 1926. She discovered through journal keeping that, "The mistake was to believe that any one expression could be the last word, for experience was always bigger than the formula." She noted that

> It was not good arguing against obsessive fears or worries, for the source of them was beyond the reach both of reason and common sense. They flourished in a No-man's land of mind where a thing could be both itself and something else...The only way to deal with them was to stop all attempts to be reasonable, and to give the thoughts free rein...in dealing with myself it usually meant letting my thoughts write themselves. (p. 156)

Another poignant example is the journal of Carolina Maria de Jesus (Moffat and Painter, 1974), who, on paper found in the trash, wrote about her oppressive living conditions in a Brazilian *favela* or ghetto:

> ...I classify São Paulo this way: The Governor's Palace is the living room. The mayor's office is the dining room and the city is the garden. And the favela is the back yard where they throw the garbage. (p. 293)

Her diaries were first printed in a newspaper, then published as a book, at one time outselling all others in Brazil.

Another sub-type of the personal diary is the apologist's journal, which proclaims the rightness of one's position or justifies an unconventional point of view. Falling into this category are the tapes or, as referred to by Mallon, the electronic diary of Richard Nixon, and the written diaries of Arthur Bremer, George Wallace's attacker, and Lee Harvey Oswald. (Even Bremer's copyright notice attests to his public intent: "© copyright 1972 Arthur H Bremer entire contens (sic) pages 1 - 248 inclusive or parts or portions there of may not be reproduced without the written consent of the author.") (Mallon, 1984, p. 183).

Two modern and rather large communities have used and/or endorsed the personal journal: those centered in the women's movement and those in psychotherapy. The flexibility of the journal form and its usual protection against outside intervention have helped women find their voices. With the publication of Anaïs Nin's diaries and her speaking appearances, a community of women, aware of their own involvement in a diary keeping tradition, was established. Today journal activities have become recognized and valued in women's studies courses, consciousness-raising groups, journal keeping groups in which people might read entries, and at least one periodical, *Journal-Journal*.

In the US, clinicians practicing Jungian and behavioral therapies as well as psychosynthesis include journal or journal-related writing as a part of their treatment, either within the sessions or as homework; journal consultants have also become available. Journals have been used to rehearse for and synthesize the work of the therapy hour, to generate more widely-based material than is usually discussed during the sessions, and to speed up treatment for some patients. Nichols (1983) suggests that journal writing lowers the client's dependency on the therapist and can aid the client as a "bridge" out of therapy. In addition, poetry therapy, which includes some aspects of journal writing, has been used for treating both psychosomatic illness and drug abuse. In Japan, journal writing is part of Morita therapy, which is the treatment for obsessional fears, anxiety neurosis, and neurasthenia. The treatment consists of a forty- to-sixty-day clinic stay in a four-phase program of increasing interpersonal involvement. The diary is the only place in the treatment where the patient is allowed to discuss previous traumatic events. In a sense, the diary is jointly authored because therapists include their own comments evaluating client progress and suggesting behavioral changes. Marriage Encounter, an international couples' communication weekend workshop, founded in the mid-1960s, uses as its primary technique journal writing on assigned topics followed by discussion.[5]

Finally, Ira Progoff, founder of Dialogue House, an international journal writing center, has created a series of workshops on the writing of a multi-dimensional diary. This diary includes, among other sections, a daily log; dialogues with persons, the body, events, situations, society, circumstances, and an Inner Wisdom figure, dreams. Each of these subsections has a different purpose and each requires that the journal writer shift in time and dates, audience, literary form, and level of thinking. Progoff believes changing perspectives aids the journal writer in establishing a new relationship to the events, people, projects, and ideas in his/her life. The Intensive Journal and its modifications are being used by pastoral counselors, public school teachers, and thousands of other individuals.

Observations

The journal or diary is not an isolated phenomenon, unrelated to cultures or government. Although usually written by one person, it can reflect on and respond to prevailing societal issues, beliefs and constraints. Certain conditions, particularly times of crisis and/or exploration, tend to promote writing. When the writer's living space shrinks, that is during imprisonment, punishment, or reduced physical mobility, as well as when the living space expands, such as in traveling, the writing often begins.

While some diarists intend only themselves as readers, it seems equally clear that for other diarists, another person or persons, God, or "posterity" is the audience. Since some diaries contain poetry, other literary efforts or art forms, it is worth asking what characteristics diaries share with art and under what conditions, if any, diaries should be considered as art. As history, diaries are, at best, only the diarist's perception of truth. This truth, particularly in the spiritual diaries, is focused through the lens of a culture or community. Especially now, with the publication of so many diaries, it would be interesting to explore how the form teaches and reinforces group values and community tie-building and when diary readings may be the preferred forum for fostering this education. Finally, it is important to remember that diaries begin with particular diarists, in particular settings; thus, diary readers should always consider how best to work with others' diaries in order to preserve their original contexts and meanings without distortion.

Notes

[1]For both more discussion and a fuller citing of references and footnoting, please refer to pp. 1-77 in Sharyn Lowenstein, "The Journal-Journal Keeper Relationship as Experienced by the Journal Keeper: A Phenomenological and Theoretical Investigation" (Diss., Boston University, 1982).

[2]Plutschow, 1973, p. 152, revised translation.

[3]Leslie Stephen, ed. *The Works of Henry Fielding Esq. Vol. VIII*, p. 83 (London: Smith, Elder, 1882) as cited in Robert Fothergill Private Chronicles (London: Oxford University Press, 1974), p. 27.

[4]The principles as described in the text are noted in Thomas F. O'Dea, *The Mormons* (Chicago: The University of Chicago Press, 1957). For the application of the principles for Mormons' journal use I am indebted to Cydney P. Quinn, member of the Church of Jesus Christ of Latter-day Saints.

[5]For this information, I am grateful to Rose Leone, Marriage Encounter booking, telephone interview, June, 1985.

References

Assagioli, R. (1977). *Psychosynthesis*. Harmondsworth, U.K.: Penguin.

Bacon, F. (1958). Of travel. In *The essays: or counsels, civil and moral: and the wisdom of the ancients*. Boston: Little, Brown.

Baxter, B. (1976). *American revolution experience: A critical study of diaries and journals of American prisoners during the Revolutionary Period*. Dissertation, University of Delaware.

Couser, C.T. (1979). *American Autobiography*. Amherst, MA: University of Massachusetts.

De Jesus, C.M. (1962). *Child of the dark, the diary of Carolina Maria de Jesus*. Trans. by David St. Clair. NY: E.P. Dutton.

Fothergill, R.A. (1974). *Private chronicles: A study of English diaries*. London; Oxford University Press.

Haller, W. (1957). *The rise of Puritanism*. NY: Harper and Brothers.

Howe, M.J. (Ed. and Trans.) (1977). *The intimate journal of George Sand*. Chicago: Academy Press Limited.

Johnson, C.R., Jr. (1970). *Samuel Pepys and the diarist's art*. Dissertation, University of Virginia.

Johnson, E.C. (1978). *The great secret and the patterns of life: Journalcraft as a psychotherapeutic tool*. Dissertation, California Institute of Asian Studies.

Kagle, S.E. (1979). *American diary literature, 1620-1799*. Boston: Twayne Publishers.

Kimm, R. (1976). *The private journal as a form of philosophical communication*. Dissertation, De Paul University.

Kora, T. & O'Hara, K. (1973). Morita therapy. *Pyschology Today.*

Latham, R.C. & Matthews, W. (Eds.) (1970). *The diary of Samuel Pepys.* Berkeley: University of California Press.

Leedy, J. (1969). *Poetry therapy: The use of poetry in the treatment of emotional disorders.* Philadelphia: J.B. Lippincott.

_____ . (1973). *Poetry the healer.* Philadelphia: J.B. Lippincott.

Leone, R. (1985, June). Interview.

Mallon, T. (1984). *A book of one's own: People and their diaries.* New York: Ticknor & Fields.

Matthews, W. (1945). *American diaries: An annotated bibliography of American diaries written prior to the year 1861.* Berkeley: University of California Press.

_____ . (1950). Comp. *British diaries: An annotated biblography of British diaries written between 1442 and 1942.* Berkeley: University of California Press.

Maultsby, M.C. (1971, fall). Systematic, written homework in psychotherapy. *Theory, research and practice, 8,* 3, 195-198.

Metzger, D. & Meyerhoff, B. (1979). Dear diary (or listening to the silent laughter of Mozart while the beds are unmade and remains of breakfast congeal on the table). *Chrysalis, 7.*

Miller, D.J. (1979). *The intensive journal: A new tool for ministry.* Dissertation, Lancaster Theological Seminary.

Milner, M. [Joanna Field]. (1936). *A life of one's own.* London: Chatto & Windus.

Moffat, M.J. & Painter, C. (1975). *Revelations.* New York: Vintage.

Morgan, E. (Ed.) (1970). *Diary of Michael Wigglesworth.* Gloucester: Peter Smith.

Morris, I. (Ed. & Trans.) (1977). *The pillow book of Sei Shonagon.* Harmondsworth, U.K.: Penguin.

Moulton, P.P. (Ed.) (1971). *The journal and major essays of John Woolman.* New York: Oxford University Press.

Nichols S. (1973). *The personal journal: A mental health proposal.* Dissertation, California School of Professional Psychology.

O'Dea, T.F. (1957). *The Mormons.* Chicago: University of Chicago Press.

Pearson, L. (Ed.) (1965). *Use of written communications in psychotherapy.* Springfield, IL: Charles C. Thomas.

Plutschow, H.E. (1973). *Japanese travel diaries of the Middle Ages.* Dissertation, Columbia University.

Progoff, I. (1977). *The well and the cathedral.* New York: Dialogue House.

_____ (1979). *The white robed monk* (2nd ed.). New York: Dialogue House.

_____ . (1980). *The practice of process meditation.* New York: Dialogue House.

_____ . (1981). *The star/cross.* New York: Dialogue House.

Quinn, C.P. (1980, April). Interview.

Rosenwald, A. (1979). *Three early American diarists.* Dissertation, Columbia University.

Simons, G. (1978). *Keeping your personal journal.* New York: Paulist Press.

Weintraub, K.J. (1978). *The value of the individual: Self and circumstance in autobiography.* Chicago: Univeristy of Chicago Press.

Part II

Journals and the Teaching of English

Journals have long been used by teachers of English and the language arts for a variety of reasons: to help students gain fluency in their writing; to teach them to observe and document their personal experience; to collect notes, impressions, and ideas for both creative and analytical assignments; to begin the early drafts of formal papers; and to reflect on and speculate about poetry, fiction, and drama. The teachers who wrote the thirteen chapters which comprise this second section generously illustrate these practices—plus a few more—in classrooms ranging from first grade to college.

The first three chapters, 9, 10, and 11, focus on the use of journals in college literature classes. Pat Belanoff's "The Role of Journals in the Interpretive Community" describes how she uses journals to help students document their progressive understanding of the texts they are reading. Leon Gatlin's "Losing Control and Liking It: Journals in Victorian Literature" describes the author's progressive immersion in the journal technique as a way of teaching the novels of Emily Brontë, William Thackeray, Anthony Trollope, George Eliot, Charles Dickens, and Thomas Hardy. The late Gary Lindberg describes his use of Berthoff's dialectical notebook to teach a variety of works from William Faulkner to Carlos Castaneda.

The next three chapters, 12, 13, and 14, focus on journals in the college writing class. Mary Jane Dickerson's "Exploring the Inner Landscape," demonstrates the relationship of the private, informal journal to the more structured, formal writing students produce in this course. Judith Fishman Summerfield's "Golden Notebooks, Blue Notebooks: Re-readings" is a journal entry within a journal entry within a journal entry, as the author takes us on a tour of her own history of teaching with journals. Christopher C. Burnham's "Reinvigorating a Tradition" begins with the sources which influenced his development of the "personal development journal," including Britton, Bruffee, Perry, and Progoff, and concludes with a detailed description of how this highly structured journal works.

Chapters 15, 16, and 17 describe some possibilities for using journals in middle and high school English classes. In "Building a Dining Room Table," Nancie Atwell compares the dialogue journals in her eighth grade class to the lively after-dinner talk at her dining room table—and finds both rewarding and intellectually stimulating. In "I

99

Hear Voices: The Text, The Journal, and Me," Phyllis Tashlik examines the influences of contemporary reader-response criticism on several kinds of literary journals assigned to high school students. In "Respecting Opinions," Virgil Davala suggests that journals can help middle school students learn about literature, grammar, and group process all in the same class.

The last four chapters in this section offer some ideas about using journals in elementary classrooms. Ruth Nathan's "I Have a Loose Tooth" presents journal selections written over the course of a semester by a first grade student. Chapter 19 is written in two parts: the first part, Toby Fulwiler's "Writing and Learning, Grade 3" offers a father's look at his daughter's 3rd grade journal; the second part, Megan Fulwiler's "Still Writing and Learning, Grade 10," offers his daughter's perspective on keeping a personal journal for eight years. In Chapter 20, "Fifth Grade Journals," Patricia McGonegal demonstrates, with generous examples, how journals work across various subject areas within her team-taught middle school classroom. Chapter 21, "Choice Produces Result," by Bill Reif and James S. Davis, reproduces the remarkable fictional journal of a sixth grade Iowa girl and describes the process that generated it.

9.

The Role of Journals
in the Interpretive Community

PAT BELANOFF

I thought that this was an OK assignment. The only thing
that I got frustrated at was trying to figure out what you
wanted. I'd like to hear more of your interpretations of the
stories and poems that we read. That has been my biggest
frustration all term—trying to figure out what you wanted to
read in our papers. I wish I knew so that I could do a paper
that I spent a lot of time on, and know that I did the right
thing instead of wondering.

from a student journal

Writing (or trying to write) what they think their teachers want
them to write cuts students off from the source of their own writing
strength: the impulse to express themselves. Reading (or trying to read)
the way they think their teachers want them to read cuts students off
from the source of their own interpretive strength: free interaction with
the text in front of them. I use journals in literature classes as a way to
help students stay connected to direct expression in writing of their free
interaction with a text.

A majority of my students have been taught (and have learned well)
that their immediate personal responses to a work of literature are
"wrong" or, if not "wrong," inappropriate in a literature classroom.
The corollary to this is that "somewhere out there" is a "right" response
to every piece of literature and that their task as students is to discover
what that "right" response is. The student who wrote the lament
opening this article was crippled as a writer and a reader by her
conviction that her task in a literature course was to listen to a teacher's
interpretation, understand it, and write it up to submit for a grade. She
assumed that I knew the "right" interpretation and that I wanted her to
figure out what it was. She spent much time in my office playing some
student version of twenty questions, hoping she could piece together my
interpretation. Meanwhile she consistently protested that she never knew
what anything meant and therefore had no base upon which to build an
interpretation of her own. It was as though she were blindfolded and
manacled.

Many times this student told me what I have heard too often from
other students as well: "I like reading, but not 'reading for an English

101

class.'" They like reading, they tell me, because of what happens to them *while* they are reading, the feelings stirred up in them by the words and situations. "Reading for an English class" means reading to answer correctly questions posed by some authority about the "meaning" of the text. Their assumptions are confirmed by the format of most anthologies used for introductory literature courses which follow selections of short stories, poems, plays, and novels with questions about various aspects of each text. Students deduce (can we blame them?) that the purpose of reading text is to answer the questions that follow it. For the most part they don't particularly enjoy doing this, but they do believe that if they can answer the questions correctly, they know what the text "means." For many, this task is such an onerous one that I have even heard them say they don't like "reading for meaning"—unaware of the truth that reading is by definition the creation of meaning.

It isn't only the questions at the ends of selections in introductory anthologies which limit students' interpretations to mirror images of accepted ones. As teachers, we too have interpretations which it is only too easy for us to hand over to students during letures. Or we can "tactfully" guide them toward our interpretations as we read through a text in the classroom with them. Students often tell me that they deliberately do not read a text until *after* a professor lectures on it because after she lectures, they'll know what to look for as they read.

Through all this, we rob students of their role as readers; we don't really give them the opportunity to read in its truest sense. No wonder so many of them say they like reading, but don't like "reading for an English class": the teacher expects them to attend to what they consider unimportant and to see things in the text which they find impossible to see. Meanwhile, their attempts to do this preclude their enjoyment of what they read.

The underlying issue here is one which some consider sophomoric even to raise: What's the study of literature all about? Why do it? What's the purpose of knowing "the" interpretation of *Hamlet*? Of what value is it to a student to know what Professor X's interpretation of *Ulysses* is? What are we doing in our literature classes? Very few of the students who sit before us will need to know authorized interpretations of works of literature. Even those who are English majors will not make the study of literature their life's work; what they offer society will be superior literacy skills: the ability to read critically and write effectively. A majority of the students in our classes are likely to be physics, mathematics or biology majors satisfying a humanities requirement. (In today's world, most of them seem to be computer-science majors!) But we do hope (or, at least I hope) that they will find a place in their lives for literature and the humanistic approach to life that it fosters. Try as I may, I cannot find that place for them—I can only create an environment in which at least some of them may discover it.

Consideration of all this has led me to place journals at the heart of my literature classes. Journals belong to students; in them, they can record *their* thoughts about literature, their thoughts as readers. By reading their journals, I can discover what they do as they read and help them discover that too. In this way, they can learn to sharpen their own natural way of responding to a text; they build on their own strengths. The journals are never graded. Students share their responses either with the whole class, with a small group within the classroom, or with me in conference. (They are always given the right to select which parts they wish to share; if they don't wish to share any of it with me, I require them to write me a note explaining their decision.) In class and in conference, I try to focus the discussion on what the student is doing as he reads and what in the text is causing him to react as he does. Formal writing assignments ask them to analyze their responses, trace their development, and present them clearly to an audience. My goal is always to make them see their journals as the basis of all interpretation, i.e., to see their personal responses as the basis of all interpretation.

The first thing students need to become consciously aware of is that when they read, they enter into a conversation with the text or—if you prefer—a conversation with themselves about the text. To make this clear, I require students to write in their journals *as* they read and give them practice doing this in class. For this in-class exercise, I ask them to write first a response to the title and author, next a response to the first sentence, and third a response to the second sentence. Thereafter they must stop periodically to catch the thoughts going through their minds. The following sample reactions of three students are a result of an in-class reading of "The Brother," a short story by Robert Coover. For those who may be unfamiliar with it, it is a first-person retelling of the Noah's Ark story by an unnamed brother of Noah. It is written in dialect and does not use any sentence-ending punctuation.

First reaction is about family—how for some reason I think it has to do with a brother in the church. Author doesn't do anything for me—I still think it's about some church thing. So far I think it has to do with 2 brothers—one who obeys the other—who always does what he says—I'm not sure who's older. I thinking the narrator—speaker, about the brother is older—or younger—oh—I'm not sure—but it really doesn't matter. What matters is the influence of the brother. For some reason this narrator does whatever his brother wants—Does he look up to him? Is he intimidated—or insecure? Does he wish he was his Brother? Why isn't he his own person? Why doesn't he help his wife instead of his brother—building a boat. Does he dislike his wife? Does she want a boat? Well I guess the brother is older. It seems as though the younger brother dreads helping him all the time. Why do it then? He's got his own life—he says he was 20 when the narrator was born—but yet (the narrator) leads him—?—Does he think his older brother is incapable? Or is he just incapable and doesn't realize he's being lead. "Am I my Brother's Keeper?" —Ahh—Noah's Ark!!—of course!—it's blatantly obvious—the animals on the boat....

Janice

"The Brother"—I would expect it either to be about a monk or someone's brother. I don't think the brother will be narrator. Robert Coover—never heard of him. It's pretty hard to read with no punctuation. I found out that the story is going to be about a

particular   brother and younger brother (narrator) who always
winds up getting caught in his brother's schemes. The younger
brother did this all his life. I guess it's going to tell about certain
things they did. They're building some boat in the middle of the
field. It seems so stupid. The younger brother wants to spend time
with his family but his brother makes him feel guilty if he doesn't
help him. So far there are no names. The brother is weird. He
makes his wife sit on a hill in the rain so she can see God. Maybe
he's just trying to be a good person. His intentions are good
anyway. The older brother is 20 years older. That's a big difference.
He must be a pretty old guy now. The younger brother's married
and his wife's going to have a baby. I wonder if we're ever going to
find out why the man is building the boat. The wife seems very
kind. I guess she's tired of asking her husband not to go help his
brother. Maybe the older brother has some kind of mental problems. I think it's the story of Noah's Ark. That's what it seems
like anyway.

                                                          Juanita

The Brother—the title—about someone's brother! or about the
brother of someone. Robert Coover—nothing, nada, never heard of
him—American that's it. This story is damned annoying! It's
probably about 2 brothers, ignorant and unschooled working—
trying to do something in I think a field. What is he trying to do?
He is building a boat with his brother, even though he doesn't
want to. His wife doesn't want him to either, yet she still supports
them. I can't stand this story! The bad grammar totally interferes
with my concentration. I know they're building the boat to go and
catch food, but why don't they just grow it in the field instead?
Why is the brother so *tired*? How old is he? Sounds old. Why does
he keep working on this boat? Why must passersby help. O my
God—Noah's Ark! They *have* to build....

                                                          Jill

   In class, we analyzed these three responses to the beginning of this
story and concluded that 1) Janice delays resolution of her questions
about the text; 2) Juanita repeats pieces of the story and tends to make
decisions about characters; 3) Jill makes judgments about the story itself
and the action in it. When these three students looked back at previous
journal entries, they realized these responses were fairly typical of
themselves as readers: Janice tends to read for a "message"; Juanita likes
to be able to identify with characters; and Jill looks for plots she can
relate to her own life.
   As we probe these responses more deeply, students begin to realize
that Janice's assumptions about literature are quite different from those
of Juanita and Jill. The two latter students consider literature—all art—
as a reflection of the world outside the text; they respond to events and
characters in the text as they would respond to them in their own lives.
Janice sees a text differently; she sees it as creating its own world; what a
text offers her is the chance to draw analogies between it and the world
she lives in.

One of the reasons I use this particular story is that responses to it allow students to think about different ways of approaching a text while also realizing the role the text plays since all, in approximately the same amount of time, realize that it is a retelling of the Noah's Ark story. This encourages students to see that there are common elements in the way they read as well as differences; they are able to isolate those features of the text which almost all of them respond to and discuss the reasons for these common reactions. This also helps each one to isolate those features of a text which seem particularly meaningful to her and think about why that is so. I make no value judgments on the ways of reading; in fact, I work toward validating all ways of reading. As a result, students begin to treasure their journals.

> This journal made me think. It forces me to write down feelings, opinions and thoughts—without real pressure (no grade *per se*). While I have to admit, I didn't complete all of my entries at the proper time, nonetheless I learned something. I learned about expression—that it isn't always difficult (just most of the time.) Many times I really wanted to write about a story or a poem because ideas came into my brain (a unique experience) and it felt good to get them (or something like them) onto the paper in front of me—so often it happens that I forget my ideas—this process reduced that possibility, and thus made thinking and its expression a little nicer.
>
> Tim

Once students become comfortable with using journal writing as a way of talking to themselves about a text *as* they read, they can begin using their entries as a way of talking to others about what they read. Students read their responses to the class or to a small group and then later record their reactions to the ensuing discussion in their journals. I encourage them to focus on whether or not the discussion of their journal entry has caused them to alter their original response in any way. This forces students to reconsider their first responses rather than seek to justify them as they're required to do in many literature classes. Not that I frown on such justification, but on the fact that it's something we often require of students prematurely. If students have a conference with me, I also require that they talk in their journals about how that may or may not have affected their own reading of a text. Here's an edited version of a student's record of her changing perceptions of Tillie Olsen's "I Stand Here Ironing":

> *(After first reading)*
> I thought that this was a sad story. Emily was the author's daughter and the author wrote about Emily's sad life as a child and the hard times and how she grew up.
>
> Maybe Emily was someone famous and her mother was being interviewed. I'm not sure who Emily was or what her story was about.
>
> *(After second reading)*
> I read it again. After reading it twice I understand the story more. I caught things that I didn't see before. The story was the same, and

I'm still not too sure what it's about but I think I understood it more. Emily was some sick girl who's 19 now and I don't know what her problem is. I'm still not sure who her mother is. Who was the mother speaking to? What happened to Emily? Where was Emily now? What was the significance of the last paragraph of the story? I know it is important but I really don't understand it.

(After small-group discussion)
After discussion of "Ironing" I realized a couple of things I didn't before. I also decided what I was going to discuss in my interpretation. I'm going to talk about the mother's relationship with Emily. The ending explains that the mother did not have much hope or faith in Emily. She thought it was okay for Emily not to live up to her potential....I condemn the mother for feeling this way towards Emily. She also had a disappointing, fatalistic attitude towards life. I wonder how a mother could just give up hope on a child that had a potential to live up to. The mother is wrong in her attitude towards Emily's life.

(After class discussion)
Now I think different. I was convinced by Regina that the mother did the best that she could and she couldn't be condemned.
    She always did what everyone thought she should do. Now she's not listening to anyone and leaving Emily alone. Emily has to be left alone because she has been ruined by society. All through the mother's upbringing of Emily, she only wanted the best for her daughter. She did what everyone thought was right for her to do.... Not only do I feel sorry for Emily at this point, but I feel sorry for the once condemned mother. The iron represents society —hot and stinging. Emily's life has to be straightened out.

(Final interpretation)
I realize that my first interpretation is the more favorable one and now I have more evidence to support my original conclusions. I realize why the mother said, "Let her be." But now I ask, why must the mother stop trying to help Emily just because other things have failed in the past?
    I believe that the mother was more than just the dress on the ironing board: she was the iron too. She did to Emily what life had done to her. She was treated badly and wrongly, and that was how she treated Emily, except that she did not take responsibility for it. She created Emily's life and her personality by treating her this way throughout her life. Emily's life is like her mother's—and unless she does something about it, she will continue to be the dress on the ironing board, helpless before the iron.

(Reflections a week later)
I just realized now, what the *real* reasons were that explain why the mother treated Emily the way she did. Emily was the only child out of five to have such problems. Maybe the mother mistreated Emily because her first husband left her before Emily was one year old. The mother condemned Emily throughout her life for the pain and

hardships that she received from Emily's father.

Throughout the entire story there is also a subtle change between past and present. I believe that it makes the story more real. First, the mother tells us about the phone call she received, and then she **goes into her thoughts of the past and keeps going back and forth** between past and present. I believe she sees it all as one thing. The past is as real to her as the present. We get it all mixed up too and that's why it's hard for us to see that things can change for Emily— or for her mother.

Rhonda

By using journals this way, students begin to see them as re-positories of their own developing thoughts. In fact, in reflecting on their journals, this is a development they often find fascinating: the way their own minds work.

At times, a rough idea can be seen changing and evolving in the short course of one fifteen minute entry. First there will be one idea, then a similar one, and so on until there is a final idea drawn. Sometimes, I notice, I will realize that something is wrong after I write it down. Something about the writing it out makes me realize that it is not so—like I can see it physically and then mentally know that it is wrong.

Saul

The next step is to help students use the interpretations of others in conjunction with their own. This is a step that can only be taken after students have made their own interpretation. What happens too often in traditional literature classrooms is that students are assigned a work to read and interpret and the first thing they do is run to the library to see what others have said about the particular work. I want them to see that that should be a final step, not a first step. For this assignment, instead of using the interpretations of experts, they use the interpretations of other members of the class. Each student selects a work to interpret and then joins a group. Here are some comments about how that worked:

I've learned to listen to a lot of people's ideas, combine them, sort them, add or subtract from or to my own, and poof—I have my own theory! Other people are very helpful. They help you recognize yourself.

Jill

As a final assignment, students must pick a piece of text from a work we're reading and justify their choice of it. The piece of text must be what most conditioned them in terms of their interpretation of the entire work. The point of their analysis is to discover the connection between the way they read and the features of a text which impress them as significant.

My basic purpose in all this is to help students realize that whenever they read, they interpret; that, in fact, reading *is* interpretation. What I've discovered is that the greater their awareness of this becomes, the more rewarding it becomes to them to follow through on their interpretations: they begin to own their interpretations. They come to understand that they've always had the power to interpret literature and always will have, that finding meaning in texts is not some mysterious, magic power that only English professors have. And, finally, I hope they'll become more aware that sharing their reactions with others broadens and deepens their intepretations. In truth, I hope they'll discover they are a part of an "interpretive community" and that belonging to such a group can enrich their sense of themselves and their relation to others. Some of them will, of course, join my "interpretive community"; that's fine, but I neither expect nor want all of them to.

Journals are as valuable to teachers as they are to students. We can learn more about our students as interpreters of literature from their journals than we could ever learn from their papers. Students who distrust their own abilities as readers tend to play it safe when writing papers which will be graded. In their journals they dare to write what they consider inappropriate, too exploratory, too far removed from the text or too personal. Sometimes when I'm reading students' finished papers, I wonder why they did not take a good idea farther, why they didn't see other ramifications of what they were saying. Here, for example, is a student writing about *Mill on the Floss* and its main characters:

> Later in the novel she (Maggie) is once again restricted by her family, in that she promises Tom that she won't associate with her friend and his enemy Philip Waken. Tom is also a victim of being restrained and not able to do his own thing. He is directed by his father in what school he shall attend and what course of studies he shall pursue. In addition to Maggie and Tom both being directed by the family they both are also influenced by society. They live their lives not as they wish to but as they think they should, as a result of society's influence.
>
> Janice

In her journal, Janice reflected on these same conclusions:

> All these stories we're reading have to do with the influences of society. How much are *we* influenced? Am I the way I am because of my society? Ya—I guess so! —Pretty wild!—Gosh—Everything is a factor of why you are the way you are—the people, the place— Everything contrives to form you—but since everything is different —so are we!—Yeah—We're all incredibly infinite and crazy!

When I asked the student why she had not included these ideas in her finished paper, she answered that she considered them too personal. How she might have integrated these thoughts into her views of Tom and Maggie is not my right to decide. I do wish, though, that she had been willing to risk trying. I often see this pulling back from ideas when I compare students' papers with their journals. I'm not saying that students should include, in their final evaluations of a text, every bold move away from traditional interpretation. What I am saying is that journals provide a place for such ideas—otherwise they might never be written down. And if they never get written down, they cannot be examined for possible inclusion. If I had seen only this student's paper, I wouldn't have known that her mind was coping with conclusions more comprehensive than those she included in the paper. Papers let me see what students have under control; journals allow me to see what they don't yet have under control.

Before the course is over, I feel it necessary to warn students that their personal interpretations may not be acceptable to others, particularly to other professors. We practice at least once writing a "formal critique," but I insist that it grow out of responses in their journals. I want them to understand that they can tailor their responses into impersonal, critical statements about a piece of literature. If they leave my class believing that their journal responses are unsuitable for the sorts of formal critiques required in many literature classes, then I've failed. In fact, I hope they believe me when I say that those are the *only* responses worth full, critical treatment.

I need to address one final problem with my approach which I have not learned how to solve to my satisfaction. Just as there are students who want me to tell them exactly how to "do" a paper (exactly what should be included, how it should be begun, ended, organized), so there are students who want me to tell them how to read, what to look for, what to think, what to conclude. I sidestep their questions as best I can by saying that I'm not going to give them my interpretation. (I know, of course, that I cannot totally hide it either.) Some students never adjust to this; they have become quite good at discovering what teachers want and giving it to them; they have become quite good at feeding back to a teacher her own interpretations if that's what she wants. This process has earned them good grades; small wonder they resist abandoning it. After a struggle, some of these students readjust and find greater pleasure in working out their own interpretations than they had found in parroting a teacher's. Still, some do not adjust and leave the class quite convinced that I'm either stupid or stammeringly unable to explain what I want. It is usually these students who most resent writing in a journal; they rarely feel any personal connection to it. One student jotted the following note to me at the end of her journal: "There is no need to return this journal with my paper." I used to be tempted to give in to these students' demands for "canned" interpretations, especially since some of them are quite sincere and hard-working—but I don't give in anymore and have resigned myself to their usually poor opinion of me.

I certainly don't want to end on that negative note. So I'll end instead with an excerpt from a student's journal which illustrates my most basic purpose: the integration of literature into a student's everyday life. This is a journal entry in response to reading Housman's "Terence, This Is Stupid Stuff."

> I have absolutely no idea what this poem is about. "A.E. This is Stupid Stuff." I guess Terence is a fellow poet who writes bad poetry, who's the cow, and what does the story of Mithridites have to do with beer? Ale's the answer. I don't know. All I know is Terence is spewing forth poetry I think about his friend's death, A.E. Housman, has gotten drunk in his lifetime and has passed out in a mud puddle, and that Mithridites took small doses of arsenic and strychnine so no one could poison him. Where's the connection? You've got me. I'm on my break right now at work and this

day has just been extremely annoying. All I hear right now is that electronic bell going throughout the store that drowns out the **MUZAK** which is some groovy organ version of a Jefferson Airplane tune. It's amazing how many people leave their houses on a Sunday afternoon when the sun is shining and there's a nice breeze out, it's crisp, and go to the Mall. The mall, the famous Smithhaven Mall is where you can leave off your kids to play Motley Crue at volume 10 or 150 Wah stereo systems and not have to worry about them for six hours. Why can't people go to the beach or a park or even sit home and play risk or do a puzzle? Retail is no picnic. I don't get paid to get yelled at and I don't get paid to babysit. I hope this day ends soon or else I may crack. I should have taken small doses of annoyance with every meal for the past few years to build up my tolerance for these people.

Chris

Almost without being conscious of it, Chris has found a message for his own life in Housman's poem. Occasionally, I come across a student who becomes consciously aware of the power of a journal; when that happens, the student usually states my purposes far better than I can:

Thumbing through my journal and looking at it all at once I feel good. This has been the first "real" journal I've ever had. Nice, neat (for me), and ordered. I can look back and point to what I've done, try to figure out how I was thinking—to analyze what made me do what I did so that I can control it better next time, that is, have some degree of mastery over my creative juices—let them run, but run where I want them to. Just having a journal is a step in that direction. I find it's not always what you write, but that you write. I find that the words and content come after a time. You watch yourself getting better and better. It's like a clock. You can't really see the hands move, but they do and soon the hours start piling up. I also recognize that you have to keep it up. I've fallen behind on entries several times and I notice the difference when I start up again. Again, it's the process that's important. Think process, process, process. But think while you're thinking about it. I don't know about you, but I'm keeping one over the summer... and beyond....

Fred

Couldn't what I have done with journals be done without using journals? Yes, I suppose it could, but since students would need to keep all their writing in one place, they'd put it in a folder or something similar and in the end they'd create a journal. In other words, doing what I do would create a journal even if I didn't call it that. And the wonderful thing is that students usually leave class with many empty pages in their journals and with the knowledge that they don't need an "assignment" to use their journals. And so they're encouraged to keep one "over the summer...and beyond...."

10.

Losing Control and Liking It: Journals in Victorian Literature

LEON GATLIN

I had known about reading journals for a number of years. I had read Ann Berthoff and the other journal theorists, and I had encountered many teachers who used some form of journal writing in their instruction. Confident that journals were a Good Thing, several years ago I cautiously introduced them into my courses in Victorian literature. I had sound motives: I hoped journals would sharpen my students' abilities to read and learn on their own, and I also hoped I would have to give fewer tests and written assignments.

But I wasn't prepared for what happened. At first most of the students dutifully recorded entries in their journals with me, the professor, clearly in mind as audience. The writing was not spontaneous, it was too formal and correct, and it was timid. I tried to explain what was needed to make this technique work—"Just write down, freely and honestly, any thoughts that occur to you in the act of reading the novels in the course. Write for yourself; reflect on paper; ask questions. Try to write during each period of reading, or at least just afterwards, to catch fresh impressions." But most of the questions I got about the journals concerned how long they had to be, or what form they had to be in. Only a few of my students seemed to reveal any engagement and involvement in their reading.

Realizing that I must do something to break this pattern of passive, timid responses, two years ago I began sharing my own journal entries in class. At first I thought I would simply model the kind of activity I wanted from them, but it quickly became apparent that it wasn't as easy as I had imagined (or required of them). It was only when I read aloud my own journal entries that things began to click. Here is a sample, about *Jude the Obscure:*

> What upsets me so is that I recognize that Arabella is one of the survivors of this world (without the distraction of irrelevant "higher" feelings, such as idealism or tenderness), and Jude's idealism and humanitarian instincts will doom him to extinction. Arabella forces me to face some very unpleasant realities about life, and her methodical, efficient approach to life alarms me because it is so successful. I hate her, hate her because she might be right.

The result was dramatic, because the rest of the class not only experienced a real example of a journal entry, but they began to regard me as a fellow learner, not just an authority figure. This broke some thick ice in the class and brought about real improvement in their journals and in our class discussions.

As their journals became more honest and spontaneous (also rougher and longer), I discovered I had to modify the way I was responding to them. I found it even more important to respond regularly, to keep a real sense of dialogue going; and I also found that short, more personal notes to them seemed to work well. Instead of comments beginning, "You might consider what Richard Altick has to say about this," I found myself caught up in the excitement of their reading. I began responding with comments such as, "You really do seem to like the presence of the narrative voice here. I'm glad, tho' just a little surprised. Could you share some of these thoughts in class?" Or "I think you're right. I hadn't noticed how consistent this pattern of passive men and active women was in this novel." As the semester progressed, I was pleased to see most of the journals develop in several ways. For example, almost all of the students became more confident in expressing personal reactions and insights, as the following excerpts (concerning novels by Trollope and Thackeray) illustrate:

> The first chapter of *The Warden* establishes the setting and some of the characters. Mr. Harding seems to be a fairly generous man but so far his life appears to be rather routine and mundane. I have, for some reason, developed a dislike for his son-in-law the Archdeacon.

About a month later in the course, the same student wrote this about *Vanity Fair:*

> Thackeray's little interjected sermons are interesting especially when they deal with his views about women. Women today are much the same as Becky except with less cunning and a lot less class. And Amelia reminds me very much of Esther in *Bleak House*. . . . I think I would rather spend my life as an old maid than marry someone like Jos. . . For some reason I feel positive about Becky. She seemed at first to be sort of rebellious and bratty, but now I feel she was resourceful and almost what I'd call brave. . But she has risen to the height of her bad qualities when she flirts with her best friend's husband. I still can't bring myself to dislike her for some strange reason. I think it's because she has so much more life and spontaneity than anyone else in the novel.

These comments reflect a growing ability to read alertly and to reflect on the transaction taking place between the reader and the text. Typical of many students in my classes for the past several years, these entries also reveal more confidence in speculating—about the novel itself, and about the active role of the reader. Encouraged by comments from me and by the support of increasingly lively class discussions, the majority of these students increased their personal confidence and pleasure in reading fiction.

Deeper Learning

Some of my students, however, have reached much deeper levels of involvement in their reading. Apparently building on the solid foundation provided by a close and accurate recording of their responses as readers (illustrated by the examples above), some readers have found their journals to be a powerful means of generating new dimensions of inquiry and understanding. Often this is seen in the form of questions or observations that probe more than just the reader's own personal response, although that response is almost always there, thoroughly embedded in the entries, too. These two examples, by different students, are reasonably typical of this kind of response:

- Thackeray at times seems willing to admit to lesser human deceptions as long as it is aptly juxtaposed to some sort of consummate evil, such as the cruel and lecherous Lord Steyne. It is confusing, also, that sometimes Thackeray is omniscient—he can tell the inner thoughts and schemes of someone like Becky, who is quite devious. Then he begs off on revealing the thoughts of a simple-minded twit like Amelia.... Becky tells herself that she could be good if she had 5,000 pounds a year. It is doubtful if she would be, however. I think she would try to con people if she were queen. It is in her blood. It would help the reader to understand why she is that way if Thackeray gave more insight into her, but he doesn't. I don't think he is concerned with why people act the way they do so much as he is interested in giving an accurate picture of how they act.

- There is something about Hardy's writing (in *Jude the Obscure*), however, I found myself suspicious about and that is the way he handles literary or classic references... I may be off base here, but it reminds me of the sexual portions of modern day novels. In order to sell a novel, it's been said publishers take a good story and then at random, almost, throw a little sex in. I feel a bit of a haphazard feeling regarding literary references in Hardy in much the same way.

It's significant, I think, that both these students introduced these ideas into class discussion with no prompting, probably because the journal entries recorded thoughts that were reaching out, going beyond an intimate or personal level. In both cases, it seems there was a need to engage others—a wider and more public perspective. The discussions in class, concerning Thackeray's narrative method (and his moral perspective) and Hardy's use of the literary tradition, were lively and good. As teacher, I felt pleased that I had not had to initiate a discussion of these two subjects, ones which are certainly valuable enough to plan to "cover" in a course of this kind. Since the students had discovered these questions for themselves, we engaged in a discussion that was remarkable for its honesty and sincerity. Without the stimulus provided by journals, I don't see how this degree of active questioning and learning could have taken place.

Another student's journal reveals a characteristic of some, although by no means all, of the class's experience: a series of comments that slowly emerge into recognized patterns. These entries, from a journal on *Bleak House* that ran more than 30 pages, show an increasing interest in Dickens' style and use of point of view. Even in these brief excerpts, however, the comments are seen as thoroughly immersed in other questions and perceptions—about the unfolding suspense plot, Dickens' view of human character, and so on.

(2/1) Chancery allegorized as fog. I like the rolling, moving effect of his style in establishing the omnipresence of the fog, lack of light, mist, density associated with the Court of Chancery.... The description of Sir Leicester is witty—Dickens' poke at the British Aristocracy. Lady Dedlock marries into wealth and position, but what is her connection with the Jarndyce case?...

(2/3) The sudden switch to the 1st person narr. (Esther) had me confused and annoyed. I wasn't ready for it...

(2/5) I suppose it's good he has caught my interest—I'm beginning to get pulled in by the novel because I want my developing questions answered!...

(2/6) The style found in the first two chapters is intense, forceful, bold, energetic. I LOVE this style and feel abandoned when it is not there...

(2/10) Ch. 7: Here again I find energy in Dickens' writing. His constant use of light imagery in references and descriptions of Bleak House. Also, I'm intrigued by the wind image constantly juxtaposed with Jarndyce. Does the wind represent Jarndyce's wish to escape anxiety, disappointment and deceit? The REAL world?

(2/12) I've found the best description of a bird's eyes, which have always fascinated me: he refers to the canary's "bright, sudden eye." The use of "sudden" is great, because birds' eyes do seem to have a constant sense of the sudden. Good job, Dickens!...

(2/13) Again, I think his brilliance is better seen when he is away from the 1st per. narrative. I like the incomplete sentences...

(2/15) I'm wondering about the "eyes in the shutter" in the room where Nemo died...

(2/16) Ch. 14: Mrs. Jellyby, et. al, bring "the wind" to Jarndyce. The wind as symbolic of disorder?...

(2/17) Jo looks up at the cross of St. Paul's Cathedral "so high up... so far out of his reach."...

2/19) Wow! Superb description of summer woods & moonlight shining through trees. "High cathedral arches fantastically broken." The poetry in it is magnificent. Energetic.

I'm not sure how journals like this one come into being. This student followed prescribed procedures given to everyone, yet it's very clear that these entries reached dimensions of probing, questioning, and learning that go substantially beyond the norm for the class. Since no more than a third of my students seem to reach this level of involvement in their journals, I discussed their experience with a number of them after the course was over to try to find out how and why it happened. The answers don't provide a blueprint for cloning this achievement, but they provide real insights into what took place. The students reported that they got caught up in the process of writing in their journals—so much so that, despite the extreme length of novels such as *Bleak House,* they found themselves writing more and more. They became addicted to it, they felt that their reading experience was becoming deeper and more visible, and that they had to look for ways of putting all of their accumulating impressions into some kind of order. They read and reread their journals frequently, looking for connections; and they often were surprised at what they had written. The near-unanimous impression seems to be that the journals forced them to become more active and careful readers. Their personal experience in reading a novel was richer, yet the journal also stimulated better analysis. "I had more to work with," one student said, "than when I just made marks in the margin. I could find things better." And another wrote "I found I was reading more carefully, and paying more attention to details that quite often had greater importance later." However it happened, it's clear that their reading became more confident as the semester progressed and they used their writing to build better questions and better insights.

Papers in Different Modes

Something else I was not fully prepared for was the appearance of unusual papers in my classes. For many years I encouraged my students to write in modes other than critical analyses or research papers if the subject seemed to call for it. But rarely did anyone take me up on this offer, even though one student told me, "You're one of the few profs in this department who will accept off-the-wall papers." But about two years ago my students did begin writing papers in different forms and modes, and there is clear evidence that they did so when reading journals became a thorough and integral part of the course. Although the majority of my students continued to write traditional analytic papers, a substantial number began to write papers strongly characterized by personal responses, and many even wrote in the poetic mode: letters between characters in novels, short plays or stories, even ballads and other poems.

Some of these efforts were indeed off-the-wall, such as a series of letters from Will Shakespeare to George Moore, which one student wrote apparently to try to illustrate his idea that tragedy was incompatible with prose fiction. Fortunately, the student agreed that this idea was pretty shallow—little more than a gimmick without much to sustain it. But other papers began to appear that were more than gimmicks. One student re-wrote the last chapter of *Esther Waters,* originally intending just to make an implicit criticism of the plot by changing the ending, but found in the process that she had to come to terms with Moore's language, style, and conception of character and fate to a degree she had not anticipated before she began writing. It was a very successful paper, interesting not only as a piece of imaginative writing but also as a persuasive comment on Moore's art.

Another student wrote a paper in the form of letters exchanged between a married couple in Trollope's *The Warden* detailing their courtship and marriage prior to the time of the novel. She also had to become much more involved in the author's style and language than she realized at first, and she was forced to research relevant Victorian courtship patterns in order to write the paper. In these cases, and in many others similar to them, the idea for the paper first appeared in journal entries. Also, the decision to write an imaginative piece, rather than an expository analysis, seems to have evolved in response to a genuine search for the most appropriate way to explore the idea. With these papers, as well as with many of the conventional expository papers my students wrote, there seems to be direct connection to the journals: having identified their own questions or ideas to explore, the students developed their thoughts independently as far as they could, then sought advice and additional information from others in the class, from me, and from further reading. They felt more in control of what they were doing and had a better sense of what they really needed to carry their projects through.

A particularly clear example of a paper emerging from journal entries is revealed in these excerpts from a long journal on *Vanity Fair:*

> *(3/1)* What interesting things we are learning about Becky's character! She is obviously the antithesis of Amelia. It's sort of like a Scarlett O'Hara and Melanie Wilkes relationship: Melanie is by far the more admirable character, but Scarlett the far more memorable...
>
> *(3/3)* Becky reminds me more and more of Scarlett with all of the ploys and tricks she uses to win over Joe. Like Scarlett, she's hardly a "poor harmless girl." In fact, her behavior around Joe is almost exactly like Scarlett's behavior around Frank Kennedy...
>
> *(3/5)* Here's a woman—like Scarlett O'Hara again—who needs mastering by a man, and instead she rules over him...
>
> *(3/8)* "Fiddlededee"—straight from Scarlett O'Hara's mouth...
>
> *(3/11)* Becky scoffs at Rawdon's affection for their son much as Scarlett jeers at Rhett's devotion to Bonnie...
>
> *(3/13)* It amazes me how many aspects of this novel remind me of *Gone with the Wind.* I'm toying with the idea of doing my last paper on this subject in some way.

The paper that finally emerged consisted of several letters from Becky thanking Scarlett for her hospitality during Becky's visit to the United States and offering her some advice about life, men, and money. Becky is the older woman who recognizes Scarlett as something of a disciple, and the letters stop at a point just before Scarlett meets Rhett Butler. When I interviewed this student to find out more about how this paper came about, she said, "Without the journal, this wouldn't have happened. I would have noticed similarities, but keeping a journal emphasized the recognition; otherwise I think it would've somehow gotten lost." When asked about the form of the paper, she said she "liked the idea of doing a creative paper because I thought the similarities between the two women were so strong, I wondered what would happen if they knew each other. I made Becky older because Becky and Scarlett wouldn't get along if they were the same age. They would be rivals. I also think the letters Becky wrote in *Vanity Fair* suggested the idea of the paper." Although this paper was an unusually sound one in the probing of character and relationships, it does illustrate a pattern typical of many students in my courses: journal entries slowly developing into a pattern of "recognition," followed by reflection and a search for a form appropriate for the expression of that idea.

Even if I hadn't kept careful documentation of the experiences my students and I have had during the last several years, I think there would be clear evidence of improved learning with reading journals an integral part of the course. I no longer give tests, because I have abundant evidence about what my students have read and understood. Class meetings have changed dramatically, too; they are more like a voluntary reading circle in which I am only a relatively prominent member; discussion is responsible, lively, and systematic. I lecture very infrequently, only when I think some important element has been overlooked—and even then I usually just introduce a specific topic for discussion and rely on the class to take over responsibility for examining it. And I hope it is clear that there is better writing—not only the journals themselves, which sometimes reach astonishing lengths and depths of perception, but also the papers: varied, interesting, confidently written. I am also satisfied that criticism and scholarship are used at least as much as in conventional courses.

Transformed Class Structure

Yes, journals are a Good Thing. No doubt about it. But their presence in a literature course doesn't guarantee success; this isn't a technique you introduce and then sit back to admire the results. I have found that organizing a course around reading journals requires much more effort and carefully thought-out, systematic procedures than I anticipated. Also, my students and I agree that we sometimes find it hard to get used to the radical transformation in class structure and atmosphere in a successful journal-based course. Even though we value what has taken place—a major shift toward placing the responsibility for learning in the hands of the entire class—we still find ourselves almost longing for the security of a conventional structure, with lectures, note-taking, tests, and familiar paper assignments.

And then there are all of the off-the-wall and other unusual papers. I think I know how to evaluate a critical analysis or a research paper in Victorian literature, but how do I assign a fair grade to a paper consisting of a letter from a Dickens character to the author complaining of unfair treatment in the novel? I am trying to find ways to read these papers to determine if real learning about the subject is present, but it is not easy.

Even the most exciting part of my journal-based course—reading the students' journals and witnessing the powerful impact this literature can have on them—is sometimes unsettling. Like many of us in this profession, I have often paid pious lip service to the traditional value of literature as a reflection of the Human Condition, but until recently was only dimly aware of my students' responses, primarily because I was too busy analyzing flaws in Jude Fawley's character or patterns of imagery in George Eliot. But it is another matter altogether to sit up half the night reading and thinking about a journal in which a young woman experiences a genuine crisis while reading *Wuthering Heights*—pouring out her agonized thoughts as she identifies her own lover with Heathcliff and recoils in terror. (She asked for an Incomplete in the course and simply disappeared. I don't know if I will ever see her again.)

Does this mean that there are problems and consequences involved in using journals in a literature class? Yes. Does it mean that the effort is not worth making? No. Despite some problems and frustrations, I look forward eagerly to every journal, every class meeting, and every paper— even the off-the-wall ones. Besides, there's no turning back now. Next semester I may find out that I have both Heathcliff and Cathy in the same class.

11.

The Journal Conference:
From Dialectic to Dialogue

GARY LINDBERG

Using reading journals in my literature courses has changed my students' experience more than any other innovation I have tried as a teacher. It makes their reading and learning personal. And as they attend carefully to how they read and to what they personally make of their reading, they are charmingly surprised to find that such things can count in the classroom. Evidently their earlier education had convinced them that real knowledge must be impersonal and unmalleable. By watching their own reading move from puzzlements through approximations and misreadings to more and more satisfying interpretations, they gradually develop a more realistic sense of what readings and interpretations are, and in class discussion they more readily share readings and build on each other's perceptions instead of naively worrying about who is right and who is wrong.

But to keep a reading journal is an unnatural activity. It contradicts the principles of knowledge implanted by the educational establishment, and it disrupts the culturally acceptable pace of following a story. Students need explicit instructions at the outset and monitoring and reinforcement along the way in order to make the adjustment to working with a journal. I first learned about the classroom uses of the journal from Toby Fulwiler (1982), and I adapted the form I find most workable from the double-entry journal or "dialectical notebook" described by Ann Berthoff in *Forming/Thinking/Writing* (1982). My own innovation has to do with that process of monitoring and reinforcement. In an effort to keep track of what students were doing with their journals and yet not to compromise their privacy and thus their freedom to be deeply personal when they wished, I decided to follow and respond to their work by conferences. It is this approach which is my central concern here, but its significance will be clearer if I begin with a more general description of how I use reading journals in a literature class.

Here is the set of instructions I give to students in the syllabus (the particular course is on American short stories):

The Reading Journal

The core of your work in the course will be composed in your reading journal. I'd like you to get a separate spiral notebook just for this journal and to keep it together over the term. Choose one that feels good to you, that makes you want to write in it. It is essential to the course that you do the reading *before* the class for which it is assigned, and that you take notes in your journal on the readings *as* you read them. You don't need to take notes on every story, but I want you to take notes on at least one story per class meeting. You can also add notes to the journal in class. There is one *rigid rule* about the format of the journal—I want you to use the facing pages in a special way. Take all your reading notes on only the right-hand pages. Leave the opposing pages blank for later. (You may want to reverse this if you are left-handed.) The basic difference is that the right-hand pages are for comments on the story. The left-hand pages are for comments on the right-hand pages. Keep the difference clear and make use of it—don't write continuously from front to back of the sheet.

What to Put on the Right-Hand Pages:

1. Times when your reading changes:
    You see something you didn't see before.
    You recognize a pattern—the images start to overlap, gestures or
        phrases recur, some details seem associated with each other.
    The story suddenly seems to you to be about something different
        from what you thought.
    You discover that you were misreading.
    The writer introduces a new context or new perspective.
2. Times when you are surprised or puzzled:
    Something just doesn't fit.
    Things don't make sense—pose explicitly the question or prob-
        lem that occurs to you.
3. Details that seem important and that make you look again.
4. Ways in which the story makes you speculate about life.
5. Your first impression of the ending—what "ended"?

When writing in the journal, use full sentences instead of phrases. The demands of the sentence will help you draw out your thoughts fully. Be explicit about the nature of your change or surprise or puzzlement—what caused it in the text? The journal will seem less of an intrusion in your reading if you follow the natural rhythms of reading. Sometimes we are carried along by the flow of the story. But the things I've asked you to note are all signs that it's time to pause and reflect. No fiction is designed to be read straight through at uniform speed. Only machines work that way. The journal is a device to help you make more of those moments of reflection and to preserve them for later reconsideration.

What to Put on the Facing Pages (left side):

Whereas the right-hand pages involve your direct reactions to the text, your first gestures at making meanings out of it, the left-hand pages are for a completely different activity. When you finish a story or a group of stories by the same writer, go back and use the facing pages to comment on your original observations and to make something of them. Is there a pattern to the changes you experienced? Does the ending tie them together? Why did you misread when you did? Then reflect on yourself as a reader—what do you focus on? What do you care most about? What do you disregard? Where do you have to strain to follow the story sympathetically? Finally, as you make these reflections on your reading experience, discuss your emerging sense of how the story works and what it's about.

From course to course I vary the specific description of what to include. That way I adjust the pattern of observation and interpretation to the genres and skills that I am emphasizing in the course.

Students draw on their journal entries regularly in class discussion, and in turn they work out in their journals new issues that come up in class. More formally, I ask one student, chosen at random, to begin the day's discussion by a selection from his or her journal on that day's reading. And from time to time I have the students in groups of four or five spend the first fifteen minutes sharing their journal work with each other. Then the rest of the discussion grows out of their mutual discovery of problem areas or favorite interpretations. In these ways they see how what they do individually in their journals builds into a communal act of interpretation.

I usually count reading journals for about one-third of the course grade. (I also require more formal interpretive essays, which in turn often emerge from work in the journal.) I base my response to the journals entirely on conferences. Here are the instructions I give students in the syllabus:

Conferences: Presenting the Journal
Since the journal is *your* gesture of making meaning, I will not grade it directly or read through it systematically. Instead, I want to respond to your own responses to what is going on in the journal. At three points in the course we'll have individual conferences for fifteen or twenty minutes. You'll summarize for me the high points of your journal and interpret yourself as an interpreter. And I'll probably ask you some hard questions about your responses and name for you what I see in your summary. At the end of the course, instead of a final exam, we'll have a final half-hour conference. Your work in the journal will count about a third of the final grade, and your grade on the journal will be determined by how you can present it to me in that final conference. In other words, you'll want to prepare by reviewing it, selecting especially signifi-cant parts to read to me, summarizing and interpreting your work so as to show me what you made of the course for yourself.

Before the final conference, the students usually need more explicit suggestions about ways of preparing for it, even down to such details as numbering pages and marking passages so they can find selections they want to read to me.

Is it fair to base a grade of written work solely on oral conferences? What are the advantages of using conferences instead of reading the

journals thoroughly? First of all, I am not grading the journal itself—
that would contradict its nature as informal expressive writing. I am
grading the student's *work* in the journal and more precisely what the
student *makes of* that work. The three conferences and particularly the
final conference are the occasions on which students make something of
their work. If I simply read the journals, I would not have that
intervening interpretation, nor would the student necessarily make it.
The selections and emphases for my comments would be mine instead of
the writer's. In practice, the student's preparation for these conferences
becomes a more and more integral part of the journal. If the left pages
are reflections on the right pages, the conferences are reflections on the
reflections, and those successive acts of transcendence affect the ways in
which the writer returns to the journal for future writing.

Of course all that burden on the students creates some apprehension, particularly before the first conferences when they're unsure of
what they've been doing. My first effort in conference is to put them at
ease, to show them that sharing interpretations is a pleasure. I let them
know where their observations delight me; I share the questions about
which their readings start me thinking; I keep reminding them that it's
important to me to know how they feel about their reading and their
work. Then as they gradually take pride in their efforts at interpretation
and start to believe in the freedom allowed by the journal form, I begin
to push them further. I ask what the journal writer meant by a puzzling
passage or phrase. I take up a question the writer raises and help him or
her follow it up by further probing, so that the journal and the question
can become more truly speculative instruments. I never contradict a
student's reading in the journal, but at times I will offer some alternative
interpretations or perspectives and ask the student to compare them.

As in a writing conference, the subject is not some ideal interpretation but the writer's own process of making meaning. I take my cues
from the writer's sense of what's important and what's a problem. The
conference allows teacher and student to zero in quickly on the major
areas for discussion and to engage in constant exchange. What began in
the journal as a kind of personal dialectic through the use of opposing
pages, becomes in conference an actual dialogue. The student comes to
see the complete continuity between personal work in the journal and
public exchange about readings. In fact, for many students the embarrassment about certain private or "off-the-wall" journal entries
breaks down as they discover how much they can learn by later public
exploration of these unguarded perceptions.

Journal conferences help students understand dialectical processes
in a natural way. By their left-page comments, they get outside of their
own observations. By interpreting the journals in conference, they get
outside their own earlier interpretive frameworks. That double transcendence illustrates dialectic as a never-ending process of transformations,
out to a more inclusive context, and back again to the immediacy for a
fresh look. This is a difficult concept for students to grasp abstractly, but
they pick it up in practice by the series of dialogues in which they make
something of their journals.

One final selfish justification for the use of journal conferences—it takes less time than reading them and writing comments; one's interventions as a teacher are concentrated more efficiently; and it is fascinating. I have never had so individual and fresh a sense of each student as a reader.

There have been some surprises to me in watching students work with reading journals for the first time, and three of these seem particularly instructive. The first is how much they change between the first and second conferences. Most students begin by being very hesitant and apologetic about their observations, unsure that they are doing the "right" thing. And they tend to have done little with the left pages. It surprises them to learn that they can't be wrong and that I am genuinely interested in the individuality of their style and approach. But my more active intervention at this point is to try to help them do more follow-up. Frequently they are so happy to have posed a good question that they let it rest instead of trying to answer it. I suggest using the left pages to try working out some of these questions, so that they can feel the power of doing something about a problem instead of passively being puzzled by it. And if I note some consistent qualities in their readings that they haven't seen, I point them out as another possible subject to work out on the left pages.

They come in to the second conferences much more confident. They know it's all right to be interested in their own readings. And having done much more work on the left pages, they are eager to try out their interpretations with me. They know how they've begun to change as readers, and this reflexiveness about the process has made them more accepting of pauses and reflections as they read. In more general terms, they seem between the first two conferences to have accepted the journal form and to have begun to explore it more freely. It is the striking contrast between conferences that convinces me that students need some systematic reinforcement to get used to the possibilities of the journal. I should add that although the pattern I've described characterizes the majority of students, many make the change more slowly between the second and third conferences. And a small minority refuse consistently to spend enough time with the journal to make it work for them.

My second surprise occurred because of an accident of scheduling. In order to have students make use of two class periods I had to miss to attend a professional convention, I asked them to meet first in small groups and second as a full class to share the highlights of their journals and to consolidate as a class some of the major things they had learned so far and some of the major issues we should now pursue. The idea was that they would teach the course back to me on my return. The surprise was that they didn't want me back at all. They had found so much stimulation in exploring how other people had used the journals, what kinds of entries were particularly productive, that they wanted to continue working by themselves. In one sense, of course, this is exactly what we want teaching to accomplish. It is also a sign that certain days in a course using journals could be profitably set aside for class scrutiny of such theoretical issues as what makes a good journal entry, how one gets going when one's mind seems blank, what the chief difficulties are in working with the journal. But there is a catch in this shared enthusiasm for the journal as a form. In the pleasure of taking one's feelings and flounderings seriously in an academic classroom, one can easily become self-absorbed. If conventional education leaves the reader too much out of the dialogue of reader and text, it is possible for journals in turn to move so far into the reader as to leave the text behind. This is why I came back into the class even when the students wanted me out.

The third and most important of my surprises involves almost all of the students I have conferred with about their journals, and it only emerged in conferences, not in the journals. They begin by deeply resenting the intrusion of the journal in their reading, and many at first simply refuse to write in the journal until they have finished reading the text. At first I thought this was a matter of marring their reading pleasure, and of course that's part of it. But they express their resistance more as a matter of principle. There is a kind of experience they have with a text in which they move along quickly, having what they think of as quite clear ideas "in their heads." This experience is sacrosanct. To violate it by pausing and writing down those ideas is "to break the flow." They all use the same metaphor. Good reading "goes with the flow."

What does this attitude mean? That it is so widespred a belief suggests that it is socially indoctrinated. Perhaps the most obvious cause of it is the rapid pace of contemporary life in general and the pace of the popular media in particular. To follow TV, radio, advertisements, and often newspapers as well, we are conditioned to make rapid associations and instantaneous connections among images. These mental experiences resemble ideas as long as we don't inquire closely, and there is no time to inquire closely anyway. It seems to be this kind of experience that students want to have with literary texts as well. As sheer habit, that would make sense to me, by why the stubborn moral fervor about it?

It was in thinking about the pedagogy of Paulo Freire (1970, 1975) and Ira Shor (1980) that I was able to make some sense of this moralism. They argue that social orders erect barriers to critical consciousness on the part of the populace because such consciousness makes people less manipulable, more resistant. The subtler of these barriers are internalized checks on one's own thoughts. Thus, to pause and scrutinize is a "bad" thing to do to texts, and writing down one's thoughts as one reads "violates" the reading experience.

Until I started to have journal conferences, I had no idea how widespread and entrenched these attitudes were, and the discovery made me see the political importance of the reading journal. Going with the flow is a perfect metaphor for passivity. In contrast, the reading model implicit in the journal is dialogue, give and take. The habit of pausing when things change in the text or when something surprises one, slows down one's pace, creates more tolerance and space for critical reflection, sets one actively at odds instead of passively in the flow. When I realized how difficult it was for students to make this adjustment, I made my directions more explicit about the places in reading where it is natural to pause. And I became more insistent that they use full sentences in the journal. One doctoral student in a seminar with me explained in her first conference that she took shorthand phrases for notes while she was reading because her thoughts were clear anyway and she could keep her "sense of the text" coherent if she took notes very quickly. I asked her how she knew what the phrases meant later, and she tried to show me. She found to her frustration that after two weeks her notes were incomprehensible. At the next conference she had full sentences in the journal. Most of my students have been surprised at the effect of stopping to write full sentences about the patterns they are discovering or the surprises they encounter. What they tell me is that their "clear ideas" about the text while reading weren't yet ideas at all but only occasions when an idea could be formulated. The more they actually write out those ideas and later reflect on them, the more they are developing their own autonomy and breaking out of the passive role socially conditioned in them.

Let me close by giving three brief examples of such development. The selections were made from different parts of their journals by the students themselves to make a point in their final conferences. They transcribed them for me at my request to be used in this paper. The first excerpts are by Chris Bensley. She had followed my suggestion in the syllabus of pausing part way through each novel and writing about what an appropriate ending might be and then later comparing the speculation with the actual ending. She was surprised at her changes as a reader.

Interpretation	*Observation*
	on Roszak, *Where the Wasteland Ends*
Here I tell myself I can't always get answers, but I still go on believing that an author has the power to give me answers if they want to.	He cannot provide us with all the answers, but making someone aware is a huge step to educating them.
	on *Absalom, Absalom!*
Expectations, expectations! This is what I have trouble shedding!	At this point, a satisfactory ending to the book would be to bring the various stories together in some kind of interaction. I have a feeling it won't happen this way, that instead I'll be left hanging, and the bringing together will be left up to me as a reader. It makes me wonder why I expect the book to end as orderly, organized and with a clear message. I think Faulkner has something else in mind.
	on *The Color Purple*
Celie's expectations for miracles change by the time the book ends.	Everyone else thinks of "worldly" ways to get Sophia out of prison.

She looks at the world much more realistically. I can see myself changed in a similar way through this course. I always expected some kind of resolution if not a happy ending to a book, where all things would come together neatly in the ending, or if not there, in my mind. I have been able to see this much more realistically now that my journal has repeatedly questioned and pondered endings. I realize that it isn't up to the author to miraculously provide me with answers, but rather it is up to me to work out my own solutions, whether it be my own answer, or a continued process of thinking on the issues.

Celie thinks about rescue by angels who come down and carry her away.

Here a student works out on her own one of the transitions that theorists of cognitive development see as central during the college years—giving up models of authority and final answers to take on her own responsibility in a more open-ended world. The journal provides the means for successive returns to the issue and gradual reseeing of herself, and it allows her to work out the change at her own pace.

Cathy Turnbull's selections include her later comments to place them. They involve two overlapping themes:

On page 29 (right) of my journal, while reading the poetry of Zbibniew Herbert, I record a thought that becomes thematic in my journal. What kind of audience is it that reads the poems/novels of a "sensitive"; isn't it just other sensitives, and is that enough? What *is* one supposed to do with a higher consciousness? (Is it enough to increase the Solidarity of the Sensitized?)

In another six pages (43, right), still on *The Teachings of Don Juan*, I chide Don Juan for spewing out a large, long TRUTH. Too much, I say, to be properly absorbed. Truth must come in little bits. That phrase, "little bits" will appear again and again in my journal.

Then I don't talk at all about getting knowledge or giving it out until about 43 journal pages later (left page), where I ruminate a little about how the way I read has changed since beginning the journal. "I have begun to read everything like I read poetry—much slower, paragraph by paragraph, with much more emphasis on the stuff 'to the side' of the immediate words (the stuff that belongs to *me...*). Everything is a poem, and truth, which comes in little snatches, pops out at me. I pay attention to the little snatches."

The class read *Shikasta* next, and I dove wholeheartedly into the issue of what those who don't fit (alias "sensitives") are supposed to do. They've got a function which is imposed by some outside force, and a purpose, which bubbles up from inside them. If purpose and function are the same, the sensitive will be able to accomplish something for the good of the world. Mostly, they seem to keep connection with other sensitives, helping those others merge *their* purpose and function. I wonder over and over if it's *enough* to reach only the sensitives, since it's never them who are screwing up the world—shouldn't the sensitives be doing more? This is where the purpose/function paper appeared—long after I wrote that first comment about Herbert's "Five Men."

In another ten pages (right), I say again, "I didn't like that sort of vomiting up of 'this is the way life IS' all at once. I prefer my truth in little bits—I need to chew and digest it a long time before it can be mine, so I'd rather not have it dumped in my lap in great piles."

Her concern for the fate and responsibilities of the "sensitives" is clearly not just with a course theme but with a life theme as well, and when she recognized it as such she wrote a very searching paper on the subject. The other theme—the bits of knowledge—involves the direct convergence of issue and journal form. It shows how the slowed-down pace of work with the journal changes the experience of reading and makes possible a new autonomy.

Finally Lucy Morris's reflections in a course paper show what the experience of the journal did for her self-awareness and control. One couldn't make a more straightforward case for the political significance of the reading journal:

To re-see our own worlds requires that we examine how we, as individuals, perceive things. I find my belief in the importance of self-examination reinforced by the use of the left hand page of our journals. Only through examining ourselves simultaneously with what we come in contact with can we find deeper meaning, the expansion that is potentially available through reading good literature.

It is the imaginative works of the novelists and poets that precipitate change within us, because through the imagination the possibility for change is realized.

While everyone can't be "right" in what they do, everyone has their reasons based on the facts of their situation. I must then look at myself and say, "I am as everyone else is, with all of the 'reasons' that my situation has created. The only way to become unmechanical and begin to gain control of my actions is to observe myself simultaneously with what I experience and as I respond to situations."

I believe the more we understand what happens within us, the easier it will be to understand the processes around us. One way to keep in touch with, or find what we are, or lose what we've become, is to keep a left-hand page in our minds as well as a left-hand page in our journals.

References

Berthoff, A.E. (1982). *Forming/thinking/writing: The composing imagination.*
Montclair, NJ: Boynton/Cook.

Freire, P. (1970). *Pedagogy of the oppressed.* New York: Seabury Press.

_____ . (1973). *Education for critical consciousness.* New York: Seabury
Press.

_____ *(1975). Cultural action for freedom.* Baltimore: Penguin.

Fulwiler, T. (1973). The personal connection: Journal writing across the curriculum, in T. Fulwiler & A. Young, eds., *Language connections.* Urbana,
IL: NCTE.

Shor, I. (1980). *Critical teaching and everyday life.* Boston: South End Press.

12.

Exploring the Inner Landscape: The Journal in the Writing Class

MARY JANE DICKERSON

A journal is a record of experiences and growth, not a preserve of things well done or said....The charm of the journal must consist in a certain greenness, though freshness, and not in maturity. Here I cannot afford to be remembering what I said or did, ..., but what I am and aspire to become.

Henry David Thoreau (January 24, 1856)

...the function of language is not to inform but to evoke ....What I seek in the Word is the response of the other. I identify myself in Language, but only by losing myself in it like an object. What is realized in my history is not the past definite of what was, since it is no more, or even the present perfect of what has been in what I am, but the future anterior of what has been in what I am in the process of becoming.

Jacques Lacan *Speech and Language in Psychoanalysis*

Through writing in my journal, I have not only discovered trends and characteristics in my writing, but also characteristics in myself. Allowing time every now and then to look back on my journal entries lets me discover things I never knew about myself.

David Majcen (December 16, 1985)

For several years, students in my literature classes have made the journal a valuable part of their learning experience; yet, during that same time, students in my writing classes have rarely made their journals more than a perfunctory gesture. "Too much writing in this writing class" is how one student put it. Unwilling to admit defeat without one last try, I revised my introductory composition course for September 1984 and made the journal its central feature.

What appears to be the most significant finding by December 1985 is evidence of a rigorous examination and evaluation of the self that takes place during the writing process. This examination of the writerly self in the journal stimulates a changing, growing and learning process that I believe may be crucial for maturing and creating a positive attitude toward the act of writing.

From the beginning, most students expressed positive responses to keeping a semester-long journal. For example, by the end of fall semester 1984, student Molly Dunne had this to say about her 99-page journal:

> Another important, almost crucial aid, was the daily writing in our journals. My journal was my diary for things I just had to get "off my chest," my calendar of events, my outliner, my time organizer, and simply my place to write anything that I wanted. I feel that I used my journal evenly in all of these areas, yet the one that seemed to help me the most was my use of my journal as the structural organizer of my papers. For example, when I was brainstorming over what Donald Hall meant in his poem, "Kicking the Leaves," I came up with several interesting points and wrote them down. Those points, after adding detail, an explanation , and organization, became the whole basis of my paper. I think that my journal writing has improved throughout the semester, however, the focus toward the second half was more of a log of how and what I did on my papers. My journal writing was a good method of self analysis.

Here, Molly mentions the two areas that most students have recognized as those most significant for their writing progress: 1) the journal as stimulus of ideas and material for pieces of writing-in-progress; 2) the journal as stimulus to examine the inner landscape undergoing intellectual and emotional growth.

Of these, the most significant finding is the way the journal becomes related to what Molly Dunne calls "self analysis." It is the journal as record of a semester's writing experience *and* as record of the developing self that students most readily identify when they refer to the journal writing assignment. For these reasons, the journal serves a complex dual role in the development of writers and deserves a place equal to any other assignments. The journal offers itself as a natural place to encourage the dialogue with the private self necessary for the creation of the public self, the kind of development that Robert Viscusi identifies when he says "The process of making one's own voice other *is* the process of writing" (Hays, 1983).

To help students get a clearer grasp of the journal's potential, I have adapted Toby Fulwiler's suggestion sheet so that under *What Is a Journal?*, students read the following description:

> A place to practice personal expressive writing; a place to keep a record of an educational experience such as what happens in a writing course; a place to record intellectual growth in the ongoing connections between talking, listening, reading, and writing. Most of all, the journal is the place where the writer can reflect on the relationships between the self and the world and explore the implications of those relationships.

To provide students with such an opportunity to get in touch with themselves is to make the "journal...a record of experiences and growth" so that the most persistent refrain throughout the journals becomes a variation on Thoreau's "what I am and aspire to become." Students explore their own processes of reading and writing as they create a unique text of their individual learning experiences. Student

David Majcen sums up what takes place: "A journal has helped me to enjoy the writing I do, while I'm writing and when I read it again." Clearly his journal writing represents an active pleasure in such communication with the self—this "shaping at the point of utterance," to use James Britton's phrase (Pradl, 1982).

For developing and shaping meaning that might not happen in any other way (*even* in the writing class), the journal becomes a unique vehicle for students to chart the mind's movement from the descriptive toward the evaluative. In this regard, the journal itself becomes the most valuable invention process that writing teachers have at their disposal—a readily available place to set into motion a variety of structured and unstructured invention processes.

Used in such creative ways, the journal exemplifies what James Britton calls "the value of spontaneous inventiveness":

> The two words, "spontaneity" and "invention" as we ordinarily use them must surely have in common: an element of surprise, not only for those who encounter and respond to the act or expression, but also for those who originate it....rhetoricians...may be underestimating the importance of "shaping at the point of utterance," or the value of spontaneous inventiveness (Pradl, 1982).

Journals-at-work in the writing class reveal valuable information about their role in the producing process that bears out Britton's speculation about the value of journals to shape "at the point of utterance." Through this producing process, students learn how to develop conceptions of the self through language. This knowledge, in turn, enables the writer to undertake the deliberate act of writing as public communication with other selves.

But to fulfill the journal's potential, teachers should make use of the informal and expressive nature of journal writing beyond its usual role as generative device in the writing class. Placed at the center of the writing course, journals become the nucleus of writing as act, setting the recursive nature of composing into motion and resulting in texts both inside and outside the journal that show writers beginning to sense the power of their language. Journals, therefore, encourage dialogues between the writers and the texts being written so that writers can gain a richer understanding of themselves as makers and shapers of meaning. The journal is both text and meta-text.

When students begin to regard themselves as writers who make meanings, their attitudes toward writing can undergo radical changes. Student Molly Dunne credits the writing course with its journal assignment with having allowed her "to start writing with a different, more open attitude. Because of this attitude I have been able to produce writing that I never thought possible, and, for the first time, I am actually proud of the papers that I completed." She goes on to say, "I have a better opinion of my own ability to write as well as my writing itself." Her journal reflects Molly Dunne's changing attitude toward writing as she becomes more involved in its possibilities and as she becomes more aware of the ways writing in the journal can help her tap available inner resources: "Thinking aloud in my writing. I should try to write in my thoughts of what was happening to me along with the flow of what was going on" (September 6, 1984).

Frequent journal writing encourages students to trust in "language close to the self" (Britton's definition of the expressive function) so that it can become the origin for writing outside the self. To see how student Molly Dunne explored her relationship with an autobiographical poem, Donald Hall's "Kicking the Leaves," through a series of journal entries on their way toward a more formal reading of the poem is to begin to understand something of what Britton suggests when he refers to that element of surprise in "spontaneous inventiveness" for the originator as well as for the one who responds to what happens.

For the first journal entry on the poem each student chose, I asked them to write about the poem in any way their reading experience prompted them to. Molly Dunne responded as follows:

Tues.   Sept. 18, 1984

Kicking the Leaves - Donald Hall

I remember with the help of this poem. The leaves and their description of colors, taste, and smell remind me of when I was young and when we played in the leaves. The leaves represented a period of time after summer freedom and before the coldness of winter. Cider was a major fall activity. We would go and pick apples and get paid by the (bushel) (I think) I believe it was a dollar for each bushel, the last time I did it in 8th grade. Before that it went down about 10 or 15¢ each year. The fresh apples bitter yet crisp to taste. So good. A time of family togetherness. I remember when my grandmother, grandfather and I used to rake the huge expanse of the lawn near the cliff over-looking the beautiful chilled lake with a pillowy-cloudfilled bright blue sky. The coldness of the wind and the comforting heat of the sun. We sometimes needed to wear a sweater. The leaves would stick to my grandmother's handknitted sweaters that we all would wear. The leaves would stick in my hair and make it look like a rainbow of red, yellow, green and brown. The feel of the leaves as they went down my shirt and stuck to my sweaty back—scratching and tickling at the same time. The way he describes the country side & surroundings along with the memories of the past that are brought about each year as the colors and leaves reappear.

Certain features of Molly's initial entry stand out. First, she thrusts herself into something resembling the same composing act as the poet Hall engages in—both in the meaning of "Kicking the Leaves" and in its unfolding structure. By writing about reading in this way, she puts herself into the mind of another (an-other) and then proceeds to compose her own act of recovery through memory. And in so doing, she once again follows the actual sequence of events and memories that make up "Kicking the Leaves." She submerges herself into her family past and then returns near the end of her own prose poem to the creative act of the "he" (Hall) as she writes "The way he describes the country side & surroundings along with the memories of the past that are brought about each year as the colors and leaves reappear." And finally, Molly's sentence structure begins to dissolve into phrasings that in no way intrude on or obscure the meanings she is making. Instead, her language comes closer to creating its own poem as she composes: "The fresh apples bitter yet crisp to taste....The coldness of the wind and the comforting heat of the sun....The feel of the leaves as they went down my shirt and stuck to my sweaty back—scratching and tickling at the same time."

For their second entry, I asked students to respond in a more specifically directed way—"Identify and narrate what's going on in the poem." Here's what Molly wrote:

Thurs.   Sept. 20, 1984

I believe that Donald Hall was looking at his surroundings in autumn and the leaves brought back memories of the past as he watched them fall or as he raked his yard thinking. I know that certain things remind me of other times, in the past, of a similar situation. The leaves are a constant whereas our lives are constantly changing. I think that Hall mentions that or says that underlyingly through his poem. Memories of when I was young are brought back to me as I read the poem again & again. The seasons go around but we adjust and so do the trees adjust. We adjust to changes of growing older etc. Whereas the trees only have to adjust to the seasonal changes in temp etc. I think the leaves falling represents another year gone and another beginning—the cycle of life goes on.

Again Molly goes right to the center of Hall's poem in several ways. First she echoes what Hall represents as he narrates watching leaves fall and as he remembers raking leaves in the opening stanzas. Also, she once more responds by identifying herself with Hall even as she became his daughter in her first entry through the detail of the color of her hair and the colors of the leaves: "I know that certain things remind me of other times, in the past, of a similar situation....Memories of when I was young are brought back to me as I read the poem again & again." By the end of this entry, Molly has examined the varieties of ways that Hall has shaped continuity and change as they characterize "the cycle of life."

For their final journal entry, I asked students to write about the feature of the poem that most seriously affected or interested them. Molly chose to go further in her personal exploration of the implications of "death and dying":

Wednesday,   Sept. 26, 1984

Reading Kicking the Leaves makes me think of death and dying. I wish death didn't have to happen and so does everyone I suppose. My grandmother is really old. She doesn't act old at all. She goes shopping, drives her brand new Cadillac, plays poker, goes to movies, and does all kinds of stuff. I want to be just like her when I get old. She is very aware and not going senile at all. She has a bit of a hearing problem but wears a tiny hearing aid that isn't visible. She doesn't like to wear it most of the time because it makes her aware of her age. Donald Hall doesn't feel this way about death at all. Kicking the leaves demonstates how we all should feel about death, relaxed. I don't feel relaxed about death. I hated it when my grandfathers both died. I remember quite vividly the funeral, and wake, and all the sadness. I loved my grandfathers but I wasn't half as close to them as I am to my grandmother. I know she's going to have to die sometime but I really hope it's not for a long time.

Molly chose to write about her very much alive grandmother (Hall centers his poem around the deaths of his father and grandfather) while remembering her grandfathers' deaths. She expresses her closeness to her grandmother and her desire that she not die "for a long time." It's interesting to note here how Molly separates herself from Donald Hall because she's in the process of resisting the knowledge she recognizes in his poem—that death is part of that inevitable cycle just as the grandfather who was once an active part of her own memory of leaves is now dead and the grandmother who knits the sweaters to ward off the autumn chill will also die.

Molly reenters the creativity of the journal's role as she distances herself from death she knows will one day be hers to face. She distances herself by portraying a yet vibrant grandmother—"I want to be just like her when I get old"—by remembering the funerals, the wakes and sadness of her grandfathers' deaths, by saying "Reading Kicking the Leaves makes me think of death and dying." Like Hall, Molly engages in the act of writing so as not to die, "taking a place/in the story of leaves" (Hall, 1978).

To get into her formal essay on "Kicking the Leaves," Molly Dunne made further use of her journal as a place to write down her reading-in-progress: "I need to chart or write out some of the ideas & sort which go & those that don't." Selected examples from six pages of Molly's "chart" show her continuing to merge her self with the poet's self. She jumps first to a reference to a line in part 6 of the poem: "uncovering the lids of graves—the leaves are like the key to his memories." Listing what lies under "the lids of graves," she ends this section of her charting with these words: "The generation going from grandfather to father to himself, dying. The cycle of life for us lasts longer. We have more time than a leaf does. That cycle continues and we all will die someday." And finally, she does her own "recovering/from death" when she writes:

> The leaves are already dead that he must fall into but are still there. They do not disappear even though they are dead. We will not disappear mentally to others after we die....The leaves still have colors and...they bring back memories. The existance of memories is a parallel to the existance of the leaves after they die. Death is not to be feared because even after we die we exist in the memories of others....as our children's memories of us are stirred by the leaves we are remembered. The leaves tell a story, a different story to different people, but a story just the same.

Molly has internalized Donald Hall's poem so that she "has" the poem for life.

And once again, Molly's writing about Hall's story compels her own "story of leaves." While Molly never remarks on Hall's use of the ocean as a metaphor in the poem's last stanza with its evocation of the unconscious as "night heaving with death and leaves," and its evocation of a return to the womb as "the soft laps of leaves," the effect of writing her way through a reading of the poem resembles all the metaphor implies. She has opened herself up through implicating herself in the ebb and flow of memory. She is learning to trust where language might take her.

For her formal reading and writing of "Kicking the Leaves," Molly chose the title of her essay to be "The Falling of Leaves and the Passing of Life." Here is her opening paragraph:

> Death is a very difficult subject to deal with for most people. The idea of death makes us very apprehensive and instead of looking at death straight on, we try to avoid the subject. Donald Hall has a very relaxed attitude about death, those already dead, and his own death. I feel that he believes death is a natural experience and unavoidable, so the only thing to do is to try and make the most out of the present and live life to the fullest.

From reading her earlier sequence of journal entries, we know how Molly has earned this paragraph. She goes on to compose a commendable essay in which she analyzes what the poet expresses in "Kicking the Leaves." I have read many such essays; quite often I learn something about reading from these explications of texts. Yet, I am glad that I also had the three journal entries so that I could follow the inner landscape of Molly's reading and writing her own way toward "Kicking the Leaves." For this reason, I should like to work with journal entries so that, as part of their composing processes, young writers might begin to make greater use of this language shaped "at the point of utterance" as they make meanings to share with other writers reading. Molly's journal entries and the "charts" make richer readings than does her essay by itself.

As the texts in Molly Dunne's journal illustrate, the journal in the writing class gives students access to what writers actually do as they write. With their insights, student writers can learn to move beyond such formulaic structures as the five paragraph essay, always writing to prove a point, avoiding the forbidden "I," and many others too numerous to mention. The journal pushes students toward writing in a more intimate and exploratory way so they will have that option when they need it—to "discover things I never knew about myself" in the process of evoking the other. If successful, the journal in the writing class can become a repository of the self that enables play with language as well as control over the language—a vehicle for moving back and forth between the play and the work of a language—a place for writers to grow and expand their capacities as shapers of the self. In her journal entries, Molly Dunne demonstrates how writing about Donald Hall's "Kicking the Leaves" enables her to create her own "Kicking the Leaves." Journal writing thus takes her further than explicating another's text: Molly creates her own.

Exploring the inner landscape may be what we most need to encourage our beginning college students to do in the writing class. The journal may be the single most important activity to encourage that inner synthesis of self and the world necessary for creative learning to take place. To regard the messy informal prose in journals as having no value except as a way to get to neat formal prose may seriously undervalue the potential these texts have for developing the writerly self.

References

Hall, D. (1978). *Kicking the leaves*. Harper & Row.

Hays, J.N., et al. (1983). The other speaking: Allegory and Lacan, in R. Viscusi, ed., *The writer's mind: Writing as a mode of thinking*. Urbana, IL: NCTE.

Pradl, G.M. (Ed.) (1982). *Prospect and retrospect: Selected essays of James Britton*. Montclair, NJ: Boynton/Cook.

13.

Golden Notebooks, Blue Notebooks: Re-Readings

JUDITH FISHMAN SUMMERFIELD

February 1, 1985

Talked with Dad about the Chagall catalogue; thought he'd enjoy seeing Chagall's representations of the Russia where he too grew up: the Russia before the Revolution. Dad's eyes are Russian eyes: he saw things I'd skipped over, like the water carrier in the village wedding. That was the custom, he told me, to make sure that the bridal party passed by a water carrier with full buckets of water: "They foretell a full and happy life," he tells me. Dad reads his culture in the paintings. To me, the water carrier is just a water carrier.

Been thinking a lot these days about journals—since Toby F. asked me to get an article going, and since Geoffrey* said the other day, "I don't understand why your students bother to keep them; you're so casual about them, and yet they turn out pages and pages." He set me wondering how it all began, the journal, that is, and why I assign journals in every course I teach, why they've become part of the "culture" of my teaching.

February 3, 1985

Feedback, that's how it must have started. Feedback and the late Sixties: it was part of the times, and I remember now that I introduced a "feedback notebook" into my classes at Bronx Community College. I don't even use that word anymore, but *feedback* was in, as was open classroom, consciousness raising, women's lib, encounter groups, student-centeredness, free writing, sitting in a circle, Carl Rogers, Fritz Perls, Ira Progoff, relevance. The Sixties hit me like a thunderbolt: began to put myself on the other side of the desk: I wanted to know what my students were learning, how they were learning, what mattered, what didn't. Eventually, I pushed the desk aside and sat with them (and still do). How to find out what they were learning—that was the question— and I devised what today would be called a "learning log." After each class, students would reflect in writing on their impressions, reactions, questions, concerns, suggestions, etc. about the day's session. I learned from their notebooks about what seemed to be working, what wasn't, which lessons made sense, which didn't.

*Geoffrey Summerfield, my husband.

137

February 5, 1985

A memory search, actually a file-drawer search: spent the whole afternoon sifting through stuff I've saved. Why do I save *everything?* Dear Journal, you should have seen me sitting there in the study, surrounded by notebooks, file folders, boxes, all the way back from my first year of teaching. I found "lesson plans" from Schenley High School, Pittsburgh, Pennsylvania, 1963. The years flood back: Walter Cabbagestalk and Herman Sherman—they could just about write their names. Every brand-new teacher was assigned a "remedial" class, and I quickly discovered that my readings of Coleridge, Pope, and Dryden weren't going to do much for them. What *was* I supposed to do with them? I asked the chairman of the English department. He said to teach them how to use the phonebook. I asked the superintendent of English instruction. She said to assign a "new" book about teen-age problems. So we read about how Suzy didn't have enough money to buy a dress for the prom. These were kids who didn't have enough money to buy a pair of shoes. I was convinced that I could do better: what did they want to do? I finally asked them. They knew right away: they wanted to read the same books as everybody else; they wanted to read *Julius Caesar* because that's what all the other tenth graders were doing. So we read *Julius Caesar.* Walter played Brutus. I forget who played Cassius. But that's when I learned that if you want to find out—you ask. Students are a lot smarter than teachers give them credit for. (I chuckle now to think of Lauren's* teachers sitting around trying to figure out what's wrong with her tenth grade class; there's something wrong with the whole, entire class: counselor meetings, teacher meetings, board of education meetings. But nobody asks the kids.)

Found a couple of folders labeled *Students' Writing, Before 1972,* and there I actually found some of those feedback notebooks—funny, though, to think again, to realize that the patterns were set even before 1972: the feedback notebook/learning log was obviously an extension of my early impulses—to find out what I could about students' thinking, to *ask* them. I re-read now (a little embarrassed) entries from 1972: here is a young teacher trying to turn decisions over to the students themselves, students who were so shaky as students that they wanted authority in the classroom. They hardly wanted a teacher who asked them what they wanted to do. I'm sure I caused a lot of confusion. Here's a student writing back in 1972:

> *March 6, 1972*
> The entire period was spent trying to decide what we should write about. Take a topic of this sort among 10-15 people, and you usually end just the way we did, with nothing. We all had some idea about what we wanted to write about, but after hearing so many different comments, complaints, and criticisms about them all, I wondered whether or not we should have been making the decision in the first place. I left the class with this feeling, thereby writing nothing for the next class.

*Lauren, my fifteen-year-old daughter.

March 8, 1972
Next class session, the teacher had planned the work and together
we worked the plan. A brief guide for writing papers and suggested
topics was very helpful to me, and I got more from this session
mainly because it was planned.

March 13, 1972
A great session! We spent the whole time learning how to use
library resources, and I now know how to write a footnote. The
teacher was very well organized.

As I re-read, I remember that it was an up-hill climb, a steep hill there in
the Bronx as I sat with students whose expectations were far different
from mine: I wanted to open the world with them; they wanted to learn
about footnotes. One student writes a retrospective on that class:

> I remember when I first came in the class. I took a seat next to the
> window and five minutes later, the professor came in. She was a
> woman, very young and friendly. I was disappointed because I
> thought that a college professor was a person in the 40's with a
> very conservative thought. And my professor was young, a woman,
> and a Liberal.

Patrick B—I can't read the name, and I can't recall his face, and I'd
forgotten until now that I had asked for this kind of self-consciousness.
How, for example, could they *reflect on* what they had "learned" while
they were still in the midst of it all, while they were still participating?

It was a time of self-consciousness, and I was guilty; I blush to re-
read my journal entries of that time: the ones I kept on my teaching, the
one about my giving my "all" to my students, and then that one day, I
noticed that one student, Cornelius, was sitting in the back of the room,
staring out the window; he wouldn't join the circle, and I figured that he
was bored, and then after class, I spoke with him, telling him that he
seemed "out of it," and he told me that his cousin had been shot and
stabbed on 125th Street and that he'd been in the hospital with him for
the past 24 hours. "I as a teacher," I write in 1973, "tend to forget the
lives of students outside the classroom; my perspective was exceedingly
narrow. I looked at him and thought *I* am boring him. Since that day, I
know, he looks at me differently (or perhaps I perceive him differently);
anyway the waves between us are different, I think, because I responded
to him as a person."

Re-reading—I hope I didn't sound so ridiculous as I represent
myself then. Waves! Funny, now, to re-touch those "selves" of a dozen
years ago. It isn't the compassion or the caring that's changed: it's the
language, the posture, that comes through these lines. The "I" sounds so
formal, so stiff ("my perspective was exceedingly narrow"); but, at the
same time, "she" was trying to be with it ("waves"), trying so hard,
registering each nuance, in herself, in others, in the "world," trying,
straining, to make sense of a chaotic, disordered, erupting world, 1973.

February 3, 1985

Doris Lessing, that was another part of it. I don't remember when I first began to keep a journal; I have journals dating back to 1964, 1965. I remember spending long stretches of time pouring over notebooks in book stores, searching for the perfect one: the right color, the right margins, the right spaces between lines. The most ambitious notebook I began in 1973, styled after Doris Lessing's *The Golden Notebook*. There, in my notebook, I tried to compartmentalize my life:

the pink section for my life as a mother of young children
the blue section for my life as a teacher
the yellow section for reflections on reading and for
    my own "writing"
the green section for my life as a woman, etc.

If I'm not careful, I'll be up here in this room with these 20 or so journals, re-reading and re-reading for the next three months; they're filled with tid-bits of my life:

Observations of my children, growing, changing; their conversa-
    tions; our conversations, their bright sayings, their discoveries
Reflections on my inner life
Shaky attempts at poetry and fiction
Reflections on reading
Jokes
Ruminations on the state of the world: Viet Nam; the women's
    movement;
Civil Rights; history; politics; the news
Words I want to remember
Books I want to read
Letting off steam
Things I'd like to say to my mother-in-law!
A few drawings
Lists of what I want to do
Drafts of a paper I'm writing
Notable quotes
Imitations: trying my hand at a Woolf or a Joyce sentence
Promises
Dreams
Interpretations of dreams
Plots of stories I want to write
Questions
Answers
Plans for changing the world
First lines I might do something with one day
Bits and pieces of conversations I overhear
Secrets
Venomous outpourings I have to contain
Memories

I re-read, re-touch, re-live this self of those dozen years ago; I lose myself in my children:

Lauren at 3½: she delights me—her sense of time still erratic. The other day she disappeared with Sharon (her sister) and returned saying, "I was gone for lots and lots of years, and I just came home yesterday."

Am I going to school yesterday? Is today Sunday or Saturday? Did I go to school last year?

Sharon at 6: her front tooth is loose. Every three minutes, she wants to know if it's still there, or if I ever swallowed a tooth.

Sharon beginning to read: My head hurts, Mommy, cause every word I see I have to read.

That was yesterday! The journal brings them back; the memories sharpen, as I infuse them now with my own keen awareness of time passing. I wish back that innocence, their innocence; I wish back those moments, so that I could do things differently. Why doesn't Sharon (at 18) want to read? Why can't Lauren keep track of time? It still slips through her fingers like sand, and she still doesn't know if it's Saturday or Sunday. I feel with Woolf that merging of the "I now" and the "I then." And I find the patterns, the same promises, then as now:
I will stop smoking next week.
I will read a book (for pleasure) every week.
I will try to do more for the "world."
I will stop holding things inside; get them out!
Be quiet.
Walk; don't run.
Learn more names of birds, flowers, trees. (I find flattened leaves with the names—beech, birch, elm—next to them.)

I meet a rather studied, self-conscious prose—again, as if "she" is trying too hard:
Spring plunges the squirrels, rabbits, racoons, onto foreign territory—the highway—and into a darkness deeper than winter.

How can I order my existence? I feel like Ishmael—trailing after the funeral procession. Call me Ishmael!

Does Lessing have to plunge her characters into madness so that they can find the light?

"Man does; woman is," Robert Graves.

All this in 1973: so the journal must have entered my classes out of my own experiences of keeping a journal. I had come to believe in the power and the privilege of writing, of stopping time, of capturing Woolf's "moments of being"—the journal obviously cut through the moments of non-being in my own life, through the days when my mind felt like cotton-wool, so that I felt more alert, more alive. I'm certain that is what I must have said. Ellen M. said it last week in class: she had been fighting keeping a journal for a whole semester; now she was taking another course with me and she showed me her journal filling up and said, "The journal makes me observe better."

February 11, 1985

I'm determined to find out what the next step was in using the journal in teaching, but before I do, a note about now: Lauren's keeping a journal in her tenth grade English class (Advanced Composition); she handed it in to her teacher, and he handed it back with a grade and every run-on sentence circled. That's not a journal: that's co-opting a journal for error-hunting. Not one comment on what she had written; not one word of support, encouragement; not one human touch from a reader reading! And my students sit in composition courses at Queens College—constipated, inhibited, terrified that they will write run-on sentences. And, again, last week I asked them all to write down on a slip of paper what they think a run-on sentence is. Here's one:

A run on is when a sentence or sentences run together as one. Example—I worked late, and did not get home until ten o'cock.

The only way to find out: ask.

Anyway, back to the search, leafing through the pages of these miscellaneous journals, where the compartments are not delineated, I find this entry:

September 1975

I introduced the journal into English 001: all open admissions students. A sea of faces. We all free write in this class. I write, too. They're surprised. "This is the first page of 100," I say. They are not amused. Their fingers ache, they complain. "Fluency," I say. It will come. I hope. How many will drop the course? 100 pages of a journal for open admissions students. I must be crazy. Maria says she can't do it. I tell her to complain in her journal.

November 1975

Maria shows me her journal. 76 pages. "It's okay," she says.

January 1976.

Final day of class. Maria shows me her 100 pages. I carry home 17 journals; they're mostly filled.

For five years or so, the journal is on center stage in my classes: it's no longer a feedback notebook, written for me—it is more and more their own notebook; I call it a notebook because I don't want them to think of it exclusively as a diary. I collect notebooks in the middle of the term and at the end. I read every page, make comments, encourage, support, praise, provoke. Every week I take time for students to read from their journals; I read from mine. The journals are never corrected: they are read avidly, keenly; they are shared. They are not private—for students know I'll be reading.

Some students fill more than the 100 pages; some begin another notebook; some come back the next semester, the next year, to show me they're still keeping a notebook. Fortunately, I'm only teaching one or two courses, and so I can spend time reading all those pages.

The best time of all those years was with Dexter*, when he and I

---

*Dexter Jeffries, an undergraduate team-teacher and now an instructor of English.

were team-teaching. I can't now find the entries, but I remember; he was just back from the army, from two years in Germany, and he was tough. We wrote in class a first journal entry. And then we all read around the room. I read mine; it was a delicate little anecdote about my childhood in Pennsylvania. Dexter's was about a brawl he got into in a bar in Germany; he was almost killed. I remember he used some pretty rough language, and those kids were shocked. Mary Lum—where did that name come from!—looked as if she was going to cry. Others gasped. We hadn't planned it, but what we said that day, implicitly, was that you can do all this with words: you can be gentle and soft; and you can be brash and loud.

Sometime later, Dexter said that he'd keep reading from his journal if the others would, too. Half a dozen agreed. So Dexter read about his cab driving adventures in New York City. He had picked up a little old Russian woman, and she reminded him of how he had imagined his Russian grandmother, who he had never known. I remember that the class was spellbound. Others read.

The journal took over; we spent more and more class time reading journals—I remember wondering if that was such a good idea; I remember wondering how the formal requirements for freshman composition would be met: the research paper, footnotes, bibliography, when we had spent so much time on Dexter's journal and his cab driving. They were going to know a lot about the streets of New York.

Saving scraps is worth it. I find this note tucked in one of my notebooks:

May 15, 1980
Mary Lum's research paper on energy was superb! She's a senior, Chinese. Her father's a chef; she works in a laundromat. Computer science major. She came up to me the first day of class and said she was terrified, had put off taking freshman composition for three years. Now she had to. She almost cried today. Wrote 100 pages in her journal and said she was going to keep writing.

Writing brings back more fully what my memory had opened; that semester stands out so clearly now, what with Dexter's journal, with the possibilities that were opened, with how pleased I was that their "academic" writing was so strong, with the fact that the journal itself had been so successful.

February 12, 1985

What next? Still thinking about Dexter's cab driving; he's trying to publish some of those journals. Kathy Lee from that class went on to NYU for a Masters in journalism. She sends a Christmas card every year. What next? The literature courses that I hadn't taught for some time, and the quick realization that I could no longer teach *any* course without having students write journals, and so as I keep leafing through this hodgepodge of notes and reflections, these, now, are what I come up with:

October 1982
Keeping track. Reader-response. Writing. Reading as composing.

Every class session the journal becomes a text to consider in relation to another text. Primary texts and response texts. It works. Cut down, though, to 50 pages. Too many pages to read. It's not a journal—remember; it's a notebook (haven't thought about *The Golden Notebook* for some time). Open admissions needed to write and write and write. These students need to, also, but the charge is different. They don't really believe they have anything of value to say about what they read; they keep looking for the right answer, for the elusive main idea. The notes they keep; their own reactions to texts *show* them they *can*. Also—encourage them to keep a personal notebook, to keep track—the journal/notebook becomes multi-purpose—they discover for themselves its uses and possibilities. (Of course, I keep nudging.)

February, 1983
Creative writing class. First day—got "golden notebook" going, only it's a dark blue notebook. I have found the perfect notebook: blue, hardbound, numbered pages, opens flat, narrow-ruled. I assign *this* notebook! Assignment of a pen would be too much. 50 pages. An "outer" book, I tell them. And an "inner" book. Their first charge is to eavesdrop, to record a conversation (as Fitzgerald does so well). I'm encouraging them to observe, to listen to voices, to get down the stuff from the daily worlds in which they live. You don't have to go to Paris to get material. We read from Fitzgerald's notebook, from Kafka, Virginia Woolf; talk about Trollope (how he wrote for himself for 15 years and discovered that he could write, that he was fluent); May Sarton (too narcissistic for me, but some women students like her); Anne Frank; Dorothy Wordsworth. So, they're armed with blue notebooks and told to be snoops. Hope no one gets picked up for peeping Tomism. Do same with journalism class tomorrow. Important here to encourage them to go outside themselves to what's right in front of their noses; otherwise, they moan and fret about what they don't have to write about—or they invent characters and situations that are so far removed from them that they are lifeless, voiceless, un-actualized. All they have to do is listen in on one conversation in the cafeteria to pick up the richness of language: the human conflict, tension, humor, it's right there. (I did say that if anyone could not stand the blue notebook, that I would consider letting them use another!)

September, 1984
Three classes and a Mellon fellowship: no way can I collect and read journals from three classes, no way. Also, students (for better or worse) always aware of my reading their journals; no way either that I can give it up. Dave Bartholomae had a good point about students re-reading journals, seeing them not as experiences but rather as texts. So, I tell them: write fifty pages in the blue notebook, but rather than collect them, I'll have them write a reflective text on their reading of their journals. Will not tell them though until the end.

February 14, 1985

So, an experiment: the journal slips out of the center and recedes into what Geoffrey calls "casualness." The journal/notebook I co-opt for class exercises. In the literature class, students react to primary texts: they write personal responses and critical responses as they build up their "meta-language." They enter the texts; they use the journals for their own wrestlings with a text. And they keep the journal for themselves, as well, for their own private reflections about whatever they choose.

In the composition course, they write memory texts, as we explore the dimensions of memory, and one memory leads to another. In creative writing, they represent the outer world as they experiment with poetry, fiction, drama. The notebook becomes a sketchbook, a workbook, a doodling book, a coloring book: they draw lines for texts; some they finish, some they don't.

The blue notebook is present in every class, but I wondered how many would discover its possibilities if I was not there to read every page. I'm still not sure, but their reflective essays are encouraging. Most of them (80%) *say* that keeping the notebook taught them about themselves, about reading better; they could experiment and take risks; they could try out varied voices; they could "lay out" all their thoughts in front of them for reading and re-reading, for re-considering; they could read their own writing as texts. As one student says in his reflective essay:

> Yes, keeping a notebook is okay. At first I didn't think so. The last two days before the journal was due were actually very interesting. I had to fill up the remainder of the fifty pages, without much time or any particularly good ideas of what to write about. For a while I just wrote down very rambling thoughts—anything that came into my head. After a while, I sort of got used to writing things and just went through my memory banks, picking out my thoughts and fairly easily writing about them.
>
> I guess if I could lay out all my thoughts in front of me on a piece of paper, it would be very helpful. I could arrange them and make outlines and discover what I am, where I am, and how I really feel about it. Then I could read what I wrote that moment, in *that* text. And then who knows? I really would like to do that some day, but right now I've got these finals, and besides I'm feeling tired, and...

February 20, 1985

To invoke Woolf: The *I now* meeting the *I then* in re-reading. Not bad for an experiment; most of the students discover ways of making writing work for them, of discovering, as well, that they can become readers of their own texts, and for those who haven't—well, writing isn't the only way.

The whole format of keeping a notebook is now looser than it was in 1972, but more realistic: I've moved a long way from having students write for *me* in their notebooks; now, *if they want them*, they're *theirs*. And they tell me how they're using their journals: some write poetry; some write lyrics for songs; some write "difficult" letters that are never sent; some practice their verb tenses; some draw; some write fiction, philosophy, history; some write reactions to film, to the news, to events, etc. Casualness, yes, but to be fair, the journal/notebook gets a big play during the first weeks of the semester and then is present every class session. In my mind's eye, I see students at the beginning of each session, leafing through those blue books—some read to each other; some ask, "How many pages...?" Although I no longer formally read their notebooks, students ask me to read a passage or two, to take their book home with me over the weekend. (Andrew, from last term, stopped in yesterday; he asked me to read a continuation of a text he had begun in December.)

We *use* the notebook in class as we do more and more spontaneous exercises; at the end of the semester, they have a book of their own writings, 50, 75, 100 or more pages. And this is part of the culture of the course. So, casual, yes, in that I don't check every book. I know, as well, that not everyone will buy in. Some will fight the whole business. That happened before too. I make no bones about saying that I hope writing will become part of what they *ordinarily* do in their lives outside the classroom, after the semester is over, that the journal/notebook can be theirs—no constraints—a very cheap, life-long pleasure. Also, this way, the journal *is* theirs; they don't have to write for a public—in that sense, the whole enterprise is more in keeping with how writers actually keep notebooks.

Enough. Last week, I said in class that the journal will be there for us in 20 years' time, to read and re-read, to re-touch parts of our selves, representations of our lives, that in actuality are gone. One of my older students (he's a 67-year-old retired government worker) said, "Pray, let us *all* be here, as well as the journal," and he walked out of the room carrying the blue notebook.

Afterword

Being a keeper of a notebook/journal; being a believer in the notebook/journal in the teaching of composition and literature (and creative writing, film studies, history, philosophy, biology, etc.); being invited to contribute to this collection of writings on the journal, I decided that the journal form, which I know intimately, was appropriate to the task. As I now read these entries upon past entries, I am struck by a number of observations: the journal texts are raw, uncooked; they were often written in a heat (in fact, I decided to remove several that seemed to me too naked, too exclamatory, too intemperate). Although some of my satisfying moments of writing are often marked by such excesses, in such moments of absorption, involvement, and intense participation, that I don't hear the telephone ring or my children calling, I generally consider this work to be *unfinished*. The finished text demands more than the intensity of such participation; it demands the cool, distanced re-reading that can come only after a period of rest, so that I can reflect upon, re-think, cross out, weigh and measure, balance, remember my audience, fiddle with a phrase, hear the rhythm of a sentence, read aloud, copy-edit, shift around, scratch out, re-write—all the possibilities open to me as I consider and re-consider this text in this situation. I am now a spectator.

The first sentence of this afterword I shaped: as I moved out of the (fictive) situation I had *allowed* myself for writing this article, I immediately became aware of a shift in voice, role, and frame of mind. The journal voice had felt different: because I have been an inveterate keeper of journals: because my research for the article had uncovered a plethora of past writings, I could easily move into that role. Significant, as well, was my editor, Toby Fulwiler, who upon seeing a first draft, said, "Yes, go ahead, this looks promising." The context then: my experience, my file-drawer full of writings, my audience, all made possible the writing of a relatively raw, unrestrained text.

It seems to me that the matter at hand—using journals in the teaching of composition and literature—involves two frames of mind: the near and the far; the close in and the move away, the raw and the cooked, the momentary heat and the reflective cool, the participant and the spectator. Our students, I believe, need both.

14.

Reinvigorating a Tradition: The Personal Development Journal

CHRISTOPHER C. BURNHAM

Writing instructors have their students keep journals in composition classes almost as a matter of tradition. As with many traditions, however, both the origin and the purpose of journal keeping have been lost to the fog of recurrent practice. Reinvigorating this tradition motivated my research into the theory and practice of using journals both to promote personal growth and improve student writing.

Theoretical Background and Evolution

My earliest experiments with journals originated in my belief in the relationship between good writing and psychological development. Moving beyond basic considerations, grammar, mechanics, and language etiquette, the importance of higher level thinking becomes obvious; the writing we call good—writing which is thoughtful, informative, challenging, and evocative—requires a complete range of cognitive skills, especially synthesis and evaluation. Good writing requires a depth of thinking—an awareness of context, relevance, and implication—which is unavailable to the cognitively immature. Keeping a journal provides students opportunities to develop higher order thinking skills while also encouraging self-awareness and psychological growth.

Initially, I connected some writing and learning theory with some developmental and depth psychology. My first assignments used James Britton's concept of expressive writing, distilled from *The Development of Writing Abilities (11-18)* (London: Macmillan Education, 1975), and Kenneth Bruffee's adaptation of collaborative learning theory, presented in *A Short Course in Writing* (second edition, Boston: Little Brown, 1980). The assignments directed inexperienced writers to probe their pasts in the comfortable environment of an unevaluated personal journal. In such journals the writer is the audience and the primary purpose of the writing is discovering material, integrating this material within the self, and beginning to shape the material for more distant and formal audiences. Journals are Britton's expressive writing in action. Ideally, as students probe their lives, they discover the sources of the values and beliefs which govern their current behavior. According to developmental psychologists, such awareness eases the transition between the unexamined, poorly formed systems most students bring with them to college and the more thoughtful beliefs and values available through continued education.

That writers should probe their pasts derives from work by William Perry. In *Forms of Intellectual and Ethical Development in The College Years: A Scheme* (NY: Holt, Rinehart, and Winston, 1968), Perry establishes a four-category model of the intellectual and ethical development of undergraduates, tracing the growth of students from an initial dualist world view, through a period of multiplicity, to a relativist view, eventually arriving at commitment within this relativism. My concern was helping freshmen begin to move along the scale, so I targeted the first two categories, dualism and multiplicity. As dualists, students live in a world of absolutes, of "we-right-good vs. other-bad-wrong." As multiplists, students begin to accept various points of view, but they are unable to evaluate or justify them.

The first step toward moving beyond dualism is to become aware of the source of the absolutes governing behavior. That source is the past and the influence of family, church, school, and community. Writing about the past allows students to dredge up particulars in defense of their absolutes. Aware of the particulars underpinning their absolutes, students begin to discover how generally weak this support is, and they can contrast their absolutes with better developed belief systems. Only then can they begin to challenge the truth-value or utility of their absolutes. The challenge reveals incongruities and makes possible the expansion or dissolution of current cognitive schemas in the light of new information or experience. Awareness precedes challenge precedes growth, and journal writing serves as the instrument for accomplishing all of these.

The collaborative learning element of the exercises derived from another Perry insight: most dualist and multiplist students suffer from "community shock." Having left the comfort of their home community and having not yet been assimilated into the new environment at college, these students often feel isolated and alienated. These feelings do not foster growth and learning; rather, they cause disengagement and retreat. The collaborative element of the journal exercises allows students to develop a sense of community.

In collaborative exercises, students share their insights about the past and discover the foundations of their absolutes. At the same time, they healthfully discover *diversity*. The other members of their groups come from different backgrounds and value systems. Students discover differences and begin to understand that, though different, their peers are not murderers, monsters, or political radicals. Awareness of diversity precedes acceptance of diversity. Opening pathways for questions and challenges makes growth possible. Me vs. them becomes us. Isolation evolves into community.

The theoretical soundness of the journal exercises was borne out by their early success. Working through the journal assignments, students probed the past, discovered their values and beliefs, and shared them. In fact, the formal expository writing of some students moved from crimped, over-generalized absolutist writing to writing characterized by context-specific generalization, relevant evidence, and sound illustration.

In the same batch of papers, however, I would discover just as many examples of the same old absolutist crap. Examining these writers, I discovered they did not balk at the journal exercises. In fact, they responded positively. Their journals displayed signs of awareness and growth, but these were not realized in their formal writing. They missed the larger purpose and did not sense any relationship between one exercise and the next, nor between various subparts of the exercise.

The partial success of the journal exercises encouraged me to search for some solution to the problems of purpose and structure. I discovered certain answers in Ira Progoff's Intensive Journal Program. Progoff's primary metaphor for growth especially informs two of his works, *At a Journal Workshop* (NY: Dialogue House, 1975) and *The Wall and the Cathedral* (NY: Dialogue House, 1981). He conceives the individual as a well which is connected below the surface to an underground stream— the collective experience of the human species—and which shows itself as a stream running along the earth's surface—the experience specific to the individual. Through the Intensive Journal individuals sound the depths of the well, discover their connection to the underground stream, and in so doing establish a dynamic of growth based on the connection of the individual with the species and the present continuous with the past and the future. As a depth psychologist, Progoff uses his expressive journal writing exercises—private writings addressed to the self and couched in telegraphic, image-laden language often incomprehensible to others—to move writers away from particulars, from the distraction of the everyday, and towards the symbolic.

Despite the abstract and somewhat mystical nature of his aim, Progoff's Intensive Journal is highly structured and directive. Writers are presented a task and a specific procedure to follow to accomplish it. Writers are directed to persons, places, events, or things in the past for the present and instructed in how to engage them and what to do once engaged. The Intensive Journal provides a structure that informs its purpose, making the task manageable for the writer. In sum, Progoff presents a model for using journal writing purposefully to achieve psychological growth.

The Personal Development Journal: Overview

Returning to my own challenge, I borrowed from Progoff the sense of purpose and structure, reexamined my journal exercises, and redesigned them as a "Personal Development Journal" or PDJ. The PDJ is a fourteen-day cycle of expressive writing exercises in which writers systematically explore their present, probe and analyze their past, and imagine and plan their future. Its purpose is more expansive than Progoff's. As well as fostering self-awareness and psychological growth, the PDJ helps develop specific thinking and language skills required for effective formal writing.

The PDJ breaks into four major sections: *Centering,* in which students write about the present, *Reminiscence,* in which students consider the past, *Cinema,* in which students project the future, and *Reflections,* in which students evaluate the experience of working through the PDJ. Specifically, the sequence helps students 1) establish their immediate context, the now, 2) determine the various individual, parental, familial, and community influences that dominated the past, a past which continues to influence the now, and 3) project a future by creating scenes which can be used to establish goals and plans of action to accomplish those goals. The cycle fosters personal awareness, which according to Perry and other developmental psychologists is a prerequisite for effective learning and intellectual growth, and which I insist is a prerequisite for good writing.

Through the cycle, students complete one exercise per day following the chronology provided. Generally students report completing each exercise within one or two hours. Knowing the particular substance of each assignment is not as important as seeing how the cycle knits considerations of the present, past, and future together.

Day	Exercise
1	Centering One
2	Reminiscence: Place
3	Cinema: Milestones
4	Centering Two
5	Reminiscence: Person
6	Cinema: Youth
7	Centering Three
8	Reminiscence: Dialog
9	Cinema: Acceptance Speech
10	Centering Four
11	Reminiscence: Myth
12	Cinema: Maturity
13	Centering Five
14	Reflections

While directing students through a systematic investigation of their personal lives, the PDJ also causes students to develop and practice cognitive skills required for higher order, formal writing. Each exercise requires writers to first discover a glut of information—details, examples, characters, etc.—through brainstorming a particular topic. Then they must select, connect, and combine that information into a formal writing structure—an extended metaphor, narrative, dialog, letter, speech, or myth. Finally, they review and abstract, summarize, and evaluate what they have written. Each exercise requires creating, structuring, and finally evaluating material, the cognitive skills required of higher level writing/thinking. These are the same skills and procedures used in the composing process. The journal exercises are composing in the microcosm.

Use and Evaluation

The PDJ is designed to provide a sense of self to serve as a basis for subsequent writing. Students complete it at the beginning of the semes-

ter, after establishing procedures, bookkeeping, icebreaking, and completing some trust-building exercises. I collect the PDJ, read it quickly,
make some general comments, and assign S or U grades on the basis of
completeness. I return the PDJ and arrange conferences with each
student. In the conferences we discuss significant insights and conclusions. Should any problems needing professional attention become
evident, I provide references to the counseling center, social service
agencies, or local clergy using a list compiled with the help of one of our
university's counselors. This list has been a major asset during PDJ
conferences.

The real benefit of the PDJ is that it serves as the center of the
course. Students use it as a seedbed, a source for the formal writing
required in the course. And these formal papers are submitted to peers
who consider not only composition qualities but also intellectual credibility. This collaborative framework maintains the benefits of the previous expressive writing exercises. Now, however, collaboration occurs
only after the student has probed the present, past, and future sufficiently to have a sense of self and context. Students grow intellectually and
psychologically while developing their skills as writers. Growth in all
three areas is interconnected.

In fact, growth in all three areas is the ultimate end of the course.
The final paper, a personal essay modeled after those of Montaigne,
Emerson, Thoreau, and Arnold, requires students to incorporate what
they have learned about themselves and their values into a longer
statement of belief informed by research. The purpose of the paper is to
cause students to "stake a claim" on some subject—be it religion,
patriotism, education, or whatever. In these papers, students move
beyond the safe clichés they brought with them from previous experience, state a belief, and defend it. Their purpose is to change minds, to
cause others to believe as they do. At least, the reader must understand
the writer's belief. Integrating the PDJ through all the elements of the
course causes it to become the primary instrument for personal growth
and thinking/writing skills development through the semester.

Student Writing

The true test of the Personal Development Journal, however, is the
ability of students to use it to grow and produce good writing. My
experience is that students are able to follow the procedures and in the
process produce some remarkable writing. Some illustrations follow.*

The *Centering* exercises require students to go to a quiet place and
relax, and then to brainstorm a list of their current feelings and sensations along with their sources. Having created a substantial list, they
then review the brainstorming, determine a dominant sensation, and use
it to create a metaphor putting the writer in relation to the sensation. For

*The complete PDJ including the sequence, instructions, and more ex-
amples of student writing appear in *A Whole Course in Writing* (NY:
Harcourt Brace Jovanovich, Inc., 1986)

example, from the brainstormed item, "confused—new campus and people," one writer portrayed herself as:

a jackrabbit
frozen in the dark
in the middle of a two-lane highway
headlights approaching from both directions.

Having created the metaphor, writers are then asked to analyze and evaluate it, to use the metaphor as an instrument of awareness that will help them deal with the present. From *Centering* exercises writers gain a sense of awareness and control.

Here's an example produced by a first semester student away from home for the first time. Her brainstorming includes sensations common to new students: "pushed—cramming everything into little time," "homesick...My dad isn't here to help me out," and "computerized—I'm taking everything in and remembering it until the times comes when I'll really use this information." These sensations coalesce in the following metaphor, a metaphor remarkable in its ability to accept the current unrest by considering the ultimate product:

A bottle of wine in a dark creepy cellar. Hidden from view by crates and crates of bottles filled with the same thing. This bottle holds its flavor, its color, and its scent until someone decides it's time to put it to use. Then someone will enjoy its fruitfulness and realize just how wonderful it really is.

In the analysis, the writer's calmness and sense of direction contradict the frenzy of the brainstorm:

Everything will have a use. Everything I'm learning will one day be of real importance. Right now a formula for lines on a graph might not seem too important, but maybe someday three years from now I'll need it. That is when I'll be glad I learned it and I'll realize how important it really is.

Temporarily confused by the avalanche of physical and emotional sensations and overwhelmed by all the new information and experience, this writer has discovered a center and gained a sense of her context and purpose.

Similar insights occur throughtout the PDJ. Often these involve writers dealing with ghosts from the past which haunt them still. Such is the case with the following exercise, *Reminiscence: Person*. Writers are asked to relax and brainstorm about a particular person who has had an effect on their lives. Then they take that information and construct a vignette in which the person remembered plays a significant role. Finally, writers abstract from the brainstorm and vignette a short statement summarizing the impact that person has had upon them.

An example remarkable in its intensity involves a young man dealing with the ghost of his father. Though the writer has left home, he still feels the influence of his father. The brainstorming suggests some of the difficulty he experiences:

Dad—Judgemental, pessimistic, too hung-up on trivial matters. Not a listener; no room for difference of opinion. Irrational, stubborn, jumping to conclusions, reading things into others' actions. Thoughtless of others.

The vignette focuses on one incident in which the father gets very upset about some business deal with the neighbors which has fallen through:

> As soon as I come home I hear discontented gripes about the same thing as last time, trivial worries and incorrect analysis of situations and of people. I can't help but wonder how he made it this far. Always he has some dim opinion of what somebody, what *everybody*, is doing. And whatever it is, it's not right because he's too close-minded or jealous (it's usually not hard to figure out which) to see that there is nothing wrong with it. "Damn Murphy contracts with a company to have his lawn landscaped for $6,000 when we could have done it for practically the cost of materials."

> He's upset because: a) Murphy didn't hire us and we need the money, and b) he thinks we could do a better job, even though we've never done that kind of work before. And Murphy's a fool if he thinks we can't do a better job. (But Dad never does the work, he just volunteers his "boys.")

> He's irrational—gets upset when we help neighbors voluntarily, without pay. Thinks that you have to get something monetary for every task you complete, even if you're just being neighborly.

> He does very little to help with other people's problems; he's only concerned with himself. Instinct has completely taken over.

> Can't help but feel frustrated and used, like I might end up like *him* if I stick around too long. I rebel by *not* living by his rules while there and challenging his narrow verdicts on others. And by getting out as quick as possible.

A key insight here lies in the recognition of the similarity between father and son. What is resented in the father the son fears may be part of himself. This is an insight the writer can put to use.

But there is love evident also, as noted in the abstract, a summary of sorts, explaining this love/hate relationship:

> He seems to be the exact opposite of what I believe in. When I was little I can remember saying about him and my older brothers, "Whatever they do or say, I am going to do or say the exact opposite." And in a way I have and I am *glad*.

> Seems very selfish, closed minded. But at the same time honest. Hard to explain.

> Very frustrated and disillusioned. Now looks at worst of things so he won't have fallen hopes.

> Someone that you can never leave altogether because either a) you feel sorry for him or b) you know there is something great in there that has been suppressed and beaten for ages but every now and again looks like it's going to climb out.

Note how in reflecting upon his father and the common experience many of us have with our parents and families, the writer addresses his rebellion and tries to explain it rationally. He describes this relationship with an intensity characteristic of the best use of the PDJ. He is getting things off his chest but at the same time discovering what is really important about his past—what he ought to spend more time thinking about.

Student Response and Reaction

I hope these sample student responses illustrate the potential of the PDJ to generate writing of significance. Several colleagues and I have used it with enough students to allow several statements. First, students are excited by the PDJ. Despite its complexity and the demands it makes of writers, all students—from basic writers to graduate students—have completed the cycle. Most can cite several important insights from the PDJ experience. In fact, most freshmen consider the PDJ a "friend," finding it an important "place" where they can go for solace, and a means of "gaining a sense of control" over their lives. In addition, many report that they plan on completing the PDJ cycle again.

One student's response in particular demonstrates the odd turns growth can take. She submitted a complete but undistinguished PDJ; her responses seemed superficial, formulaic. She created for herself an archetypal mainstream American life with marriage, career, children, and a "happily ever after" existence. Through the semester, however, her work contradicted the superficiality of her PDJ; her formal papers were thoughtful, almost always dealing with some conflict from her life or our readings.

In a conference near semester's end, she began talking about her PDJ. She confirmed my suspicions that it did not reflect her real thinking and feeling, that she had been writing a fairy tale. In fact, the castle she had built herself in the air had crumbled. In the course of the semester she broke up with her boyfriend, moved out of her parents' home and into an apartment, and changed her major. These had been the most frequent topics of her journal writing, though they had always been presented in idyllic terms. She claimed her inability to deal seriously with problems and incongruities in the PDJ helped her conclude that changes were necessary. She said she was tired of pretending all was well when it wasn't. In her evaluation she writes: "I really enjoyed working through the PDJ even if I was a might confused as to what I was writing that I wanted and what I really do want. Now that that's cleared up, I really plan to work through the PDJ again...it's a great way to learn about yourself, especially if you let it sit for a couple of months." Evidently she is sold on journal writing. If nothing else, the PDJ gives writers a comprehensive introduction to journal keeping procedures and purposes.

Concerning writing and thinking skills *per se*, we have found evidence of growth in the formal writing of the PDJ students. Generally, students who complete the PDJ write better papers. Their essays are more complex and thoughtful, better structured, better defended and qualified, and more rhetorically sophisticated. All these are characteristics of higher level writing, and the PDJ students produced writing of this kind much more quickly than normally. Their writing illustrates the benefits of an intensive journal writing program both in terms of intellectual sophistication and writing skills. The journal proves its worth on every level.

I don't advertise the Personal Development Journal as a panacea for the thinking and writing problems of our students. It is, however, a model that writing teachers who are not sure why or how to use journals, who have forgotten the roots of the tradition, can adapt to their individual teaching styles and purposes.

References

Britton, J., et al. (1975). *The development of writing abilities (11-18)*. London: Macmillan Education.

Bruffee, K. (1980). *A short course in writing* (2nd ed.). Boston: Little Brown.

Perry, W. (1968). *Forms of intellectual development*. New York: Holt, Rinehart & Winston.

Progoff, I. (1975). *At a journal workshop*. New York: Dialogue House.

———— (1981). *The well and the cathedral*. New York: Dialogue House.

15.

Building a Dining Room Table: Dialogue Journals About Reading

NANCIE ATWELL

One summer weekend some friends from the Bread Loaf School of English drove over to Maine for a quick visit. During dinner Saturday night my husband Toby discovered that one of our guests actually read and, better yet, appreciated his favorite novelist. Long after the table was cleared, the dishes washed and dried, and everyone else had taken a long walk down to the beach and back, Toby and Nancy Martin sat at our dining room table gossiping about Anthony Powell's *Dance to the Music of Time*. This didn't help me appreciate Anthony Powell, but it did open my eyes to the wonders of our dining room table. Not sitting there, I saw it.

Our dining room table is a literate environment. Around it, people talk in all the ways literate people discourse. We don't need assignments, lesson plans, lists, teachers' manuals or handbooks. We need only a text and a literate friend. And our talk isn't sterile or perfunctory; it's filled with jokes, arguments, exchanges of bits of information, descriptions of what we loved and hated and why. The way Toby and Nancy chatted, the way Toby and I chat most evenings at that table, were ways my students and I could talk, entering literature together. Somehow I had to get that table into my classroom and invite eighth grade readers to pull up their chairs.

I had already taken steps toward establishing my classroom as a literate environment. I'd shelved my reading curriculum, along with its standard issue anthologies, and stocked the room with individual titles of paperbacks—novels, histories, biographies, poetry. I'd turned over the time scheduled for whole-group literature instruction to silent reading of books selected by individual readers. Now it remained to build a dining room table, to create a forum in school where readers could engage with me in congenial talk about books, authors, reading and writing.

I think it's crucial that students have opportunities for literary talk with the teacher; it's not enough for schools to simply make time and space for independent reading. For too many kids, sustained silent reading programs are little more than a nice break in the day's routine. With nothing happening before or after the reading, the context in which readers read doesn't support or extend their interests. As Donald Fry observes, the teacher needs to keep the ball rolling, "to be resourceful and responsive to what (the student) does in order to maintain that interest and allow that process to bring about change and not stagnate" (1985).

Recreating my dining room table, being resourceful and responsive to what seventy-five individual readers were doing, presented problems of logistics. Class size averages twenty-five, so one-to-one reading conferences during the workshop allowed students to do little more than provide quick plot synopses of their books. There wasn't enough time or teacher to go around. And I discovered that even when the opportunity arose for an extended discussion between a student and me, readers had real difficulty moving beyond telling what happens. In talking with me they rarely analyzed or critiqued what they'd read or articulated what they liked or valued, a phenomenon also observed by Applebee (1978), and Whitehead (1977). I spent reading conference time trying to stay awake through retellings of novels I came to know too well.

At the time I was struggling to orchestrate meaningful discussions with my kids about their reading, Dixie Goswami, my teacher at Bread Loaf, pointed me toward Jana Staton's dialogue journal research (1980, 1982). Staton studied the written dialogues that a sixth grade teacher sustains over every school year with each of her students, letters written back and forth in a bound journal. In these dialogue journals I recognized what I'd been looking for: a way all seventy-five eighth graders might pull up their chairs and join me at my dining room table. The following September I gave each reader a folder with a sheaf of lined paper and a letter from me clipped inside. In my letter to them I said:

> This folder is a place for you and me to talk this year about books, authors, reading and writing. You're to write letters to me—at least one a week—and I'll write letters back to you. All of our letters will stay here together, arranged chronologically, as a record of our thinking, learning and reading. In your letters, talk about what you've read. Tell what you thought and felt and why. Tell what you liked and didn't like and why. Tell what these books said to you and meant to you. Ask me questions or for help, and write back to me about my ideas, feelings and questions.

I invited written dialogues about literature because I had some hunches about the combined possibilities of writing as a way of reflecting on reading, and teacher-learner correspondence as a way of extending and enriching reflection through collaboration. I suspected kids' written responses to books would go deeper than their talk, that writing would give them time to consider their thinking and that thoughts captured would spark new insights. I knew writing to be, in Emig's (1977) phrase, "a unique mode of learning," different from speaking, listening and reading. I also suspected that a written exchange between two readers, student and adult expert, would take readers even deeper inside written texts. As a teacher of writing I'd learned how writing conferences—the dialogue between writer and teacher—helped students to consider and develop their thoughts. As a teacher of reading I welcomed another opportunity to engage my kids in what Vygotsky termed "mediated learning" (1962), cooperating with them as an experienced reader in this special context. Finally, I believed this special context—a teacher initiating and inviting first-draft chat—would provide a way for me to be responsive to every reader as well as a specific occasion for them to write and reflect: a genuine and genuinely interested audience who was going to write back.

The dialogue journals between my kids and me confirmed my hunches. Over each of the last two years we've exchanged thousands of pages of letters. In our correspondence we've gone far beyond plot synopses and traditional teachers' manual issues as genre, theme and character, to give accounts of our processes as readers, to speculate on authors' processes as writers, to suggest revisions in what we've read, to see connections between a published author's work and our own writing, to see connections between books and our own lives. We've taught each other.

From my students I've learned about adolescent readers' interests and concerns. I've learned the names of authors who write well for adolescents. I've learned the value and necessity of allowing kids to read as real readers do, choosing, skimming, skipping and abandoning. And, maybe the hardest lesson of all, I've learned how to authoritatively respond to what readers are trying to do without coming across like a teacher's guide or an examination. Instead, I can affirm, challenge, gossip, joke, argue, recommend and provide the information I see a reader needs. I can also offer some well-placed "nudges," Mary Ellen Giacobbe's word for the gentle guidance that moves learners from where they are to where they might be.

Through our dialogue journals, my students learned, too, about the world of written texts—what good writers do, what good readers do, how readers talk, what books are good for and how kids can get in on it. When I asked eighth graders to be specific about their literary knowledge, to spend a few days reading through our letters and making categories of the kinds of things we talked about, they named over 150 literary topics. This, finally, is the greatest of all the benefits of our letters about literature: the range of talk in which we engage in school is much the same as the genuine literary gossip of my dining room table. The following section features eighth grade readers' responses on a sampling of subjects, illustrating how written dialogues about literature can work to open up texts to young readers and compel reflection.

Literary Gossip: Kinds of Talk About Books

In their letters, readers often connect stories about others' lives to their own feelings and experiences. This response to literature isn't often encouraged or accommodated in school; it is, I think, one of the surest signs of a reader's involvement. For example, Jon responded personally, and intensely, to the loyalty and love among roommates in *The Lords of Discipline*.

> Pat Conroy puts four boys in a room, changes them into men, and then puts them against the world. But there is a tratior amongst them, which is a startling blow because there is so much love in that room. That is another thing that I liked. Conroy put an incredible amount of feelings in this book. The roommates love each other an incredible amount. When the main character exposes

a secret organization, you have an immense feeling of joy for that character because he succeeded in doing the right thing; he put himself against men in power and he won. I just can't stop thinking about how much love there was floating in that room. It isn't like they are gay, they just care an incredible amount for each other, and Conroy illustrates this excellently. Normally I would have dropped a book like this, but this book has changed my way of thinking. I don't think that one boy caring for another boy is weird now.

Jon's personal connections with books ran the gamut. Here, the same week, he connected fiction and life as only an eighth grader can connect.

I have an uncanny experence to tell you about. I was going up to Sugarloaf/USA, and I took *Live And Let Die* with me. I came back on Sunday (I went up on Friday), the book finished. On Sunday, *Live And Let Die* was on ABC-TV!! I really couldn't believe it!!

Students also connected literature and real life by responding to the specific information authors presented via fictional narratives; they learned some things about the world around them through stories:

I finished *Goodbye Paperdoll*. It is a great book. It's very informative and I think helps alot in understanding anorexia nervosa, like *Deenie* taught me about scoliosis. (This was one book I really enjoyed the ending. It wasn't your typical, everythings all better, she gains thirty pounds type of ending.)

I finished *Cache Lake Country* last night...It tells every little detail about the wilderness. Its so discriptive, it tells about every little sight, sound or smell. For instance how a squirrel turns a mushroom around while its eating it. I saw a squirrel do it Saturday. Its wonderful!...And I have tried to make some "baking powder" can lanterns that are in *Cache Lake Country*. They look kind of sloppy but I got the idea.

Their dialogue journals elicited another kind of personal connection that I'd never observed in eighth grade readers. In their letters they began to reflect on themselves as readers, to become conscious of and articulate how they learned to read, their reading rituals, and their processes as readers, the ways they went about reading and thinking about what they'd read:

I just can't remember how I got to like reading so much. It might be that way because of my mother always reading to me until I was in fourth grade. I remember I always seemed to love listening to her read.

When I read it's a special time for me to be alone. I sit on my bed with a pillow leaning against the wall and another one on my lap so I don't have to hold my arms up. I get completely relaxed. Also, after I finish reading, I just sit for a while thinking about the book...The only thing that bothers me is when I get a phone call or if it's time for dinner and I'm right in the middle of a good book. I try to get the interruption over with so I can get back to reading. How about you?

When I pick up a mystery novel, after examining all of the charactors, from the leading lady to the gardiner, I make a logical asumption of who I think did the dasterdly deed, and many times I'm rite, like in King's novel I'm reading now, I assume something like "Boy! CHRISTINE's gonna get them!" and usually it happens, so thats why I like King's work, because I can have a say in the ending. King I feel is trying to have people asume, and that's what makes him so great. What do you think?

Dear Theo was a collection of letters written by Vinsent Van Gogh to his brother, and it tells me many things I didn't know about him. He was a gifted artists who led a mostly terrible life...The letters were arrainged in the days he sent them. I picked the ones I wanted to read by skimming down the pages.

This was my second reading of *Conan the Warrior*. And this time it was different to me! I read things I missed or didn't think much about the first time when I mostly wanted to see how Conan was going to live through danger.

I've sort of noticed "trends" or "cycles" in my reading. Right now I'm in a Paula Danziger "cycle". At the beginning of the year I was in a Science Fiction "cycle."

I just finished *Accident*...The only thing is that at the end I don't think she would of (in real life) been as calm as she was about having a limp, but theirs lots of things I still wonder about like—(1) Will she have a limp? (2) Will Adam and Mike be friends? (3) Will Adam ever go to Harvard? (4) Will Jenny change her mind and go with Adam?

While I was reading this book *(About David)* I could imagine what David looked like. I could picture the town, the houses, the school, everything. Like in *The Language of Goldfish* at the end they let you think what is going to happen. I like that, it makes me part of that book. You have to let the reader do some of the writing. Let them be a part of the book their reading. That way they will like the book more.

Advice to authors and comments on how authors wrote—their processes and styles—is probably the most frequent response eighth graders make in their letters. I often wonder if this would still be the case without the other half of the junior high language arts program. Every student has a daily writing workshop (Graves, 1983) in addition to the daily literature program, so besides dialogue journals they're also writing their own narratives, poetry, plays, essays and so on. As authors themselves eighth graders make choices and have a lot to say about the choices professional authors have made. The excerpts below—touching on character development, credibility, subtlety, authority, titles, suspense, and use of language, description and conventions—show students' emerging criteria for good writing.

The only problem I found with *Hitchhiker's Guide to the Galaxy* was that I think he could have developed the characters a little more. I didn't care about them as much as in some of the other books I've read. I think its humor is the only thing that makes this book work.

Everyone in this book *(An X-Rated Romance)* was too, too childish. The dialogue was bizarre and the plot was barely okay. I mean some kids develop crushes on their teachers but don't do things like trying to seduce them. Also the part about the camera, when Emily came out with it around her neck and her mother was too dumb to suspect, sheesh!

I think that some of Auel's situations were a bit silly. One thing that bugged me was how Ayla discovered things, like building a fire with flint, riding Whinney, etc. You knew exactly what she was going to do next. When she gets on Whinney you just know that's going to lead to riding her, then using her to chase animals, then to hunt. She makes it so obvious! (Do you understand what I'm trying to say?)

By the end of the story you got the reason why the author wrote this piece, like the book was only written to show An Important Lesson About Life and the author just fitted the rest in. NOT EXACTLY SUBTLE.

Glendon Swarthout is really good. He was probably writing about some of the things that he and his friends did. He probly went through alot of problems like the kids in this book. I think it is important that authors as well as kids write from their own experiences because they know just what to write. Especially their true feelings and thoughts.

I just finished the sequel to *The Cat Ate My Gymsuit*, you know, *There's a Bat in Bunk Five*. I think the titles of both of these books were stupid. They have nothing to do with the major plot, and I was sort of lost by how the title and story differed. I don't think Danziger wanted me to spend time being confused by that.

After what seemed like ten million years (but was only a month) I finished *The Chancellor Manuscript*. This has been the only Ludlum that I have been disapointed with. It seemed to me that it just dragged on and on forever. There were also some pretty disgusting parts in it too. It's like your on a train travelling at a certain speed. With all the other Ludlums, the train would speed up as you got toward the end of the book (or destination). With *The C. Mans.*, you stayed at the same speed throughout all the book and when you got to the end, you stopped dead. Usually, when you reach the end, you are travelling ten times faster and when you reach the end you have to rest to catch your breath. Do you see what I mean? I'm not going to drop Ludlum, but I will most certainly hope that the next one I read will be better.

One thing I like about Pfeffer's writing is the way she ends her chapters. If you look through you'll notice the short, one-sentence paragraphs. This really adds a lot of force to what she's saying.

There is one thing I don't like about Adams' writing. I would just be getting to a really exciting part (of *Shardik*) and he would stop and give this long metaphor and I was so anxious to find out what happens I would skim it. Adams is a very descriptive writer, and I think he sometimes gets carried away.

I love the way King puts thoughts in italics and parenthesis, and sometimes runs all the thoughts together into one sentence. It gives you a feeling of what's running through a person's mind. Have you noticed him doing this?

Part of kids' education as reader-writers was sorting out such issues as genre, formula and point of view. Sandy used her dialogue journal to articulate the differences between gothic romances and novels, both of which she was reading and enjoying but for different reasons.

My analysis of a love story is: a book with a simple plot, not much you have to go by, and the same book as alot of other only the title is changed.

A novel is: a book which one enjoys reading because of an interesting, different plot. A book where characters are different and each has a quality (whether good or bad): themselves. A book you don't know the ending to just by reading the first couple of chapters. Something that has substance, that you can grip onto rather than fall through. A surprise ending. Also, not a book that has between 100 and 150 pages so that you can zip through. Maybe, something longer, with a theme that keeps you interested.

I've shed most of my anxieties about adolescents' attraction to formulaic fiction over the last two years because I saw readers passing through this stage of their histories as readers in the pages of their journals. Amanda discovered the formula of her once-beloved teen mysteries, and Jenn discovered the Sweet Dreams recipe.

This book was alot like a Nancy Drew's. I saw them (Susan Sand mysteries) in a magazine and the ad said "Getting tired of Nancy Drew's from your mother's time?" There almost exactly alike. And Every Single Nancy Drew is The SAME. When I was reading them alot, I could tell exactly when things would happen like when she would get captured near the end ect. ect. It drove me crazy. These weren't that bad, but if I read them alot it probably would be. The girls are *so* perfect. Then the author makes them have dead parents or something so it won't be so perfect, but the girls don't even care. It's dumb.

I have read many, probably just about all, "Sweet Dreams" and "Wildfire" series. It used to be all I ever read. As you keep on reading so many I realized that basically they're all the same. I'm quite surprised with myself lately. I haven't been reading any.

During this time, I've read other books I enjoy more. Stories with more of a plot than, a boy and a girl fall in love, have some problems, and at the end get together again. They are so boring. My mother is happy I'm getting over my love stories and into interesting novels. Although I don't know why, she usually reads Harlequins.

A big piece of their dissatisfaction with formulaic fiction stemmed from a growing awareness of narration and point of view. They wanted to believe in, trust and feel close to a central character, especially if that character were also the narrator.

I really like a book that tells alot of description about the person who is telling the story. It makes it easier to relate and have feelings towards them. It also helps to know what the characters are feeling. During this story, Leslie never mentioned her feelings about what was happening to her and the way she looked. I needed more of a person from Leslie.

I've decided I like a book that has a one person view. *Killing Mr. Griffin* could have been better if a character involved told the story from his or her view. I like a book with more feelings; I like to know what a character is thinking rather than just his or her actions.

I think this is going to be my last which-way book. When your reading this your thinking to your self during the whole book that this would never happen. But when your reading a novel you picture your self in the person's spot that your reading about and in this book you can't unless you really have a wild imagination.

As the school year and correspondence progress, students have more to say on an ever greater range of literary topics: the length of a chapter, what makes a main character a main character, copyrights, jacket copy, type size, leads and conclusions. When they gain experience and reflect on that experience, a new diversity of issues affects how readers approach and perceive written texts.

I hate the way they just picked a picture for the cover. You can *tell* it's no one in the story. Isn't an illustrator supposed to read the book he's illustrating?

I've decided I prefer paperbacks. One of the things I don't like about hard-covers is that when I'm reading it the cover sometimes gets in the way and I have to take it off to concentrate on reading.

Alot of times I've noticed that by the title of the book that it's going to be a good one. Like the two books I'm going to read. One is called *White Fang* which sounds exciting and the other one is *Me and Fat Glenda* which sounds hilarious.

It used to be that I'd go into the library and just close my eyes and grab a book. A thing I've noticed is how I've gotten fussy. It's not just that I know what I like, I know authors I like. Now I ask for Cormier or Hinton or Myers or for some author like them.

By the way, did you watch *Watership Down* on TV? I saw some of it and thought it was rather disappointing. I didn't like the comical beginning and they shortened the exciting parts so much that they lost all their excitement. I don't think they'll ever make a movie anywhere close to the quality of the book. (Is it possible to make a movie close to the quality of any good book?)

Many of their letters about good books were letters of recommendation, sometimes in the form of advice to pass on to other readers in other classes, sometimes in the form of warnings:

Another book I read over the weekend was a book by Farley Mowat, called *The Barrens*. I thought it was a very, very good book. I would encourage you to take a look at it. It was about two hundred pages long and I liked it so much I read it all in under two hours. I don't exactly know if that is good timing or not; I just know that it was a very good book.

I recommend the series starting with *A Wrinkle in Time,* by Madeleine L'Engle, to Jenny, if she hasn't already read them. But they are a little different from *A Ring of Endless Light.* They're a little more fantasized, but excellent. If she's already read those, she could try *The Arm of the Starfish* which is more like a good guy, bad guy book. But it has some characters in it. The best one to read after *A Ring of*...is *Moon by Night.* It has Vicky Austin in it, *A Ring of Endless Light* is its sequel. But you can still read the second one first.

I also read *Flowers in the Attic.* I don't know if you've read it or not, but if you haven't "don't". I don't think it's a book you would like. I don't think you would like any of the characters.

The responses eighth graders most often wanted from me were answers to their questions. These were the letters that brought me the most satisfaction: when my students asked me to teach them. They asked for my recommendations of good books—funny, scary or sad stories, or a book like one just finished, or other books by a particular author or on a particular topic. They asked for information, about how books are published, about the length of time it takes for a hardcover to be released as a paperback, about various genres, about strategies like skimming and speed reading, about conventions like epigraphs, epilogues, flashbacks and foreshadows. They asked for my theories about why authors had written in particular ways. And they did a lot of comparing notes, wondering if I'd noticed or experienced something they had in their reading.

I especially liked "Crosbey Dream", one of the stories in here. That was about the best even though the others were right up there too. I wish there were more of these books around. I looked at Edgar Alan Poe's book and said "Forget this!" It was too hard. I know I've asked this before but, do you know of any other short horror tales?

In two books I've read lately *(Heads You Win, Tails I Loose* and

Dinky Hocker Shoots Smack) they've talked about "A Street Car Named Desire" or something like that. What is it, a play, a movie or a book? I think it was a play but I'm not sure. Is it in a book (or even a script)? Do you have any ideas on how I could get it/Who is the author, ect.? It sounds like I might like it. It's supposed to be funny isn't it?

Bell Jar ended so abruptly when I wanted a more flowing ending. Do you know what I mean? I guess I wanted a fairy tale ending. After I read the biography in the back about Plath my happy feelings about the recovery of the character soured. "The bell jar descended again" and Plath succeeded in killing herself. Well, maybe Esther did too. How are you supposed to read an auto-biographical book? If Plath died can Esther live on?

Writing Back

Over the last two years I've had to re-learn my role as reading teacher. I've had to put a stop to teacher talk, to spitting out questions like a computer and lecturing my kids about what they're supposed to see and appreciate in the literature they read. There is no one set of questions to ask every reader; there are, instead, individual readers with their own strategies, questions, tastes and styles. There is no one correct way to approach or interpret a text; there are, instead, individual readers with an incredible range of prior knowledge and experience. Through the dialogue journals I've discovered alternative ways a secondary English teacher can talk to students about literature. The letters I write to readers are personal and contextual. That is, what I say in my half of the dialogue journal comes from my knowledge of how the student reads and thinks, of what the student knows. Response grows both from what I've learned about a reader and how I hope to move the reader's thinking.

At the same time as I've learned to respond specifically and personally, I've also discovered some general principles of writing back. The first is not to respond too personally. Toby Fulwiler reminds teachers that "journals exist somewhere on a continuum between diaries and class notebooks...Like the diary, the journal is written in the first person; like the class notebook, the journal focuses on academic subjects the writer would like to learn more about" (1980). Our dialogue journals focus on the academic subjects under consideration in my course: books, authors, reading and writing. I'm not a counselor, and the purpose of the letters is not to invite students' personal problems or offer counsel.

Neither is the purpose of the letters to test reading. Students' most perfunctory letters were responses to letters of mine that read like a teacher's manual, bombarding kids with questions. One good, thoughtful question is more than enough. I received my most interesting letters when I responded as a curious human being, asking a question about something I really wanted to know, but also when I leveled with students about my own experiences, tastes and opinions as a reader, sharing freely and frankly, agreeing and disagreeing.

Neither is the purpose of the letters to test writing. The dialogue journals were conceived as first-draft chat, not polished pieces of writing. I make no corrections on students' letters, but I do comment if I'm having trouble reading them.

My role as correspondent strikes a careful balance between experienced reader, mentor, and teacher responsible to her adolescent students. This means sharing what I've learned about reading, offering my advice and expertise, and nudging—sometimes hard—when I think a student might be in need of a nudge. The several exchanges below illustrate this balancing act.

Dear Dan,

Is *Watership Down* feeling too long to you? You seem to be making little progress. It's okay—it's more than okay—to abandon a book you're not enjoying. I know I recommended *W.D.* to you, but that doesn't obligate you to finish it or tell me you like it. If it's getting boring, please put it back. Does this make sense?

Ms. A.

Dear Ms. A,

Yes, I think it does make sense. Yes, even though I liked *Watership Down* it got too long for me and I was getting pretty discouraged. I put it back and got this other book I really liked by Farly Mowat, *Never Cry Wolf.*

Thanks.

Dan

Lance wrote to me about the conclusion of S.E. Hinton's *Rumble Fish:* he didn't understand why Motorcycle Boy freed the zoo animals and the fighting fish at the novel's end.

Dear Lance,

When Motorcycle Boy frees the animals, you have to figure— because of the strength and intelligence of his character—that he's doing it for a reason. To him the animals represent something else, someone he wants to set free of cages and walls that keep them captive, but can't. Can you begin to figure what animals and piranha represent to him?

Ms. A.

Ms. A,

Yes, I think he thinks about himself and the other boys in the gang as trapped in a cage, a cage of fights and puzzlement. A cage that men build around themselves and even Motorcycle Boy with all his brains is stuck inside it...

Sandy was similarly confused about the conclusion of Robert O'Brien's *Z for Zachariah:*

Ms. A.

I'm trying to decide whether or not this book was too deep and whether or not it was written for kids my age. I'm trying to think if maybe there was something there, like the answers to my questions and I just didn't realize. I was really disappointed by the ending. I felt she gave up what was rightfully hers. I felt she could have had more guts. Also, I didn't like, to me, an unanswered ending.

Sandy

Dear Sandy,

I often think: is there something wrong with me or something wrong with this book? This most often happens when I read something I didn't entirely understand. Sometimes I'm tempted to write to an author and say, "Would you mind revising this? I don't get it the way you've done it here," or "I don't like how it came out."

I did like how *Z* came out—the fact that it didn't become a futuristic version of Adam and Eve. The girl and man didn't live happily ever after because they couldn't. Even those two people couldn't live amicably; the man had to initiate his own, private war after the big one had managed to wipe out (probably) the rest of the world. To me the novel was about human nature, about how our basic instincts lead us to suspicion and competition rather than harmony and cooperation. I think O'Brien is essentially pessimistic, like Wm. Golding's *Lord of the Flies,* but although I'm interested in this theme I don't think I agree with him.

Ms. A.

Ms. Atwell,

I agree with you. I'm awfully glad they didn't make the story out to be a happily-ever-after book because life isn't like that. Also they get boring after reading so many of them.

The book was different from any other book I've read and I decided I liked that. I liked the change. Your statement makes alot of sense to me. I guess I really didn't try to look at what they were getting at until now. Your opinions helped me a little more to understand parts.

Sandy

Some of my letters contain more explicit nudges, as in these three excerpts dealing with, respectively, "Which Way?" books, a student whose first letters consisted of lengthy plot synopses, and a reader who complained about a change I made in his seating plan.

These "Which Way?" books are driving me crazy. I'm using the term "book" loosely. I hated the one I read. It was just arbitrary— the characters never developed, nothing built toward anything with any logic, and my involvement was minimal and artificial compared with the way I get involved with a good main character. I came away feeling as if I'd spent thirty minutes reading the backs of cereal boxes. I bought a couple of books last week I think you'd like. One is *Friends Till the End* by Todd Strasser. It's in the classroom library if you'd like to give it a try—a good and surprising story.

By the way, your letter was a little book-reportish, mostly recounting what happened in this book. You've got to keep me in mind, Kellie. If you're writing about a book I've already read, it's a little boring for me to read an account of the plot. And if it's a book I haven't read, it's particularly exasperating because you've told me the outcome and ruined the story for me. Do you see what I mean? I'm mostly interested in your reactions: what you liked, didn't like and why; what you think; what you wonder about.

You can't sit on the floor anymore because you read less when you sit on the floor. I've been worried that you haven't finished a book in well over a month now. I want you to read a lot and get better at reading—and pass this course, too. Your chances of accomplishing these things are better if you work in your seat.

Conclusions

My students include all the eighth graders at Boothbay Region Elementary School; our special education students are mainstreamed for the reading course. Every student is responsible for keeping a dialogue journal, and everyone must write at least one letter a week as the bare minimum for passing the course. Grades are based on the fulfillment of this requirement as well as depth of response, use of classroom independent reading time, and progress made toward individual goals established at the beginning of each quarter. I expect all my students will read and will join me at that dining room table, but I back up my expectations by inviting their participation just as sensibly and generously as I can. Dialogue journals play an important role in encouraging students to pull up their chairs and become readers, to enter the world of written texts and make it their own. And dialogue journals allow me to respond, pointedly and personally, to what my students are doing; dialogue journals allow me to teach every reader.

Kim was one of my students last year. Classified as a slow, low-comprehending reader, she'd spent a lot of time in remedial reading programs. In my letters I nudged Kim hard to employ alternative strategies, to abandon books she didn't enjoy, to try novels her friends and I knew were great stories. Kim read twenty-one books that year and showed three years' growth on the standardized reading test our school administers each spring; most significantly, Kim knew and could describe her growth to fluency and her right to a place at the dining room table.

Dear Ms. A,

I just finished *E.T.* and again I really liked it, the only problem was my mind kept racing ahead. The part I like best is the last chapter, when every thing starts to get going. Excitement builds and at the same time your getting every ones (including animals) thoughts and feelings. It's great.

I have changed so much as a reader this year. I think I changed as I read but also when you were talking to me at the beginning of the year. "When you read you should take the words in groups not one at a time." You said, "And don't go back just keep reading, don't read over and over what you've just read." And also you incouraged me. "Keep reading, but don't read a book you don't

like. Find one you do and read it as fast as you can." And I also
found with your help some books that I couldn't believe how much
I liked. Thanks, Ms. A.

Yours,
Kim, A Reader

References

Applebee, A. (1978). *The child's concept of story*. Chicago: University of Chicago
    Press.
Emig, J. (1977, May). Writing as a mode of learning. *College Composition and
    Communication*.
Fry, D. (1985). *Children talk about books: Seeing themselves as readers*. Phila-
    delphia: Milton Keynes.
Fulwiler, T. (1980, December). Journals across the disciplines. *English Journal*,
    69.
Graves, D. (1983). *Writing: Teachers and children at work*. Portsmouth, NH:
    Heinemann.
Staton, J. (1980, May). Writing and counseling: Using a dialogue journal.
    Language Arts, *57*.
———, Kreeft, J., Shuy, R., & Reed, L. (1982). *Analysis of journal writing as
    a communicative event*. Final report, National Institute of Education Grant
    No. G-80-0122, Center for Applied Linguistics, Washington, DC.
Vygotsky, L.S. (1962). *Thought and language*. Cambridge: MIT Press.
Whitehead, F. (1977). *Children and their books*. London: Macmillan.

16.

I Hear Voices:
The Text, The Journal, and Me

PHYLLIS TASHLIK

For more than a decade, now, literary critics have been shifting their focus from the text and the author's intention to the response of the reader. Their theories have corroborated what many classroom teachers have long observed: reading (like writing) is an active process of making sense or making meaning. The text is not an autonomous object that in itself contains meaning: it is the reader, actively engaged in the reading process, who creates it.

Each reading, then, at different times and among different readers, seems to offer the potential for a wide range of individualized responses. These responses, however, are not as individual as we think. They have been influenced by myriad external conditions (historical, political, academic) barely conscious in us when we interpret a text. When we read, we do it in a social context; when we create meaning for a text, we do it from within the particular community we are a part of.

I sought a way to apply these ideas to the junior high classroom, an environment often inimical to the goals of reader-response theory. Schooled in New Criticism, we teachers were trained to view the text as a hallowed object, one that required the interpretation our professors approved as "right." There seemed to be an "ideal reading" against which we were judged. Unfortunately, this notion still pervades our classrooms. Too often, instead of opening up possibilities for our students to explore literature, we tend to close them down. We surround our students with questions that we hope will elicit just the "right" answer.

Journal writing became my primary method for developing a literature curriculum based on reader-response theory. I relied on my familiarity with James Moffett's work (especially point of view exercises: *Student-Centered Language Arts and Reading*, 1976; *Active Voice*, 1981) as well as my own experience with the writing process. In fact, it was my years of involvement with composition theory and my students' writing that had led me to investigate new ways of integrating writing into the literature units and nurturing the natural connections between reading and writing.

When I began teaching *The Crucible* I asked my students to invent a character who had lived through the events of Salem's 1692 witchhunt and to write a series of fictional journals from that character's point of view. The range of characters they chose included believers and non-

believers, servants and slaves, children and adults, a cat, and even the
devil himself. Sharing journals in class, whether in small groups or as a
whole, encouraged those who had felt unsure about the assignment to
give it a try. These readings eliminated the specter of the right answer
and allowed students to engage themselves in creating new texts based
on their reading of the play.

When I read Jonathan's journal, I was impressed by the fictional and
imaginative leaps he was able to make in his writing:

> I was returning to my home after a hard day's work today. Master
> Cobbler was attempting to show me the fine arts of the high boot. I
> can put the boot together well, however I have problems in the way
> of making the boot pleasing to the eye. Finally, master became
> exasperated and sent me on my way. Anyways, I was on my way
> home and passing by Rev. Parris's home—it was late at night, and
> I saw there was much commotion at hand. This verily suprised me,
> seeing as Rev. Parris and his family are rather quiet, 'ceptin' for
> that neice of his who...anyway, I decided that something must be
> afoot, but I dismissed it for the moment.
>
> On my way back to the Master's, as I passed the Parris house and
> I saw huge crowds of people there, risking my Master's wrath, I
> decided to dawdle. I asked Goodman Thomas what was going on
> and he said that Betty Parris was bewitched and that she and some
> other girls had been caught dancing. "I seen her fly!" Thomas said,
> "Betty Parris were flying."
>
> I had to go then, but my curiosity was interfering with my work
> so master sent me on my way early.

Like Jonathan, most of the students tried to capture the "voice" of the
17th century as depicted by Arthur Miller in his dialogue. Below is a
portion of Alice's journal, written from a child's point of view:

> People are saying there are witches in the town. I heard father
> telling mother that some children say they have seen the devil, and
> now they know who is evil. He said that Goody Simms has been
> accused. Once when I picked a flower from her hedge, she chased
> me and cursed at me. I could tell that she was bad.

Kerry chose to portray the consciousness of a "believer":

> Today I also bear serious news. Many townswomen have now been
> accused of being witches and most of them are, for when they enter
> the courthouse, I near want to faint.

Soon she confesses:

> Many times I do want to faint but my body just won't do it and
> since Abigail and all the other girls are fainting, I feel that I must
> also. Therefore, I pretend.

Josh conceived his journal as a series of letters to his fictional brother,
Jonathan. His introduction provided some background information:

> I am a 16 year old boy in Salem, Mass. named Josh. Betty and I are
> good friends, and I happen to have my eyes on her for a wife. I
> don't particularly like Mr. Parris; Proctor, yes. But I don't take

kindly to Abigail. Jonathan is my older brother, a merchant in another part of Mass.

In his last journal, his outrage was eloquent:

John!! Jonathan!!

Proctor has been hanged!! He held his head high, he held his pride up—FOOLS!—this man was no warlock, he was no wizard. And yet he hangs, his body limp and left without life, and he hangs.

Abigail shall rot for this!

This man died with pride. John was a brave, proud man, a righteous man, and he dies, leaving the sniveling accusors—those who were too blind to see, too guilty to confess, too broken for pride—THEY—THEY!!! are the ones that should hang. But those who held the town together, those who really believed! I have done nothing, condemned no one, yet I hide IN GUILT! I live among those who have no conscience, those who do not deserve to die, they must live on and watch the world rot in decay from the wound they caused.

MAY EVE POINT THE GUILTY FINGER AT THE SERPENT WHEN IT IS SHE THAT LOWERED HERSELF TO EAT?
MAY SHE COMPLAIN ABOUT NOT LIKING LIVING OUT-SIDE OF EDEN WHEN IT IS SHE THAT CAST HERSELF OUT?

Let them pay every last ounce in pride or respect they have, and let *THEM* live in *HELL!*

Josh

Clearly, students enjoyed this assignment and willingly entered into the language and consciousness of another time and place. Still, I was not satisfied. I was uncertain if the imposition of a fictional device had interfered with their reading. I wanted to offer a method that would give them an even greater opportunity to explore the text.

For the next assignment, then, on *The Glass Menagerie,* students kept what we referred to as reader-response journals in which they wrote after every one or two scenes. Memories, associations, symbolism, feelings, pleas to the characters or playwright—all were acceptable terms for discussing the play. I, too, kept a journal and though I had re-read the play months before, I refrained from reading it again so that my entries could be fresher. When I read my journal to the class, they applauded! We were off and, I hypothesized, the response journals would bring them into an even more intense interaction with the play than the fictional journals had allowed for.

As opposed to the dry essays students often write about reading assignments, their journals were lively, moving, and in some instances revealed an innovative approach to the play that, despite my extensive training, was outside my "range of choices" of interpretation (Michaels, 1980). For example, the setting of the play, in my mind, is firmly rooted in Tennessee Williams's South during the Great Depression. A group of students, however, moved by the descriptions of the setting, felt as if the story could have taken place today. Rubén wrote:

> The stage directions did evoke some memory within me. I remembered the South Bronx and how most of the buildings are burnt out and how most of the neighborhood is gone.
>
> If I did have a chance to talk to the playwright, Tennessee Williams, I would ask him if he meant it to be a kind of a place like the South Bronx, as it is today.

Similarly, Joseph wrote in his journal:

> When I read it I learned it wasn't a good scene. It was like the Ghetto with alleys and bums. It made me think of New York or Chicago who have the worst slum areas.

When Joseph read this journal aloud in class, Irma, one of the students, said that she thought the story had taken place today, just around the corner. That would have shifted the drama to East Harlem, 1984, a very intriguing approach to the play and one, I believe, that breathes new life into the doomed family's situation. For some students it made sense: a single-parent household, the consequences of unemployment, a rebellious son who refuses to be responsible for the family, a sister without the man her mother desparately wants for her. It is especially interesting that when the classroom is open to individual reader-response, so many students produce a *shared* response, a reading of the play that they share within their own "community of readers" (Fish, 1980). While the play includes specific references to the '30s and the beginnings of World War II, and I never hesitated to point them out or explain them, their reading indicates a possible modernizing of the play which, I am sure, many directors would be interested in.

Like the fictional journals, the reader-response journals allowed for a variety of "voices." Nava chose to direct some of her journals to the characters:

> Amanda, why don't you leave everyone alone? Tom regards your forever reminding him how educated you are and what a good family you came from as one does a buzzing, annoying fly. Too trivial one thinks to bother with, but as time goes on, and the sound does not cease, the anger wells within and threatens to burst its jailer and flee in the form of uncalled for anger. I think that Tom gets just so fed up with the nagging that he has little outbursts every once in a while: all that annoyance being repeated day after day, so often in the same form. I don't think it is as if Tom doesn't take notice one minute and then flies into a rage in another but that he is always with his comments ready—just not always wanting to pursue an argument that would most likely amount to nothing....

Andrew used his journals to explore the play's symbolism, which he seemed to delight in, and to make tentative guesses about where the play might be heading. Below are some excerpts from his journals:

> The Wingfields live a dull, common life symbolizing many families during the Great Depression of the 1930s. All of the

curtains in the play show how closed off and withdrawn they are from the world.

The beginning of the 6th scene describes Laura as a piece of glass. This shows how close she felt towards those glass animals. The next sentence points out that glass is not realistic, only pleasing for a few moments.

Amanda puts handkerchiefs in Laura's bosom to deceive the gentleman caller. This contradicts what Amanda said in an earlier scene about not liking when Laura practices deception.

When the gentleman caller, Jim O'Connor, arrives, he is shaken. He sees a girl, Laura, run away from him and then a mother who has jumped thirty years into the past and practically pounces on him. I think Amanda's going to end up with a new husband.

Happiness, like the beauty of Laura's glass menagerie, only takes place for a moment. In the last scene, the glass menagerie, especially the unicorn, becomes almost a part of Laura. Mr. O'Connor is breaking Laura's shyness and makes her feel normal. When he breaks the unicorn's horn he is making it regular. As Laura says, "Maybe it's a blessing in disguise."

Daniel's journal overflowed with emotions:

"This is the climax of her secret world," said Tennessee Williams in the stage directions. This struck me very hard. It made me think of Laura in her glass world and how this short scene could be so important for her.

When Jim told Laura how he was going to be married, I could feel the disappointment flowing through her. The fruited future she thought she was going to have with Jim turned into a barren desert. For one brief second she was living in reality. Now Jim pulled her from her shell into the world and then slammed her right back and threw away the key.

I curse Tom for leaving his family—how horrible and depressing the two women were. They would be crippled without him. So much hardship with him, imagine what it would be like without him.

And finally, the critic's voice, Zach:

Nothing personal to Tennessee Williams fans, but I don't like him at all. Let's be honest, at first all of his symbolic stuff was cute, but now it's getting out of hand. Okay, so Laura's glass menagerie breaks—am I as a reader supposed to associate that with the death of Laura's hope and soul? I hope not. And how about dear ol' dad—is his smiling face supposed to tell us that there is hope in the Wingfield's squalid house? Let's not be silly.

As a researcher as well as a teacher, I asked the students to evaluate the two reading and writing experiences believing, like Culler (1980), that when we make explicit what we do when reading and interpreting, we gain "in self-awareness and awareness of the nature of literature as an institution" (p. 116). I made up questionnaires with ample room for

written explanations of their answers. Like literary scholars, they offered
their responses to the responses.

To my surprise, twice as many students enjoyed the ficitonal journals as enjoyed the reader-response journals. They discerned that while
they enjoyed *The Glass Menagerie* more, the ficitional journal for *The
Crucible* was still the one they preferred! Many of them wrote explanations similar to Isabella's (their classmate): "With the fictional journal I
got to take the story and use my imagination to explain it. It was a lot of
fun and creative"; and Kena's, another classmate: "I enjoyed the fictional
journal because writing it I could become a significant member of the
play."

Pedro wrote, "I like the fictional journals because I like writing a
story about the play instead of just writing *about* the play," and
Matthew explained in a group discussion, "If I make up my own
character I feel like I've taken part in writing the play which helps me
understand it because I feel I collaborated with the author." In fact, what
students enjoyed most about the exercise was that they were actively
creating something they could identify as a new text; they transformed
into written language the mental activity of creating a text that occurs
whenever we are reading.

They seemed closely aligned with what Jane Tompkins (1980) describes as the classical response to literature: "response conceived as
action." Not that they took political action or changed their moral
behavior, but as Miriam wrote about her experience with fictional
journals, "I felt like I was part of the action." While I realize that
fictional journals still do not testify that the students experienced the
text as a "force exerted upon the world" (Tompkins), they did feel that
writing about the text as if they had participated in the action was
empowering and gave them an opportunity to "do" rather than just to
"signify."

Those students who enjoyed the reader-response journals more saw
it as a chance to "write about your inner feelings" (Mechelle) and "from
your heart" (Chris). Very often they considered the fictional journals just
a summary and were not able to reach the point that Gemma explains so
well: "I felt the fictional journal wasn't so fictional because I was
writing my ideas but in someone else's brain and time."

In answering the second question of the questionnaire, Which
journal helped you to understand or become more involved with the
play?, the ratio changed and, while a small proportion felt both journals
helped, most favored the reader-response journal. In other words, while
the ficitonal journal was more enjoyable, the other was more "educational." But their reasons were more varied than uniform.

For the third question, I asked students whether they perceived the
constant writing about the plays as an aid or a hindrance to their
understanding. Only fifteen out of the ninety eighth graders polled felt
the writing a hindrance. Lisi described what I hypothesized might occur:
"If you became involved with the play you were forced to cut yourself off
and write." But almost all the students agreed with Ethan: "I thought
about it more when I was forced to by the writing," and Alfonso: "The
more I wrote, the more I understood," and Deirdre: "I have a habit of

speed reading through books but doing the journal made my reading less of a routine." As Eva explained, "You could keep your thoughts organized and you didn't forget how you felt the minute you read a part."

The complementary nature of the processes of reading and writing becomes obvious when students are engaged in them concurrently. Lê (1984) explains that "reading is not just to 'comprehend.' It is also a meditative process," a process with a continual "flow of thoughts." Writing, too, provides us with a meditative process (Tashlik, 1975). In writing about reading, then, we can literally see how we have constructed meaning recursively and how we go on to project meaning forward. As my student Paul explained, through the journals he "could focus on what occurred so far and was more prepared for the rest of the book." Jacob wrote that the journals made him "think of the coming scene and that would add suspense to the reading." Matthew thought that through journals you could "go back to what you had previously written and...remember it, then build on what you had said or contradict it if you changed your mind." Adrienne said the journals helped because "you think faster than you write, so when you write you go slower and you feel how you're trying to put it down and how it will make sense not only to you but to the person who's reading it."

Literary journals offer students an active and concrete means of participating in the text. Through their writing, students add their own voice to the voice of the author. The writing helps them make the connections needed for a deeper understanding and knowledge of the work and, indeed, to discover new connections is to make discourse (Knoblauch and Brannon, 1984). The students feel themselves engaged and take ownership of the text, even a text they do not necessarily enjoy. I think this "action model" of literary discourse can provide us with a new means of conceptualizing our literature curricula. Active interpretive modes, including journals and fictional journals, deserve more than just lip service; they ought to occupy a central position in our literature and reading programs. Unfortunately, they do not.

True, it is easier to assess multiple-choice grids or look up the "right answers" in teacher's editions of texts. But we must consider what it is we want our students to experience through reading and through literature. If all the questions have already been asked and all the answers are already known, what is the sense of exploring a text and creating meaning? Both students and teachers are diminished by depending on others to define and interpret what we ourselves have read. If teachers are willing to take risks and have a classroom come alive with energy and creative thought and "interpretation battles," then developing criteria for assessment becomes possible and rather easy.

Too often teachers minimize the opportunities for "action model" assignments because we lack the experience of interacting with texts in other than traditional ways. How many of us have written fictional or response journals while reading a novel or a play? Our own training militates against this sort of experience. We tend to teach as we've been taught, especially in a field as sacred as literature (for secondary teachers) and as imposing as reading comprehension (for elementary teachers).

The more often we do use the action models ourselves, the more we will understand the profound effect such writing can have on our comprehension of a text.

We need to trust the imagination more, to come to terms with the way in which the imagination works actively to help us understand what we've read. To read fiction and to deny the demand it makes upon the mind's creativity is a contradiction of terms; yet this is what we do daily in our lessons and in the types of reading and literature tests we devise. Reader-response theories clearly show that reading is a creative act of the mind at work, and the students' writing and testimonies show that literary journals tap the energy and excitement of the imagination and add a whole new dimension to what we teachers think of as reading and literary discourse.

References

Culler, J. (1980). Literary competence. In J. Tompkins, ed., *Reader-response criticism*. Baltimore: Johns Hopkins University Press, pp. 101-117.

Fish, S. (1980). *Is there a text in this class?* Cambridge, MA: Harvard University Press.

Knoblauch, C.H. & Brannon, L. (1984). *Rhetorical traditions and the teaching of writing*. Upper Montclair, NJ: Boynton/Cook.

Lê, T. (1984). Cognitive and meditative aspects of reading. *Language Arts, 61*.

Meyers, M. (1983, June). What action research is (and is not). The National Writing Project Network Newsletter, 5.

Michaels, W. (1980). The interpreter's self. In J. Tompkins, ed., *Reader-response criticism*. Baltimore: Johns Hopkins University Press, pp. 185-200.

Moffett, J. & Wagner, B.J. (1976). *Student-centered language arts and reading*. Boston: Houghton Mifflin.

————— . (1981). *Active voice*. Montclair, NJ: Boynton/Cook.

Tashlik, P. (1973, October). Writing as meditation. *Teachers & Writers Magazine*.

Tompkins, J. (Ed.) (1980). *Reader-response criticism*. Baltimore: Johns Hopkins University Press.

17.

Respecting Opinions:
Learning Logs in Middle School English

VIRGIL DAVALA

When I introduced learning logs to my seventh and eighth grade students during the past two school years, I wondered how they would respond. Would they see their writing as a means of making connections between their personal experiences and what they were reading and learning in class? Would regular expressive writing in these logs make their learning more memorable? In other words, would the logs really make a difference?

Making Connections

Students through writing *do* make connections between their personal experiences and those encountered in the classroom. When Jennifer states, "I write about stories and things that have happened to me," she is expressing those connections. Similarly, Danielle M.'s comment that "we get to write down what it feels like to be that person..." reflects the same kind of relationship. Students *are* better able to identify with the characters and situations they encounter in their readings when they discover similarities in their own backgrounds. They "tune in" to the curriculum when they explore it personally.

For example, to introduce a unit on Jack London's *The Call of the Wild*, I asked my seventh graders to do a focused freewriting on one of four concepts—survival, leadership, courage, success—which I considered important to their understanding of the novel. I directed them to define the term(s) of their choice and try to recall and describe a personal experience the word(s) brought to mind. For Bill, the suggestion triggered a personal memory of what it felt like to be lost in unfamiliar surroundings:

Survival—when a person or any other living thing is *trying to stay alive in a place where that person is "lost."* When I survived— Colorado, 1982—my classmates and I were going on a field trip to the mountains. We were all trying to reach the peak. High school students were at the lead, some others and I were right behind them, the others were far behind. Our small "team" stopped to rest. When we started off, we lost eye contact with our guides. We decided to keep going.... But at one point, the main road we were following became two narrow paths. After minutes of thinking, we decided to go to the left road. After one hour of hiking, we were

absolutely lost. We didn't know where we were. So we decided to
go back, but on our way, we met many crossroads. After a long
time (about three hours) we thought we were lost forever. We
decided to just keep going down. . . . Many hours later, we found
the other students and teachers.

Recalling his own experience provided Bill with a frame of reference for
better understanding Buck's difficulties in the novel and sharing his
feelings and those of the other characters. After reading several chapters,
Bill wrote this response, identifying with the "human-like personalities"
of the sled dogs:

I think Spitz is doing what I would have done, which is to show off
how strong he is by pushing around someone who is not as good a
fighter, Buck. I think Buck did the right thing by fighting with
Spitz. At first Buck wanted to stay away from any fights, but after
his victory against Spitz, he wanted to show off like Spitz did. I
think this change was good since he could fight so well. But still,
this change could have brought him a lot of trouble.

Within the framework of scheduled reading deadlines, my students
completed the novel at various rates, their assignment being to write and
turn in a response after reading each chapter. I suggested a few concepts
and questions to focus their responses but kept these minimal, mainly
requesting their feelings, opinions and questions to which I in turn
briefly responded. The two samples which follow show the personal
involvement and understanding these students experienced with their
reading; their written responses were the means of communicating those
connections to themselves and me.

Right now I am almost to the third chapter, and between the
second and third all the stuff is interesting. It is unusual to see that
a dog is *learning* so much. I have even benefited from the story. I
know now that if I am stuck in the cold and there is snow on the
ground I would bury myself in it.

Jack

I've just now finished chapter four and I think it is the best so far.
In this chapter Buck is now the leader and has somewhat aged.
Spitz is now dead, "courtesy" of Buck. Dave gets sick and is killed
by the revolver. Buck builds up confidence and accepts the fact that
he will not return to his old peaceful home. Buck also has
flashbacks, especially those of the "cruel" man in the red sweater
and of the fight that took place between Spitz and himself. Buck is
now very wise and respected by his drivers and by the other sled
dogs.

Dan

As we finished the unit on *The Call of the Wild,* I asked students to
share their opinions on keeping response logs to the novel. Three
reactions in particular show how students valued their log writings as a
way of organizing concepts in a more personal and meaningful way:

The log responses I wrote were helpful in getting the story together and to flashback the chapter. For the test all I had to do was look at my logs.

Adam

I think the log responses made me think more about the story. Your comments were helpful and made me understand the story a little better. At first writing logs was a pain but then I enjoyed writing them.

Susan

I enjoyed *The Call of the Wild* immensely, even though I've read the book before... The comments you made on the responses made me feel good because you can realize the way I feel about the story and agree or disagree with it. The responses to the story in each chapter arranged my thoughts so I could have a clear view of the story, and at the same time realize my own feelings.

Alex

Alex's response especially intrigued me when he commented that his log helped him "realize his own feelings" about the story. I sensed his recognition of writing's power for clarifying ideas and connecting them to the reader's experience.

Expressing Feelings

When classroom journal writing is done regularly, students develop a routine that enables many to see value beyond a teacher-initiated requirement. Because I expected that seventh and eighth graders might have difficulty disciplining themselves to view learning logs seriously unless I provided an initial incentive, this year I made this the first required section of their English class notebook. I was not surprised by these log responses to questions I asked early in the year, "What kinds of things do you write in your logs?" and "Why do you keep a log in English?":

I write in my learning log things that relate to the subject matter.... I keep a log because I can use it as a reference on a notebook quiz. I also keep it because I have to.

Miguel

We write about stories we've read in class and other stuff we have to write about. We keep a log because we have to. I wouldn't if I didn't have to.

Lisa

As the year progressed, I still found that most students needed the incentive of meeting a course requirement to keep writing going, but there was less questioning about what *I* wanted when log writing was done. Many students were writing much more and for a longer time than I had earlier observed. While not all became equally involved, most seemed to be serious about their writing and saw their logs as something important. Nicole's observations indicate this kind of personal meaning responding in journals gives:

> I write a lot of things in my learning log. Most of it is freewriting.
> I like to write in it. Our class writes on stories we have read, how
> we feel about things, and others. I feel it is important to do this. I
> enjoy writing very much in my log.

The learning log, then, provides a place for students to express
feelings freely. They verbalize their satisfaction, success, and happiness
when things go well. And they comment that their logs are a means of
releasing other emotions—tension, frustration, anger, resentment—of
getting their feelings out and making them recognizable and acceptable
on paper:

> I like to look back at it and see what I wrote, and if there's no one
> to listen to what I have to say, I can write it down, and it will make
> me feel better.
>
> Missy

> I write in my learning log because it helps me get some things out
> of my mind.
>
> Courtney

> I think writing about my report put me at ease because I had all of
> these mixed feelings bottled up inside of me.
>
> Jon

These responses together indicate to me how important it is to provide
outlets for students at this stage of their educational and personal
development. Missy's comment reinforces what I observe so many times
in adolescent behavior: the significance of peer approval and support.
Courtney's and Jon's reactions similarly point to the value this writing
can have. These students appreciate the log as a place to express feelings
freely. "Viewing" feelings on paper appears to make the difference, as
Anji indicates when she writes: "I think that in writing this log entry I
realized a lot of feelings that I never would have just thought about in
my mind."

Because writing provides evidence in front of them, students can
keep track of progress effectively and positively. Many see their logs as a
means of keeping track of where they are and as a way of measuring
growth:

> I write about what I do in class and what I have learned...I write
> in it because Mrs. Davala tells me to but mainly so I can remember
> what I learned.
>
> Victoria

> I write what I'm thinking about, I write down my thoughts
> basically...it's fun to go back and see what you've written....
> Anji

> I keep a log so I can look back and see how I've improved as the
> year goes by.
>
> Danielle W.

Danielle's comment in particular reflects the kind of honest assessment
the learning log promotes, as do the following responses to presenting
oral book reports and writing about those presentations:

I think oral book reports are fun. The only thing is that I don't think any one else likes them. I don't mind getting up and talking or performing in front of people. I did have some butterflies in my stomach but they went away when I went up. As a listener, I enjoyed hearing the book reports. Some people were boring and took too long. Other people were too nervous and sped their reports up. Then there were some people who did really well, whom I liked to hear.

Linda

I personally hate speaking in front of a group. I find it an ordeal, to speak in front of my friends especially. I have all the classic nervous symptoms: dry throat, sweaty palms and a dull nervous feeling in my stomach. The worst part is when you get up your nerve to go to the podium and get in front of the class, you say your title and get a groan. Then you wonder if you will survive.

Sarah

My speaking in front of audiences has always been not one of my better things. For hours during the day I worry about speaking in front of twenty-six people. In the last few minutes and as I walk to the front of the room I feel as if the whole world can hear my heart beating.

I enjoy being a part of the audience much more than giving my book report. I enjoy listening to others interpret their books.

Marianne

Writing in my log helped me understand my grade a little bit more. When I got the grade, a 42 [B], I was really down on myself. But when I started writing about my book report I realized why I got that grade.

Marcelo

I felt that it [log] gave me ideas about how I was going to do my next report and what I should do better than my last report...

Susan

These reactions point out the way in which log writing helps students view honestly and constructively their accomplishments and set goals for improvement. This same kind of attitude is expressed in these responses to individualized study of a skills lesson on verbs. Although perfection was not necessarily achieved, the logs reflect positive feelings about accomplishments and encourage students, through their writing, to verbalize and communicate questions about confusing parts of the lesson. From my perspective as teacher, their responses helped me assess their individual needs as learners.

I think I am well ahead on verbs. I believe this because I didn't get any wrong on the diagnostic test. I feel it helped me a lot. I understand the past, present, and past participles.

Miguel

As of now I feel quite comfortable with verbs. I'm confused about things such as the past tense of words like swim, drink, and sink. Words that behave this way are hard to remember.

Carol

Verbs to me have always been confusing, but after the class discussed some pages in the book and did the diagnostic test, I understood verbs better. The main thing that concerns me is the words of past tense and when to use them and where. After I missed the five problems on the test, I had to do some exercises in the book. This was very confusing and mixed me up. I would much rather we discuss the verbs together as a class.

Jill

...I really enjoyed working by myself. Working by myself helped me understand verbs better. It gave me time to stop and think about what I was doing. Verbs are not my favorite subject but they weren't as hard this time. I understand them a lot better and I won't mind doing them again. I cannot do great with verbs but I'm doing better.

Danielle M.

This last response particularly interested me when Danielle said individualized study "gave me time to stop and think about what I was doing." *Writing* about these studies further provides that "time to stop and think."

I also found "time out" for writing effective in helping my students assess their progress in developing group process skills. As we worked toward the goal of building effective reading/writing groups, I directed them upon completing various tasks to respond in their logs to their group's performance. I asked them to comment honestly on things that went well, helping and hindering behaviors, and skills needing improvement. The following observations indicate varying degrees of group success, but all demonstrate that writing aids clarification of progress and encourages students to assume responsibility for continued improvement.

Our group seemed to me very frustrating; no one really listened to anybody. Our group did complete the task. We all got to read and answer the questions on our cards. Not everyone participated, and a lot of people usually interrupted....

I don't have any idea of what my group felt like. But they all must be pretty bored. Next time our group will have to pay attention and not interrupt. From five to ten I rate my group a six.

Rob

Our group completed the task, and, I think did it quite well. Everyone participated and was helpful in getting things done, although there was a little bit of dominating. We agreed to rate it a 7.6. I think that we will work well together.

Carol

"Owning" Learning

When learning logs become a regular part of classroom activities, students take an active part in their own learning. Writing physically involves each and every student and so calls for active participation in class. Sharing writings likewise increases participation in discussion when *each* student is required or encouraged to share from his or her log. While I still observe some reluctance to share, having words on paper in front of them appears to alleviate the hesitation many students feel:

> I was not as nervous talking about how I felt as I was in giving my report.
>
> Bobby

> As we discussed reports, I felt better....I know that everyone felt the same way at first.
>
> Miguel

> ...when we had the discussion in class it really helped me out because I think when I just talk out it's harder, so the log just helped me because when it was my turn to talk then I just had to read off my paper.
>
> Victoria

Stephanie's comment that "we got to hear other people's responses" points again to the value these students place on peer opinions. It further indicates to me that the sharing of their logs promotes a classroom environment where respect for the value of each person's opinion is nurtured. Miguel's response emphasizes the security that is fostered by such an environment; Victoria's shows how writing before sharing opinions can build confidence.

Implications

I believe that learning logs *do* make a difference for students in the English classroom, so much so that I plan to continue to make them an intrinsic part of my program. Since I still feel strongly that the incentive of a course requirement is needed to keep writing going, I will continue to make the log a mandatory section of the English notebook.

I found the learning log relatively easy to work into my grading system by checking the writings in the same way I evaluated other homework and classwork, with full credit ($\checkmark$) awarded so long as the log requirement had been met. I discovered I could quickly glance at papers and make the rounds of the room within five minutes, no more nor less time than I needed to check other tasks. Sometimes I collected writings, skim-read them, and returned them with credit noted. And occasionally I varied the pattern by giving credit as logs were shared informally in groups or with the class. Here the requirement was to "volunteer" something orally from the written work; I awarded full credit simply for sharing and did not look at the papers at all. To accommodate the learning log, then, the nature of some homework or classwork assignments had changed, but I found that the concept fit more easily into my classroom system than I had expected.

I also found the idea of keeping a learning log easier to introduce and more quickly understood by students than I had anticipated. During the first days of school, we brainstormed together, recording ideas about what a "learning log" might be. We discussed both parts of the term and defined it as a special kind of journal, a record of learning. We began to establish this section of the English notebook as a place to record thoughts, feelings, interests, observations, etc. We read aloud excerpts from Donald Murray's *Write to Learn* (1984) and discussed freewriting and focused freewriting. I encouraged students to choose their own formats for their logs by accepting their lists, outlines, charts, pictures, phrases, and writings in various forms. While many selected lists, phrases, or a mixture of phrases and sentences as a pattern for their writing, others experimented on occasion with poetry, dialogues, and short story forms.

While the log didn't work equally for all students, I am encouraged by the positive responses many students wrote about keeping their logs. I hope to find ways of using classroom journal writing to help others develop greater responsibility for—and ownership of—their learning.

When I encouraged my students to respond openly in their logs and to listen to each other when writings were shared, they discovered that their opinions had value and would be respected. In turn, I gained an understanding of my role as a facilitator of learning. The learning log has helped us to build a cohesive classroom environment where we can work together so that real learning can occur.

References

Ellis, K. (1984). *Writing to learn about group process.* This workshop/presentation was shared during the North Virginia Writing Project Summer Institute at George Mason Univeristy, Fairfax, Virginia. It has been an invaluable resource containing suggested ways of using writing to aid in the development of group skills.

Fulwiler, T. (1982). The personal connection: Journal writing across the curriculum. In T. Fulwiler & A. Young, eds. *Language connections: Writing and reading across the curriculum.* Urbana, IL: NCTE.

Jones, J. (1982). *Writing before reading.* This handout, produced during the Northern Virginia Writing Project Summer Institute, contains excellent activities. The suggestions for writing before and in response to reading poetry have been particularly helpful.

Murray, D. (1984). *Write to learn.* New York: Holt, Rinehart and Winston.

Special thanks to my seventh and eighth grade students at Longfellow Intermediate School, Fairfax County, Virginia, and particularly to those quoted in my paper. I appreciate their permission to use samples from their logs and to identify them by name. In some instances, names have been changed.

18.

I Have a Loose Tooth and
Other Unphotographable Events:
Tales from a First Grade Journal

RUTH NATHAN

For about three months, Janet Edwards and I worked together in her first grade room encouraging her children to write. We introduced a writing program where the youngsters eagerly chose their own topics and invented spellings that enabled them to write any word they wanted. Daily, we read first-rate stories to the class, the best our culture has to offer; talked about being authors ourselves; modeled writing strategies; and encouraged plenty of oral language play. In other words, we created a dynamic and interactive literate environment.

In addition to all of this, the children wrote in journals. For ten to fifteen minutes each day they scribbled, doodled, drew, or wrote about whatever they wished. Mrs. Edwards read their entries and frequently wrote back. In the interest of science, I began to copy a few journal entries, one here, one there, so captivated was I by the sheer power of what I believed the children were teaching *themselves*. What follows are brief extracts from Claudia's journal, one of Mrs. Edwards' twenty-eight children.

9-26-84
MY FAVRet food is lamChoPs

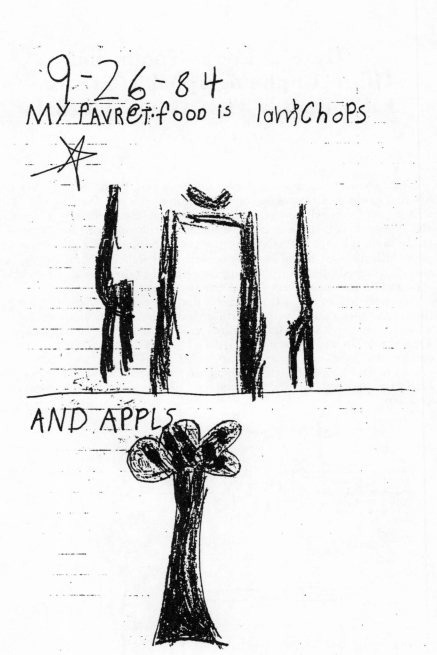

AND APPLS

11-26-84

I Had a Good time ug north

12-20-84

tomro is My BiRthDay my Grama and
Grampa are Comeing we are having
Chines food and cake

Start 1-4-84

This is a stry aBowt
an oid man and a old Wamin
Tha livd in an old howse
Tha were pore and Ther
howse was not prety
Tha Bothe had gray her
and Blue ees and Tha
livde in The woos and
Tha were Frens wthe The
animis The Animis liked them

This stry is aBowt Wen
a man Coid up The old
man it was a rony Day
he askt if He cooe
wrcke for him The old man
Sad yes I Do want To
Wrke fonyou The old man
and Woman wen So happy
now We will not Be pore
The nexDay The old man
Went To Wrck in The
Evng He came BaKe with
Two Doors The oid womin
was so Happy and The old
man side He liked his Work
He Began giting more and
more monny and soon Tha
wernt pore any more and
That is The End of my story
aBowt The old man and
The oid womin By Clauia

The End

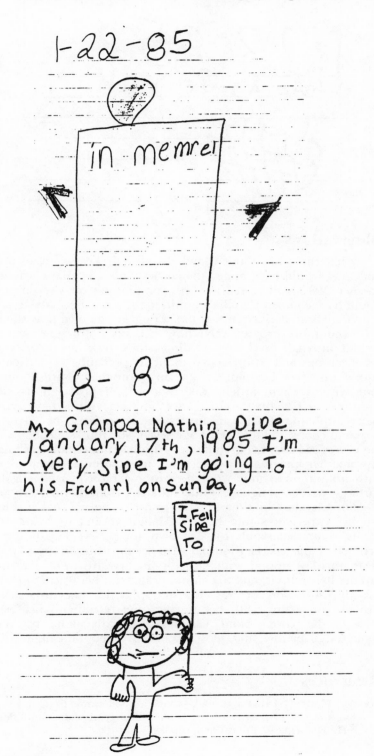

1-22-85

in memrel

1-18- 85

My Granpa Nathin Dive
January 17th, 1985 I'm
very Side I'm going To
his Frunrl on Sunday

I Fell
Side
To

1-23-85

I have a loose tuth

Observations

What can I say about Claudia's journal? Years ago, as a doctoral student, I would have mined the entries with a scholar's zeal, as Garth Boomer (1984) said he did with his son Simon's pre-sleep transcripts. I would have counted Claudia's t-units, done syntactic analyses, structural analyses, vocabulary counts. I, too, would have noted how she built up her word units progressively; how her story structures expanded to include internal, psychological dimensions; how her pictures enlarged her meanings and incorporated thoughts probably too difficult to put into words. Now I cannot do this, any more than Garth Boomer (1984) could in his recent article. Like Boomer, "I just want to show."

Look at Claudia's journal. See how her entries have captured so many unphotographable memories: she is an artist; her favorite foods are lamb chops and apples; at age seven, she thinks elephants are cute; she is very sad over her grandfather's death. And see how her journal has captured her imaginative wanderings: forest animals living comfortably with an old man and woman, rainbow monsters having birthday parties,—written language quite different from normal school work.

For Claudia, the time to write in her school journal enabled her to put her experiences into her own language and to create imaginary events, some remarkably like her own, for her ever-expanding array of fictional characters. Her journal gave her the opportunity to try on new ideas; to play around with difficult literary structures, like stories; to explore her feelings; and to communicate with her teacher in a thoughtful, unrushed sort of way. She has played, associated, shared, and created, interacting with her teacher, and often with her classmates, through the written word. Claudia, essentially alone, teaches *herself* about language, life, and, most importantly, about the interaction of the two.

References

Boomer, Garth (1984). Piggy nick—that's a good word. In James Britton, ed. *English teaching: An international exchange.* London and Portsmouth, NH: Heinemann Educational Books.

19.

Writing and Learning, Grade Three

TOBY FULWILER

Look with me at Megan's journal and watch how she uses language to explain her experience to herself. Megan, a third grader in a Michigan elementary school, wrote in her journal several times a week, usually in response to a prompt from her teacher, Jean Chilcote, and saved this personal, nongraded writing in a red pocket folder. I have chosen to look at four entries, written at different times during the year, because they illustrate well the possibilities for using journals "across the curriculum," to help young students become more aware of themselves as writers and learners. These entries are not examples of precocious eight-year-old perception. Rather, they represent language use more normal than not among children in the early elementary grades—which is precisely why they are important: they suggest writing that is possible for many, rather than exceptional for a few.

In the following journal entry, Megan wrote about her reaction to the first fire drill of the year, in September:

> Yesterday a fire drill went off. We all lined up at the door it felt kinda skary and exiting at the same moment we went out-side and I still had my pencil I thought it was funny! Then we went in to work again we were all talking at ounce it was fun

This piece has the basic narrative structure of child talk, with simple sentences and a few conjunctions. Megan recounts her experience about the fire drill as she would tell a story: "Yesterday this happened....And then this happened..." and so on; in doing so she keeps her chronology intact, using past-tense verb forms with apparent ease. Since narrative is how most of us, adults and children, store and recall experience, we are pleased that she writes both comfortably and correctly in this mode.

We might notice where Megan adds important, personal information to her narrative: the experience "felt kinda skary and exsiting at the same moment," a phrase which reveals Megan's ability to express well conflicting emotions. We also see her laughing at the incongruity: "I still had my pencil" (out here on the grass, outside the classroom, far from any paper). "I thought it was funny!" Her ability to separate herself from her tangible experience, and even laugh gently at herself, suggests a healthy self-awareness. The teacher who reads carefully even such simple and informal texts as this, learns just how her students look at themselves, their world, and their place in it. She can then build more elaborate, formal, and individualized assignments based on this knowledge.

If the omissions in punctuation and errors in spelling bother some adults, we might point out what those omissions and errors tell us: first, it is evident that Megan thinks out loud in whole sentences; she does forget a few periods, but she uses both periods and exclamation marks successfully elsewhere. Practice will provide the periods. The misspellings (kinda, skary, exsiting) are phonetic, based on hearing spoken words; she's using a good rule base to figure out untried words. Practice and time will take care of the spelling too.

Look at another entry, written a few days later, and enter again the writer's mind. Here Megan responds to the teacher's direction: Write all the words that come to mind as rapidly as you can in the next few minutes:

> Words on my mind snuwd,
> slusly, wet, cloudy, school,
> sickness, cold, toothbrush,
> hairbrush, comp, spoon, mom,
> lunch, dad, work, map, clock,
> desk, dress, mad, sad, glad,
> supper, sock, calk, white, milk,
> flower, meat,

At first I'm amused—and then I'm impressed—by this simple activity. Megan's words allow us a glimpse of her early morning train of thought; we see in quick succession: (1) a catalogue of Michigan weather, (2) states of health, (3) morning bathroom rituals, (4) family breakfast activities, (5) parental sex roles, (6) a classroom inventory, (7) rhyme games, (8) color games, and (9) free association with food. The mind ranges widely in a few minutes of writing.

But why would this quick bit of writing be important to either student or teacher? (Well, at the very least it's a helluva comma exercise!) This free-association writing lets the writer both survey what's on her mind and capture it for examination, manipulation, and development. From any one of the word clusters listed above, the writer, with or without teacher help, could move in several directions: writing family stories with accurate, telling detail; sharing with classmates mutual morning rituals; writing poetry based on rhyme, rhythm, and association; exploring the meaning, history, and use of familiar words; and so on. Practiced often, such exercises help children locate and shape mental images into concrete language.

At mid-year, Megan and her classmates listened to an oral reading of Harriet Tubman's biography, which tells the story of the underground railroad. In response to the teacher's request to write about the story in any way they wanted, Megan chose to role play how she would have felt were she the slave or master. Here is what she wrote:

> February 8, 1979
>
> The color black, nothing
> The color white, everything
>
> If I were a black slave I would
> feel like who are these people? What
> do thay want? If I were a
> slave master I would get the family
> together and take one at a time
> to the North in a car with a
> blanket over them

Again, the journal writing assignment allows the third graders to stretch themselves in whatever direction they choose, without risk of censure or correction. Here, unlike the previous assignments, the writer chooses to make judgments based on some developing scale of values. No doubt the book, teacher, classmates, and her family provided a controlled context in which to make decisions. But by reacting in writing, young Megan was forced to find her own language to express her views, both to herself and to the teacher who would, at some time, read the journal. And in finding her own language, she selects and discards and arranges and rearranges her thoughts and emotions until some formulation seems just right: "I would feel like who are these people? What do they want?" Good questions!

One could argue that Megan did not really understand the role of the "slave master" in this tragic drama (do we?). No, he would not "take one at a time to the North in a car," would he? But eight-year-old Megan would. And if she might be questioned about whether or not they had cars in the mid-nineteenth century, she might, of course, respond: but I'd have one now. Or Megan could have misunderstood and confused the phrase "slave master" with "slave leader" (like Harriet Tubman). If so, of course, the teacher now has good material to introduce a clarifying discussion to the whole class—and once again the writing feeds the talking and leads to understanding.

Let me emphasize again the importance of asking for *writing* in conjunction with such a discussion: at the very least, it allows the writers to find and rehearse their thoughts before they speak. It may also commit the writer to a more firmly held position because she worked hard to establish her stand in concrete black-lettered language. Finally, the private reaction in writing, prior to public discussion, allows the writer to explore the issue without being directed first by other people's opinions; as a result, I believe, more personal writing is a direct route to more autonomous thinking.

Look at one more of Megan's journal entries, this one written in May, near the end of the school year, about a trip to the local newspaper:

> Dear Journal,
> We went down to the mining Gazette yesterday to see the printing and stuff. We all got a free newspaper and these little peices of medalle with words on it raised on it, backwords. Did you know that before thay print it the photograph and words are ~~waxed~~ waxed on like this: Waxed, Waxed, Waxed and so on.
>
> [a drawing of a framed box containing three small boxed labels reading "Waxed," "Waxed," "Waxed"]

Like the very first entry we looked at, Megan again writes about an experience which happened the day before, beginning in narrative voice: "We went down to the mining Gazette yesterday...." But something quite interesting happens midway in this piece: she switches to expository mode: "Did you know...." and so attempts to explain (to herself? her journal? her teacher?) what they do when they put a newspaper toegether. Here is a task quite different from straight narration, the language in which most of us structure yesterday's experience. While she may often explain things orally to her friends (how to hold a jump rope, how to cross a street), the same act in writing demands a new consciousness; Megan must now address an audience she cannot see.

Since Megan cannot use facial expressions or hands, she resorts to equivalent gestures in the drawing which accompanies the writing—her first "technical writing." Of course, she is not entirely successful in her description of the waxing process, resorting, as she does, to a repetition of the word "waxed" to make the most of her point. But who would intrude here with lessons on technical illustration? That may come later, if at all, and surely in another context. Here and now, Megan is writing to a safe and trusted friend, "Dear Journal," to whom she will explain just as much as she needs to.

One last point about the mechanics in this entry. While our young writer still misspells a few words, she continues to do so according to rules—or rules momentarily confused. More importantly, look at the freedom with which she uses words she wants to, that she believes are hers, and so uses with authority: "peices" and "meddle" just haven't shown up yet on those weekly spelling lists. And look at the punctuation: the periods are now in good shape, the commas in place, and even a perfect colon—which some of my eighteen-year-old college students still struggle with. Looking at these four entries, spread out over the year, I am most pleased with the progress—the progress of progress—I see, much of it through informal writing, in that third grade year.

I especially enjoyed writing about Megan's journal because I so enjoyed watching her try to explain, in words and sentences, what was happening in her world. I enjoyed it then, in 1978, as she wrote it, and again now, in 1984, as I reread it. In fact, I even feel just a little nostalgic, as a father does now and then, as I, too, reexperience that year of fire drills, list making, story reading, and field trips. But that's something else journals do so well—take you back in time, to the moment of the writing, to since forgotten thought, as well as to that cold, "slushly" Michigan weather.

Megan, now fourteen, is my older daughter, and I still remember Jean Chilcote explaining patiently to me how she worked the journal in among the lessons in reading, spelling, mathematics, social studies, science, and composition. She assigned journal writing daily, often first thing in the morning, to help students explore, on their own, whatever subjects they wished to. As a college English teacher, schooled by James Moffett, James Britton, and Ken Macrorie, I already knew journals belonged across the curriculum, in the compartmentalized subject areas of the higher grades. Jean convinced me, as she had convinced Megan, that journals also belonged in grade three. For Megan, all year long, journals proved a safe place in which to think freely and play with language. Megan, now in tenth grade, has written the following piece reflecting on the journals she has kept since then.

Still Writing and Learning, Grade Ten

Megan Fulwiler

Last night Dad showed us slides from his Ft. Lauderdale trip when he was eighteen. He and his friends all looked so cool. I wonder where those shades went to? Told Dad he looked good with a bleached blonde crew cut. Those long shorts were great! Then there's Dad on his silver motor-scooter. And the red '53 Studebaker all shined up in the driveway. Mom thinks it's great that Dad has records of his past. Me too. I'm already planning my Ft. Lauderdale trip. Maybe that's why I keep a journal. (No, not to go to Ft. Lauderdale. To have a record of my past.)

I used to have a diary in elementary school. In fact, Dad wrote an article about some of my third grade entries from my school journal. In a way, my own slide show. What Dad didn't show you are the entries from my personal diary, which include such profound thoughts as:

February 16, 1978
I and my friend Jennifer Foster had 4, fights today. And we foght
and foght. She even said that I was dump.
February 28, 1978
This week I take cold lunch. So does Jennifer foster. It is fun.
March ninth, 1978
I hate Jennifer Foster!

I didn't start keeping a journal regularly until sixth grade. It started
out as a place to write down story ideas and a record of the day's events.
Dec. 6, 1981
I'm class president!! I won by one vote. Tomorrow is our first class
meeting, we have to discuss the Christmas party. Missy Archambeau,
who is class secretary (yuck!) wants our class to invite all the other
classes into our room and have a dance. I'll bet the only reason she
wants that is so she'll see Jamie R. (double yuck!)

But gradually my journal developed into a private place where I
could write to myself. It became an extension of my mind. It was
somewhere I could work out my feelings, ask questions, find answers
and write down and organize all my floating thoughts.
March 24, 1983
Sitting here by my open window, I realize that there will always be
people better than me and it's too exhausting and it's not worth it
to compete with them.

And a place to write about my newest boyfriend:
November 25, 1983
You will not believe this. I am going out with Sean. Can you take
it?! He asked me out Nov. 22, after school.

And to record my summer trip to England to visit my best friend
Anne:
July, 1984
Right now I'm in England! I've been here not quite a week now.
Went to Bath today. God do I love it there! The Royal Crescent is
absolutely goergous! When I graduate I want to live in Bath for a
year, be on my own and totally independent.

And a place to vent my frustrations:
December 4, 1984
I still feel sick about school. I have this nagging feeling that I'm
wasting some of the awesomest years of my life getting up at 6:00,
going to school, sitting in tedious classes (not boring, I mean I
don't get straight A's). What is a "grade"? Where is it going to get
you in life? How can someone be categorized by a letter? I hate
being categorized.

Sometimes I wouldn't write for days, sometimes even weeks, it was
impossible for me to make up for missed time but I didn't have to. This
was for me and me only. I've kept a journal now for almost five years. I
love reading my old entries. They jog my memory and prove to me that
my problems are never as bad as they seem. For example:

November 11, 1981
With my short hair, Matthew, Craig and Dean are calling me
Elmer Fudd. I don't like it at all. I mean, I don't want to be called
Elmer Fudd, who does? I'm sick and tired of being called names.

I can laugh now at something that seemed to be the end of the
world four years ago. The older I get, the deeper some of my questions
get. Last summer I wrote this while spending three weeks at our cottage
in Michigan on Lake Superior:

July 29, 1985
What is a person's soul? I was thinking about that down at the
creek. It's so peaceful when I'm down there alone. Soul. Soul. I
used to think it was located somewhere around the kidneys. Maybe
it's *you*. Not your body or anything visible, but your ideas,
thoughts, likes/dislikes, experiences—the voice inside your head
that are words/concepts, not really a voice. I'm getting really tired
& this is getting really heavy.

Lately, I've been writing a lot of poetry, trying to figure out what's
going on in my life. The journal is a good place to do this in:

my name is megan fulwiler
i'm a sophomore
and this is a poem about
me.
i love to dance
listen to U2
eat oreos, whole
read a great book, like
Gone With the Wind and
cry when i watch the movie
alone.
running is something i do
but not love
school is something i do
but not love
people are the cherries on top of
old smokey and
the telephone was
a great invention
i called ann
dad showed me the
bill, 27.85
pretty neat, huh.
going barefoot is the
only way to go
swimming is fun but
chlorine is not
pasta was a great invention too
i think love is great
but i doubt i've ever
known the real

true kind
do you wonder, too
if i ever will?

clothes are an obsession
money and time are
precious gems in a
dirty snowbank
i get my licence in
less than five months.
life could easily be lived
in sweatpants. Hmmm, I'll
have to think about this one.
i think boyfriends are
like brussel sprouts. Hmmm,
you'll have to think about
        that one.

Looking back, I see that my entries became progressively more personal as I became more comfortable with writing. My journals have become a record of my life, of my growing up, of problems, pains, and joys.

Thanks Dad, for a great idea.

20.

Fifth Grade Journals:
Results and Surprises

PATRICIA McGONEGAL

My twelve-year-old son, Joe, is going off to study in a Russian classroom again today. He is to wear a white shirt with a red kerchief, like all the other kids in his class, and for one social studies hour today, his name will be Yuri and he will pretend to be a Russian child. He will learn what Russian children learn, play some of their games, taste the kind of food they eat. Joe's bright, energetic teacher knows something I am fast learning about education: doing it and being it beats studying it.

I'm an English teacher. I want my students to know what it's like to be writers. I want to show them that they can be writers, and successful ones, by looking around, thinking, and then writing down what they think. Later, together, we can work on polishing: finding better ways of saying what they said. But for now, early in fifth grade, I want to give them the idea that they can do it. They can *be* it.

Informal journal writing in all their subjects seems to give students this idea. Since the first day of school, when my partner, Grant, and I handed out clean new composition books to 42 ten-year-olds, we have asked them to write nearly every day in at least one of our academics: in social studies and math (Grant's disciplines), in English and science (my subjects).

We have made it clear from the start that anything they write in these journals is valid. We respect and encourage their thoughts, questions, digressions, dreams, complaints. These are the things that writers write and they are writers. They write enthusiastically and, I think, comfortably, because they see us writing while they write and hear us read our own imperfect words.

Naturally our questions and topics vary greatly. But our writing sessions follow a standard form. We pose a question or a suggested statement that springs naturally from a current topic, then ask the students to answer it, develop it, argue or dream on it for five minutes or so.

Early in the year it was necessary to insist they discipline themselves to keep writing constantly for this five-minute period. Into the third month of school now, this no longer seems necessary in most cases. They know that their words are valued and valid. After the time is up we share our writing; either in pairs (the most relaxed and non-threatening way), in small groups, or all together. Only constructive comments are made— a cardinal rule. No put-downs or rudeness.

From the first journal assignments of the year, the children gave us insights into what and how they were thinking, though these early writes were terse, taking fewer risks than they took later on.

What do you know about nouns?

There isnt a lot about nouns, well there isnt a lot about nouns that I know.

Shannon

What is a scientist?

A scientist is a person who figures out things about science and mixes potions and makes different kind of potions and figures all different things out.

Matt

On one of those early September days I wrote in my own journal: Answers were brief, hesitant. Nobody wanted to share, so I read mine, then let them discuss with a partner the main idea of what they wrote. I realize what is going to help a lot is my modeling. I read my entry, showing how informally you write in a journal, revealing humanity, vulnerability.

A major breakthrough was getting some students past the catch phrase "it was fun" in reply to recall-type questions. After a while they found it more interesting to share specifics. Audience reaction is better.

From our science observation unit:

Tell how you feel about our smell observations yesterday.

The vinegar smelled like a lemon mixed with pickles.

Angela

Explain to a newcomer what we did in science yesterday.

Yesterday we went outside and looked at trees. We took queens anns lace, broke it, and smeld it. It smelled like carrot.

Jason

Now that they were starting to communicate, I began using the journals to reach for some of my goals in teaching the content areas.

Assessing what students already know

A pretest in an atmosphere of journal writing is stress-free enough to give a very accurate picture of what they learned in "the other school."

Tell me what you know about sentences.

I know that a sentence has a period at the end of it. Every sentence has to start with a capital and I know a sentence is a statement. Also a line of words that tell you about stuff like for an example (The cat ran across the street) that is a sentence.

Jenny

Making knowledge part of student lives

Instead of teaching research skills in isolation, a teacher does well to give an assignment and illustrate research tools as they are called for in an assignment.

Before we started, however, I tried to get the children to think of research as pursuing information one needs in any part of life, in or out of school. I asked in the journals:

What might you like to do research about in your own life?

They gave back hopes, fears, ambitions, interests. What is the history of my family? How many gallons of water in the Pacific Ocean? Stars, horses, ornithology. Scott wrote out a big array.

...how war began and what caused it. I need to find out about indians and cowboys and everything that is in the past. Id realy like to know who bilt the first house and how you can make a motercycle because I don't got one and how you could make plastic or rubber or stickers.

We focused for a while on how to pursue those areas they brought up in the journals. I showed them the reference section of the library. We fooled around with the almanacs and encyclopedias. We talked about primary sources: Does anybody know a motorcycle expert?

Later on we thought about how to use these research tools to cover curriculum topics.

What would you like to learn about trees?

Some then gave themselves their science research assignments.

I'd like to know why palm trees grow only down south. Everybody says because they only live in warm climates. I bet if I brought up to maybe Virginia it would live well at least for a while.

Jason

I want to know about the silver maple. I wonder what bug live on it and what color bark and why the silver part is more soft and what is the sticky stuff inside the leaves it is gray too.

Heather

Valerie showed me she had little use for trees at all, except maybe as graphics.

I want to know what kind of wood the egypt. I want to do a report on Egypt. I could care less about trees. Trees are pretty boring.

Finding out what students have really learned

Here is our report card. After all manner of brilliant input, the journals can show what has sifted down into the long-term memory.

Tell me about latitude and longitude.

Latidude is some imaginary lines that go east or west. The lines are parallel and they go by every ten like 10-20-30 and all the way up to ninty degrees latitude. The lines go all the way around the world. Latitude helps people to tell were sailers are but it would be hard to find them without longitude. Sometimes you can mix them up so be carfull. Longitude goes up and down or south and north. There not parallel lines. They start from the north pole or south pole and end at the south pole or north pole. Longitude you can remember by the word long.

Brittany

Monitoring self-images

A week or so before report cards, we asked our students to write their perceptions of how school was going so far, and how they felt they were doing. With report cards we get into some very heavy issues. Their answers showed that many of them see themselves as successful or not primarily in light of what others think. Of course, much of what we do in school, from giving report cards to asking this type of journal question, conditions the children to think this way.

All this philosophy notwithstanding, they did tell me how they feel about themselves in their journals, as students never had done for me anywhere before.

> I did okay but I might get in trouble. I think I did pretty good. When I get C's or D's my dad will talk for hours about school days of his life...the reason I got an S on my exploritories is because that I was afraid to use the tools.
>
> Angela

> I was scared when I was getting my report cards because I thought I was going to get a bad grade. I think my mom and dad will be happy.
>
> Dwayne

After school on the day of this write, the following page was left on my desk.

> School ben hectce sense it started. I now I haveent got good grades on my report card. You gis think I am going to lerne fast but it takes a wiyell for me to cech on. S.S., Science and English I donot to very good on test. Those three are my brobblom. I fell so stuped when you let other people see. like wen we are cheking them sometime you let other people cjeke it. I do not dar ask for help because the kids or Mr. A. mit think I am stuped. I donot spell good ether, you broble now that all rety. Like in this Journal rite. Some times I get frostrated.
>
> Mary

I was moved and changed by this write. I gave Mary a long letter the next day, telling her I heard everything she said, and how much I admired how well she said it. Mary and I can help each other this year.

Determining cognitive ability

I want to find out on what levels these children can think. Can they make connections, evaluations? Can they create whole new scenarios, applications? Do they take things apart and analyze them? Do they understand?

They demonstrate all these abilities when they write in the journals, at least as often as when they recite facts.

1. EVALUATION

When I asked in science class which tree each of them will choose to study closely, Jenny tells me

> I'm going to adopt an oak tree because it feeds animals.

Grant asked his math students if they thought a test he had just given them was fair. Ray's review:

> Yes I think the math tests were fair because we reviewed and we should have study and the people who didn't study well its their tough luck.

Writing about *Stone Fox,* a story I read them about a little boy's heroic attempt to save the farm, Genevieve writes

> It was sourd of sad at the end but I'm glad he won and I'm glad his grandfather got better. $500. is not a lot for taxes for 10 years so I thought it was wierd but mabey it is a lot I dont no about taxes so I mabe wrong.

2. SYNTHESIS

From my September journal:

> We talked generally about the essence of a poem, favorite poems (read and heard some) what makes it a poem, etc. I finished with a write: "Choose some words carefully to describe something you feel strongly about." (Our definition of a poem).

Crystal wrote three or four in that five-minute period. The last one:
My mom and dad care about me. They don't live together but they do in my heart.

After a field trip to some fast-food places, we asked them to *Create the perfect fast-food restaurant.*

> ...It would have famous paintings and a jukebox. I would have a place where the people could look at whales and sharks, crab, lobster, fish and other things that live in water. I would have all kinds of animals in another room. I would have fancy chairs and tables with a red tablecloth. The name of my restaurant would be Genevieve's Fast Food Restaurant Zoo.
>
> Genevieve

3. APPLICATIONS

When Grant did the unit on latitude and longitude, several children invented situations to demonstrate the usefulness of these measurements.

> If a ship was sinking the capiton would tell the coast Gaurd what line of laditude and longitude he is on so they can rescue him.
>
> Jeremy

Ben took his journal and applied some of the research skills I have been teaching. He went to the back of the book and wrote an index of all the journal questions we had asked so far, in chronological order, listing the page numbers for each.

Index
1. What do you expect in English class
2.
3. What map experiences have you had?
   What is a scientist?
   How was school yesterday?

5. How was math?
   What books have you read over the summer?
   How was Social Studys?
   Poem
7. Smelling observation
   How was Social Studys?
   What do you expect to see and smell outside?
9. What do you know about sentences?
   What did you do in science class today?
10. What do you expect in the taste tests?
    What was your favorite plant on our walk?
11.
12. What do you think we will do at Camp Swampy?
    What was your faverite part of the filmstrip?
    What do you know about compound sentences.
13. What do you think about adopting a tree?
    Tell Mr. Goodrow about the field trip.
14. If I could create an Ideal Rest.
15. Do you think the math tests were fair?
    How did you like Stone Fox?
16. Write a poem about Camp Swampy.
    Tell me about nouns.
17. What did you find out when you did your drawings today
18. What did you learn from the movie and how can you use it?
    Why did the uncle change his mind?
19. Tell me a few things about pronouns.
    Tell me about latitude and longitude.
20. Write about one item on the bullitin board.
21. What are your hopes for your school maps?
    Write about your best our of this long weekend.
22. Tell how you would choose adjectives for an ad.
23. What do you need to do research about.
    What was the hardest thing about latitude and longitude?
    How has 5th grade been so far?
24. Tell me all you know on New England States.
25. What would I like to know about trees?
26. How do you feel about Report cards?
27. Write your feelings about *Summer of the Swans*
    Mrs. Math?
28. Tell me.

Ben

4. CONNECTIONS
From my October journal:
After reading the children a story about a country boy with an abusive uncle, they wrote on "why the uncle changed his ways" when the boy finally stood up to him.

Answers expressed the uncle's recognition for the boy's rights, feeling, at long last, for the boy's dead father, his brother, and suspicion that the uncle "had a trick up his sleeve."

Genevieve extended the story further and speculated on future events, in light of what had already happened.

> I wonder what happened later on did he start doing his work wright or did he still make mistakes and get hit.

Raymond is a great connection-maker. After a trip outside to survey local flora, I asked them,
What do you remember about the plants we saw?

> Red pines you can see the branches and they are together like my relitives and me, white pines are spaced out and you can't see the branches like distent relitives and me...

Soon after our poetry lesson we took a field trip to the nature center. The next day, Ben wrote his recollections in poetry instead of prose.
The Tree Next to the Telephone Pole

> It stood there, the living peice of wood,
> Standing there, exactly like it should.
> In the perfect form it is, on that field,
> With a telephone pole for a shield,
> With a telephone pole for a shield.

Here are some of the advantages I see journal writing giving our kids:

Everyone is thinking at once when they are journal writing. Nobody is "on vacation," as some can easily be with another form of class discussion. Even the most devout daydreamers have opinions about things, and when given a non-threatening way of expressing their opinions, well, they do it, as they wouldn't do in front of the whole class. They are thinking while they're writing. They are thinking while they're sharing.

A lot of peer teaching goes on during the sharing intervals, forcing me to surrender some control. At first it was hard for me, with my rather rigid background, to accept that they were all talking at once. But having them all talk at once, and many tutor at once, pays off.

They seem happier at school, more at ease, because of the acceptance our journal format requires. They may feel freer to take risks with writing because we never correct spelling, punctuation or grammar in the journals. I feel this gives them access to the entire language. "Why don't you correct their spelling?" asks my husband. It would narrow the field of words they feel comfortable with.

I feel I know these kids better, faster than I knew others. Again, they feel free to say anything and everything they want. Jeremy, in our tree explorations, tells me:

> I can feel it, touch it, look at it, smell it, climb it. That's whats how I can learn about it. I don't like the fact about adopting a tree that is for little kids with nothing to do. The tree is not really yours.

Matt is more subtle in his suggestion:

> I think compound sentences are fun as long as you don't give more than five.

Walter—a boy with loads of problems—when asked for his thoughts on a book I read aloud:
>It was a good book. I wish I kud red that book but I can not red good.

They are discovering, as they write, some things about themselves. After an observe/sketch session in science, Jennifer writes,
>I always use to say that I draw terrible but nowthat I drew Angla and my sneark [sneaker], I have to face it, it is pretty good afterall.

And I am coming face to face with problems they freely confide to me:
>One day I was doing my homework and Mom and (her friend) were having a fight...

It is mid-term as I write this and I'm not sure where to go with that kind of thing. We talk in my school of how today's children could benefit from a teacher advisory system. I think this kind of writing shows that need, and it may also hint at how to implement such a system.

The children are learning that they can use writing to tell someone their problems and to seek help. When Mary did this in her poignant note, she and I were both helped a lot. Jennifer sent me a similar plea just this week. Our reading group's current book, *Trumpet of the Swan*, is a little more difficult than our last book. On the back of a homework assignment, Jennifer wrote,

Dear Mrs. McGonagal,

>I fell this book is harder than every thing else what can I do about this

From Jen

I took a closer look at the book and altered my plans. Both Mary and Jennifer are shy, quiet girls who found a way to communicate very nicely in writing.

One day Valerie, who is especially quiet, found her voice. For reasons that baffle us, Val never speaks above a whisper and rarely volunteers a comment or an opinion. On report card day, however, Valerie received two grades that infuriated her. Listen to Valerie's new voice answering the journal question.

How do you feel about your report card?

>I dont like my science and reading grade
>I want to know why I got those grades.
>I got C's! I NEVER GET C's! Only once did
>I get a C and it was a C+ too. But 2 C's?
>It's rediculous. I DONT BELIVE IT!
>I CANT GET A C! I read Grown up books!
>I have a humongus vocabulary!
>(Science is what I got the C+ in last year
>but that's okay) I dont mind getting a C
>in science because I stink in science.

BUT READING? I JUST DONT BELIVE IT!
It's imosible!
I love reading (I hate science)
My dad minds if I hate science because
that was HIS favorite subject.

Writing is traditionally used in school to extract factual information, sometimes to test comprehension of those facts. My students are taking these facts and running with them: figuring them out, comparing, connecting, creating, complaining, dreaming and working the dreams out.

Writing is traditionally the domain of the English teacher. Every day, in one class or another, my fifth graders are asked to do some thinking on paper. In science, in math, in social studies, in English, they tune in, they think, they wander around in their thoughts, they make discoveries, they work things out, they write it all down. They show it to somebody, and get some feedback.

The next day, in a different place, they do it again.

They are doing it. They are being it.

They are writers.

21.

Choice Produces Results

BILL REIF and JAMES S. DAVIS

The Teacher's View: Bill Reif

Allowing students freedom and latitude within an assignment produces amazing results. For the last three years I've been teaching in a unique program entitled EXPO (Expanded Pupil Opportunity), which provides a two-year alternative educational program for average and above-average, socially adjusted fifth and sixth grade students. The thrust of the program is to horizontally enrich each student through an activity-oriented approach. We do encourage autonomy in the pursuit of individual excellence.

My students have three weeks to do reading, writing, and project goals around each theme in our Scott Foresman *Reading Unlimited* series. "Goals" allow students to extend and enrich their writing and reading skills as they further develop the reading theme. They allow students to explore beyond the basic text. I always give a list of broad goal choices. However, students are allowed to rewrite a goal, subject to approval, for they have their own great ideas. Allowing students choices, input, and freedom places responsibility for the learning where it belongs—on the learner. Task commitment and quality are just two byproducts of the ownership this creates.

Jill is one of the most gifted students I've ever had. She entered the program for the last half of her sixth grade year, adapting extremely well to the program's need for students to be organized, flexible, and committed to task.

Section 1 of *Reading Unlimited,* Level 20, centers on relationships between "People and Animals." It was the second theme Jill faced in EXPO. She never lacked creative ideas nor the motivation to extend and present her work.

From four writing goal choices for the "People and Animals" unit, Jill chose

2. Find information on a reptile of your choice. Develop an interesting report on the reptile you've become an expert on. Use the reporting technique we used in doing the "Conference on World Problems." Don't forget the use or need for diagrams. I can't wait to learn about reptiles! (Teacher prepared Goal Sheet.)

The cycle of three goals for a three- to four-week period is intended to provide time for reflection, for individual work both in and outside the classroom. Ideally, students develop responsibility and time man-

210

agement skills as they learn the processes inherent in each goal. Earlier in the year, we used ideas on report writing from Lucy Calkins's *Lessons from a Child* to prepare for an "EXPO Conference on World Problems." Report writing resurfaced during a Writer's Workshop in my classroom, when Jill and I discussed her rough draft. She was stumped as to a format for her "People and Animals" writing goal. She didn't want anything that sounded like it came from *World Book Encyclopedia.* She wanted something unique. Knowing how Jill enjoyed writing in her journal, I asked her, "How do you think Jane Goodall first wrote about her chimpanzees?"

"In a journal," she answered. We talked about how a scientist might keep such a journal. We discussed the importance of reading about the Sahara Desert where this snake lived, so that everything she was writing about would fit together and be realistic.

Jill returned to her desk and thought about our conversation. Soon she was in the library collecting reference books. She spent an enormous amount of time reading about the sidewinder and the Sahara Desert. She recorded sheets of notes. Her task commitment was especially noticeable when she had to stop working and rejoin group activity. As soon as class was over she was back at her desk or in the library. Tuning out her surroundings she was into her research.

After several days Jill's first draft was begun. She worked at home as well as at school. She revised her first draft after getting responses from her peer group and parents. The process of response and revision was repeated four times, each effort pleasing her more. The applause from her peer group after her final presentation of this goal was spontaneous. Her product validates student choice and ownership.*

THE SAHARA SIDEWINDER

A Personal Journal By:
Nikki Lagene Katerena

Photographs by: Nikki Lagene Katerena

March 3, 1985
Sahara Desert—Africa

I arrived here at 1:30 in the afternoon. My guide was waiting for me at the airport and drove me to the desert where my research is to take place. My guide's name is Mungo and he seems to be very experienced. He took me to a small oasis where only one family lives and then Mungo wished me good luck and left. There was a small vacant house nearby where I was to make my home for the next two months during the time I was to research the venomous snake, the sidewinder, for National Geographic.

The Sahara Desert is awesome. It's full of contrasts with its moun-

* Publisher's note: The format Jill created for her piece is a remarkably authentic looking facsimile of *National Geographic* magazine, complete with captioned, full-color photos. We ask that readers *envision* such a context, inasmuch as it would have been too costly to reproduce the original.

tains, rocky plateaus, and gravelly plains. Plants aren't as rare as I thought they would be. And neither are the animals. Some of the plants and wildlife are strange to me yet, but soon I will research them. I have to get settled in and rested. If I saw a sidewinder, I would be even more eager to start researching at once. I'm so excited about this opportunity because it is my first really important reporting assignment. Two months will hardly be enough time to get everything done.

Well, tomorrow is going to be a busy day. I'd better get some sleep.

March 4, 1985

I haven't seen the sidewinder, but I did research the various plants and animals nearby. There are only three types of plant life growing around here: aristida grass, had bush, and the acacia tree. Desert lark and mourning wheatear are the two birds found on the Sahara. Two types of lizards reside in this desert: the spiny-tailed lizard and the fringe-toed lizard. The jerboa is another animal I've seen today. It resembles a mouse and a kangaroo. Two other animals are types of deer. The first one I saw was called an addax, and the second was a dorcas gazelle. The last type of animal is a fennec, which is a type of fox. I hope to see a sidewinder tomorrow when I'm out looking around.

March 6, 1985

I saw the sidewinder yesterday! I was so absorbed in what I saw and excited about seeing it, that I didn't take the time to write in my journal. Tomorrow I'm going to try to capture one. If I do, I'll be able to study its reactions.

Also, tomorrow I am going to introduce myself to my neighbors.

[PHOTO]

The first oasis I passed in the Sahara. It is in Algerian Sahara.

March 10, 1985

I met Mr. and Mrs. Tahayo and their daughter Kanea on the 7th. Mr. Tahayo offered to help me capture a sidewinder. I told him that if he wanted to, it would really help. He went out with me on the 8th and we captured a sidewinder. I think I could have captured the snake without Mr. Tahayo's help, but only because the snake was wounded. It has a small hole in the side of its body which made it a little handicapped. Mr. Tahayo and I agreed that the hole was made by the spiny-tailed lizard. That lizard has a tail that ends in a sharp point. The snake and lizard must have gotten into a fight.

March 13, 1985

The house I am living in is very primitive. My light source is a gas lantern and I carry my water from a nearby well which is shared with the Tahayo's. Mungo just left a few minutes ago. He comes once a week to leave me some canned food and my mail. I really am grateful that he comes because besides him, the Tayaho's are the only people around me. I feel like I've been locked up and kept away from the rest of the world.

I still haven't been able to capture a healthy sidewinder, but the one

I have has given me a lot of information. Sidewinders, which are little rattlesnakes, are different from other snakes in three ways. One is the hornlike scales which are found above their eyes. Another is their habit of burying themselves in loose sand. And, the last is the way they move over soft, shifting sand better than the more usual snake motion. The way they move is hard to explain. It's like holding a short rope by one hand and flipping it across the ground with circular wrist motions. When they're moving, the snake's head points at right angles to the direction he's traveling. With the help of other sidewinders I've seen, I've come to the conclusion that the snakes are seldom over 20 inches long and dur. . . .

April 11, 1985

I've just barely recovered from being bitten by the sidewinder I had captured earlier. Lucky for me, Mr. Tahayo was outside and heard me scream. He rushed in and did what he had been taught to do in case of an emergency. He made me lie down and keep quiet. He tied a band firmly around my arm just above the bite to restrict the spead of the poison. Then he sterilized a sharp knife with a match flame. He later told me he could have used iodine or alcohol, but he didn't have any handy right then. He made a cross-cut incision about one-quarter inch long through each fang mark. Since he didn't have a suction cup, he sucked the poison out with his mouth. Because there was no way to get me to a hospital, the Tahayo's cared for me until Mungo came seven days later. He rushed me to the hospital as I was still very weak and not always aware of where I was. I remained at the hospital for two days.

[PHOTO]

The jerboa is a small, desert living rodent with several kangaroo-like features. Its hind legs are long and made for jumping, but the front legs are extremely short and aren't used much in helping it move. The front legs are used to catch food.

[PHOTO]

The sidewinder, or horned rattlesnake, is a venomous snake that dwells in the deserts of the U.S. and Africa.

Mr. Tahayo said the sidewinder I had captured escaped and, since it was wounded, it bit me. Unfortunately, I don't have enough time remaining here on the Sahara to capture another one. I have only one week more to finish my researching assignment. If I work extremely hard, I should be able to finish in time. The doctor told me to stay in bed until tomorrow, so that will slow me down a little, too. I'm going to have to work *very* hard these last six days.

April 12, 1985

Well, for the first time since March 13th I've been able to get out of bed. I went out and took additional notes on the desert. Mr. Tahayo came with me because he was concerned about my health. While I was out, Mrs. Tahayo and Kanea fixed me a nourishing lunch.

I observed some more interesting facts about the sidewinder today. The weather was a little cool this morning and, for some reason, I didn't see any sidewinders. I asked Mr. Tahayo about the mystery and he told me to look in a small cave in a rock we had come across. I looked inside and saw approximately six sidewinders sleeping. Mr. Tahayo explained that this type of snake hibernates during the cooler weather. They hibernate in holes and caves. Sometimes they crawl in the same one year after year.

April 13, 1985

It's unbelievable that I have only four days left until I return to the States. The time has gone by *so* fast! I still have some researching to do regarding the sidewinder's eating habits. I plan to go out tomorrow night. I'm sure they eat during the night. I'd go out tonight, but I still tire easily and need to get some rest.

April 14, 1985

It's extremely hot today! For the day, that's not unusual at all. Parts of the desert reach daytime temperatures as high as 110°F. The desert cools off at night which is lucky. I couldn't stand it being 100°F at night! Winter temperatures in the Sahara average from 50°F to 60°F. I'm glad it's not that hot in the States.

Tonight is the night I will discover what the sidewinder eats. I plan to rest this afternoon so I will be alert tonight.

April 15, 1985

I made my final discovrey last night. As I thought, the sidewinder eats at night. They eat lizards and mice. To devour these animals, sidewinders (like other snakes) swallow their prey by unhitching their jaws. The snake's teeth are very sharp and slightly curved inward. They are not used for chewing, but are perfect for biting and holding. When its teeth are fastened into something, the snake slides one side of its jaw forward. Then the snake bites again and pulls this side of the jaw back, drawing the food inward. Next, the sidewinder slides the other side of his jaw forward to pull in the food. When the food is in his mouth, the snake may use both sides of his jaws at once. The snake's body is expandable. When a snake swallows an animal that is bigger than his body, everything stretches to make room for it.

[PHOTO]

The addax is an antelope with a rather heavy body and loose-jointed legs that give it an awkward appearance at first sight. This impression is soon corrected when a herd of addaxes vanishes at full gallop and creates a minor dust storm.

April 16, 1985

Since my work is practically finished, I was able to rest today in preparation for my journey home tomorrow. I don't want to leave because of the friends I've made. Kanea just left a few minutes ago. Mr. and Mrs. Tahayo had to go to the village to get a few supplies. Kanea didn't want to go with them, so she stayed with me. She's a nice girl and I will be sorry to leave. I hope someday I will be able to come and visit them again. I'll miss Mungo, too. He was friendly and very helpful.

April 17, 1985

Kanea just came over. She is going to help me finish packing. Mrs. Tahayo is packing me a lunch for my journey home. Mr. Tahayo and Mungo are helping me put my boxes and suitcases into Mungo's car. I just can't believe I'm actually leaving today. With the exception of my accident, everything went wonderfully. I wish there was some way I could repay the Tahayo's and Mungo for their helpfulness.

April 18, 1985

I'm back at my own house. I got home at 12:30 last night. It's nice to be home, but I miss the Tahayo's and Mungo already.

Work today was wonderful. My boss loved my research article and said it would be published in the May issue! I can hardly wait to start on my next assignment!

[PHOTO]

The awesome Sahara.

An Observer's Reflection: James S. Davis

Jill's remarkable "Sahara Sidewinder" reflects growing control of writing as a choice making, decision making process. She found information on this particular snake in a general reference book on reptiles and initially intended to do two models of reptiles for her project. Upon deciding to do a story instead, Jill produced three pages of carefully handwritten, numbered notes on the Sahara and its plant and animal life. For example, "2) mourning wheatear (bird)" in her notes becomes "Desert lark and mourning wheatear are the two birds found on the Sahara." Jill had difficulty finding an adequate vehicle for the information she had gathered so she initiated a conference with her teacher, Mr. Reif. His sensitive and timely question, "How do you think Jane Goodall first wrote about her chimpanzees?" legitimized a journal form which Jill already enjoyed. Still, the journal/magazine idea came very late in the research phase of her project and about halfway through the time Jill had allotted for this particular goal, approximately 2.5 weeks.

Jill's first draft was fifteen pages of handwritten text. Her review of the draft led to many deletions and additions in preparation for the second full draft, over three pages of single-spaced, typed copy. Jill conferred with Mr. Reif and with her mother about revision as she moved through multiple drafts. Her mother in particular helped with proof reading and urged alternative wording for several phrases. Jill gave some attention to the magazine format in her first draft, but the cover design came after the second full draft, as did an index and captions for photographs. *National Geographic* is a fixture in her home and she recognized it as a natural, credible context for her article. Jill shared the final copy with two other **EXPO** students before presenting it in class.

Jill's writing process is a problem solving process. The snake bite shortens the total number of entries and effectively skips almost a month in the chronology. Jill candidly asserted that, although she set up a two-month expedition, she "didn't have that much to write" and "wanted to get some of it over with quickly." She was left with a manageable, more dramatic manuscript which included most but not all of what she knew about her topic.

I believe the snakebite, a consciously chosen dramatic convention, is one clue to the other complex aspects of "Sahara Sidewinder" and its author. Jill is a quiet, private person. She is neither talkative nor demonstrative in the classroom, yet she has control of the entire classroom when she does speak. According to Mr. Reif, "You get to know Jill through her journal." And indeed as with other students, Jill's personality influences her choice of goals and her style of working on them. Moreover, her choice of the journal form makes this piece particularly interesting to consider in terms of the function categories proposed by James Britton and the Schools Council Project research team (*The Development of Writing Abilities*, Macmillan Education Ltd. 1975). Within the world of her classroom, Jill fulfills the transactional function of reporting, demonstrating the breadth of her research and her control of information. She even adopts the genre of an article in a specialized publication. Teacher and peer audiences are part of her rhetorical situation, and she clearly meets a requirement within a given set of goals. However, her choice of the personal journal form for the article shows Jill's familiarity with expressive writing and its conventions. Not only does she date and set the stage for journal entries with a phrase or opening sentence, the entries themselves are reflective and descriptive. They are remarkably consistent in tone throughout the piece, despite the scientific information she must include for more transactional purposes. Indeed, Jill acknowledged that it was "easier to put the information into a journal than a story." However, her accomplishment involves the poetic function as well, for the journal also carries a story. Jill projects a character who writes the journal from experiences Jill creates for that character. The reader is clearly offered a narrative which includes, but also exceeds, the scientific expedition. Jill obviously identifies with her character and projects herself, potentially into a comparable situation or career. She makes newly researched information into a story she could live, in some ways does live, and thus makes the learning her own. She is a participant in her own learning, certainly, but she is also a spectator seeing how new information might first come into existence—for her character, for herself as that character. "Sahara Sidewinder," as piece and as learning experience, demonstrates why writing needs to have a fluid, flexible place in classrooms, whatever the content area. It also suggests that all the "functions" of writing can serve the function of learning.

Jill is a sophisticated young learner and writer. However, writing served her as a learner throughout the development of "Sahara Sidewinder" because of the classroom context. The pace and structure were hospitable to the writing process, to multiple functions writing can serve, and both the written product and the writer were valued. The piece is indeed an accomplishment—of student *and* teacher.

Part III

Journals and the Arts and Humanities

The important questions in some fields of study can seldom be answered yes/no, right/wrong, or true/false. In disciplines such as history, philosophy, religion, literature, art, and music, the answers are more obviously matters of intepretation and judgment than fact. Journals make especially useful assignments in these studies because they provide students with the opportunity to think, wonder, speculate, question, and doubt—in their own terms and in their own language—without fear of penalty for not having a right answer. In this section teachers in elementary school, high school, and college discuss how journals help promote the learning so characteristic of the arts and humanities.

The first set of chapters, 22, 23, and 24, describes journals in historical studies: Henry Steffens's "Journals in the Teaching of History" explains how journals promote better class discussion and better term papers in college history classes. Bernadette Marie Mulholland's "It's Not Just the Writing" puts the reader in her 11th grade American Civilization class and lets the students do most of the talking. Richard Sweterlitsch's "The Honest Voice of Inquiry" describes how journals in a college folklore class helped students to delve more deeply into living folklore traditions than had been possible through more formal writing assignments.

Chapters 25, 26, and 27 are written by teachers of the visual arts and music. Christopher Thaiss's "A Journal of the Arts" provides an in-depth examination of one freshman writer's experience keeping a journal in a course called Reading the Arts. Catherine M. Larson and Margaret Merrion's "Documenting the Aesthetic Experience" describes the use of music journals in elementary and junior high schools, while Jane Ambrose's "Music Journals" focuses on journals in her college music classes.

The next set of chapters describes journals in philosophy classes: In "Student Journals and the Goals of Philosophy" O. T. Kent makes the argument that journals are the student's turf, a place where they can practice philosophical speculation without risk. In "The Philosophical Journal: Three Case Studies" Stephen M. North, an English teacher, studies the journals of three freshman writers in a colleague's philosophy course to examine the relationship created between student writer and teacher reader. In "Journal Writing as Person Making" Fred Halberg describes his use of intensive personal journal in his courses on the philosophy of psychology and religion. Laura Fulwiler's "What's a Horny?" offers a look at how guidance counselors can use journals in small- and large-group settings as well as with individuals.

This section concludes with two chapters presenting more controversial uses of journals: in "The Team Journal" Jean Graybeal explains how students in a college religion class divided into five teams of six each and kept one "team journal" for each group. In "Letting Them Write When They Can't Even Talk?" Karen Wiley Sandler outlines plans for using journals in foreign language classes, including both first year and advanced classes.

22.

Journals in the Teaching of History

HENRY STEFFENS

History would not exist without writing, for "doing history" means writing history. Unfortunately, while historians recognize the importance of writing, students frequently do not. And, in fact, it would be unreasonable to expect otherwise. How can students who are asked only to write for purposes of evaluation appreciate the important role of writing in history? All too frequently, we insist that they write about questions which we set for them, generated out of our own interests, in the context of our own understanding. Our questions are not the students' questions. We seldom develop the context of our questions fully enough for the students to appreciate what we have in mind. They assume that we already know the answer to our own question, and that there is only one good response. They believe they must reproduce "our" answer, rather more than less exactly, leaving little room for innovative or original thinking. Students don't acquire a sense that they are writing a piece of history of their own. Such writing is usually far below our expectations and even further below our hopes.

Without doubt, student writing needs to be evaluated. Students need to produce examination essays, term papers and reports to be evaluated for both form and content. But these transactional language exercises are not the best vehicles for teaching history, or for learning history. Our writing assignments often separate students from both the enjoyment of exploring ideas and the enjoyment of writing. Our writing assignments allow students to display information, but don't promote personal involvement in the process of writing and learning history.

More informal and expressive forms of writing may be better suited to teaching and learning history. Informal, expressive, loosely structured writing is the form of writing closest to thinking. Informal writing allows for the exploration of ideas, for speculations about implications and variations, for the development of ideas in increasing stages of complexity, and for the recall of information from previous experience. Informal writing permits writers to express feelings about a topic, and their degree of commitment to an idea or point of view, in a way that thinking and talking do not. Through expressive writing, students have the opportunity to develop ideas, to "see" those ideas for the first time, and to decide whether they disagree or agree with themselves.

We know a great deal more history than we can usually recall immediately. Informal writing, free from specific evaluation, encourages us to explore ideas and to think about the richness of the historical past.

It helps us to think as we write, stimulating our imagination and generating ideas. As we write in an expressive mode, we often digress to follow an idea, to pursue a connection, or to come to a realization which didn't exist before we wrote. Expressive writing helps us explore the connections between ideas and information that we already possess. Writing may also be helpful in revealing what we do not know, or what we need to know more about. The best writing, and the most valuable in terms of learning, occurs when the writer is involved in the subject matter. Expressive writing is a way of interesting and involving students in the content of history.

Journals in Small History Classes

The student journal is one of the most effective formats for informal writing in small classes. Journals can be the core of a successful small history class, as well as make history seminars work "at a seminar level." Student journals for small classes can be divided into four distinct sections: (1) entries written in class; (2) entries written at home related to reading assignments; (3) comparative entries written at home relating the reading assignments to previous classes or to previous readings; and (4) more personal entries which allow a full range of questions, doubts, speculations, emotional responses, etc. The primary reason for keeping a journal is to enhance the learning of the "content" of history courses.

The key to the successful inclusion of a journal in a small class is supervision and organization. In planning the course, decide what you hope the students will accomplish and structure the journal accordingly. Decide on the size and nature of the journal. The full-sized looseleaf notebook is good because the larger pages seem to encourage more writing and "larger" thoughts. It is also easier to include clippings and other outside material into the larger format. Have the students make, or purchase, separators for the notebook, so that the sections can be clearly marked.

During the first class period, give specific instructions on how each journal should be organized and what each entry should contain. Insist that each entry have a number, a date, and a brief title or label. The title is best chosen before the writing of the entry, for example: "Tuchman's view of history," "Real causes of the Boer War," "Contrast between Sassoon and Remarque as novelists." Ask students to write continuously for a minimum of five minutes for each entry they make. Longer entries should be encouraged; as the semester progresses, it will be the rare student who does not write many entries longer than the minimum five minutes.

Encourage students to include materials in their journals in addition to the assigned readings in the course: book reviews from newspapers and magazines, appropriate clippings from any source, comments about movies or TV shows that relate to the course, or to history, recollections of visits to museums, travel or other experiences. Try to encourage the relationship between the student's "life experience" and the topics in the course, to help to break the separation between "what I do in school" and what happens during "the rest of my life," maintained by most students.

Journals provide the professor with a sense of the intellectual vitality of each student, an impression seldom conveyed by an answer in a Blue Book. Reading the journals also provides a sense of which topics in the course are most interesting to the students, which topics elicited the best response, and which need to be approached differently.

Types of Journal Entries

1. Entries to start a class

The section of the journal written in class helps the teacher start discussions and focus attention on particular topics; it helps students respond to slides, movies, and music, and helps them draw connections between the assigned readings and the class material. Start each class with a five-minute write on a question related to what you want to accomplish during that class. These beginning writes transform the opening of a class into an active discussion group; students have to be active during the writing process, and after the five-minute write, they actually have something concrete to offer for discussion. Ask students to volunteer to read their entries to the class. You might read your own entry to the class to start things off for the first few sessions and occasionally after that. It is crucial that you write along with your students during each in-class write; when they see you writing with enthusiasm, they will take their own writing more seriously. Students will soon volunteer to read their entries on their own. Have them read their entry just as it was written, without paraphrasing or making apologies or disclaimers. This will save time and give a better sense of what the student meant to say in the entry. The following is the complete list of questions for in-class journal entries I asked of my seminar "European Cultural History, 1880-1930":

1. What are your personal goals for this seminar, this semester?
2. What three terms come to mind when I say "European Cultural History, 1880-1930?" Write a paragraph about each.
3. What aspect of George Sherston's life struck you the most?
4. What aspects of technological change struck you the most in the Hale readings?
5. Write for 10 minutes on a possible paper topic, and how the topic might develop.
6. Why was there such diversity of opinion and attitude in Europe at the end of the nineteenth century?
7. What aspect of Vienna in the readings characterized the city for you?
8. Why did Schorske devote himself to the study of Vienna?
9. Where am I now on my research?
10. What was wrong with Klimt's University panels?
11. Vienna of the 1890s has been stigmatized as the training grounds of Adolf Hitler. Was Paris of the 1890s any better or worse?

12. Tuchman's chapter is called "Neroism Is in the Air." What do you understand "Neroism" to be?
13. What is the most interesting thing that I have come to, so far, in my research paper?
14. What aspect of science around 1900 interested you the most?
15. For ten minutes, start your paper. Write the introduction, or make some start.
16. List all of the things for which Einstein is famous.
17. What do you think are the most important ingredients in Einstein's early education, as portrayed in the film?
18. Mach reduced all knowledge to sensations. Why was his insistence upon sensations thought of as incomplete by 1900?
19. What major differences do you see between Sassoon's novel and Remarque's novel?
20. What are Janik and Toulmin's views on the "professionalization of culture" after World War I?

2. Class Entries to Develop Ideas for Term Papers

Journal entries during class can be used to help students formulate term research paper topics. See questions 5, 9, 13, and 15 above for a possible sequence of questions. This sequence helps to keep the students going. The first and second class entries make them realize that they had best be getting on with the project! They will usually come and talk about their topic after these two writing opportunities.

3. Journal Entries During Class

Journal entries during the course class period can redirect attention to a new topic or area. A journal entry may be used to summarize the discussion to that point, or to allow the students to reach some conclusions on their own. If a subject has been discussed fully, a new entry will get everyone thinking along new lines.

Journal entries after the showing of slides and movies or listening to music are very constructive in small classes for two reasons: they allow the students to draw some conclusions about the experience, and they allow them to make some connections between the new material and the class topic. For example, after a short film, *The Expressionists,* students in my cultural history class realized just how much the paintings looked like the slides we had seen on Fauve artists two weeks previously. Writing a journal entry on the comparison served to make that comparison specific and allowed students to reach their own conclusions. A journal entry after a class experience also makes the students more attentive during the experience. Knowing that they will have to write about what they see or hear, makes the students more attentive. No more nodding when the lights are low.

4. Journal Entries at the End of Class

"End writes" are primarily useful to allow students to draw conclusion and to reach closure on a topic. These entries may be used to start the next class period. Have students read their conclusions, and see if the class can reach a consensus. A discussion which attempts consensus often clarifies ideas and beliefs. Students have their positions in writing, so there is little ambiguous assertion or gratuitous comment. Ask the students to read just what they wrote last time, as a basis for discussion.

5. Entries at Home Related to the Reading Assignment

In my senior seminar, I assigned three five-minute entries per week on the assigned readings. Students could choose whatever they wanted to write about, but the topic had to be taken from the reading assignments. Students reported in their evaluation sheets at the end of the semester that knowing they had to write about the readings made them more active readers. They could no longer simply "do" the readings. There were at least three things about the readings that they needed to select for themselves and write about on their own. Students came to class with at least those three aspects of the readings prepared and personalized.

When we discussed the readings, I asked the students to read one of their entries about the readings. This served to make the discussion informed and concrete. It was also interesting to the students to see what others had chosen to write about. Students usually supplemented their entries with more traditional reading notes. But because their entries were self-selected and written in their own words, students most often referred to their journal entries, rather than their reading notes, for information in our class discussions. They were usually proud of at least one of the three entries they had written, and were pleased to read that one to the rest of the class. Reading entries and then discussing them took less class time than asking the class to "say something" about the readings. Discussions were far more informed and informative to the class. An example of an entry of this type follows:

#21—Dreyfus and Zola, March 6, 1985

> Once again Tuchman has selected a topic, the Dreyfus Affair, and allowed the reader the pleasure of penetrating the complexities and ambiguities of it. It is the first time that I realized how deeply the Affair permeated the depths of all of French society—that it was an issue that one had an opinion on, that it was endless, inescapable and threatening. The existence of the affair polarized and emphasized the underlying realities of life in France, by pitting the idea of justice against injustice and calling into question the nature of admirable ideals and concrete reality—the army, political factions, the church etc.
>
> Many times I have read about Zola's courage without ever absorbing the content of it. I read Germinal many years ago and applauded Zola's depicting of the poverty and struggle of the working classes without connecting that natural sympathy he had with his stand in the Dreyfus affair. Last class we discussed the connection between art and life and in J' Accuse Zola transcended the distinction. He was capable of expanding the boundaries of art to include life.

This very useful comment on the reading assignment, written from the student's own point of view, shows a level of introspection and recall of information seldom shown on an essay examination. The journal allowed the freedom to compare and to venture an opinion.

6. Comparative Entries Written at Home

The students were also required to write at least three five-minute entries each week comparing the reading assignment with previous readings, or comparing the assignment with class discussions, or anything else related. These were the most difficult entries for the students to write, but they were also the most interesting entries to read and discuss in class. The following entry gives some idea of the range of comparisons possible:

#17—*Schorske and Tuchman, February 17, 1985*

> Seems to be a common theme between Schorske's Chapter on "Politics in a New Key: An Austrian Trio" and Tuchman's Chapter on "The Idea and the Deed"; although the end results were entirely different, what the Anarchists, the Pan-Germans, the Christian-Socialists, and the Zionist movement had in common was their reaction to the rigidity and rationality of liberal politics, and their creation of "the sharper key"—a mode of political behavior at once more abrasive, more creative and more satisfying to the life of feeling than the deliberative style of the liberals. All four movements indentified themselves with some sort of pseudo-religious myth; Anarchism in its most idealistic form, In the "Kingdom of God" analogy of Kropotkin, in which the apocalyptic acts of the anarchists would bring about the perfect society—a "heaven on earth" so to speak, similarly, Schonerer appealed to the collective mythic past of the Germanic peoples in his call to arms, placing himself as the "Knight of Rosenau" at the head of the battle between good and evil. Lueger also appealed to the image of the medieval Catholic social order in his combat against liberalism. Finally, Herzl (who in fact was inspired by anarchism in France) viewed himself as the Jewish messiah, the "new Moses" who would bring about a new and better life for the Jewish peoples. As Schorske so adroitly points out, all three of these men, as well as the anarchists, transcended the purely rational politics of the liberals, performed the magic of summoning the "forces from the deep" of society's collective past, to satisfy the needs of an "irrational mob" who wanted a better life, but knew not how to find it. In some ways, these three men are like the charismatic leaders of new religious movements in present-day America; they appeal to a mass audience, tapping into the mythic past to find solutions to the modern problems of moral relativism and anomie.

Another example begins with brackets to show the writer's awareness of a digression:

> [This will probably sound really off-the-wall, but it just occurred to me that Sherston's world is in some ways like that of the

Kalahari bushmen in "The Gods Must Be Crazy." Like Sherston, their world, for all practical purposes, is composed of the distance that can be traveled in a day, and having no contact with people from other parts of the world, they naturally assume that they are the only people on earth. Although there are many obvious differences between a bushman and an English fox-hunting man, the essential similarity is that they both consider themselves to be the only thing in the world that matters, the only entity that the gods, in all their wisdom, favor.]

This was an early entry in the journal. Later in the semester, the writer did not feel the need to bracket digressions of this type. The comparison between the movie and the Sassoon novel was both accurate and memorable. Even students who had not seen the film appreciated the vivid contrast when this entry was read in class.

7. More Personal Entries

This is a section which could be kept by the student and simply removed from the loose-leaf notebook when the journals are read by the professor. The students should be given the option of handing this section in with the rest of the journal or not. More personal entries are certainly not part of the subject matter of the course, but they can be helpful to the student, especially a student working through a problem with the course. Here is the first entry by a former history major, now returned after a break, as a graduate student:

All through college there were courses which one knew would involve keeping a journal. They tended to be theater courses or English courses or other such ones that blatantly involved creativity. Interestingly, history, which requires a large element of creative and reflective thought to tie together the scattered facts, was one area of academics that never required a journal. (Or at least the numerous courses I took as a history major never did.) And yet ironically, there is probably no better topic suited for journal writing than history. By reflecting upon readings and integrating class discussions, along with tying in ones own subjective perspectives and experiences, one becomes much more personally involved in the historical process than an otherwise passive incorporation of the historical facts combined with the needed reflextion for putting together papers or answering an essay question. Having never kept a journal in an academic environment, or for academic purposes, I feel somewhat apprehensive, I have no reservations about keeping a journal and look forward to those moments of reflection, however I am apprehensive about writing in class and perhaps more so about reading entries in class. Actually our first entries the other day were not difficult to write. I felt mine were a bit stilted or cliche, but then.... Those that read theirs out loud had no problems doing so, and I guess I could easily have read mine out loud also, but I always hate the echo of my own voice when I read out loud something I have written on paper. It's as though my written thoughts were meant for paper and their tone is awkward when vocalized. However, the fact that reading our entries out loud is subtly required within the requirements of keeping a journal I suppose I shall deal with this and hopefully not find it as foreign as I fear.

Evaluating Student Journals

The success of journals in history classes depends, perhaps unfortunately, on the student's realization that they "count." Journals need to count, both in terms of the student's and the professor's opinion, and in terms of the final grade for the course.

In small history classes, where the number of students permits the careful reading of the journals, they may be counted as much as 50 percent of the grade. Since some evaluation must be made, in addition to just reading and responding to the journals, broad criteria of evaluation are most helpful. Regularity of entries, length of entries, and appropriateness are three useful guides for evaluating journals in small classes. The journal should show a continuous involvement with the course material throughout the semester; there should be no "holes," nor should there be any obvious and extended lapses of interest or effort.

Broad, holistic evaluation should be matched by broad grade ranges. The usual A, B, C, D grades are useful if you use only the letter; it is remarkably easy to conclude that a student has kept an excellent journal the whole semester, or a good one, or just a satisfactory one, or a poor one. Students usually reach the same conclusion about their journals and their degree of involvement with the course material in their journals as you do. Since the journal is all their own, they know very well how it should be evaluated.

It is very important to collect and read the journals early in the semester, perhaps during the second week of classes, to see that everyone is going in the right direction. For this early reading, select one or two of the best entries and write a short, positive comment to the student, right below the entry. Date and initial your comments. "I enjoyed reading your entry on the Sassoon novel. Sherston was an unusual character. I wished that you had developed your comments about Sherston's world more, because I was interested to see what you could have concluded. HJS, 26 Jan 85." Remind them to date and title their entries, if they are not doing so at this point. You might want to collect just one entry from time to time, to check on the quality of the entries. Just have the students clip the page out of their notebooks and put their name at the top of the page. You might write only "fine entry" on the good ones, but you might want to give some suggestions to the students who need improvement. You might collect the whole journals, a few students at a time, about mid-semester, and at the end of the semester.

The use of journals will modify and improve the learning environment in any class. They are not quick fixes because they must be taken seriously by both the professor and the students. They must be kept regularly and they must be valued. Journals will help students to become more active learners, and they will help to produce a more personal involvement with the subject matter of the course. Reading the student journals will unite the professor and the students in a shared "voyage of discovery" for that whole semester.

23.

It's Not Just the Writing

BERNADETTE MARIE MULHOLLAND

"Okay, everyone, please get out your logs and put today's date on top of a clean page. This is 8/29/84." The immediate response to my instructions is the noisiest part of the assignment: Students search purses and pockets for pens and pencils; pop three-ring binders for clean paper; and move chairs about to find comfortable positions for writing.

"What's today's date?"

"Did she tell us to write yet?"

"Do you have a pen I can use?"

"Can we write in pencil?"

"What are we supposed to be doing?"

This is the second day of school. My eleventh grade American Civilization students and I spent the first day writing and talking about writing; reading articles by Elbow and Macrorie on free writing and focused free writing; and sharing our responses to these articles in small groups. Writing to learn, to explore, to discover is new to these students. They are full of questions. I give them two or three minutes and ask for quiet. "Put today's date on the top—8/29/84—and then write the title, 'What is history?'" There is momentary silence while they write the date and title, and then the questions begin again.

"What do you mean, 'What is history?'"

"Do you want a definition?"

"*What* is history!"

"I don't understand."

"Write whatever comes to mind about the idea of history. What do you associate with the idea of history? What words, phrases, sentences can you use to describe history? Think about what history is for. If you are not sure what to write, start that way. 'I'm not sure what to write.' This is writing to explore, to understand, to think out loud on paper. Let the writing help you discover what you think about history. You'll be asked to share this with at least one other person."

Soon the room is quiet and students are writing. I write with them. I write in a teacher's log I keep about what they are doing, how they reacted to the assignment, and what I think about the activity. These class observations are invaluable to me in trying to plan what to do next and in understanding what's going on with the students. I also write the assignment with at least one of my classes. I like to have something to share with them.

Ten minutes go by, and they are still writing. "Please begin to finish." In another minute I ask them to read what they write to a partner of their choice. I walk around the room to see and to hear what is going on. They read quickly and self-consciously to each other.

"You go first."

"That was good."

"This isn't very good, but...."

In five minutes, everyone has had a turn, and I ask if anyone would like to share with the whole class. I emphasize that students receive credit for sharing: a full-credit check in my grade book for class participation. I open my grade book and pick up a pencil. A few seconds elapse while the students decide how they are going to answer my question. Four or five raise their hands and read. These are excerpts from what was shared:

> The word history makes me think about time and the events that occurred, events that are worth remembering. I think history serves a great purpose. For one thing, history enables us to keep in touch with our backgrounds and reality. Like everything else—even though many of us never experienced the American Civil War, but with history, we can imagine what it was like.
>
> Mai

> History is composed of famous men, inventions, important dates, wars and different concepts of things. History is something everyone possesses.
>
> Melissa

> History is, in a general sense, the known past. However, "known" is rather vague—sometimes people perceive the past incorrectly. The ultimate example of this is Orwell's *1984* where the past is changed frequently.
>
> Duane

> When I think of history, usually I think of things that have happened a long time ago or usually even a couple of years ago...I like to know about how people acted and what they were like way back when.
>
> Marni

I acknowledge each writing by telling what I hear by saying, "So the main idea was...." and ask questions like: "Melissa, you mentioned that history is something that everyone possesses. Could you tell me more about that?" or "Mai, I really like where you say, 'But with history, we can imagine what it was like.' So, history, in a way, is imagination, putting ourselves in the other person's place."

As a follow-up, I ask the students to read "America Revised" by Frances Fitzgerald and "In Search of History" by Barbara Tuchman. They read and respond to each article. Using the student responses, we started off with a discussion about the differences between high school texts and high school texts as history.

> The history texts in themselves are a part of history because even though one may have been written in the early 1900's and another in 1950, they were each written at a certain period of time when people held different views on history...
>
> Melissa

We also discussed the differences between primary and secondary sources and the importance of being aware that written history, as such, will always be someone else's point of view, no matter how objective the historian. The class asked questions like "What is truth in history?" and "How does each age reinterpret history?" and "How can we tell the difference between fact and interpretation?"

Is it possible for someone to be in control of history?

Mai

Could it be that a search for history begins with a search for yourself?

Melissa

We talk about writing history beginning with a topic of personal interest.

I can understand...how it (writing about a topic you love) can really improve your writing because you can write about something you know, understand and enjoy.

Melissa

Our discussion took us from a view of the historian as writer to the nature of historical interpretation: analyzing, synthesizing, hypothesizing, asking questions and solving problems.

The History Log

I want my students to read their history text at home as a background for what we discuss in class. But I don't want them to mechanically outline the chapter or to answer "reading and comprehension questions." I want them to think about what they read, so I ask them to respond to their chapters the same way we respond to in-class readings: write what you learned, what you thought about it and any questions you have. We had been responding to primary sources and essays in class, but somehow a textbook had a different meaning. Respond to the textbook? What would happen? I am never sure—and neither are the students. I set up a weekly reading schedule and collected the first set of responses the following Friday.

When I read that first set, I found a variety of student approaches to the assignment—anywhere from jotted lists of facts or summaries to reflective pieces in which students were asking questions, giving opinions and making connections.

The papers in the last group were a delight to read. The students were really thinking. They were going beyond summary to interpretation, analysis, synthesis and hypothesis. I wrote brief comments in the margins next to sentences which showed students connecting, personalizing and interpreting history. When students raised questions, I wrote brief answers or suggested they bring them up in class. I acknowledged opinions and insights by writing "Yes" or "I agree" or "Interesting" or "I never thought of it that way." I underlined or marked with double lines in the margin especially important concepts that they brought out. I gave checks (✓) to summaries or jot lists and check pluses (✓+) to true responses. Here are some sample entries and comments:

9/17/84

The colonists I find hard to believe in this chapter because before the reader was left to believe that the American forces were barely united and not composed of that many troops; yet when the reader moves to the next frame of the picture, it is as if something has been omitted; specifically how did all the colonists get together as quickly and in such larger amounts than before?

This is really a key question—be sure to bring this up in our discussion.

Melissa

9/23/84

I don't see how just because they met alot meant that their organization became part of the "Constitution." What is the true link or reason, that's what I want to know.

It's part of the unwritten Constitution.

Craig

9/23/84

I also noticed that the text related George Washington to the reader in the same boring way as a list of facts, not anything like what the books I read (for a research project) made him out to be at all.

Would you share this with our class during our discussion?

Joey

11/20/84

By the way, why didn't he (Hamilton) just start from scratch with new money? He could have set up an exchange rate, like for every 20 Continental dollars you have, you receive one new dollar. Perhaps this would have brought the dollar up in the monetary scale. I guess it just wasn't that easy, but that seems logical; to redistribute money so that its value is greater and then allow the use of the old money. Why wouldn't that work?

Scott, bring this up in class.

Scott

11/15/84

The Federalists use logic similar to that in the resolutions (Virginia Resolutions), saying that since people created the government, the government should answer to the people in the form of the Supreme Court. A good practice I feel.

I agree.

Mai

12/10/84

We went to Mexico, beat up a few people, and paid $18,250,000 for the land. We *won!* Why did *we* pay?

Because we got the land we wanted.

Jennifer

After I return the papers, we discuss the differences between the papers with checks and those with check pluses. I ask students to read aloud what they had written and point out where in the writing I heard connecting, questioning, thinking. Students also share how they do the assignment. There are many different approaches. Some respond in short bursts as they read. Others read the chapter twice—once to get an overview, another time to think about what they would respond to. Still others take notes as they read and respond later.

I look forward to reading the logs. Each student's log is different. They are interesting, original and informative. As the year goes on, the entries become longer and more thoughtful. This is the beginning of a process by which writing to learn in history logs becomes an integral part of our class. Writing in logs is one way students use their own language to personalize history. Equally important is the talk they do about their logs—talk that takes place most effectively in small groups.

The Group Connection

At the beginning of class the room is full of students talking, laughing, writing graffiti on the board or catching up on physics homework. My voice is no match for a room full of lively sixteen-year-olds, so I write on the board: "I need to see the group leaders now. Please get into your reading/writing groups." I like talking with the group leaders while the rest of the class gets physically settled. It saves time and having the group leaders deliver the instructions focuses on the importance of the groups. While the rest of the class begins getting into groups, I give the leaders these instructions:

1. Individually read your responses to Chapter 9. As you read, underline ideas that for any reason seem important or significant to you and mark places where you have raised questions.
2. Choose one of these ideas or questions to do a focused free writing on.
3. Take turns reading your responses to each other.
    a. Tell the writer what the main idea of the response is and what you thought was most interesting about the response.
    b. Discuss these main ideas and answer each other's questions, if you can.
4. Choose one of the group's responses to share with the rest of the class.

The instructions are familiar ones. We had been working in groups for two months by this time and students were used to the basic responding method I had learned from reading Donald Graves:

1. Say back what you think the piece is about.
2. Tell what the strongest parts were.
3. Tell which parts you'd like to know more about.
4. Ask questions about parts that you find confusing.

I adapted these four responses for the history chapters, but the idea was the same. And I found them to be very effective discussion starters.

I wait a few minutes while the groups get settled. Getting into groups is not a quiet process. Tables get moved, chairs bang, and books are dropped while students negotiate for places. Then they need time to look through folders for the right papers and to ask for directions.

In about five minutes the room becomes quiet, and all I hear for the next twenty minutes is the sound of pens moving across paper. During this quiet writing time, I write in my class journal about what's going on with the class and with me.

Students begin to finish and the room fills once again with student voices as they share their writings. I walk around from group to group to listen and answer questions. This is an excerpt from a group sharing their responses to a chapter called "Launching a New Ship of State." It is about issues facing the United States during Washington's first administration, 1789-1792.

Brian: Of course the Republic was a "New Ship on Uncertain Seas"; they had just become a new nation, open to all sorts of problems. I think the main problem was finance—the government quickly had to get a good monetary system going and all the debts paid off or it would go bankrupt in a hurry. Response, questions, comments, what?

Vida: Keep on going.

Wendy: Wait a second. "Bankrupt." No, that means we would lose all our money.

Vida: Wait a minute. The government, you mean the government would lose? They all wanted to have one monetary system. 'Cause the—it was the states which had their own money.

Wendy: Monetary. Is that like m-o-n-i-t-a-r-y?

Brian: M-o-n-e-t-a-r-y.

Vida: Why did they all want one though?

Brian: They had to. So they could have stable finances. I mean, if you have, like. . . .

Ben: You know, you know. . . .

Wendy: Money.

Ben: Yeah, you know. (Laughter)

Brian: Washington was a good guy, although I'm sure history *has* beefed him up a little. I pretty much know about his cabinet already, although I didn't realize that Hamilton and Jefferson were such enemies.

Ben: Enemies or animals?

Brian: Both. (Laughter) No. Enemies. They had like different philosophies. Hamilton was crafty indeed. I agree that although "Funding Fathers" is probably an appropriate name for Congress, they had to also help the nation at hand, which Hamilton's bill did. Also $54 million for a national debt seems like a lot for the time period and a nation so young. . .was it also money owed from the Revolution?

Alisa: I have absolutely no idea.

Wendy: Was it money. . .what?

Vida: What else could they owe?

Ben: Well, that's what I was about to say. What else could the debt be? I mean, before the Revolution, it [the textbook] said that the colonies were...that their economic status was better than that of England, wasn't it?

Vida: Wait a minute. Who did they owe this money to?

Alisa: Probably France.

Vida: Who did they owe the money to? It [the textbook] says "also $54 million for a national debt." It seems like a lot for the time period. So who did they?

Alisa: France. France. Read the next paragraph.

Brian: Hamilton's plan moves on—assumption, D.C., logrolling....

Ben: What is that?

Brian: All of Hamilton's plans jibe nicely with the fact that he wanted a strong central government for the rich. His taxes and customs duties greatly support these ideas.

Wendy: Well, what about the poor people?

Brian: He didn't care about them. He thought that only rich people should be allowed to vote.

Ben: Now there's a clear-cut Republican for you.

Brian: Yeah!

Wendy: I don't like Republicans.

Ben: I don't either.

Wendy: The Republicans of today are like the Democrats of a long time ago, and the Democrats of today are like the Republicans.

Brian: Hardly.

Wendy: Yeah, they are.

Ben: Where did you get that from?

Alisa: History.

Wendy: I don't know. I've heard that before.

Ben: She read it in the latest *National Enquirer.*

Wendy: That the Republicans of today are not the same. They don't have the same values they did a hundred years ago.

Brian: Well, what it was...it's like they used to be Whigs, okay? The Democrats and Republicans way back in chapter 8 were in one party called the Democrats. There were the Republicans and the Federalists.

Wendy: The Democrats of today have the same values as the Republicans hundreds of years ago.

Ben: What was Hamilton at this time?

Brian: He was a Federalist.

Ben: A Federalist?

Wendy: Why do all the Democrats today hate all the Republicans?

Brian: Because there's two separate parties. But look....

Alisa: The Republicans have become like the rich....Why don't you continue reading?

Brian: Hamilton seems to be getting what he wants all the time...his banks, his taxes...he was pretty powerful. However, all was in the name of a strong federal government which was important. The Whiskey Rebellion shows me old colonial feelings, which were "any central government has to be wrong." It was put down easily but did have its consequences...the government got respect and Jeffersonians came to vote. The government got respect because the military put down the rebellion. Good thing all of Hamilton's plans worked. That's all this chapter has talked about. Was Washington a Federalist? It wouldn't seem so, with the book saying that Federalists were against the masses having any power and were even Loyalists! Hamilton sure seems different from what I would expect a strong American patriot to be.

Ben: Hold it. At this time, what were the two political groups? There were the Federalists and the Republicans?

Wendy: So the Federalists are like the Republicans, I mean the Democrats.

Ben: No.

Alisa: The other party, not the Federalists, were the Democratic-Republicans.

Brian: Right.

Wendy: See, I told you the Democrats were like the Republicans from a long time ago.

Brian: Look, back then they had the Federalists, and, for our purposes, we should call them Democrats, but they were the Democratic-Republicans, okay? The Federalists eventually died out and the Democratic-Republicans stayed like one party. Then the Whigs showed up, okay? And the Whigs evolved into modern Republicans and the Democrat-Republicans just came into Democrats. And you have all your weirdo parties out there somewhere.

Wendy: Yeah.

Vida: But why was Hamilton different from what you would expect him to be?

Brian: 'Cause I didn't expect that a guy who was so key in our government, in our central government back then, he didn't support pure democracy.

Ben: That's true. He wanted rich and aristocracy.

Brian: I mean, he was that way during our whole Constitutional Convention.

Ben: Are you done?

Brian: Jefferson was basically Hamilton's opposite; However, he didn't want everyone to vote, either: only the educated. Okay, I'm through. Now you can talk about...

Wendy: Well, that's true. Look. If you have a bunch of uneducated people voting, you're not going to get a true vote.

Brian: Right.

Wendy: Understand?

Brian: Yeah.

For the most part, I am not needed; they are on their own. They listen, discuss and answer each other's questions. When they get stuck, they call me over or get a book from the shelf. This sharing goes on for another twenty-five minutes. After a short break, I ask students to volunteer to share with the whole class either their chapter response or the writing they had just completed. I tell them to listen and to take notes from each other. They no longer look to see if I am marking a check in my grade book. And I'm not because students value how much they learn from each other, and I no longer need to mark the checks to show the importance of participation.

After a student reads, I respond by pointing out how she is interpreting history, making connections and predictions. When appropriate, I ask her to explain a point or to offer more evidence to support a conclusion she has drawn. If she has a question, I throw it back to the class. Rarely have I had to be the final authority; and I will very often ask the class to respond to a log entry instead of my responding to it. Students begin to see the classroom as very much their own.

Conclusion

> Writing helps me to understand more what I don't understand about something. When I write something out, it clears my mind ....You have more than facts. You have what you thought about it. I think it helps me to write the history responses because I remember...what I was thinking of as I read it and what it helped me to realize or to make connections or whatever about the topic. And that's more valuable than just taking straight notes because you have more than facts. You have thought about it.
>
> Jennifer

For writing to learn to be effective, and for it to make a substantive difference in what happens in a student's learning, we need to look at other factors at work in the classroom. In my history class, it's not just the writing. It's the language connection. Students learn from listening to each other, and the groups afford the greatest opportunity for this interaction. Students write their logs and read them aloud. They listen and respond to each other. All four language modes are at work: writing, reading, listening, speaking. This language connection enables writing to learn to play a central role in the history curriculum.

Appendix

I found Jennifer's log interesting because of its evolution. Her first entry was a listing of facts from the chapter. She included terms and definitions and a brief description of the topics covered in the chapter on colonial society. This is an excerpt from that first entry:

Nov. 15, 1983
Ch. 4 The Character of Colonial Society

birth rate high - large growth
large families (10-20, etc)
 many infant deaths

Colonial Melting Pot
 mostly English - some German (Philadelphia)

Scotch—Irish, French Hugenots, Welsh
Dutch, Swedes, Jews, Irish, Swiss, Scot Highlanders
Africans - carried in chains to America
slaves - 90% in the South

Jennifer's second entry was written after we had a class discussion
about the differences between summarizing and responding. She included notes and lists as she had originally done, but this time she wrote
the following at the end:

Nov. 20, 1983
I found this chapter interesting but a little boring. It really amazed
me how "strong" the Americans were mentally. They wanted
independence and freedom, and really went after it. It did surprise
me, though, how much they were complaining over trivial things.
After all, they were there *for* England to *benefit* England. What
gave them the right, or courage to rebel?

She started out with a judgment and then draws a conclusion about
what was going on in the minds of the Americans. The Americans were
"mentally strong." She is interpreting what was going on in the next
sentence: "Complaining over trivial things," and then asks an important
question: "What gave them the right, or courage to rebel?" Jennifer is
beginning to think like a historian—analyzing, interpreting, asking
questions.

As we used the responses more and more as the basis for discussing
the chapters in the text, I noticed a shift in what Jennifer was writing:

Feb.8, 1983
James Madison and the 2nd War for Independence 1812:
Chapter 11 Response
I am going to try a new technique: responding every so often. First,
I don't really understand the theory behind Macon's Bill No. 2. It
doesn't really make all that sense to me. One big mistake the
American made was going to war against England. First of all,
they really had no reason to—why not France? They had also been
tricked by Napoleon, and were a divided nation—New England,
especially was against the war of 1812. How could they think that
it could possibly work?!
I tend to question the sincerity of the war anyway—it seemed like
the War Hawks just wanted to fight—the issues weren't tremendously significant—at least they didn't seem that way to me. I never
saw a real *solid* purpose. (impressment, etc.)

The Post-War Upsurge of Nationalism 1815-1824
Chapter 12 Response
The beginning of this chapter seemed to be saying what I had
expected to happen after "ch. 11." There was quite a great feeling
for America—a pride, even though they hadn't exactly accomplished everything they wanted out of war—it was still a unifying
factor. This was probably the first time this sort of nationalism was
experienced, as the people considered themselves *Americans* first—
the impact of these feelings was very important to America's

growth and development. I didn't completely understand the Tariff of 1816, so I need to go over that again.

Jennifer here is consciously shifting into a more reflective style of responding which includes asking questions which get at the heart of understanding the War of 1812: "They had no reason to—why not France?... How could they think that it could possibly work?" When she says, "The beginning of the chapter seemed to be saying what I expected to happen after ch. 11," Jennifer is anticipating and predicting what would happen next. She is asking "what will be the consequences of these actions?" She had already related winning the War of 1812 with a feeling of national pride, and this was confirmed by her reading. And she is becoming aware of what she doesn't understand by asking questions about the Tariff of 1816.

Within six to eight weeks, Jennifer's entries became longer and more thoughtful. They grew from lists of facts to one-page summaries to entries which were anywhere from two to four pages and which truly engaged the material.

Drifting Toward Disunion 1854-1861
Chapter 21 Response
There were so many big ideas in this chapter—it went through all the events leading up to secession and Civil War. The last paragraph was very interesting, as it drew parallels between the 11 colonies seceding from the Union and the 13 colonies breaking away from England. Believe it or not, I was thinking the same thing earlier in the chapter. It seems as if no one is ever satisfied— but then again I suppose if we were ALWAYS happy, nothing would ever change. *Uncle Tom's Cabin* by Harriet Beecher Stowe had a great effect on the people. I suppose it was quite shocking and devastating for the people to read—and an eye-opener sort of effect. James Buchanan was elected President. The Kansas-Nebraska Act, and the following compromises came into play. The Missouri Compromise (bans slavery north of 36°30′) was nullified by the K-N Act. Abe Lincoln and Douglas caused an important conflict with Republicans and Democrats, the North and South, etc. I was surprised to read some of the things about "Old Abe." It seems like I always think every President in the beginning of America was such a great guy—they're not all they're cracked up to be in 5th and 6th grade classes! John Brown did seem to be insane—his idea made a little sense, idealistically, but it's hard to believe he actually tried it—a good cause, but no common sense. Finally, the very important election of 1860 (Lincoln and Douglas). If Douglas had been elected, the Civil War probably would never have occurred. The Crittenden Compromise sounded feasible to me, but I guess Old Abe was just too honest to go back on campaign promises (What happened to that honesty today??!) Secession and disunion could now begin. What actually did the South want? (Just to keep slavery or what—they seemed determined to make it their own.)

Jennifer goes beyond summary to interpretation and analysis. She had already begun to draw her own parallels between secession and the American Revolution. She assessed the importance of John Brown: "He made sense idealistically, but it's hard to believe he actually tried it. A good cause, but no common sense." She makes connections to her own world: "What happened to that honesty today?" And she asks the question throughout? "What actually did the South want?"

Jennifer's log changed over the semester from a place for notes on the highlights of the chapter, to a place where she writes to connect, to question, to evaluate, to speculate. But I think what happened with Jennifer had a great deal to do with what else was going on in the classroom. Jennifer's log grew, I believe, because the logs were used in small and large groups as the basis for discussion; because of the kind of comments she received from peers and from me; and because the logs were valued as a truly important part of our curriculum.

24.

The Honest Voice of Inquiry: Teaching Folklore Through Writing

RICHARD C. SWETERLITSCH

> First of all, this journal seems to be a compilation of the information that I have learned this semester. Many of the writings go beyond the "learned-stage" and enter into understanding and relating to my life.... This journal is a growing experience. [The entries] change in mood and style, but all of them contain a sense of understanding or wonder....Hopefully this journal expresses my excitement in learning. It was an expansion of ideas involving old and new and related to much more than just the classroom.
>
> from the journal of Tom O'Hare (December, 1985)

Tom's final journal entry marked the end of a fourteen-week writing project for him and an experiment for me.

I had taught an introductory folklore course for ten years, presenting each time the major folklore theories and concepts. And students were required to write the usual research papers based on their own field and library research. But more recently I wanted to develop students' awareness of living traditions and to train them to use folklore theory to understand better traditional events occurring in their everyday world. I decided to experiment with journal writing. The informal nature of the journal provided a context where students could write freely, unencumbered by the demands of formal essay writing.

I required students to keep a journal in which they wrote reflections on their own experiences with folk traditions and *reviewed* them in terms of the folklore theories presented in the course. Such writing, I hoped, would encourage drawing upon personal experiences, identifying folk traditions in the "real" world, and applying and testing ideas presented in lectures and in assigned readings. The students' primary concerns in this assignment included reflection, analysis, and synthetic thinking, all without the restraints formal writing assignments place on an author. My primary concerns were explaining the assignment well and developing questions or assignments which would meet its goals.

In the first week of class I explained the journal assignment and the philosophy behind it. I showed examples of my own journal entries and characterized the kind of journal writing I encouraged as *writer-oriented*, that is, written by the writer primarily for himself. I would occasionally collect the journals and look, as it were, over the writer's shoulder, maybe raising a question here or there regarding some of the entries or encouraging more thinking and reflection in others. In the end, the journal would be graded as an informal journal, evaluated chiefly in terms of its thoroughness and thoughtfulness. It was worth 80 percent of the final grade, with the remaining part of the grade based on class participation. I was serious about discovering the value of the journal writing as a learning experience, and I wanted the students to take the assignment seriously, too.

As the course progressed, I designed questions which I thought would encourage reflection and various modes of thinking. I gave the entry assignment during the class lecture and sometimes devoted time in class to writing and sharing entries. On some occasions, I suggested a "free write," meaning students could write about a topic of their own interest. At all times, however, students had the option of writing on their own ideas drawn from the readings, class presentations, or something relevant from outside the classroom which particularly struck them. I wanted them to take ideas and go with them as far as they could, but it was important that students left the classroom with the option of a particular topic. I would like to share four assignments, some student entries, and some analysis of the entries.

Example 1

January 18—Second class meeting. There was a general class discussion of what "folklore" meant. I noted that even folklorists have disagreements among themselves regarding specifics, but most agree on some general ideas. Students were reading the introductory passages of Richard M. Dorson's *Bloodstoppers and Bearwalkers* (Cambridge, 1952) and his *America in Legend* (New York, 1973). Assignment: you have signed up for a class in folklore. First write down what you think folklore might be all about. Then review the two definitions/descriptions provided in Dorson's texts. Where do you and Dorson see eye to eye, and where do you differ?

Jim, a freshman, spent a summer hiking in the White Mountains of New Hampshire, sleeping, as he put it, "on the ground with the locals," and learning their lore. He reflected on that experience in terms of its meaning to him and to his studying folklore. He wrote in part:

> To me, there is no better way to learn than by doing and being a part of what you are learning. That is what folklore is: it is a "doing" experience. Through folklore we can learn how the commoner was affected by the economy, culture, and changes in society. We can gain insight to the beliefs, customs, traditions, secrets and thoughts of a group.
>
> Dorson describes folklore as being literally the history of a folk or a closely tied group. It is much as I've said, actually. We, through folklore, can learn a people's traditions, customs, anxieties, fears and beliefs. But I seemed to have left out some important points that Mr. Dorson points out nicely to us. Folklore is more than just traditions, these traditions are esoteric. Anyone outside the group fails to understand them. Now I feel I under-

stand the traditions taught me in the White Mountains although many seem silly to me. Does this understanding make me a victim of "fakelore" as Dorson has coined the term? All of the stories I heard were told by mouth thus fulfilling one of Dorson's criteria. I have yet to see if any of the tales are listed in the catalogues Dorson has mentioned. It would be interesting to see if they are. Dorson also focuses on the ordinary citizen: "the peripheral rather than the mainstream culture, with the peasant rather than the shopkeeper." In my experience I dealt with these kinds of people. I hope, through this course, I can learn more about ordinary folk in my own country and abroad. I am looking forward to reading what Mr. Dorson has compiled for us.

Jim's entry, only half of it repeated here, brought together disparate ideas drawn from his hiking in New Hampshire with Dorson's descriptive definitions. Jim perceived that his initial notion of folklore—"'doing' experiences"—meant much the same as what Dorson wrote. While the meaning of Jim's curious phrase might not have been clear to another reader or even to the author himself, he became intrigued with Dorson's observations and applied them to his evasive concept of folklore.

What happened was both reflective and synthetic thinking. Expressing his experiences with the local folk in New Hampshire as an experience with folklore eluded Jim. But he picked up on three key ideas: the common man theme he shared with Dorson; what he heard in the White Mountains came by word of mouth, and so it did meet a criterion laid down by Dorson; and perhaps the stories could be found in the catalogues, a reference to the Thompson motif and type indices. Jim wrote to connect his own experiences and ambiguous notions about folklore with some of Dorson's ideas. He concluded that he wanted to know more.

Jim took a chance with this entry. His sense of what folklore meant wasn't clear in his own head, and his entry is accordingly evasive. But he didn't hesitate to write it in his journal and then compare it with those of a professional. During the following class, Jim read his entry aloud. It, along with several others also read aloud, provided a lead-in for a constructive class discussion, which included a critique of Dorson's definitions and ended with a general sense of agreement over the meaning of "folklore."

Example 2

January 22—A section of *Bloodstoppers and Bearwalkers* dealt with Native American lore regarding love potions and charms. This provided the context for the question: *What is your reaction to the Native American belief in love potions? Do we Americans use potions or similar love charms?*

Discussion in the following class was very lively, to no one's surprise. I began by asking several willing students to share their journal musings.

Several wrote that they found the Native American belief very strange, if not outright humorous. Yet, a number of them wrote they had heard about Spanish fly and green M&M's arousing sexul passion. Few failed to mention advertisements for perfumes and aftershave lotions. Several of the male students who had attended boarding schools talked about saltpeter secretly put in mashed potatoes on dance nights. No one came away from the assignment without realizing that the tradition of using charms and lures to attract love partners—or with saltpeter to curb lust—was a part of the folk and popular cultures in the modern world. The question posed to the class before had the students thinking about their own lore, and this established a context which helped facilitate my presentation on esoteric/exoteric factors in folklore.

Example 3

About midway through the course I dealt with the folk heroes, drawing primarily upon nineteenth-century American figures. At the end of the unit I contrasted those heroes with more modern ones. I began the class with an in-class journal question: *What is the status of hero worship in this country today?*

"Today, we can't really come up with personal heroes," wrote Tina. "We recall folk heroes but don't really know much about them. This is sad in a way because a lot of our heritage can be detected in the stories of Davy Crockett, Mike Fink, Sam Patch.... The people and their work today in America are so varied and diverse that we are unable to focus on a single representative figure that we can admire and humanize enough to enable everyone to take part in the 'hero making.'"

Sandy wrote: "Truly we live in a time without national heroes.... The hero of today is Bernhard Goetz, the vigilante killer. Everywhere I go I hear people talking about him, arguing over his decision to take the law into his own hands.... The American hero scene is a big mess. When I try to think of a national hero that I look up to my mind draws a blank. Mass media distort personal integrity to the point where natural heroes are invisible."

This particular question occasioned several interesting points in the entries. Was notoriety equivalent to being a hero? How important are the mass media in making public figures heroic? Tina lamented what she saw as a failure to maintain in our heritage an association with folk heroes. Sandy calls the situation a mess, blaming the problem on the mass media which distorts personal integrity. Both writers came to grips with the current phenomenon of a dearth of national heroes. Their explanations differ, but both probed into American life and discovered that the nation has changed from the hero-making days of the nineteenth and early twentieth centuries.

Example 4

April 10-17—Jan Brunvand's *The Vanishing Hitchhiker* (New York, 1978) proved to be a very popular text. In conjunction with reading it, the class was asked to note in their journals which if any of the accounts in the book they had heard before. For Hannah, the first night of reading assignment prompted her to report a collective experience.

> Tonight I was reading *The Vanishing Hitchhiker* while sitting in a friend's room with three others who were studying. I read one of the stories about "The Hook" aloud and it set off a round of storytelling. Each of us knew a different version of the story but could not remember where we first heard it. Then I read on about the babysitter and the phone caller from upstairs. That one really hit home because we all have been scared while babysitting and sometimes for good reason like a rapist being reported in the area. As I read more, my friends commented, "I heard this one" or "I heard that one." We realized that many of these stories have been made into movies like *A Stranger Is Watching* or at least used in parts of movies such as *Halloween* and the scene with the man in the back seat. [In a marginal note, Hannah added: "It makes a horror movie scarier when you have heard the story before."] Before we even read that one, a friend told us a story that she heard from her mother. "This really happened," she said. . . .

And Hannah wrote two more pages, recounting two of the narratives she heard from friends that night. She ended with, "I'm sure these terrible things really happened to people at one time, but that's just how it starts. The stories get exaggerated and passed along until they supposedly happened in every town across the country to someone that someone's friend's friend knows."

Although I had not yet discussed the urban legend per se in class, Hannah had already touched on some important qualities of that narrative form. First, they were widespread legends and she became aware of that fact particularly well that evening as her dorm mates recounted different versions of them. Urban legends, too, centered around ordinary activities such as babysitting, so that they struck very familiar cords for Hannah and her friends who themselves babysit. Recent motion pictures have dramatized some of these legends, and Hannah as an aside adds that pre-knowledge heightened horror. Then she began to recount a series of tales, each beginning with the formulaic legend opening, "This really happened" and an ascribed living source for the narrative. Interestingly, Hannah began her entry with a note that she and her friends could not remember where they first heard the stories, but when they began recounting them, they, unconsciously obeying the formulaic opening of legend telling, ascribed them to a particular person who had told the legend to them. Her final observation about the migratory nature of the urban legends and their attribution to a friend of a friend's friend are also important marks of this genre. After I discussed some of the formal characteristics of the urban legend, Hannah was able to look back at her entry and note many of them present there.

Hannah's entry was typical. Most in the class retold in their journal at least one legend they had heard. Moreover, most of the writers recognized that those tales which they might once have believed were in fact examples of modern folklore, and they began to view them less as factual accounts and more as significant oral narratives which provided insight into modern urban fears and anxieties.

Hoping to draw upon this latter awareness, I assigned an entry in which they were to explore what these urban legends tell us about the contemporary urban world. The notion that a world view can be understood in terms of a culture group's folklore had been discussed in mid-February. Now in April the students were to draw upon that concept in order to use it to sort out some meanings of contemporary urban legends.

Shirley wrote, "Within this collection [*The Vanishing Hitchhiker*] there consists a mass of cultural symbols...many of these give insights into human behavior in a social urban environment." She discussed at some length symbolic meanings she found in the legends about the death car, fast-food contamination, and the boyfriend's death. "While these legends themselves," she concluded, "do not represent *in toto* the world of the urban dwellers, they certainly symbolize many of the concerns of urban society and contain many cultural symbols of its world." Tom saw the urban legends and behavior patterns as signs of contradictions within our society: "...we say we believe the tales, and yet we do not in any radical way change our behavior patterns." No one stops eating fast-food even though the stories of fried rats "play on the mind, when you are actually eating the chicken...." Jennifer, another student, noted that many of the tales proved anti-feminist by characterizing women as being incompetents, who jeopardized themselves by foolishly placing themselves in threatening situations. She cited several tales in which women neglecting the traditional roles of housekeeper and mother in favor of working outside the home turned over these traditional responsibilities to others and thus ended as victims of their decisions. The legends reflected anxieties resulting from a change in traditional roles. Jennifer wrote that it wasn't until she read these legends and stopped to look critically at the message symbolized in them that she fully realized the anxiety that women's liberation produced: "This really shocked me and it is one thing that I never realized until I took this course." All three of these writers looked closely at the texts and stopped to discover the meanings embedded in them. From their own perspectives they understood more about the role of folklore in the modern world, and they learned a little about seeing beyond the surface level of the legend narratives themselves.

Each student wrote a total of forty-five entries, including those in-class and out-of-class. Topics for other entries included critiques of several films and videotapes I showed in class. For example, I asked the class to enumerate the various functions that quilting had in the lives of the women presented in the film *Quilts in Women's Lives* or to evaluate the videotape *They Shall Take Up Serpents* in terms of its presentation of the world view of the cult featured in it. A videotape of *Ben's Mill* encouraged several students to write about traditional craftsmen living in the students' own town. Some assignments called for extremely close reading of various folktale texts. In one case, students compared and contrasted six international variants of "Cinderella" and then contrasted the folk versions to the one they are most familiar with. With Eudora Welty's "The Robber Bridegroom" (New York, 1963) and Arthur Miller's *The Crucible* (New York, 1959), we discussed, and the students wrote about, several aspects of folklore in literature.

Reading and evaluating the journals proved no small task, especially with fifty-five students enrolled in the class. I randomly collected the journals on a regular basis, read some entries thoroughly and skimmed the others. I wrote back to the students on separate sheets of paper, encouraging their work and stimulating some re-visioning of weaker entries. Toward the end of the semester, I asked students to write an introduction to the journal, provide an index to the entries, and point out which entries they particularly liked. A week before classes were over I collected all the journals and spent a week and a half reading and rereading entries. Actually I spent little more time reading these journals than I would have taken to read research papers. After all, I had been through parts of the journals over the course of the semester. In addition, entries were much more interesting than the usual undergraduate research paper. There was a freshness of expression and a sense of familiarity, since the students were writing on topics they knew about or with which they had some personal contact.

An honest voice of inquiry pervaded the entries, and it was obvious to me from many of the entries and some of the introductions that the students had incorporated much of the course into their own way of looking at the world about them. One student wrote, "I enjoyed writing in the journal because I think it really pulled the ideas of the class together in such a way that the writing of the journal became a focal point for the lectures and the readings." Another student, reflecting on the journal, which he dubbed "an anthology of thought," marveled with a sense of accomplishment over how much work he had done. Regular writing was a demanding task, he felt, but he decided in the end that he had good tangible proof of his growth in understanding folklore.

I believe that the experiment was a success. The type of student engagement with folklore which I sought was achieved. Entry after entry showed signs of serious questioning, independent thinking, testing, and synthesizing. Over the course of the semester, the entries grew less ambiguous and less evasive as the students became more comfortable using the critical concepts and terminology of folkloristics. And I think that those results are not bad for an introductory course.

25.

A Journal in the Arts

CHRISTOPHER THAISS

I. The Journal Artist

Reaction to *Ways of Seeing*

Narcissism was the term used, I do believe. He's got a good point. I'd love to have a dime for every minute women (or men) spent thinking "How do I look? How do I appear?" I feel that I'm especially aware of this problem having grown up in dance studios—mirrored dance studios. In those clothes, if you ate an extra portion of alfalfa sprouts everyone knows it. The hair and make-up must be in place. You are constantly judged by the image you project. Higher leg. More turns. More eyes. Every aspect of your body must work for that projection, so of course your brain is preoccupied with appearance. Unfortunately, that preoccupation does not stay in the studio. A performer's life, if gone unchecked, is quick to become one big production—everything done for the proper reaction. I can tell you that reality and your projection of reality soon become hard to differentiate. Carried to the extreme, you have the "washed up" performer who is too old, the "fat" dancer (who weighs 102 lbs.), the "has been" chorus girl who can't get that leg extension any more, who are alcoholics, drug addicts, and anorexics. THAT'S SHOW BIZ!!

from Emily Chamlee's *Reading the Arts* journal (November 1984)

Emily Chamlee has been keeping journals for years, both in school and out. At 12, she began keeping a "notebook" of "experiments" with language: "I loved to write poetry, but when I read *real* poetry I realized that I'd have to work harder with words. In my notebook I could try out anything to see how it sounded, and revise until I got the effect I wanted." She discovered for herself that the journal let her understand how she felt about things. The journal made her analyze her feelings and gave her a way to organize ideas.

She saw, and still sees, the journal as a way to achieve psychical distance from her emotions and reactions. She has even experimented in her journals with narrative styles and voices that help her enhance this distancing. "When I was in Europe, I wanted to record everything I saw as vividly as possible; I wanted to avoid my usual tendency to reflect. So

I pretended that I was one of my favorite writers, Joseph Wambaugh, writing about the place, with me as one of the characters in it. Instead of writing, for example, 'Today Jean and I walked along the Left Bank,' I'd say 'There's Emily from America, with the red pack on her back, just meeting Jean.' Then I could describe the setting. I guess I also liked the creative freedom this playing with styles in the journal gave me. I didn't have then as many creative outlets as I have now, so the journal let me be an artist."

During these same years, her high school English teachers were assigning journals. She kept these in addition to her private journal, which has always been the laboratory for her most serious, experimental writing. The high school journals, she says, were intended by the teachers to be used for the students' reactions to the class, to school, to people. "We are supposed to record our emotional ups and downs." Already experienced in journal keeping, Chamlee used these assigned journals not just to *record* her feelings about things, but to analyze the motives and patterns of her reactions. "I'd write about a problem until I'd looked at it from every side I could. I was trying to wrestle it down so that I could understand how and why I was thinking as I was. As I'd learned earlier, the writing let me admit things that I would have had a hard time saying; this process didn't always solve my problems, but if I kept at the writing it usually helped."

The high school journals also presented Chamlee with a problem that she had not had to face in her earlier journal keeping: the teacher as audience. In those and in the journals she is keeping now as a college freshman, she has found that "no matter how non-judgmental a teacher tries to be, I always feel that I'm putting forth an image of myself in the journal, and that judgments, even if they're unconscious, are coming back." She praises the usual teacher practice of not giving specific grades to the journals—this does free her somewhat. Nevertheless, she says that she would "find it uncomfortable to write, for example, about gender issues to someone in authority whom I could tell was not sympathetic." When asked how she avoids confronting a teacher's prejudice and still maintains the integrity of her journal, she says that she "gets away from emotion—the journal becomes more like a paper, in which I 'look at the facts' in order to support my argument. I wouldn't say something emotional, like 'I can't understand why things are this way!'"

One facet of the image she tries to project as a school journal keeper is that of "the non-apathetic student who does journal assignments." Consequently, she will stick to a three-entries-per-week schedule assigned by the instructor, even if this means writing three entries on three topics on one day, a practice, she says, which reduces the effectiveness of the journal, "since it doesn't allow me enough time to think about what I'm writing or about what I've written." She knows of students, of course, who will write two or three weeks' worth of entries the night before a collection day. "I don't see how they can get anything out of the journal. I'd find the exercise meaningless if I let more than three assignments pile up."

Consequently, she wishes that teachers would collect and respond to student journals more frequently, ideally after each entry is written. She sees that this might result in fewer assigned entries, but feels that more important than the amount of writing is the pride that students, including herself, would feel if they knew that each entry would be considered individually, rather than "in a bunch." However, she also realizes that her private journal has made her more fluent than other students and less in need of an external requirement to write regularly. It has also made it unnecessary for her to use the assigned journal for personal writing directed to herself; hence, she looks forward to the teacher's response to her journal and writes *for* the audience rather than *despite* it. Predictably, given her experience and accrued confidence, she doesn't fear criticism of her writing, and she particularly likes the respondent to raise questions about her ideas or to state facts that she has not considered. She also appreciates grammatical correction and comments on style, such as this that she received in a first-semester college course: "You have a strong voice; however, don't move too far away from the topic and don't hesitate to state the obvious." She appreciates this, she says, because it alerted her to characteristics of her entries that she had not recognized. She isn't satisfied, she says, merely to receive a "Good" or "Nice job" beside her entries.

II. A Journal in the Arts

As a college freshman, Chamlee, a student in the interdisciplinary general education program (PAGE) at George Mason University, has contended with one assigned journal in each semester. In the fall, she wrote three entries per week for Professor Lorna Irvine in PAGE 122, "Reading the Arts," a course which deals with the structural elements of literature, painting, and music, so that students can learn ways to perceive the arts and talk about them. As another "Reading the Arts" professor, Eileen Sypher, stated it in her syllabus, the journal in this course

> is not the same as a diary—that is, a stranger (me) will be reading it, a stranger interested principally in observing the ways the material of this course affects your perceptions of the world and the new ideas it generates.... Use your journal to wrestle with an idea that comes up in class, to respond in more depth than we did to a poem, or painting, or piece of music, or to start applying what you're learning to other "art" objects you notice around you.

To Irvine, the "Arts" journal differs greatly from the "write your thoughts and feelings about anything" journals that students such as Chamlee wrote in high school or that Irvine herself has assigned students in freshman writing classes. "This journal is far more analytic than those are, and far less open in subject matter. I still want students to say honestly that they love a rock song or that they hate abstract art, but I want them to focus on writing reasons for their feelings. Sure, I'd like them to become more appreciative of unfamiliar styles, and the journal does help this happen, but I still feel that they've learned something if 'I hate' is now followed by 'because.'"

The Arts journal differs enough from the "feelings" journal that

Irvine thinks "journal" is the wrong name for the form. "We should call it a response log or an analytic notebook. To most of the students, 'journal' means unanalyzed reactions; to a few, it means our prying into their personal lives, and they refuse to do it, until they understand what we're looking for. Maybe it's ironic, but an 'analytical' journal is much more liberating to this type of student than is one explicitly personal." It was precisely because of this misunderstanding that Irvine moved this past fall toward more directed assignments for journal entries than she had given in fall 1983, the first semester in which the course was taught. Though the general guidelines, as now, asked for analysis of reactions to works of art, many of the 1983 students, without specific assignments, tended to deal only glancingly with their art experiences and drifted toward commentaries on their courses, teachers, and friends—in short, they fell back on the framework they were familiar with. The more specified assignments this year gave the students direction for their writing without greatly inhibiting their freedom to explore points of view; e.g., "Study two paintings, one you like and one you don't like. List all the reasons why you think one is good and all the reasons why you think the other is not." Irvine sees such assignments as compelling analysis without limiting either the student's choice of material or freedom of expression.

To the extent that "journal" connotes to students a fairly unfettered, more expressive writing than the "paper" or "essay," Irvine accepts the term, since she is striving to free students from excessive concern over such discursive elements as the appearance of objectivity and the subordination of ideas. "Basically, I want the journals to show the students that they can express themselves about subjects that all of them react to emotionally, but which few of them feel they understand. The journals, in this way, fit perfectly into the course: much of our reading and our talk in class gives the students terms—language—that can clarify their feelings about works of art, and the journal, among its purposes, lets them try out those terms in relation to works they experience. The journal also encourages them to invent their own analytical language. This isn't easy. The journal entries alert me to the students who are having the toughest time translating their feelings into words; in conference I get them to talk about the works that are giving them trouble, and the talk, together with the journal, helps to open up the students to productive ways of seeing."

Chamlee's journal provides instances of this struggle to apply modes of analysis, as well as to identify metaphors that give shape to feelings. A Dali painting, for example, challenges her to follow lines of sight in an attempt to discover patterns of meaning:

> Immediately striking the viewer's eye are the three bright orange oozing eggs, with the reflection of a window pane in the gelatinous yolk. The egg suspended from a string from the heavens seems to accompany the yellow sky in giving a sunrise effect, setting up a rather crass visual pun (sunny side up, get it?). The egg "shines" on the watch, making the eyes next focus on the balancing images of the suspended time piece and the suspended egg.

Later in the course, an entry on "music in film" challenges the writer to explore the complementary effects of sight and sound. Taking as her subject Michel Portal's music for the Daniel Vigne film *The Return of Martin Guerre*, Chamlee identifies three "musical forms" that dominate different parts of the film. The first she calls "blaring orchestral sound" that heightens our surprise, while the second is made up of "beautifully understated passages that almost go unnoticed by the conscious ear":

> Sometimes it is difficult to decipher between the sounds in the background and the music itself. The instruments quite often imitate the subject of the dialogue. Bertrande is worried about the wolves coming down the mountain. Is that a wolf I hear in the background? No, it's a French horn. She is frightened by the spirits. Is that what is making that noise? No, it's a violin....I'm not sure which came first in this film, the musical score or the cinematography, but it's amazing how well the two complement each other. If one could give music a color, these passages would be the soft greens and blues of the French countryside....

Since these pieces of analysis take place in the journal, rather than in a more formal paper, Chamlee feels free to experiment with analytical frames and images; she tries to be descriptive, but does not feel compelled to persuade Irvine of the sensibleness of her observations. She can, as the *Martin Guerre* entry shows, develop notions as her mind evolves them, and the entry takes on an associative rather than logical coherence (even though most of the entry's structure follows from her introduction of the idea of the "three musical forms"). By association, Chamlee moves from her examples of "imitation" to an unstated question—"How did the collaboration of director and composer work?"—back to her statement of amazement at the complementarity of music and situation. This notion of unity leads her to a metaphor—color—by which she tries to picture what she feels. The writing/thinking process here eventually leads her to abandon the "three musical forms" frame in the last section of the entry. Her careful recollection of the film leads her to define a fourth form that she cannot include in any of the others:

> Pansette's final march to his death is made even more endless and agonizing by the a capella choral Mass sung by the villagers....It is different from all the other musical forms used in that it is not loud, it is not soft, and it does not have a pulsing beat [like the French folk songs in the movie]....It is another unexpected which prepares us for the final unexpected—the good guy loses.

The journal format gives Chamlee the freedom to move on to fresh observations suggested by what she has written (or by the very *act* of writing about the film) without having to apologize for discarding the "three forms" motif.

Because it fulfills this "discovery" function, Chamlee's journal can serve the further role of testing ground for preliminary theses to be used in analytic papers. Indeed, Irvine encourages students to use the journal for this purpose. She invites them both to plan their papers by experimenting in the journal and to use their completed entries as a source file for topics they may want to pursue further. Chamlee appreciates Irvine's invitation for two practical reasons: (1) it lets her complete one assignment (the journal entry) while letting her do initial work on another, and (2) it gives her the chance for early feedback—questions, guidance—from Irvine on ideas she can then set about confidently to develop into an essay.

While very experienced journal keepers such as Chamlee look forward to Irvine's constructive criticism, others need her patience as they struggle to apply the structural language introduced in class and to understand what she means by "analysis." According to Irvine, some students suffer from what might be called "analytical blocks," in that they don't see the connection between describing in their own words what they see or hear and trying to define structure. Perhaps because of earlier training, they tend to see analysis as an esoteric operation which *depends* on scholarly language and which necessarily takes a precisely subordinated, argumentative form. It takes much time to break down these students' inhibitions. "With some students," says Irvine, "I have to proceed slowly, being satisfied if they will write anything about a story, a painting, or a piece of music." Her written and spoken comments attain particular importance here, as she points out the ways in which a student's brief response *is* analytical, and then asks questions intended to draw out more detailed explanation of what the student has cryptically written. The journal is absolutely essential to this process, although even with its aid she doesn't reach all these students. Nevertheless, without the opportunity for ungraded dialogue with the students that the journal provides, few, if any, could build up enough confidence in their analytical ability to tackle an essay.

The journal also gives Irvine a comparative tool which can help the student understand the deficiencies in an essay Irvine has read. "Frequently, a student's journal will contain passages or whole entries that are more clear and insightful than passages in the student's paper," she says. "Sometimes a journal entry on a topic will achieve an effect that is missed in the paper that develops the topic. It's much easier for the writer to accept criticism in the paper if he or she is being praised for the journal. It also makes my criticism more understandable to the student."

Moreover, Irvine's overt connecting of journal entry with analytical essay seems to make more tangible the link between expressive and transactional writing—a link that students may miss if they see the graded, "organized" paper as "serious" and the ungraded entries as "just my journal." If anything, the experienced journal writer tilts the balance of power toward the journal, because it is in the expressive stage (though a writer like Chamlee would not see any writing as *un*-expressive) that discourse acquires that associative coherence—that dramatic intensity of the mind at work—which Chamlee, for one, calls "life." "I know that my journal entries start on one topic and then move off on tangents, so that the end is very different from the beginning. I'm glad that teachers like Professor Irvine encourage this, because otherwise there's no life, no vitality. Writing from topic to topic lets me see the connections among people and ideas." To Chamlee, revision of journal pieces into papers means getting the opinions of others, so that one might see if the flow of thought is as clear to them as it is to the self. It also means continuing to mine the same rich ground to see what new, and perhaps better, patterns will emerge. Revision does *not* mean taking the personality out of a piece, on the theory that it will thereby become more relevant to others besides the writer. As Chamlee's "Reading the Arts" journal illustrates, the general relevance of the writing expands as the personal meaning-fulness intensifies.

The journal entry that heads this essay exemplifies this point. When asked to reread this entry in order to attempt to recall her composing process, Chamlee noted three distinct stages, each change occasioned by a powerfully personal image generated by the text, an image that she wanted to articulate. Each stage does follow from the previous, but it also reinterprets and intensifies the emotion with which she began the entry. In this way, she actually revises as the entry proceeds.

The first stage, which ends with "How do I appear?" was occa-sioned by the use of "narcissism" by the speaker in the film. In writing about appearance, Chamlee says that she saw the image of herself in the dance studio and thus vivified her general remarks by describing the physical preoccupations of dancers. The third and most intense stage begins with "Unfortunately," as her focus moves out of the dance studio and through time, her scope of thought increasing through the mult-iplying of images. This change was occasioned by Chamlee's seeing in her mind two dancers, one a famous ballerina, the other a close friend, whose lives had been endangered by the syndrome she goes on to describe. Had she continued the writing, she says, she feels that she would have written about the individuals, though she admits that she cannot predict this, since the number of images generated by the journal writing always accelerates, as this entry shows. "Sometimes I stop," she says, "because I just get overwhelmed by how much there is to say."

Most students who keep the journal in "Reading the Arts" probably do not reach the level of psychic energy in their writing that Chamlee does. But this we cannot really know, even for—maybe particularly for—those few who rarely respond, at least in black on white, to Irvine's praise or her stimulating questions. Nor can we say for sure what is happening to those who write what Irvine calls "protected" journals—ones that list the periods, artists, and dominant colors of the paintings in the museum but which never describe how this one viewer's eye moves across the canvas, much less what that viewer recalls, or wishes, as he or she looks. Suffice it to say that the Emily Chamlees of a class tell us much about the potential of such journals, as they put on paper what many others may feel but do not reveal or—because they have not written—understand.

What we learn from journals such as Chamlee's and from the observations of journal keepers such as Chamlee herself is that avowedly "analytic" journals, whether in the arts or, I suspect, in any other field, lend themselves to the expression of deep emotion as readily as do journals whose avowed intent is emotional release. The key condition seems to be the receptivity of the teacher/audience, most clearly shown in the instructions given and the sorts of comments made about the journal entries. If even a confident writer like Chamlee can be intimi-dated by the journal reader's perceived prejudices, then how much more difficult it must be for the inexperienced or blocked writer to hold to the illusion that writing for a journal is writing for the self. It seems that if we teachers really want students to be "analytic," i.e., revealing their honest reactions and their best estimates of what events or artifacts "mean," then we'll have to keep giving them whatever opportunities, incentive, and encouragement that that takes. *How* to do this will vary with the writers, as Lorna Irvine's flexible practices demonstrate.

Not only do the journals in "Reading the Arts" lend themselves to emotional expression; Chamlee's entries and her comments, as well as those of Irvine, show that these journals depend on it. The writer may not be "talking about her feelings" per se, but is it really less adventurous to write about the terrifying narcissism of dancers—when one is a dancer—or to describe the "orange oozing eggs" of a Dali painting? For the student who is not a practicing artist and who feels totally unable to talk about works of art, is it not a highly emotional exercise to describe the lines of sight in *Guernica* or to analyze why he or she can't stand a Henry Moore sculpture? What I'm suggesting is that as long as we see journals, or whatever else we may call them, as tools toward fluency, for those who lack it, or toward deeper insight, for the already fluent, then we cannot see any journal as "merely" technical or as "just" practice. We have to avoid, for example, the easy equation of "no grade" with "not deserving of credit." If we refrain from giving grades because we know how much students are risking emotionally in their journals, shouldn't we also devise ways of rewarding students for the risk with more than "extra" credit?

Finally, the good news from people like Emily Chamlee is that expressive writing really does help us learn, and that nobody had to tell them that it did. They discovered it on their own and now they tell us. The troubling news, of course, is that such insights don't come easily and can take years—at least, for some of our students, more than a semester (beyond which time most of our students pass from view). Sometimes we teachers will make substantive discoveries in a class like Irvine's of the value of directed journal assignments; more often, however, we'll have to be satisfied with small gains, such as the *reasons* that students now give for why they *still* hate abstract art. But the troubling news should also encourage us, since learning doesn't stop, though semesters do, and the confidence that a student gains from journal writing and from our responses to it can only be a base for further growth.

26.

Documenting the Aesthetic Experience: The Music Journal

CATHERINE M. LARSEN and MARGARET MERRION

As keen observers, music teachers have always been able to identify that students overtly react to music with foot beats, smiling, or free dance. But what is happening inside the listener? We wondered if children could express in writing what they think and feel when they listen to music. Could writing give shape to *feelings* in addition to giving shape to thoughts? And will the act of writing about music help students wed cognitive thought with affective reactions? We believe the answer to all these questions is *yes*. In the following passages we will describe the procedures we use to incorporate expressive writing in our classes, show a sampling of our students' writing, and discuss the results of our work with fourth grade children.

To help our students learn to listen to music we start them slowly. As a first step, we ask students to generate a collective list of musical elements or expressive qualities which *we know* affect the way the music sounds or the way it makes us feel. During this class session, we compile a large, often very messy list of student responses and ideas. This proves to be a stimulating discussion, with excited students often searching for the correct musical term to fit someone's description of sounds. Regular references to titles of pieces previously studied, and musical examples of the items on our list (i.e., the crescendo in *Bolero,* the instrumentation in *Fanfare for the Common Man*) make this step a valuable review for the students. When complete, our list is transferred to a wall display. We relate listening questions to the list during preparation for listening and writing. As new lessons evolve, the concepts presented can be added to the list. The classes develop a sense of accomplishment as their vocabulary visibly expands. An example of a fourth grade list follows:

4th Grade List

Loud/soft
Fast/slow
Change of instruments—number, type or family
Rhythms—lots of activity, not much movement
Use of voices—range, quality
Accents
Repetition/contrast
Use of motives—melodic, rhythmic

254

We select the listening repertory very carefully, considering three criteria. First, we wish to integrate listening experiences which will fit naturally into the courses of study. For early writing/listening experiences, compositions which have been heard or studied previously are selected. For example, we study concepts such as dynamics, tempo, structure, and timbre. So a composition such as *In the Hall of the Mountain King* by Grieg serves as an exemplary listening experience for our writing experiment, because the children have listened to it within the modules addressing those concepts. In addition to the curricular appropriateness of the literature, we screen compositions in terms of their length. It is our intent to keep the students listening most attentively. This requires sensitivity to their brief attention span. Compositions or segments of no more than five minutes in length are chosen. Third, we limit the repertory intially to pieces having high affective potential, i.e. those with lush melodies, active rhythms, and expressive dynamics. Later, however, we experiment with repertory of a more absolute nature, hoping to elicit more subtle degrees of aesthetic response.

We find some of our compositions in published series. Most of them are recordings; a few are live performances presented by music education students doing field experiences at the Laboratory School. This list is by no means exhaustive, but gives an indication of recommended literature.

Recommended Listening Repertory

Bach	Toccata in D minor
Bernstein	Chichester Psalms
Beethoven	Symphony #7, 2nd Movement
Britten	Ceremony of Carols
Brubeck	Take Five
Cage	Fontana Mix
Chopin	Voiles
Copland	Fanfare for the Common Man
Debussy	Children's Corner Suite
Gershwin	Preludes; Selections from Porgy and Bess
Grieg	In the Hall of the Mountain King
Joplin	The Entertainer; Maple Leaf Rag
Kodály	Hary Janos Suite
Mozart	Horn Concerto in E Flat, 3rd Movement
Partch	Plectra and Percussion Dances
Prokofiev	Classical Symphony
Puccini	Selected opera choruses
Purcell	Trumpet Voluntary
Ravel	String Quartet, 2nd Movement
Schubert	String Trio in B Flat
Sibelius	Finlandia
Strauss	The Emperor Waltz
Stravinsky	A Soldier's Tale
Tchaikovsky	Nutcracker Suite
Varese	Poem Electronique
Vaughan Williams	March Past Kitchen Utensils

Vivaldi   The Four Seasons (Winter)
Wagner   Prelude to Act III, Lohengrin
Webern   Five Pieces for Orchestra, Piece 4

After selecting the musical examples, we develop a variety of listening questions. Some are very specific in nature, to guide responses to a particular piece. For example, appropriate questions for Britten's *Ceremony of Carols* might be: How do the voices in this music make you feel? Do you hear changes in the vocal tone color? What is happening? Some questions are general enough to apply to many different listening examples: What action do you imagine is taking place in this piece? What is the composer doing in this music to change the mood? What changes do you hear?

We find it helpful to guide the students through a trial run because the writing process we present differs in many ways from familiar compositional techniques. So, to familiarize the students with the journal's unstructured, unedited style of writing, we tell the students to:

- Write as best you can each thought that occurs. Phrases, or parts of thoughts are acceptable. Complete sentences are *not* required. EVER.
- Don't worry about punctuation and spelling. Get your thought down quickly, as best you can, and continue listening.
- Once the music begins, keep your pencil in contact with the paper and keep your pencil moving. Write something—anything—write slowly, but don't stop writing. Keep yourself attached to the thread that connects the sounds to your thoughts.
- Write down what you hear.
- Concentrate on our listening questions. Begin to write about whatever you hear in the music. When you run out of ideas, think about the questions again and write about another one.
- Don't worry about how well you expressed a thought. Keep listening, and continue to write. Proofreading isn't permitted.

To implement the actual listening/writing experience, we ask students to consider the selected questions as they listened to the music. The students intently focus on the music during listening. The selection is then played again, and students begin writing. Continuous reinforcement and encouragement during the "write" moments are imperative at this stage, to help students overcome apprehension about getting started, or getting the correct answer. Prompting cues such as "Keep your pencil moving...; There is no one right answer, so put down what *you* think; Now I hear...; Now it sounds like...; It makes me feel like...;" are delivered in a quiet voice while we circulate among students.

We give students a moment of quiet time to finish a thought or reflect on what they have written, and then collect the journals. Students frequently ask to hear the music one more time. We prefer, however, to limit the listening.

We carry out the follow-up step of the listening/writing experience during the next class meeting. We select entries from a few students' journals. These anonymous journal samples are transferred to transparencies and shared with the entire class. This strategy has a powerful effect on the quality of writing and listening. The students are fascinated with the thoughts and feelings of their classmates, and we often note marked improvement in subsequent entries. We also observe greater effort to concentrate, "shut out the world," and focus on their inner senses during listening.

Journal Entries

These are some unedited samples from elementary (grades four and five) and junior high (grades seven and eight) students' journals. Like pictures, their expressive writing is worth a thousand words. These entries are responses to *In the Hall of the Mountain King.*

It starts soft then gets louder. Sounds like some
going up a winding staircase crescendo
long stairs like dancing.
It's fast and loud getting faster and louder.
cymbals thunder lots of thunder
big day fireworks lots of notes
lots of instruments
soft to loud exciting moment

Notice how this fourth grade boy first attends to the musical concepts, then provides a storyline to fit the musical action:

The rhythum is slow. It is starting to get faster and louder. Now it is Loud! and very, very fast. I feel excited. This is very neat. I hear an orchestra. Someone is sad. Someone is walking down a dark road. they get scared and start to run suddnely gosts appear They run fast fast They catch him. He's fighting. He's dead.

We see this fifth grader reconciling the tempo and dynamics with the story she envisioned:

It sounds like trolls walking into the woods. It's getting faster. The trolls are walking faster. And there's a fight going to happen. And a king and queen coming and its getting louder and faster, faster, it sounds like there getting meaner and the drums get louder like there getting mad.

Another fifth grader summarizes her entry as... "a baby turtles jerny to the sea," while a fourth grader reports that the music... "makes me feel funny...tingley...dissy...I am losing control."

Total absorption, to the point of stopping the writing and just listening occurs in this fourth grader's entry:

A mouse is tip toeing to the cheese. It's getting'
souder. Someone's after him. There comeing oh no.
This is too intresting. I have to listen to it.
Mrs. Larson, the mouse IS
Mrs. Larson turned it off.

The following excerpts are from the junior high students' journals in response to Copland's *Fanfare for the Common Man.*

This seventh grade boy reports being startled yet pleased with Copland.
It scared me when the trumpets started...a king when he is
walking to get married—foot steps are gongs...I love them trumpets. The ending was neat.

Another eighth grader notices the effect upon her classmates.
The music is bold and strong. It makes people perk up in there
chairs instead of relaxing and slumping over.

The junior high students are more economical in their expressive
writing; some begin by analyzing musical elements, but often attend to
the affective import quickly. There appears to be less fiction and more
focus on the power of the music:
Sudden and very loud. The gong played. It feels very far away. To
me the picture in my mind is in the country, rolling hills, green
grass. It repeats very often. Very intense. He means something.

It sounds official...I like the drum...he lets one insterment play
and then anothr come in.

It's kind of jumpy and serious. It sounds like something big is
about to take place.

And like the elementary students, the adolescents feel free to share
aesthetic reactions:
It gives me a big, long, loud feeling of winning. American feeling.
Proud to be an American. It has a sporty mood. It makes me feel
like I'm in a long echoing room. It is very slow and careful, like it
is a graceful sound with its head held high. It sounds very important.

It sounds like there is somebody in POWER.

Here's What Happens

In sum, we find that incorporating journal writing in the music
listening process brings about three worthwhile results. First, when our
students are given an opportunity to write while listening to music, their
attention gravitates towards musical association, i.e., elements of music
which affect their feelings towards it. While the students juggle imagery,
fictional fantasies, and emotional responses, they eventually connect
extra-musical associations with musical understandings.

A second important outcome to spring from the writing is the
change we measure in the student's shift from creative writing (story
telling) to aesthetic writing-responding to the affective import of the
music. The journals reflect a wide range of responses, from a "heavenly
feeling" to a snake pit feeling. As the journal writing progresses, feelings
and emotional responses appear more frequently. We're particularly
pleased with this outcome because typical general music activities sidestep any analysis of feelings.

The third outcome is our students' receptivity to the whole process
of expressive listening/writing. Each experience seems to yield active

participation and positive response. In fact, students often initiate re-quests to write in their journals and ask to re-listen to compositions. The fact that our students uniformly look forward to the listening/writing lessons (even at the sophisticated junior high level) assures us that the experience is truly enjoyed, holding promise for nurturing music appreciation.

In sum, we value writing as a learning tool because it brings about outcomes that are difficult to facilitate in the general music setting. For example, although our students can easily describe instrumentation, metric organization, and other characteristics which commonly emerge during analysis, they rarely describe how the music affects them. In the privacy of their journals, however, they freely express their feelings and sensations. The writing seems to act as a conduit for thoughts and feelings about music. The writing process removes students' reluctance to discuss the affective import which music has on each individual. Indeed, expressive writing gives students the freedom to go beyond the clinical analysis of music. At the junior high level, in particular, this result proves most welcome.

With the use of the music journal, we are able to tap and more precisely interpret covert reactions to music listening. The journal allows students to shape reactions to music individually and personally. It provides a medium for sharing an aesthetic experience. The teacher in turn can examine entries as measures of aesthetic growth—a valuable bonus.

Since this act of writing fosters an expressive outlet for emotional responses to music, our students are becoming more adept at expressing their emotional selves through language. We find that ability to do this creatively is not linked to the students' performance in music nor other academic areas. While some of our special students, for instance, have difficulty finding appropriate vocabulary to express their thoughts and feelings, they invent devices to convey what they mean. We note that the disabled as well as gifted draw figures of abstract shapes, conjure up new words, or sketch complex diagrams to express themselves.

We find the music journal to be a highly useful activity for the general music class. It is an activity which can be employed at intervals throughout the year, rather than in a unit format. The familiarity of the process, together with the flexibility of the type of music chosen, provides a refreshing break in regular class routines. As new concepts are introduced, we can return to the journals for synthesis. The listening/writing process enables students to incorporate the new threads into the fabric of their musical understandings. Best of all, it is time efficient. It fosters the refinement of listening skills, the synthesis of musical con-cepts, and the development of affective awareness, all at the same time.

We are sold on this process. Our students respond to music in a more relaxed, assured, and controlled manner. Externally, we can change some listening behaviors; internally we can take a rare glimpse at the thoughts and feelings which occur during a listening experience. Now we can better answer the question: "What happens when children listen to music?" We believe the sole purpose of music education is to increase our students' potential to feel the power of music. Since the journals allow our students to express this, we could not ask for a more useful tool.

References

Fulwiler, T. (1982). Writing: An act of cognition. In C.W. Griffen (Ed.), *New directions for teaching and learning*. San Francisco: Jossey-Bass Publications.

More information can be found in:
Fulwiler, T. (1980, December). Journals across the disciplines. *English Journal, 69*, 9.
_____ . (1984, February). How well does writing across the curriculum work? *College English, 46*, 2.

27.

Music Journals

JANE AMBROSE

"What were you going to write to me?" Monica asked...

"How would I know?—if I had written," Sheila said, licking her lips nervously, "I'd know: doing is knowing, after all."

Joyce Carol Oates; *Solstice*

In preparation for this paper, I have thought about my own experiences with journal keeping through the years, partly because I am old enough to enjoy thinking about the past and partly to prepare myself for my new venture in asking my students to keep journals. I have begun journals (perhaps they were really meant to be diaries, and that was what was wrong with them, at least for me) several times in the past, but never found them particularly helpful or enjoyable, and this is at such a premium in an academic's life that what is not required and not enjoyable is definitely something to be stopped. The last time that I made a serious commitment (interesting that I should use that word—it was not premeditated) to a journal was at the beginning of my last sabbatical. The first entry was written even before commencement— "Marvelous feeling to finish last set of exams today and to think that the next 16 months are my own!" This journal-diary soon became an obligation rather than a pleasure because I felt for some reason that it was a record that I had to maintain and so I had to write in it at some length and with some frequency. As soon as I realized that this was an obligation that I was imposing on myself, I stopped the daily record which I now know I never should have begun and kept a reading journal, something that I have done throughout my adult life with varying degrees of regularity and have always enjoyed. Somehow the concept of an occasional journal never occurred to me.

Last spring I decided to try (much more positive approach) a journal again after spending two days at an intensive workshop designed to encourage more and better writing across the curriculum. One of the suggestions was, of course, the keeping of journals. (I had added annotated bibliographies, discographies and program annotations to the more ordinary essay and term paper assignments and was glad for the impetus to try something new.) It seemed to me that I myself should try again in anticipation of my students' efforts, this time writing only when I felt like it and using this notebook to keep in one place lots of the things that I was already doing. That journal is still going strong and seems to have settled into about four discrete sections, each of which reflects a part of my personal and academic life.

261

In the first part of my own journal I record notes about concerts that are especially important or recordings that I want to remember and professional and personal observations thereon. Repertory lists and want lists frequently develop from rereading this section of the journal.

Part two is the reading journal, this time with more personal observations and rough drafts of music reviews. A new feature of this section is the incorporation of a thematic index of sorts based on scores that I have looked at in preparation for various concerts that I have a part in planning, either for myself or for my students. I use a loose-leaf notebook so that I can remove all of the pages which are pertinent to any one project and examine them together. With this arrangement I can incorporate typed pages. Part three is a record of travel to professional meetings and conferences and research travel, particularly when it relates to a grant. This section was a great help in preparing my tax return this year. Part four is idiosyncratic in the extreme and contains everything from encounters with friends who have told me something that I wish to remember to copies of poems. Recent examples include a record of an interview with a well-known composer granted to a student and me and an account of several hours spent with a charming woman who had studied in Paris with Nadia Boulanger in the twenties and had contacted me when she saw that I was performing a sonata by a woman who was her colleague there. I am quite sure that I will continue *this* journal because it has turned out to be an easy way to organize certain aspects of my personal and professional life.

I have thought a lot about what we and our students read and about how and what we ask them to write. In music literature we read books of all kinds—historical and pseudo-historical in the form of novels or imaginary biographies such as Esther Meynell's *The Little Chronicle of Magdalena Bach* (JSB's beloved second wife about whom we know almost nothing), biographical, particularly revisionist in the last several years as biographers have tried to strip off romantic accretions in the cases of composers like Mozart (Wolfgang Hildesheimer) and Beethoven (Maynard Solomon) or to add the all-important element of psycho-biography as in the new Schumann biography by Peter Ostwald, *The Inner Voices of a Music Genius,* autobiographical (*Virgil Thomson* by Virgil Thomson or Robert Craft's collaboration with Stravinsky); reviews of concerts, books, records; essays—philosophical, historical, instructional or otherwise practical, speculative explorations of the nature of the art such as Lewis Rowell's *Thinking about Music* or George Rochberg's *The Aesthetics of Survival;* conversation books (Beethoven by necessity, others by choice), idea notebooks and sketchbooks, sometimes again the form of "conversations" such as those of Jonathan Cott with Stockhausen and Glenn Gould, and on more popular subjects for *Rolling Stone;* correspondence at all levels to and from composers and, of course, journals—most notably perhaps in this country at the present time, those of Ned Rorem. Rorem's journals serve for him the purpose of recording his thoughts and experiences. For us they are a valuable record of the musical and emotional experiences of an important and talented creator and of the musical life around him.

Now let us consider what musicians might ask students to write and what help journals might be in addition, of course, to their intrinsic value. Let's look at some student journal entries from two undergraduate classes: Music 4 is an introductory listening course which surveys many kinds of music by genre or class in a non-traditional and non-chronological manner. It is intended for students who have no background whatsoever in playing or listening to classical and non-western music. It is taken primarily by students wishing to fulfill a university distribution requirement. Music 12 is the survey of western music for majors, minors, and students with some experience in listening to classical music. The major difference between the two courses is the level of student sophistication and the complexity of the material.

The first journal writing assignment in Music 4 was to define music, a difficult task, particularly for students who listen almost exclusively to music of the last few years in the form of rock, an observation that I am able to substantitate from my reading of their journals. Most students presented a standard definition in class—most typically some combination gleaned from a dictionary that tells me that music is melody, harmony, rhythm, form and tone color. However, one thoughtful student went far beyond that and wrote in her journal:

> The other day in music class, we were asked to write down our own definition of what music was. I took a sort of phenomenological viewpoint, and wrote that music depends as much on the listener as the sound which is being created; if the listener hears a certain combination of sounds as music, then it's music....As someone else mentioned in class, music is the "barometer" of our feelings, thoughts, ideals and dreams, perhaps one of the greatest expressions of our higher selves. I think that will be my definition of music, at least for the time being; that which evokes a response from, corresponds to, or is an expression of our "higher selves."

The last assignment of the semester asked the student to compare his feelings about classical music at the beginning and end of the term. One entry read:

> The similarity of a Bach Chaconne or Pachelbel's *Canon* to blues was an eye-opener, as was the similarity between something like "Semper Fidelis" and "Eine kleine Nacht-Musik." The term "classical music" still bothers me. It just doesn't really describe the true nature of this music. I don't find "serious music" or "orchestral music" any better at defining the differences between Tchaikovsky and Chicago, for example. Perhaps one should approach all styles from the simple viewpoint of just "music."

Another final entry let me know that I had been successful in my objectives for the course for this student:

> I began casually to listen to classical music in November or October because I was so completely bored with the garbage that [the local AM stations] were dispensing. I turned on the public radio station but quickly turned that off too for some reason. The next day I found myself turning it on again—and again and again until my roommate began to complain. In a week I bought my first tape. It was three of the Brandenburgs and I was hooked. I entered

this classroom with a nodding acquaintance of the major historical periods, but I knew little about the music itself. I feel that now I have a good basic understanding of a symphony, concerto, and other forms so that I can listen with some technical knowledge. In the course of the semester my tape collection has grown to about 25 tapes! For many years I didn't even give classical music a chance, but I guess opening the mind is what the University is all about. I'd like to learn to read music next.

One day we spent our class period watching a videotape of a professional performance of Gian-Carlo Menotti's chamber opera *The Medium*. The tape took the whole period so there was not time for our usual post-listening discussion. I aksed everyone in the class to take the next free fifteen or twenty minutes that he or she could find to write some reactions to what was for many of these students a first experience with opera. One student wrote:

I enjoyed the video of the opera we saw in class. I believe that it's the first one that I have made it through. I did see Joseph Papp's *La Boheme* but I guess real opera buffs don't consider Linda Ronstadt a real opera star. I particularly enjoyed the character of the mute. I've been to several fortune tellers in my life and I hope that they were all as full of it in the way that the one in the opera was. I think that it is definitely worthwhile for us to see the operas and videos in class where you are there to explain them. I think that is the most important part. Otherwise people like me would not know what to look for and would simply watch a television show like this without knowing what we were watching.

Another wrote:

For me, viewing *The Medium* in class was a positive experience in my relationship to opera. While growing up, my experiences of opera were limited to hearing (but not listening to) my mother's Verdi and Puccini records—a lot of romantic excesses and unintelligible gibberish without the benefit of visual aids. Menotti's was the first opera in English that I have ever heard. Understanding the dialogue and seeing the drama puts opera in a whole new light. It was an emotional and intense experience.

The third entry would probably not have found its way into class discussion.

I find it really hard to write about this because I really didn't like it and I don't want to offend you. . . . Do you have any suggestions on how I could appreciate it more? There must be some aspect of it that could cause me to ignore everything I didn't like about it and concentrate only on the good parts.

Through journal entries such as these I am able to monitor class reaction and to make better judgments about materials to be used in subsequent semesters.

Students in Music 12 are more at ease with personal thoughts about music because they have more confidence in their ability to cope with its technical aspects. One angry student wrote:

I've come to a conclusion about contemporary atonal music. I hate
it! Is it fair to hate what is considered "great music"? I was asked to
play the piano for a contemporary ensemble. When I practiced, I
just got frustrated because I couldn't tell if I was playing the right
notes or the right rhythm. UGLY is what it was.

Another student found in the Sunday *New York Times* an article about
a subject which we had discussed in class:

So exciting to see in print subject matter that is familiar from class.
The subtleties of education—all my years of acquaintance with
music—it was the first time I'd really looked at the music section—
and happily I found myself in familiar territory.

A performance major used a journal to rationalize her anxiety when
she took a job as a pianist and singer at one of the local student hang-
outs. After writing for several pages about why she was finding it
difficult to be herself when in the spotlight, she concluded, "but they are
my age and I know most of them." Another student wrote a meditation
on the life of a friend who had recently been killed in a skateboard
accident. He was distressed at the incongruity of the music chosen for
the funeral relative to the personality and tastes of his friend and was
using the journal as an outlet for his hostility. Many students attend live
concerts for the first time when they take music classes. One commented
that she had enjoyed particularly an organ recital because she found that
her attention was concentrated entirely on the music because there was
nothing to look at but the organist's back. She wondered whether there
was an analog in the celebration of the Mass and said that she much
preferred a Mass where the priest was not facing the congregation.
One of my favorite entries came from an art history major:

I thought of a great idea last night for our seminar on Cistercians.
It dawned on me that music was of great importance to Bernard. It
was the one type of art he allowed in his austere monastic life. We
planned to work Gregorian chant into our lecture presentation and
what a success it was! We put on the slide of the interior of
Pontegny and played the chant. It was really effective with the
visual aid of the slide. The music seemed to echo off the walls; roll
down the nave arcade in rhythmic ups and downs. I wish I
understood more how the use of proportion and number that was
so important to Bernard fit into the use of these chants. I am not
familiar enough with the church modes to draw any conclusions. I
just know that Bernard wanted music to radiate truth and to please
the ear in order to move the heart.

At this point I inserted in her journal some suggestions for outside
reading that might help her to understand proportion (Boethius) and
church modes. A student in Music 4 made me rethink a lecture when he
wrote, "Billie Holiday rolled over in her grave the other day when, in
class, Ella Fitzgerald was ordained the greatest female jazz vocalist."

The considerable amount of time that it takes to read the journals is
frequently rewarded by a particularly thoughtful or humorous entry. For
example, one student wrote:

Mozart Clarinet Concerto - Wonderful graceful Mozartian opening. Too bad all this lovely music is leading up to the clarinet. I realize that different individuals have different affinities for different instruments otherwise it would be difficult to staff all of the orchestras of the world—but the clarinet??!!

Another wrote this comment on public radio's morning programming:
All composers have birthdays, but surely that doesn't require that we be subject to five hours of minor composer X's wretched tunes on February 1st just because that happens to be the day his mother went into labor. (I except Bach, Schubert and selected others from this diatribe).

And in the more thoughtful vein is this entry which is a reflection on a classroom listening session devoted to Penderecki's *Threnody for the Victims of Hiroshima,* an extraordinarily effective evocation of that horrifying event:
This is not a song of lamentation but an endless scream of protest. It's as if with one voice, all the ghosts of Hiroshima were crying out to us: Stop! Go back! Don't let this happen! How does one respond? One can only sit and listen and ask: Why? Why? Except, there's no one to ask and no answer that could ever make sense.

For several years I have required my students to attend at least five live concerts per semester and to write some kind of a concert review, either formal or informal. These reviews are perhaps the most important writing assignments for my students and it is here that a good listening journal will serve them well. Students may bring their journals to concerts (my colleagues are all used to note-taking attendees), but more frequently, they take notes on their programs and record and reflect on the concert later in their journals. Music students will frequently tell their teachers that they express themselves through their music and therefore should not be expected to write very much or very well, but experience teaches that those who express themselves most eloquently in words about music (Yehudi Menuhin and Glenn Gould are good examples) are usually among its most successful practitioners. Concert reviews force students to verbalize their thoughts on literal and figurative matters and to put those thoughts in descriptive and critical terms. Incidentally, they listen more carefully to a concert when they know that they are going to write about it. The new vocabulary of music is put into use and the instructor has the opportunity to assuage his curiosity about what the students thought about any particular concert.

Because the courses that I teach are largely about traditional "classical" music, I require that most of these reports be of concerts of classical music, although I allow an occasional jazz or rock concert or even a film—*Amadeus,* for example, or on a less high-brow level, *Fantasia* or *Stop Making Sense* (Talking Heads)—because the vocabulary is the same and the concert report serves the same purpose. In many lower level classes, students initially resist the assignment because they are convinced that they don't know enough about music to write about it intelligently, but course evaluations show that concert reviews turn out to be among the most popular class activities.

I would like to have you read a journal entry written anticipating a formal concert review. From these philosophical observations, the reviewer moved to a general critique of the specific performance.

Bach's B Minor Mass is the only one of his compositions that I am forced to admire at a distance. All the rest of his music has a spirit, and warmth and immediacy that draws me into its spell at once and keeps me there long after the music ends. but not the Mass. It always strikes me as an intellectual exercise demonstrating how one writes sublime music on a religious theme. No matter how beautiful I know it to be, I remain unmoved from the first note to the last. After due consideration I conclude that this is due to the ritual nature of the theme. For after all, the purpose of ritual is not to "move" but to "control."

Such an entry teaches us a great deal about its writer.

Finally here is one of my favorite reviews (despite the spelling). After several sentences about why he didn't wish to see *Amadeus,* he concluded:

Truth is, I'm prejudiced against almost any kind of classical music—that is one reason why I wanted to take this course. Well, I certainly stuck my #9½ size sneaker in my mouth again. I really did like the movie and the music is what set the mood for the whole show. Obviously, Motzart was a genious with a lot of gifts and a supreme love of life. I found myself crying as the coffin of "Wolfie" was lowered and his body dumped into the papuer grave. The requiem turned out to be more moving than Clapton's "Layla" or anything else I've ever heard. The writer, producer and director made the screen play fun to watch while the music put the emotion into it. One could sense the horrible frustration that Salieri felt when he heard a Motzart composition. God *was* speaking through Motzart and his music. There is no way that Salieri could ever top that or even compete. He was not chosen. I can now sit and enjoy the music from Amadeus and the music in class does not hurt as much. Perhaps I will gain some more culture some day.

When students keep journals in music classes, they have a means to monitor reactions to specific pieces and performances. Last semester I was somewhat surprised to find that non-majors were most enthusiastic about examples of chant and Wendy Carlos' Bach transcriptions. Journals also tell me whether students are following up my suggestions for outside listening, films, books or other artistic events. The majors made good use of their journals to sharpen their critical skills. The entries of the non-majors were homogeneous for the most part and tended to tell me things that I already knew like the fact that they listen almost exclusively to rock and think that they have switched to "serious" music if they go back in time to the Grateful Dead or (especially) the Beatles. For that class, free writing exercises and journal entries to prepare for concert reviews are probably enough.

Initially I thought of the journal as an alternative to increasing the number of writing assignments. Its benefits have been far greater than that for me and for my students. Those who have been keeping their journals conscientiously have been doing a great deal more writing. The assignments which have been handed in reflect the additional practice in writing about music and higher grades have resulted in many cases. I have had the advantage of following the students' progress toward the completion of a project and, at least as important as any of the other benefits, I am a dedicated convert myself to journal keeping.

28.

Student Journals and the Goals of Philosophy

O.T. KENT

Whether we like it or not, students perceive the classroom as the professor's territory. Discussion there is always somewhat contrived and usually involves a minority of the students. Student journals, however, bring the professor into the students' territory. I have been assigning journals for four years, and I am still struck by how different a student's *attitude* is toward her journal from that toward class discussions, essay tests, and term papers. No matter how much I fill the margins of a student's paper with helpful comments or probing questions, the paper remains a device to enable the professor to evaluate the student. But let a student put a hundred sheets of paper between two covers and call it "My Philosophy Journal" and she believes the professor is meeting her on her own ground, helping her clarify her thinking and learn.

For the past two years I have used student journals as the sole means of determining grades in my Introduction to Philosophy course. Previously I had used journals to supplement traditional term papers and essay exams. Following the suggestion of a colleague who was doing research about student journals, I decided to use the journal method of evaluation in one of three sections of Introduction to Philosophy that term. The results were gratifying, and I have used this method exclusively since.

I introduce the concept of a journal to my students on the first day of class. The primary purpose of the course, I tell them, is to *do* philosophy. Doing philosophy is thinking about one's most fundamental beliefs. Thinking, I explain, is essentially related to writing. Writing involves expressing one's ideas in words, which in turn involves crystallizing and clarifying the ideas for oneself. In this sense, writing *is* thinking. A journal, then, is a place to practice thinking. In the words of a former student,

> Journals are almost like a lab. For example, in Mechanics, we have class where we learn the material, and lab where we perform practical applications of what we have learned. The journal is sort of the same as a lab; we apply philosophy, ask questions, discuss problems and difficulties.

Having linked writing to thinking, and hence to the primary purpose of the course, I go on to answer the three questions on the student's mind at this point: "About what am I supposed write, how am I supposed to write, and, most importantly, how is my final grade to be determined?"

What Should I Write?

I distinguish three kinds of journal entries: summaries and responses to reading assignments, topics for writing on either in class or as homework, and entries initiated solely by the student.

1. A summary and response entry follows a fairly specific format. Drawn from an anthology of contemporary and classical sources, each reading is a self-contained essay in which the author argues either for or against a particular thesis. In summarizing the reading, the student is required to do three things: state clearly and concisely the main issue and thesis, clarify key terms and ambiguous statements, and describe as accurately as possible the author's reasoning. The process requires that the student evaluate the author's thesis and reasoning, either by criticizing—pointing out that the author raises more questions than he answers, is uninformed, inconsistent, or incomplete—or by defending the author's thesis. Students may do the latter by providing additional evidence, or by illustrating the thesis with examples or analogies.

2. I assign topics in class or as homework to get students to think reflectively and imaginatively about their beliefs. If class discussion is lagging, I might spontaneously ask students to write for five minutes in their journals on, for example, "the differences between faith and gullibility." Or, as a prelude to our examining the question of God's existence, I might assign as homework an entry on "How my life would change if I suddenly became convinced that God did not (or did) exist." They are encouraged to question themselves, write without censoring anything, make leaps, use analogies, metaphors, and real-life illustrations.

3. Self-sponsored entries can be on any topic the student wishes to write on, as long as it is even tangentially relevant to the course. Such entries can start with a doubt, frustration, or fantasy that the student has had; or something that has caught her attention in lecture or discussion, in her text, at a movie, in the newspaper. Examples might be "What is love?", "Can I do anything I want as long as I don't hurt anyone?", "What's wrong with premarital sex?" I make available topics for students unable or unwilling to come up with their own, by writing on the blackboard without comment a philosophical aphorism or quote that pertains to the subject currently under discussion, for example: "It is wrong everywhere for anyone to believe anything on insufficient evidence" (W.K. Clifford). I ask students to make a contract with themselves to set aside a specific time every day or every other day to write journal entries, to put aside fears and excuses and, if necessary, to force themselves to write for the entire time. Being "stuck" or frustrated, I tell them, is part of any creative process, and can be overcome by getting on with the business at hand—writing. And if all else fails, one can write about being stuck or frustrated.

How Should I Write?

In general, I tell my students to write however they want. The point is to think on paper, without worrying about spelling, punctuation, or grammar. I suggest that, if possible, they use proper spelling, punctuation, and grammar; but that they should not interrupt their thinking to edit or to worry over such matters in their journals. They should use language that feels natural, that expresses their personal voice. They should strive to write long entries, develop their thoughts fully (even going off on tangents), construct arguments, imagine examples, and use words literally to explore their minds.

Entries on the assigned readings, of course, are different. There I ask students to strive at all times for accuracy in presenting the author's views and to make clear the logic of the author's arguments. Directed specifically at the arguments in his summary, the student's response should express more than mere agreement and disagreement. It must demonstrate understanding of the author's thesis and arguments and offer an evaluation of them. I encourage students to experiment at first in their search for a style appropriate for summaries and responses—trying a dialogue format, for example.

What's the Basis for My Grade?

I guarantee the student no less than C if he does *every* assigned entry and demonstrates minimal understanding of the readings and lectures. Assigned entries include summaries and responses to readings and specific topics to be done in class or as homework. Minimal understanding of the readings involves knowing the author's main thesis and arguments supporting it. Minimal understanding of lectures means, for example, that if I show a particular argument to be unsound, that argument should not be used by the student unless she addresses my reasons for rejecting it. In these respects, the student's assigned journal entries are no different from essays he would write if I were to give him an essay exam.

One way a student may receive a grade higher than a C is by the number and length of her self-sponsored entries. Is quantity more important than quality, then? My answer is that if a student pursues a topic far enough, a breakthrough in his thinking is more likely to follow. If my hunch about the relation between thinking and writing is correct, then a student who produces a quantity of philosophical writing will also sooner or later produce a quantity of philosophical thinking. A student's best chance for a higher-than-average grade is by giving imaginative interpretations or explanations, using original examples to illustrate a point, raising provocative questions, revealing subtle problems, articulating and defending well her views, or offering alternative approaches to a problem. Not surprisingly, these are the same things I look for on term papers. But I have found I'm more likely to come across them in a journal.

The Pedagogical Advantages of Journals

Teaching is an interactive experiment between student and teacher. Educators put together a set of ingredients, call it "a course," and test it on themselves and their students. But courses are not highly controlled scientific experiments, and in humanities courses in particular, it is difficult to determine success, or even what counts as success. The journal, I believe, diminishes the realm of doubt. There are several advantages to this method of teaching Introduction to Philosophy.

1. I am concerned when a student is unable or unwilling to write (to think). Writing does not come naturally for most people and one gets good at it not by memorizing rules of grammar but by doing it. By writing in their journals every day, students begin to feel comfortable with a pen in their hands and gain confidence in their ability to write:

> I must admit that I did not look forward to using journals....It had to do with my lack of confidence in my writing. But as the entries came along, it got easier for me....It was valuable for me and I plan to use it for a long time.

> Writing has to be my least favorite thing in the world to do, but I was able to keep up with my entries and use the journal like I feel it was meant to be used, and if I can do it anyone can.

> At the beginning of the quarter, I looked upon this journal as a royal pain in the ass. Indeed for the first 3-4 weeks, this attitude held. I despised the thought of writing in it 3 or 4 times a week. I would read the articles, summarize them, and quickly jot down a few comments. Later in the quarter I began to think more about the articles and used my journal to think in. I still did not enjoy writing, but at least I was getting some good out of it.

> Looking back on the pages of writing I have done, it looks to be a large amount. Yet, it never appeared to be that way as I was writing....My writing skills have been sharpened overall through my entries.

2. Journals permit education to take place in a more relaxed, less stressful atmosphere. This is especially important in a philosophy course, where the goal of getting students to examine their beliefs can easily be thwarted by anxiety. Again, students say it best:

> [The journal] allows me the freedom to ramble a little bit while trying to get ideas straight in my own mind. I like it better than the testing method because if I mess up an idea the penalty in the context of an entire journal is much less than the penalty for a mistake in a test.

> Once I was free from the worry of grammar and spelling, etc., I was able to allow my thoughts and ideas to freely flow. I felt very unrestricted in my writing, and I was encouraged to use my personal beliefs to their full extent.

> The "first-draft phobia" is much lower, for I have lost much of the initial fear caused at the start of an assignment.

> The journal gave me time to develop my arguments more fully than I could in class or on a test when the factor of time is involved. My whole thought process breaks down when I am

pushed for time, and in this way I feel that the relaxed atmosphere in which I wrote in my journal was advantageous to my thought processes.

With the journal one has a lot more time to reflect on the subj. Once a test is over, that's it, there's no way to add more. But with the journal you can write a little on a subject and come back to it the next day and write some more.

3. Journals provide a forum for more dialogue between me and the students. Philosophers are notorious for claiming to use the Socratic method of teaching (and I'm no exception), but try as we may, we are unlikely to have the degree of success in a crowded classroom with a 50-minute stopwatch ticking that Socrates had while strolling the streets of Athens. Journals open up and keep dialogue flowing in ways that class discussions, tests, and term papers do not.

Since students write on only one side of a sheet, the page facing the student's writing is open for my comments. I never criticize self-sponsored and assigned "free-write" entries unless a student asks me for it or directs the entry to some specific point I have made on the subject. I want my students to risk articulating positions that cannot be rationally defended and that they themselves sometimes suspect are not sound. Religious and moral convictions are often of this kind, and if personal growth and autonomy is to occur, they must be examined carefully and honestly. My comments on these kinds of entries consist of encouraging the student to develop a point further, gently raising a question, amplifying the student's point with an example from my experience, or simply praising the student for her insight, argument, or honesty.

My commentary on summary-and-response entries is more academic. I correct misconceptions and errors of logic, pose counter-examples, chastise for not reading carefully, as well as offer praise for good argumentation and insight. In short, I apply my philosophical skills to the problem, and try to help the student develop his. These entries give students practice in organized, logical thinking about a subject, and an opportunity to test their thinking against the standards of a professional.

Journal "dialogue" is an extension of class discussion. Students who would never raise a question or respond to a point in class will often do so with vigor in their journals:

Journals are the best way to get things out about how the students feel....I don't know why but I have trouble speaking out about how I feel. I don't have any problems with writing down what I think, though. I wrote many things in my journal that I would never had said in class.

There have been many, many thoughts bottled up inside of me for a long time that I have finally been able to express in detail. But the best thing has to be that I get an evaluation from a professional philsopher on these inner feelings for free.

4. The journal works better than any other method I know in achieving the goals of Introduction to Philosophy: to teach students to reason clearly and to distinguish between good and bad arguments, to

diminish their dogmatism, to enlarge their conceptions of what is possible, and above all, to examine their beliefs to discover which ones are justified by reason and which ones are not.

The reason the journal method works probably has something to do with how the goals of my course relate to the kinds of writing that go on in students' journals. Writing theorist Peter Elbow distinguishes between "first-order" thinking and "second-order" thinking: "First-order thinking is intuitive and creative and strives for conscious direction and control. We use it when we get hunches, or see gestalts, when we sense analogies, or ride on metaphors or arrange pieces in a collage. We use it when we write without censoring, and let the words lead us to associations and intuitions we have not forseen."[1] When a student is asked what he is going to say, he is likely to be guided by his unconscious prejudices and unexamined points of view. He may in fact find out for the first time what he does believe about the topic. It is interesting to hear students describe this process:

> I found myself confused about topics as I began to write. This confusion, virtually every time, cleared away as I continued to write.

> I realized often that while I wrote a journal entry, my arguments would reduce significantly to the point where I sounded dogmatic.

> I would get writing, and one beginning thought would "snowball" into many related thoughts. My own sentences provoked new thoughts until I had written about everything I had wanted to about the specific topic. Sometimes I surprised myself with what I had written.

> For me the journal is not simply a place to record my thoughts, but a place to develop them. . . . It gives me a chance to develop my thoughts more objectively; it acted as sort of a mirror for my ideas.

Second-order thinking, according to Elbow, "is conscious, directed, controlled thinking. We steer; we scrutinize each link in the chain. Second order thinking is committed to accuracy and strives for logic and control: we examine our premises and assess the validity of each inference."[2] When students summarize and respond to a philosophical essay, they should examine premises or assumptions, test the validity of each step in the chain of inference, and come to some defensible conclusions:

> Writing in the journal allowed me a place to think over an argument and to understand it. I hate to use the word force, but the journal did force me to think about what I read.

> The journal drove me to read, reread, and understand the author's arguments so I could find the precise point where I would have difficulty in understanding the argument and then bring it out in the journal to work on the problem. Thus I was forced to "get inside" the author's head to decipher his argument into its components and work on the one that gave me trouble, then fit that one back into the whole argument to see if it made sense.

I have some ideas that I think make really good sense. These never really got tested until I tried to put them into words. I think that most of these ideas were basically solid (some were not). Almost all of them had a few problems, though. These problems are a lot easier to see when writing them down or trying to tell them to others. If I write something that seems obviously true to me, and someone I consider to be relatively intelligent and rational doesn't agree, one of two things are true. Either my idea sucks, or I'm not stating it correctly. In this class I have experienced both results.

First-order and second-order thinking are obviously quite different. In fact they conflict with one another. Students need to develop both kinds and be able to move back and forth between them. A student will not learn to think philosophically if he writes and revises simultaneously, if he rejects and criticizes before he even gets started. Nor will he learn to think philosophically if he never is compelled to look at his beliefs and examine them carefully.

Some Objections to the Method.

By letting students write however they want without concern for spelling and grammar, do we lower our standards of clarity, care, and attention? I don't think so. Certainly good spelling and grammar are important, but I want my students to take risks in their thinking, and I would defeat the purpose to insist that they perfect their prose first. The appropriate time to evaluate one's prose is *after* one has developed one's thoughts. A journal is a place to do the latter and not the former.

But, one might object, could I not serve both purposes simply by assigning term papers? Again, I wouldn't want to deny the importance of term papers; they can be good tools for measuring the ability of students to organize, evaluate, and think. But a student who spends six weeks perfecting a paper on the mind-body problem will not be devoting much thinking/writing to the existence of God, the problem of evil, or the foundations of morality—all topics assigned during the same six weeks. This is especially true if the grade the student would earn on the paper is proportional to the amount of time and effort I would expect him to devote to it; students will naturally spend most of their limited resources on those projects that count most heavily. One reason students take their journals seriously is that they realize I take them seriously.

If journals are so valuable, why don't I use them as the sole means of evaluation in all my courses? In more technical and specialized subjects, essay exams and multi-draft term papers are appropriate. But there is another reason. I teach several sections of Introduction to Philosophy every year, each section with thirty-five students. Reading and commenting in journals, which I have students turn in at least every two weeks, takes an enormous amount of my time. Unless a student specifically sets aside an entry as "personal," I feel obligated to read every one. There are a couple of other courses where I believe the journal method of evaluation would work, but until teaching loads and class sizes are reduced, I shall have to experiment in other ways in those courses and use the journal method where I believe it has the highest chances for success.

As with any humanistic discipline, philosophy cannot be neatly packaged and sold to students through the medium of a classroom. I have learned that if I want philosophy to touch students' lives, if I want them to experience the joys of critical thinking and to develop their own distinctive responses to the world, then I must help them to do philosophy in their own territory. Student journals provide me the opportunity to do this.

Notes

[1] Elbow, P. (1983, September). Teaching thinking by teaching writing. *Change*, p. 37.
[2] Ibid.

Appendix: Excerpts from Student Journals

[Self-sponsored entry on Descartes' distinction between psychological and methodological doubt.]

I am told that I can cast into methodological doubt my thoughts about the existence of the real world. However, I am told, I cannot psychologically doubt the actual existence of, say, a book, which I am perceiving at the moment....I have always strove for what is rational and logical. I have also always believed that I (or my mind) is a tool with vast untapped capabilities and should be able to be programmed and/or altered by me (or itself). I now perceive that I have a body and so supposedly I find it impossible to psychologically doubt my body's actual existence. However, given a few minutes of self-hypnosis, I can put my mind into a state where I can no longer perceive my body at all. Then I guess what I do is use methodological doubt to mask/overwhelm psychological belief in my body. I can close my eyes (sight is the only sense I have difficulty in negating) and I can cease to sense everything if I concentrate hard enough. In that intense state, I *really feel* detached from everything and for periods of a second or two I actually can and do psychologically doubt I exist with the "real world."...God that sounds weird! Maybe I should just be locked up. Maybe I have found a way to process my sense data in a strange way....

[In-class entry on the question "When is a person free?"; assigned prior to class discussion.]

A person is free whenever it's the case that he alone controls all thought-triggered actions. When he is presented with two choices, he can choose either. Although he may be persuaded to choose one over the other because of outside factors, the consequences of his actions stem from him, and he can choose either way. By being free, we are not obligated to take any one path through life. In order for one to be free, the choice to a decision has to come from inside, unpressured by whatever forces could motivate him to take only one course of action....

[Summary-and-reponse entry on the argument that God cannot be the source of morality.]

I want to take some time now to go over and clarify in my own mind the argument. The question that this argument aims at is: Is X good because God says so, or does God say so because X is good? If "good" is defined as "whatever God approves of," the phrase "God is good" implies only that God approves of himself. This is not particularly helpful. If this were the case, it would not be necessary for God to have any knowledge at all, much less perfect knowledge, for He could be completely arbitrary in his assignments of good and bad. Also if this were the case, tomorrow God could change his mind about anything He wished. He would have no reason to not change his mind. He could say that now only murderers will get into heaven. But, you say, He won't do that. Notice what you would reply when asked *why* he wouldn't do that: He wouldn't do that because *it would be wrong*. We must measure God *against* morality. It must be the case that God says that X is good because *He knows* it is good. He has perfect knowledge of good and bad, but is not the source of morality....It seems that one can go through God to get to morality, or go directly to it. I will say nothing about which path is easier except that they are both difficult. So it seems that it is possible for a person to be moral and not believe in God. So I hold the position that even if religion starts to crumble, morality will stay intact.

29.

The Philosophical Journal:
Three Case Studies

STEPHEN M. NORTH

When we began the task of engineering a writing-across-the-curriculum program, we found ourselves, as perhaps others have, in a rather unfamiliar promotional role. Despite the fact that participation held no tangible rewards for faculty—no released time or bonuses or lighter loads—we had to try, in effect, to sell writing. One of our most marketable items, it seemed to us, was the journal: "Have your students keep a journal! You can use it flexibly, read it when and how you like, and it will be of great benefit to your students." We pointed out to them, among other things, the centrality of "expressive" discourse in the theory offered by James Britton et al. in *The Development of Writing Abilities (11-18)*, and the opportunities for it that journal writing seemed to provide; and we suggested to them Toby Fulwiler's enthusiastic and useful article in NCTE's *Language Connections* (1981), "The Personal Connection: Journal Writing Across the Curriculum," with particular emphasis on the conclusion:

> Journals are interdisciplinary and developmental by nature; it would be hard for writers who use journals regularly and seriously not to witness growth. I believe that journals belong at the heart of any writing-across-the-curriculum program. (p. 30)

And so the program was launched, with upwards of 600 students taking what we call Writing Intensive courses each semester, and expansion planned.

Once underway, though, I began to wonder at the boldness of our promises. In theory, yes, journal writing ought to work well in any classroom, in any curriculum. In theory, it offers all students equally enormous freedom to explore some new discipline through language, to begin to make it their own. But in practice, as anyone who has ever assigned or been assigned journal writing in a classroom knows—and I've tried both—every student will react to the opportunity/obligation of journal writing in his or her own way. All we had behind our promises was theory, on the one hand, and anecdotal, albeit persuasive, testimonial evidence from people who had tried it, on the other. But we didn't really know, couldn't really predict, what students would *make* of these journals when our faculty introduced them in disciplinary courses.

It was under these circumstances, then, that I undertook case studies of three writers in one Writing Intensive course where journal writing played a central role. I chose three students, as opposed to one or nine or twenty, for two reasons. First, I needed a small enough number to be able to study each writer very, very closely. I wasn't aiming to generate a taxonomy of journal writing "types" or a model of the journal writer's composing process. Nor were my subjects intended to constitute, in any statistical sense, a 'sample'; it would certainly be possible to reduce patterns of journal writing to a set of norms, but that was not to my purpose. Instead, I wanted to understand each student as special, as unique: as someone who would make of the journal something no one else could. Second, then, I chose three simply to help accentuate each writer's idiosyncracy, to offer enough contrast to help highlight what was unique in each.

The course was Phil. 110, an introductory course of about 53 students, taught by a senior professor and a teaching assistant. Like most such courses, its purpose was to expose students to the discipline of Philosophy: the kinds of questions it asks, its history, its central figures, its modes of inquiry, and so on. In this particular class, students were expected to take a very active role in this process, by becoming—or realizing that they already were—philosophers themselves. That is, they were expected, with the help of the instructors and the textbook, to articulate their philosophical position on various issues, and then try to locate themselves in the context of the larger discipline. Crucial to this enterprise was their writing, about 90% of which was to be done in what was called a "philosophical journal":

> If we are to gain clarity about our personal philosophies, it will be necessary both to talk and to write about our ideas, especially, to write. For this reason, you are being asked to keep a journal of your philosophical thinking. By semester's end a good deal of your personal philosophy should be down in the journal.

The entire course, including the journal writing, was to be guided by a rather special Syllabus (see Appendix). It has 13 sections, with such headings as Truth, Beauty, Freedom, and so on; and under each heading were anywhere from 5-15 questions designed to help the students (a) figure out their position on the issue; (b) see, by examining their experience, how they arrived at that position; and (c) find philosophers who agreed or disagreed with them on the issue, and so locate themselves in the context of philosophical thought (as represented primarily in their textbook, the *Dictionary of Philosophy and Religion*, written by the instructor, William Reese [New Jersey: Humanities Press, 1980]).

The case studies themselves were very simply designed. I asked for three participants from the class who would agree, for a nominal $20.00 honorarium, to let me xerox all their writings, and to come in for three taped interviews during the course—one at the beginning, one in the middle, one at the end. The three writers I studied were Alyson and Yvette, both freshman, both new to Philosophy; and Mark, a senior taking this third Philosophy course. Alyson was from a white, upper-middle-class, upstate New York family, a student-athlete, and the most prolific of the three in her journal (5570 words). Yvette was the youngest of 10 in a black New York City family recently moved to this country from Jamaica (journal: 4420 words). And Mark was an economics major from Long Island—demographically, a "Suburban conservative Jew," as he puts it. His journal ran 4380 words.

The full report runs over 100 pages; I cannot offer all of that here. What I can do, however, is offer a profile of each writer that will make it clear just who they were as journal writers—what each *made* of that philosophical journal.

Alyson

I was especially interested to find out about the relationships these writers established with their readers in the journal. Of the three, Alyson seems to create an audience with whom she is most comfortable, most at home. To some extent, this is a matter of style. She consistently writes in a reflective "I" of considerable intimacy, full of self-conscious meta-comments ("Excuse me, I have to do some reading"); questions ("How come there's no Reese entry?", to the instructor, who has written the textbook, without referring in it to his own work); and assumed shared experience ("I think when Prof asked in class...").

But it's a matter of substance, too. Consider, for example, the trust implicit in her very first entry, Autobiography. She tells in poignant detail about the most painful period of her young life, the breakup of her family:

> Back at home my secure world was gradually being taken away from me. Dad was elected to a high political office in the county and family came second for him it seemed. The fighting started between Mom and Dad and the drinking, too. That continues to this day. I would call their fighting a large crisis in my life, a continuing one, and so it began, a continuing fight for survival.

Later in the same entry:

> Then Dad left home. There it went, family, friends and boyfriend. The grades that were always so good were slowly becoming terrible and I felt a confusion of hurts from my losses while the rest of the world went on oblivious.

This is powerful stuff.

Alyson's mode in her entries might best be called dialogic: She fashions for herself an audience whose presence she feels so immediately that she "knows" what they would say back to her, and writes as though they were present as the writing was being done. How the two men who actually read and responded to her journal correspond to this fictive audience, though perhaps of theoretical interest, is of relatively little importance here. What matters to Alyson is that they do nothing, either in class or in responding to her journal, to disrupt the image of them she has created.

Perhaps the most interesting effect of this dialogic mode is its impact on the way she shapes her entries. As one might expect, her strategies are essentially those of talk: She blends together the class talk, the Syllabus, and the readings as if they were parts of an ongoing conversation. And she introduces these various elements with equal freedom. I cited the beginning of this Values entry earlier:

I think when Prof asked the question, if you knew the world was going to end in an hour, where would you go, what would you do?, our answer would lead us closer to what we value the most— not so much the meaning of your life—for if that was what gave our life its meaning, why wouldn't we always be with it? Most people expressed desires...

Her entry on Beauty begins with this class-talk reference: "I have to agree with the taxi cab driver in Japan that said the world is so beautiful I can hardly stand it."

Not surprisingly, the Syllabus and the readings most often serve to create this conversational context. In her early entries, the dialogic movement is somewhat obscured by structures from other sources—the Autobiography, for instance, has chrono-logic to it. But in fact all the entries follow pretty faithfully the questions asked in the Syllabus, and later in the term, when her journal gets less of her time, their influence becomes quite clear. In her last entry, then, on Right and Wrong, she begins by answering #1 ("What is the principle, standard, rule or method you use in deciding what is right and what is wrong?"):

I thought that by eighteen, after so many mishaps and mistakes, that I'd have figured out what is right or wrong; I haven't. There are some basic principles I try to live by and some things I have decided are right for me but the decision usually comes from experience and or logic. I also like to ask persons who may have been in a similar dilema what worked for them but in the end I know that I am deciding only for myself and I will have to live with that decision.

She then gives one sentence to her own reliance on principle ("I try to decide as little as possible & act on principle."); two sentences to the importance of consistency; two to her reaction to the textbook's treatment of Socrates; and so on through question #9, which offers a series of difficult ethical issues (incest, orgies, etc.) for which she offers one- or two-sentence reactions, concluding with a final reference to her reading: "As Santayana sees ethics (right and wrong) as a rational discipline, so do I. Discipline in consistency." No need to establish or maintain an autonomous context for these entries, not even via the old school device of repeating the question. The context is a given, and shared, so she can just plunge in and expect that her readers can and are keeping up.

For Alyson, then, the journal is a place for the central interaction in the course or, as she puts it, "the journal just ties the rest of 'em [textbook, Syllabus, class talk] together." The class sessions, in which students offer their positions, and during which the instructor alternates between resource and gadfly, serve her mostly as something for "bouncing off" of. The result is that "a lot of the journal..I think the discussion in class steers my reading for the journal, and then that steers my writing, so what I write about is mostly what I read about, not really what I talk about." In one interview, she describes how she makes these entries:

A:...I could read "Self", Hume, Russell, Emerson, write; then go back and read Thoreau, *Walden*, Jung, write; go back and read,

write, read, write. Because just so it's not a reiteration I write and
then see where my writing's going so I can go to a philosopher...I
know what I'm writing about...I start reading Edwards, and see,
y'know, he doesn't have anything to add what I want to say, it's
not gonna help me, so I go to another one.

Equally important, this interaction is one in which she feels that
she can hold her own. The philosophers she reads are participants in
this dialogue, too, and they do not intimidate her. I asked why not:

A: Philosophy isn't...I think that's just the subject, the way the
subject is, that there aren't really any rights and wrongs. And I
think Prof. Reese has kind of established that...he's looking for
the way you want to look at it. There is no right or wrong.

The upshot is that she makes of the journal very much what the
Syllabus suggests she might, and so does "gain clarity" about her
personal philosophy—and to that extent, anyway, vindicates the claims
we had made.

Yvette

Yvette makes of her journal a very different thing. It certainly would
not have been easy to predict how her journal might differ from Alyson's
at the beginning of the course: if she does not make as deep a commitment in terms of trust in her 820-word Autobiography entry, she is at
least as good-willed, and even more ingenuous. Here is how she begins:

My name is Yvette Hope Johnson and I am nineteen years of age.
My island home is Jamaica and I am of Negro descendance. My
Zodiac sign is gemini and this governed my moods in a special way
because of the twin emotion that are involve. Most people can
detect my tempermental moods and deal with them if they knows
me long enough. The greatest goal in my life is to get a master
degree in Computer Science which might enable me to get a good
profession to secure my future. Being an independent individual is
something I enjoys very much.

And here is how she ends:

I value myself as a unique individual who respect nature and all
the enjoyable things that life as to offer. I count my blesses as they
go by and never take anything for granted. I believe their is a God
who governs all of our lives on the earth and give him praises for
my failure and all my successes. To be alive is a very wonderful
inward feeling especially if I am acheiving or working to acheive
my life goals. I love me very much and this help a great deal to love
others regardless of their short comings.

And yet a couple of differences do stand out. First, this seems to be a
less complicated, perhaps less troubled person. She gives no indication
that she has had to face the sorts of crises or conflicts which have had
such an impact on Alyson. We might even call her, for whatever the
label is worth, less mature, preserved in a certain innocence, perhaps, by
being the tenth of ten children in what, by her account, anyway, is a very
happy family.

Second, for all its good will, there seems to be a certain reticence here. In fact, it's far more Introduction than Autobiography. She offers description, aspiration, declaration—but little history; she traces no causes. It's hard to tell exactly why. The Syllabus prompts, after all, seem clear enough about what's expected (e.g., #1: "Who has influenced you most and in what ways?"). It's no doubt partly because she regards the assignment as more like "school writing" than Alyson does; she seems to treat the genre here as not incomparable to that required by "My Summer Vacation." She may also be, in her own way, a more private person. That is, while we could conclude that her apparent misreaction to the Autobiography assignment was simply sloppy school work, it may be that it was selective reading in response to a stronger, albeit probably unconscious, need to protect herself: to present the "correct" Yvette, the one that she thinks ought to be for public purposes. Whatever the causes, it seems clear that she cannot so readily accept the invitation "to gain clarity" about her personal philosophy with the same depth of commitment as Alyson.

In a sense, then, the course, and especially the journal, pose more of a threat to Yvette. By design, the latter invites her to complicate her life, to be reflective, philosophical. She is quite aware of what the invitation entails:

I: Where d'you...do you have some idea of where the journal is supposed to take you during the semester? I mean, what its goals are as far as you're concerned?

Y: Yeah. I think he said he was lookin' for somethin' that you can help yourself to develop it. It's like to look deeper inside yourself. Suppose you have a goal that you set for yourself and, y'know, to really bring it out...y'know, he want you to write about it so that it can be like something grounded. Y'know, he want you to get inside yourself more than you usually do in your writing. If you have like a idea, you might just brush it aside because you say it's not worth anything because it's only my idea. He want you to believe in you, really.

The problem is, she finds it hard to see herself taking on this role. For all that she recognizes the invitation for self-exploration, she suspects there must be a "right" answer. This is, after all, school writing:

I: When you write in the journal, are you worried about...is it like a formal paper?

Y: Sometimes. It's not really formal, but sometimes, you know he's lookin' for something specific and sometimes you just want to write something general...y'know, just anything that's really in your mind you just wanna write but then again, I know he has to be lookin' for something specific, y'know, to see at least you understand what the class discussion was about...something like that.

And there are other factors. If Alyson was unintimidated by philosophers, Yvette is awestruck: "...you sit there and you read all these things that people sit there and like most half their lives think about and somethin' you just take so lightly and spent half of their life tryin' to prove their point about it. Really amazin'!" These are not people to be disagreed with casually. In addition, she is constantly reminded—in the Syllabus, in class meetings, and especially in comments in her journal—that part of the process of articulating one's personal philosophy is locating it in the context of other philosophies.

In the face of these combined forces—her native reticence, her awe, and the pressure to play the class talk and her reading off of her own thinking—what happens is that she gradually disappears from her entries altogether. Thus, while in her first two entries she writes in the first person, by the third entry she's become mostly a commentator:

> The self within its natural context often replaces soul or psyche. From the Webster dictionary it is seen as the essential person distinct from all person in identity. This latter definition is what I want to use in my journal to interpret what self means to me. To me, self is clearly shown through the experiences that we have from childhood up to our adult life.
>
> According to Locke, we were all born with a blank tab on which our life experiences are written. This tab continued to be scared by our experiences throughout our life. Eventually the innocent person who was born with no incites about the world...

The first line of this entry is a garbled version of her textbook ("A term which, in naturalistic context, often replaces soul or psyche."), the second borrowed from Webster's. She finally appears in the third and fourth, but only to opt for one of her borrowings. The rest of the entry (another 350 words) plays out the implications of Locke's *tabula rasa*— "blank tab," in Yvette's rendering—for the development of a hypothetical child. In our interviews, it becomes clear that this entry represents something of a breakthrough, the discovery of what she calls the "problematic" approach:

> I think...the first two journals [journal entries] I write they were more like subtle, y'know. I didn't get like into the depth of what I think the philosophers think, y'know, I just skim on the top of what they think. But like when we get wew get down to "Freedom" we had to do it in a problematic way—like we had to come up with a problem, y'know, find different solutions for it and then we had to draw a conclusion from it.

This general strategy gives Yvette a handle on philosophical discourse. At the same time, it is clear that it resolves for her the tension implicit in her understanding of what the journal is for—"to believe in you, really" versus "you know he's lookin' for something specific"—in favor of the latter. Not once in the entire journal does Yvette directly invoke personal experience. In place of whatever *she* might think on a given issue, she offers a quoted, paraphrased, and/or garbled version of some authority—the textbook, the Syllabus, her suitemate's philosophy text. And in place of her own experience, she offers these hypothetical cases, "problems": the Lockean child, Constance the reggae singer, the person "who is seen as physically ugly," and so on. Rather than having to deal with the possible conflicts between the assertions of these authorities and her own beliefs, then, she has only to work out the implications of their positions.

As a result, what she accumulates is less a coherent, articulated personal philosophy than a series of problems within which she works out—and confirms—received wisdom, a set of what are more or less stock morals. From Self:

> If we are strong and willing to stand up for what we believe in, life would be a lot more easy to live.
>
> He [the child] will find out that everything is not handed out on a silver platter but he has to work to achieve what he wants.

From Beauty:

> It is best for all of us to take heed to others feeling and give them a chance to show us how beautiful they are before passing judgement.

Thus, for Yvette, writing her way into Philosophy turns out to be more a matter of learning a philosophical style, its forms and rhythms, than of making philosophical inquiry. Is that bad? I don't think so. It seems to have been all she was ready for, and it has left its mark. In our last interview she says "...he [the professor] like opened our eyes to these things, y'know? And at all time he challenge what we saying. Like if I say art is beautiful, he say why do I say the art is beautiful? You know, he just gets you to open up your own thinking, like you don't say something is beautiful without havin' a reason." That may not be exactly what we had in mind when we made our promises, but it may be learning enough.

Mark

Mark turned out to be a different kettle of fish. His status as a last semester senior raises immediate suspicions: What is a senior who has taken two other philosophy courses doing in an introductory course? Mark figures it was maybe a waste of time: "It was a good course...I think it wasn't the best for me, I think I was wasting my time, but for a lot of people in there it was a very good course." Given that attitude, what he says about the journal comes as no surprise: "I just essentially wrote it off the top of my head, it was stuff I already knew." The readings which should have led to journal entries? "Again, I'm a senior, I've had a lot of these courses, I'm fairly well read, so y'know, someone else may have to do the reading more than I would have to do in order to, uh, present a good picture of the subject."

By contrast to Alyson's intimacy, and Yvette's blend of awe and reticence, Mark presents a kind of not entirely secure bravado—a persona more accessible than the later Yvette, but far more prickly than Alyson. Consider his version of Autobiography, which I quote here in full:

My Life
By Me, Myself, and I

It all started when I came forth from my mothers womb in an antisceptic hospital on Long Island, some 21 years ago. At this stage in my life all I could do was cry and wet my diapers.

Although, I have not lost the aforementioned skills, it is no an unreasonable immodest claim to say that I have progressed some what since that early part of my life.

My goals in life since then are essentially an enlightened hedonism where long-run pleasure is maximized any my values in pursuit of these goals is a libertarian system constrained only where my actions interfer with another person.

The crucial event(s) which caused this character essentialy came from my religious back ground as a suburban conservitive Jew. I valued on one had the intellectual discourse of informal "minyans" held on Sunday's but disliked the pompous dead rituals of the sabbath (Saturday's).

When I realized, that almost everyone was born into a society which had a true religion "inspired" by "God" I came to the conclusion that all religions are obviously myths & not to be taken seriously.

I thus began to pursue the true meaning of life to me (pleasure) constrained by my Jewish guilt into a form of libertarinism.

The end
(Well, not quite yet?)

What are we to make of this writer? Sophomoric humor, odd spelling of familiar words, correct spelling and use of more philosophical ones; on the one hand, a flip evasiveness, on the other an attempt to locate pretty specifically the roots of his philosophy. It isn't a question that ever gets an easy answer. What Mark seems to seek in response to his journal is acknowledgement, respect: when you are older than all the other kids in summer camp, you want special recognition from the counselors, but you aren't sure whether to get it by showing off or demonstrating your prowess—or both, since the line that separates the two is often very fine. That is Mark here: he wants to think of himself as superior, as a philosopher, and he wants his instructors to agree, partly because it will save him work, but also because he seems to need the praise.

For Mark, then, the journal becomes a place to try to win or assert this status. Like Alyson, he sticks with the first person much of the time, but it is never her reflective, intimate "I." Instead, it's the almost arrogant "I" of that first entry, or the arrogant "I" trying to be humble—and ending up closer to obsequious:

> p.s. I realize that this is an intensly personal view of life's meaning and that this class perhaps requires me to re-iterate the views of the "great thinkers". If this is the case, I will graciously expand this text to include intelligent ruminations on the great learned philosophies presented in class. [End of Life's Meaning entry.]

And occasionally—again, the demand for status is clear—Mark switches to a righteous, all-of-us-philosophers-have-to-clean-up-our-act "we": "As we have *abandoned* such *superstitious nonsense* as 'impetuosity' in the hard sciences, let us also abandon such shoddy thinking from philosophy (and psychology or social sciences in general.)" (His emphases.)

Mark spends almost all of his time on the attack. He wants to get his readers to bow to the inescapable logic of his formulations; or, failing that, at least to admit that he makes an awfully good—i.e., real philosopher's—case. One of his favorite tactics, as the passages quoted thus far suggest, is to take extreme positions for their shock value. His first move in the journal is to inscribe the inside cover with

Audiatur et altera pars

—Let the other side also be heard.

Seneca

My favorites, though, are the ones he devises. Here's a syllogism he constructs:

1. A man is composed of matter & energy
2. Matter & energy are not capable of animistic "choice" or purpose
   ...Man is not capable of choice or purpose

Here's a shocker, from the end of the same entry: "Freedom is dead." And here's a third, one that could be considered the cornerstone of his philosophy: "My main point is that we are all nothing but a bunch of atoms."

The fact of the matter is that Mark doesn't really seem to be working to "gain clarity" about his personal philosophy at all. On the contrary, he seems to figure he already has that, and that what remains is to pound away at those who don't—or won't— see. His characteristically short, aggressive entries provoke the fullest responses of the three from the instructors. One comment reads, in part: "It would be best to refrain from name calling. It is neither philosophical nor scientific." Does Mark take this as friendly advice? Hardly: *"NAME CALLING!* My points were *not clear* to *you,* so my conclusions on *Freedom* & *Turing's test* were considered 'name-calling'." This is interaction, true, but it's hardly dialogue. Indeed, probably the best way to characterize what Mark makes of his journal is to say that he turns it into his end of a shouting match. And, as is so often the case in shouting matches, he never really does listen very well.

When I asked the instructor who taught Alyson, Yvette, and Mark to read and respond to the full versions of these profiles, he was both gracious and honest. He was disappointed, he said, in not having really reached, by his standards, these three kids: that they have not perceived what he was doing as he perceived it. When I pointed out that all other readers of the profiles had been really impressed with the teacher depicted, and the course, he said that well, he wanted the world—quite the response one would expect. He followed with a note:

I had supposed, naively, that in changing my course to S/U, making it self-discovery, using S/U instead of A/E to encourage work, I had avoided the games that students play. My initial shock at your research on my course was learning that the games were still going on, perhaps slightly changed. I was still the object of intense scrutiny; they still wanted to please me where I wanted them to please themselves. The question whose answer I still don't know is, how much (if anything) has been gained in thus altering the course? The new format is attention holding. Does it do anything else?

I think he can rest easy. He has simply re-learned—as I did, certainly, and as most anyone who reads these profiles is bound to do—a lesson about journal writing, and learning generally, that we return to as teachers over and over again: while we may assign students to keep journals as a way to learn about our disciplines, they will decide what those journals will be. Perhaps that's not always so easy to accept. We like to think of ourselves, usually, as initiating people into our disciplines, and to think further that that means exercising control—not only over what our initiates learn, but over how they conceive of us and our disciplinary authority, how they conceive of themselves as learners, what kinds of discourse they use to make entry. But this is always bound to be a reductive view: *teaching* may be thought of in such terms, but *learning* won't stand for it. And that, of course, is the moral of this story: *journals are for learning.*

Appendix: Sample Syllabus Section

Week 4 *The Self.*—

1. What is the object of this "I, me, mine" reference? Are you your body? But you say, "I lost my leg." (Of course, you also say, "I got hit by a car.") Apparently you will distinguish between yourself and a missing part of your body as long as you could say anything at all. So are you that central mass of brain and nervous system? But your cells replace every 6 years (except for the brain cells and they replace their material). In addition to brain cells, your genotype stays with you all your life; but is your genotype "you"? Theoretically, you could be cloned from your finger nail. Would your clone be "you"?

2. Then are you your capacities and memories, in a sense, then, a great time-worm, including your past and your prospective future? (a) But you don't remember all the parts of your time-line. You construct the early years out of what you've been told. Or is Freud (q.v.) correct here, that all is retained? (b) Can your capacities change through time?

3. Are you, then, what you think you are? But you might have committed a murder and revised your memory. Can you have a conversion experience and separate yourself from parts of your past, so you really aren't that part anymore?

4. When Sartre (q.v.5) considers the self a "project" he emphasizes purposes, plans, and the time in which to achieve them. But then when you change projects are you a different self? Can you take the same boat even if every part has been replaced?

5. Is there a difference between what you are and what you want others to think you are? Check Jung (q.v. 3, 6) on the Persona and the self.

6. Basic views of self: (a) as substantial (Socrates 5,6; Plato 3; Descartes 8,9; Kant 6) (b) as complex (Hume 4; Locke 1,8; Russell 6; Kierkegaard 2-6) (c) as functional (Aristotle 7; James 2, 3; Jung 3-6) (d) as material (Hobbes 1-6; LaMettrie 1-3; Holbach 1, 4, 6; Montague 2; Broad 3; Santayana 1, 2, 6; Dewey 4-5; Feigl 1) (e) as epiphenomenal (T.H. Huxley; Santayana 1, 2, 6) (f) Psycho-physical parallelism (Spinoza 8, Leibniz 6-7) (g) Identity theory (q.v. 2-3; Rorty)

7. What, then, do you finally think you are?

30.

Journal Writing as Person Making

FRED HALLBERG

The Problem of Unintended Effects

The use of personal journals for the teaching of writing is far more powerful and far-reaching in its effects than is generally recognized. When it works to improve a student's writing skills, it is also working to change that student's enduring attitudes, values, and sense of personal identity. These deeper personal consequences of the activity of journal work should not be minimized or avoided. Rather we should admit that personal transformation toward personal integration is the real function of education in the liberal arts. We should therefore encourage and applaud pedagogical techniques that facilitate such transformation.

There are, of course, dangers involved in the use of methods with the power to transform our students' identities. But any technique sufficiently effective to do any good will also be subject to potential abuse. I shall argue that these dangers, though real, may be minimized by the use of a few precautionary maxims.

Sources of a Theory of Personal Life

Understanding the effects our assignments have on students' lives requires an understanding of the structure of personhood in general. The account of the structure of personal life I shall be using is derived mainly from the works of C.G. Jung and Ira Progoff, who are respectively the founder of, and a practitioner within, the school of "Analytic" psychotherapy. (Progoff's general theory of the person is stated in his *The Symbolic and the Real*, especially in Chapters 5 and 6. A concise statement of Jung's theory may be found in his *Memories, Dreams, Reflections*, especially in Chapter 11.)

A Theory of the Person

To be a person is, at bottom, to be recognized, within a community, as playing a social role or set of roles. This is a sensible starting point, since as Jung has emphasized, the term "persona" originally designated the large mask borne by an ancient Greek actor, which signified his role in the drama. The playing of a social role does not, however, exhaust the concept of being a person. This can easily be shown by pursuing the question of just what are our recognized social roles. What does it mean, exactly, to be a parent or a child, a teacher or a student, a spouse or a paramour? Our attempt to specify these roles will involve the story of our relationship with significant others, the norms of the larger community, and that larger community's history and traditions. So the attempt to specify any given social role will inevitably expand into an open-ended project of inquiry involving a great deal more than a specific task at hand. Specific social roles are defined by a spreading network of relationships that appear to involve, in principle, reference to the entirety of our personal, social, and cultural experience and history. (Alex Haley's *Roots* provides an illuminating example of how individual identity depends on the larger context of history and culture.)

Besides the complicating facts of interdependence, the playing of a social role requires a degree of self-consciousness and deliberateness of participation. Acting involves knowing as well as doing. The actor knows he is playing a part, as well as what his part is.

The playing of a social role is, however, different from theater acting in that one's script is not out in advance. This is one consequence of the impossibility of exhaustively specifying a given social role. The concept of a person as specified by a network of social roles, performed deliberately and self-consciously, is a notion that involves degrees of realization. We might think of the concept of a person as lying on a scale of deliberateness and self-consciousness, with the completely articulated and acknowledged script of the theater actor anchoring one end of the scale and the completely unself-conscious role of a human neonate, or a sub-human social animal, anchoring the other.

A particular individual will be located somewhere along this scale of articulate self-consciousness. A person will always have some awareness of what he or she is about. This awareness need not be very comprehensive or adequate, especially early in life. But once the person stands up and announces "Here I am!" the question of just what this "I" is becomes inescapable. We as self-conscious beings have a built-in drive impelling us in the direction of a more adequate and accurate self-definition. To become thus self-conscious and self-possessed is to become a person in the full sense of the term and to realize the implicit meaning of our lives.

Intermediate Structures: Autobiography, Dialogue, Depth Dimension

The structure of personal life I have been describing is plausibly universal because it is so very general. As soon as we get down to cases, the variety of forms of personal life become infinitely numerous. Each person is absolutely unique in at least two respects. First, each person constitutes a center of awareness that is numerically distinct from that of any other personal subject in the universe. And second, each person's story of his or her life experiences is qualitatively distinct in the sense in which each snowflake is said to be qualitatively distinct from each other.

Between the two extremes of the very abstract generality of form on the one hand, and the absolute uniqueness and infinite variety of individual lives on the other, lies an intermediate zone of personal structures given empirically rather than conceptually. Analytical psycho-therapists listen to hundreds of hours of material from dozens of clients. Soon they begin to discern patterns of similarity among these individual case histories. Ira Progoff has put a lot of effort into his attempt to capture these frequently encountered themes or areas of concern within a taxonomic system, and he has structured his personal journal exercises to address precisely these recurrent themes. His most recent formulation of this taxonomic structure includes four main categories and sixteen subordinate categories. (This structure is outlined in the "Appendix" to Progoff's *At a Journal Workshop,* pages 301-320.) This is an impressive achievement, but its encyclopedic complexity tends to defeat the outsider who has not actually attended a Progoff workshop. I believe the bulk of the material Progoff presents can be condensed without significant loss of accuracy into three main categories. I call these "autobiography," "dialogue," and "depth dimension" respectively.

Autobiography

A large part of our self-concept consists of the narrative by means of which we remember and relate our past experiences. I am the person who built a snow fort with Doug and Henry in the winter of 1948, who climbed water towers with Mark and Clark in the summer of 1952, who graduated from college and was commissioned in the Army in 1958, who received my doctorate in philosophy in 1969, and so on. The irrepro-ducibility and distinctness of each person's life narrative consitutes a large part of our personal uniqueness. That is why actually telling our story has the therapeutic effect of "ego strengthening." The very process leads the teller to become aware that he or she is a person with a unique history of triumph and tragedy, with as yet unfulfilled hopes and projects. (Sam Keen and Anne Fox's *Telling Your Story* is a good example of the use of the technique to strengthen an individual's sense of selfhood. So too is Tristine Rainer's *The New Diary.* The technique has even been used in the context of vocational counseling to clarify goals and to enable persons to withstand the shocks and disappointments of job hunting. See John Crystal and Richard Bolles's *Where Do I Go from Here with My Life?*)

A curious consequence of actually telling your story is that the more you tell, the more you have to tell. In my experience students usually begin by doubting they even have a story to tell, or if they do, they fear it will be so poor an affair no one could find it interesting, including themselves. But once they begin to write, more and more memories become available to them, until it becomes plain it would take many volumes to even begin to tell their story adequately. This is one dimension of the infinitude, or fathomlessness, of the self.

Students don't come easily to this realization about themselves, so Progoff has worked out a stepwise procedure for leading his clients toward this recognition. He has them begin by describing, in writing, the "present period" of their lives. (Progoff, *At a Journal Workshop,* Chapter 5.) He has them get clear in their minds its temporal boundaries ("When does your present period *begin?*"). He then has them work up a title for their present period and has them write a brief summary of it. He even has them attempt to construct a visible symbol of it. (The role of the "Period Image" is described in Chapter 6.) Finally, he has them describe the detailed contents of their present period in straightforward discursive prose.

My students find this a very easy exercise which serves as a warm-up for the more demanding work ahead. These "present period" entries, however, are typically not very insightful or imaginative. This confirms what I said earlier about social roles constituting the starting point of our sense of selfhood. Students at this stage are concerned mainly with what they need to do to meet the demands of other persons. What they need to do to meet their own enduring personal needs will typically not surface until later in the process.

Two sorts of resistances often block the students' way from a superficial self-awareness of their "present period" to a more developed awareness of the autobiographical structure of their lives. They may deny their lives have any developmental structure at all by denying anything of significance has ever changed in it ("I have *always* been the same person!"). Or they may throw up so many minute details that their large-scale developmental patterns are effectively hidden from sight. Progoff neatly sidesteps both sorts of resistance by means of his "Steppingstones" exercise (See Chapter 8). He requires workshop participants to list the time and place of their birth, and then to divide the time from then to the "present period" into a small number of "chapters" or "turning points." He recommends they choose no fewer than six and no more than eight, for a total of eight to ten periods including one's birth and present period. The point of the minimum number is to force the participants to exhibit and acknowledge at least some developmental structure in their lives. The point of the maximum number is to force the participants to organize their memories into a system of priorities which manifests the interest and concerns characteristic of his or her present period.

The "Present Period" and "Steppingstones" entries constitute the first two steps of the autobiographical component of the journal process. The third and last step is to require the writer to select one past period which seems to be especially important or interesting, and to fix its temporal boundaries. The writer is then required to tell the story of that "past period" of his or her life.

Once the main outline and a significant quantity of the past period material is recorded in writing, the participants are told to survey the results of their efforts, and to write down any features which now seem evident in these components, or in the entire sweep of their lives.

By now the main idea of the autobiographical component of the "Intensive Journal" process will have been communicated. Further work filling in the blanks of this emerging autobiographical structure is typically left for the writer to pursue as a voluntary task on his or her own time. A number of participants will by now have had several powerful "A-ha!" experiences concerning their lives and their related self-concepts. The process has brought them face to face with both the absolute uniqueness and the fathomless complexity of their own lives.

This encounter typically engenders a sense of exhilaration, and markedly increases the participant's sense of self-worth.

Dialogue

The second main component of the "Intensive Journal" technique is called "dialogue." So far the journal process has been developed from a single point of view, namely, that of the "present period" of the writer's life. But these proliferating autobiographical materials contain references to many persons, all of whom had a point of view and autobiography of their own. The fact that these past encounters were two-way interactions implies they cannot be defined exclusively by reference to the writer's own consciousness. It is the very "otherness" of these other persons and the consequent ambiguity of our relationship to them which gives these relationships so much power and significance in our lives. We are haunted, as it were, by the continuing presence of all those who have strongly influenced us in the past. (Nancy Friday's *My Mother/Myself* provides powerful testimony to the way in which past relationships continue to structure present consciousness long after the actual interactions with these other persons have apparently ceased.)

The first step of the dialogue technique is to make the separate consciousness of the other person as clear and definite as possible. This is done by writing the steppingstones of the other person's life, just as the participant has already done for his or her own life. This exercise often proves difficult because of the absence of information and the presence of emotional blocks. So in this case the writer is instructed to make the steppingstone list as full and complete as he or she can. Once the dramatic life history of the other person is written, the participant is instructed to write a brief description of the essence of the relationship as it exists at the present time. He or she is requested to close his or her eyes, and to allow an image of the other person to appear in the inner arena of imagination. He or she is then requested to allow a dialogue script to develop between himself or herself and the imagined other, and to write this dialogue script in the journal. Finally, the participant is asked to read over the dialogue script and to make note of any general features of the dialogue, or of the relationship itself, which has then become evident.

This procedure may not work very well at first. But with time and patience a number of participants will have powerfully cathartic emotional experiences as they get in touch with this buried material and work through their unfinished business with these significant others from their past. These experiences will affect the participant's self-image and behavior in at least two ways. First, it will bring him or her to acknowledge a second dimension of infinitude within the self. The participant will have already encountered the infinitude of the self constituted by the fact that telling one's story is an inherently uncludable project. Now the participant encounters the fact that his or her story is internally related to the stories of numerous other persons, each of which is just as fathomless as is one's own. Second, the experience releases the energy that had been bound up in the effort to not think about old hurts or disappointments, so the participant's experience of catharsis is often followed by a sense of renewal and enhanced vitality.

This dialogue technique, once mastered, provides a surprisingly general procedure for linking the various components of our learning and experience into a unified whole. The key idea here is *personification*. The dialogue technique works by personifying emotionally significant encounters from our past, so we can relate to them imaginatively in the present. But this technique need not be limited to personal encounters we have actually experienced. Virtually anything with a beginning and a developmental history can be treated as if it were a person with a life of its own, to whom we can relate emotionally and conversationally. Besides "dialogue" with persons, for example, Progoff has his clients personify and "dialogue" with work projects, with their bodies, with important events in their past, and with troubling developments in the larger society. In each case the participant personifies the material to be dealt with by writing out its developmental history, and then converses with it, in imagination, as if it were another person. I have had students dialogue with authors of assigned texts, such as C.G. Jung and Pope John-Paul II. I have had them dialogue with historical characters like Erasmus and Luther. I see no reason why this technique could not be generally employed to establish a personal relationship with characters in literature, or with important events in history. The final result of all such dialogue exercises, which feed back into the participant's developing autobiographical materials, is to extend his or her articulate self-concept until it embraces almost everything he or she knows.

The Depth Dimension.

The third component of the "Intensive Journal" process is a set of disciplines intended to establish an articulate awareness of the apparently irrational world of our dreams and reveries. Progoff calls these materials the "depth dimension" of our experience. This way of speaking of the "depth" of our experience is of course derived from Jung's concept of the unconscious self. Jung and Progoff believe our individual consciousnesses are part of a larger "transpersonal" consciousness which we contact by means of dreams, visions, and other supposedly revelatory intuitions. It may seem question-begging to utilize such controversial theoretical constructs as part of the methodology of expanding self-awareness. In practice, however, the techniques he prescribes do not entail covert acceptance of questionable theoretical constructs. Everyone does have, after all, an inner life of daydreams and night dreams. The journal techniques for working with them simply makes one more area of our life accessible to articulate self-awareness. Some especially creative individuals maintain an ongoing dialogue with their inner world of dreams and reveries as a matter of course. This was how Kekulé discovered the benzine ring (it was "revealed" to him via a dream symbol), and how Descartes discovered analytic geometry. (See Arthur Koestler's *The Act of Creation*, especially Part II, where he uses Kekulé as one of his main examples. See Bronowski and Mazlish's *The Western*

Intellectual Tradition, Chapter 12, for the connection between Descartes' dream life and his mathematical discoveries.)

The first step in the process of dream work (or "dream extension," as Progoff calls it) is to keep a log of your day dreams and night dreams. (See Progoff's *At a Journal Workshop,* Chapter 16.) If you have difficulty recalling your night dreams, this is no great problem. All the phenomena of dream work can be reproduced by other means. There are, for example, the meditation techniques described in Progoff's *The Practice of Process Meditation.* There are the "guided fantasy" techniques described in Jerome Singer's *Imagery and Daydream Methods in Psychotherapy and Behavior Modification.* (See especially the material on Desoille and Leuner in Chapter IV.) But let us assume you and your students can remember at least some of your night dreams, and are able to collect several pages of material over a week to ten days.

The second step in the process is to peruse your collected material, looking for recurrent themes or for especially striking incidents or situations. Once you have found such a recurrent or especially interesting symbol or situation, you are to describe it in your notebook, and then close your eyes and attempt to recreate that symbol or situation in your imagination. You should allow that symbol or situation to develop or change, or even to "speak" to you, in any way that seems required or appropriate. Finally, you are to record all these experiences in your notebook.

Progoff believes these dreams and fantasy materials stand in a counterpoint relationship to our ordinary, discursive, self-conscious awareness. So these materials should provide an alternative point of view, or interpretation, concerning the significance of what we are about. In my experience, participants respond to this material pretty much as they did to each previous discovery of an additional dimension of their personal identity. They are awed and gratified to find there are yet further riches of their inner life which they did not even know they had.

Classroom Applications

I have integrated Progoff's "Intensive Journal" method into two mid-level philosophy courses, one on the philosophy of psychology and one on the philosophy of religion. One might wonder how these journal techniques could be used to enliven and motivate study of a traditional academic discipline, rather than as a separate course of study on its own. The full intensive journal technique does take time. I find even the abbreviated version of the exercises I described in the preceding section requires sixteen contact hours, or just under a third of an eighteen-week semester. Wouldn't this material simply displace one-third of the normal course content?

This isn't what actually happens. Students in my "Intensive Journal" sections seem to master and retain at least as much objective material as do students in my regular classes. The reason for this unexpected result seems to be the greater motivation exhibited by students in "Intensive Journal" sections, and the fact that students in these sections end up writing a great deal more than do other students. Improvement in my students' writing skills was not one of my original goals, but that has proved to be a very welcome ancillary effect.

I make two modifications in the structure of Progoff's "Intensive Journal" technique, beyond the simplifications mentioned above, in order to make it more applicable to my sort of classroom setting. First, I replace Progoff's "daily log" section (daily journal entries as normally conceived) with what I call a "class log." This is simply a log of the class meetings, so that a three-hour course requires three class log entries a week. These entries include class notes and exercises, plus an account of their responses to each class period. Second, I add extra journal sections for their notes on assigned readings, and for their own critical comments on the meaning or significance of these materials. I also require essays on relevant topics at both the middle and the end of the semester.

I have learned through painful experience how *not* to integrate the journal work with more traditional classroom material. It is a mistake to crowd the journal work into either the first or the last third of a semester. In the first case the students exhibit a tremendous reluctance to set aside their fascinating and emotion-laden journal work in order to return to more ordinary objective kinds of learning. In the second case they claim to be disappointed that they were deprived of the experience until so late in the semester. My most successful arrangement has been to set aside one meeting a week, which is held at a different location than the other two, for the sole purpose of "Intensive Journal" work. This arrangement avoids confusion as to what is appropriate student behavior in the two kinds of settings, and allows the levels of emotional and cognitive discovery to rise together toward a mutually reinforcing end-of-semester climax.

Ethical Problems

There are some ethical problems involved in using such intensely personal and emotional materials in a college classroom. There may be some psychological hazards as well. Does the assignment of "Intensive Journal" work invade a student's right to privacy? And does the emotional intensity of the work involve classroom instructors in activities best left in the hands of trained psychotherapists?

The potential for the misuse or abuse of these techniques is real enough and seems to result from a specific dynamic between a certain sort of group leader and a certain sort of group member. Destructive group leaders are ones who deal with their own unresolved problems by denial and projection. They say, in effect, "I'm O.K. Now let me help you put your life in order." The potential casualties, on the other hand, are dependent sorts of people who really believe such a savior could be found who could put their lives together for them. (See Lieberman, Yalom, and Miles's *Encounter Groups: First Facts*, and Will Schutz's "Not Encounter and Certainly Not Facts" in the Spring, 1975 issue of *The Journal of Humanistic Psychology* for a detailed discussion of these issues.)

When the "problem" of such casualty-producing leader-participant relationships is stated in such bald terms, the "solution" is equally obvious. It involves two common-sense rules. Trouble will be avoided if one makes sure (1) the students have the power to disclose or not disclose any personal material which turns up in their journal work; and (2) if it is up to the student, not the professor, to label or interpret the significance of these materials.

The group leader or professor must decline, politely but firmly and repeatedly, to play the role of savior for anyone. He or she must keep putting the responsibility for interpretation and decision back on the shoulders of the participants or students themselves. Gradually the great truth will sink in that no one but the participants themselves can do what needs to be done to change their present situation or to realize their destiny. Salvation in this context must remain strictly a "do-it-yourself" project.

The privacy issue is a purely technical matter and is, therefore, easily solved. The instructor *does not need to know* the content of the more intimate portions of the journal entries in order to evaluate the student's performance. He or she only needs to know whether the student is making a good faith effort to carry out the steps of the assignment. I give my students the option of stapling such sections of their notebooks shut under a title page which identifies the contents in general terms such as "Dream Log" or "Dialogue with Persons," etc. I have no trouble at all, in practice, distinguishing those students who have made a good faith effort to carry out the procedures from those who have not. Finer discriminations of differences in the quality of their performances can be made by reference to their notes on assigned readings, their evaluations of these readings and of classroom materials, and their midterm and end-of-term essays. There is no shortage of objective evidence on which to base a course grade.

Afterword

This account would be incomplete if I did not admit how much fun my two experimental courses have been to teach. I find I go to these sections eagerly and return reluctantly to my more ordinary classes. This is one area of my academic life where I can honestly believe I am realizing the ancient goal of a liberal arts education; namely, to create whole persons whose lives are oriented toward ultimate value and reality.

References

Bronowski, J. & Mazlish, B. (1960). *The western intellectual tradition.* New York: Harper & Row.

Crystal, J.C. & Bolles, R. (1974). *Where do I go from here with my life?* New York: Seabury Press.

Friday, N. (1977). *My mother/myself: The daughter's search for identity.* New York: Delacorte Press.

Haley, A. (1976). *Roots.* New York: Doubleday.

Jung, C.G. (1961). *Memories, dreams, reflections.* New York: Random House.

Keen, S. & Fox, A. (1973). *Telling your story: A guide to who you are and who you can be.* New York: Doubleday.

Koestler, A. (1964). *The act of creation.* New York: Macmillan.

Lieberman, M.A., Yalom, I.D., & Miles, M.B. (1973). *Encounter groups: First facts.* New York: Basic Books.

Progoff, I. (1963). *The symbolic and the real.* New York: McGraw-Hill Paperbacks.

_____ . (1975). *At a journal workshop.* New York: Dialogue House.

_____ . (1980). *The practice of process meditation.* New York: Dialogue House.

Schutz, W. (1975). Not encounter and certainly not the facts. *The Journal of Humanistic Psychology, Vol. 15,* No. 2. pp 7-18.

Singer, J. (1974). *Imagery and daydream methods in psychotherapy and behavior modification.* New York: Academic Press.

Rainer, T. (1978). *The new diary.* New York: St. Martin's Press.

31.

What's a Horny? or, Writing and Counseling in the Middle School

LAURA FULWILER

Well, you can put more things on paper than what you can say out loud. Even to a friend. I've said more things to a piece of paper than I ever would to my friend.

Eighth grade student

The four 6th grade boys came into my office, shuffling uneasily, their eyes shifting from each other to their neon-laced high-top tennies, to their folded hands. Jeez, I thought to myself, their teacher must've given them hell about this one. The boys had come down to see me at my request. And I had asked to see them at the 6th grade team's request; I was to "have a talk with them."

Earlier that day the social studies teacher came to me concerned about two boys whose "dirty notes" he had intercepted several times in the last two days. The teacher didn't seem very comfortable about the implications of such behavior and asked me to see them. I had some suspicions that I was being set up as the heavy (and we counselor types always dislike set-ups) but was equally intrigued by the situation.

The two ringleaders and their accomplices were penitent—and I, of course, appropriately sober about the whole thing. What the boys had done was to take a "Mad Libs"-type comic book, and insert into the dialogue balloons of Spiderman, IceMan, and FireWoman the stuff of 6th grade "obscenities." The boys were trying on their new-found vocabulary, using it to spin some pretty absurd adventures—the lack of accurate sexual information aside. I was rather amused by their inventiveness, but at the same time concerned about their noticeable misconceptions about sex. I threw out a feeler: "It sounds like, more than anything, you guys really have some questions about sex." Phew. They were relieved I wasn't going to "kick butt." The relief was good for us all, and the five of us chatted and finally came up with the idea of having a regular group time when we could talk about some of this stuff—without everybody at their lunch table knowing about it. We set a date for our first meeting and parted.

I figured that these boys, though pretty clever at scatological jokes, were going to have a rough time talking about sex when we reconvened around my office table. So when we met for our first club meeting, I handed out some paper and asked the boys to write down—anonymously —one main question they had about sex. When they were done, I gathered the notes and read each one aloud. There were comments after each one. "Yeah, I wondered about that too," or a couple of the boys made attempts to answer the questions. The written questions determined our curriculum for the next few meetings and certainly loosened things up.

The writing did exactly what I knew it would do. It provided a safe forum for honesty. It afforded each boy privacy. It gave me what I needed in order for the group to function well, without costing the student a personal price. No boy had to claim his note—or his curiosity or lack of knowledge—yet in reading them, each one gained a sense of "I'm not the only one who didn't understand that." Some of the questions that arose from our first session were:

"What's a Horny? And why are they called that?"
"Why do people use dirty words?"
"Why is sex so untalked about and so bad?"
"How do parents find each other?"

Though we made considerable progress on the first three questions, I claimed no authority on the last. (Was this a geographical, anatomical, psychological or metaphysical query?)

Rationale

Writing is a well-established adjunct to counseling. Often assigned as between-session homework in conventional therapy, writing is used to shorten duration of counseling, provide interim expression for the client, and serve as an outlet for stress (Jauncey, 1976). In addition, the act of writing gives concrete form and order to clients, enabling them to approach their lives with a greater sense of objectivity (Millard, 1976).

Teachers have used journals to establish closer teacher-student interaction, to give students a private place to initiate a request for help, and to provide signals for early intervention of a problem (Staton, 1980). As a school counselor, my role is different from both the office therapist and the classroom teacher. My clients are 5th, 6th, 7th, and 8th graders, and my interactions with students range from indiviudal counseling, to small groups, to the large classroom presentation. I have used writing exercises as an incremental part of all three models.

Individual Counseling

Sometimes I ask students to keep journals as simple logs of events. Last week Jenny came to me, concerned about all the teasing directed her way in the 8th grade. Sounds straight to me, I thought; some of those 8th graders can be pretty brutal up there. I found myself getting involved. Who was teasing her? How? What did they say? How did she deal with it? Her responses seemed vague, and so I asked her to record each time someone teased her over the next three days. I wanted her to make a conscious record of each incident. Will this merely blow it up to greater proportions? I asked myself. Am I just adding fuel to the fire?

Three days later, when Jenny came in I asked her about her reporting. She showed me several brief entries that began with "No one picked on me today" and went on to talk about other issues. Clearly too good to be true, I said to myself (I know these 8th graders!). But she insisted that this was the case. The act of writing it down gave it a reality, an objectivity, and enabled her to separate what was actually happening from "I feel like everyone's always on my case." Such an exercise does not relieve me of the responsibility to help this girl with the question of what she gains from feeling so miserable, but it does serve to illustrate for students, in a dramatic yet quiet way, how our feelings can color our perception. Her role as the recorder put her—and not me—in the role of trying to reconcile the two perspectives. Her resolution of this discrepancy was more important than if I had just offered a different interpretation of the situation.

Sometimes I ask an individual student to do a brief journal write as a way of assessing where he or she is—a kind of emotional temperature-taking. I had been seeing "Sally" weekly for several months, working with her on developing assertive skills in response to her demanding parents. In our meetings she talked about her anger toward them, her inability to measure up to their expectations, and her compulsive need to always be on top at school. But despite our seemingly productive sessions, Sally continued to get in lots of fights at school, and exhibited a self-defeating competitiveness in sports. I asked her to summarize her thoughts through a journal write. Reluctantly she agreed to pen this:

> I have trouble writing things so I am pretending to talk. I'm never assertive. I'm always afraid to say what I feel. I think it's real important to be assertive because often enough you don't get what you want, but most important you don't say what you feel. When that happens you end up carrying a load on your shoulders, you get depressed and crummy.

Though some of this sounded much like our conversations, it also alerted me to some important insights: Sally was willing to give this writing deal a try; she was getting better at making personal declarations about her own emotions ("I'm always afraid to say what I feel"); she was beginning to understand her behavior in a larger context; and she was learning how she could affect the feelings that seemed to end "on your shoulders." No, Sally didn't feel comfortable writing this at first, but it served as important information she could not have offered orally to me.

I have asked anxious and distressed students to keep journals of their feelings between our meetings. The journal serves as a companion for the student, a constant ear, and in some cases, a surrogate counselor. The journal provides continuity to our talks, a place for reflecting on what we have talked about and applying some of the ideas to daily events in a student's life. It is an extension of our relationship, as well as a practice ground for the student to begin recognizing, identifying, labeling, and expressing feelings and reactions. Often this "pairing" of student and journal will lessen dependence on seeing me, will provide comfort, and can also serve as agenda for our next meeting. The student begins to take some initiative, to share writing, concerns, perceptions with me. It signals a subtle shift of responsibility from my looking for patterns to the student's looking for patterns, from my focusing on certain events to the student's assuming this role.

The student has the right to keep the journal private or to share it with me. The privacy option is rarely taken, but is, nevertheless, very important. Young adolescents are very vocal about "their" things— possessions, room, secrets—and a private journal acknowledges this, accepts ownership as their right, and gives them an appropriate locus for such secrecy. We discuss a place they can keep their journal, a place where family members can't find it. Such planning allows them their secrets, and ironically makes them less secretive. The decision, however, remains theirs.

Small Groups

When students write in small groups, I'm able to learn about the individual worlds they each inhabit, as well as their individual needs— as seen in the Crazy Cartoonists group I mentioned earlier. It also helps me identify those students who have individual needs that are not being met in a group forum or to identify unresolved issues for particular kids.

Last week I asked a small group of 5th graders—a group which meets weekly to discuss some of the developmental stages of surviving their parents' divorce—what they would want their teachers to know about their feelings. Roger penned the following:

> I feel sad that my mom and dad got divorsed and it hurt because I don't now what happened because I was down to my cousins house and my mom came and got me and when we drove by my house picelmen were there and talking to my dad. I asked mom what was happening, and my mom said that they were telling dad to get out of the house and then I felt mad and mom said it was not your falt but I thought it was. BUT IT IS NOT YOUR FALT.

I'm not sure if Roger wanted all his teachers to know this, or even if he consciously wanted *me* to know. But the opportunity of such a private communication gave him the space to "talk" about, write about, what was really prominent in his world at the time. We had spent a great deal of time discussing self-blame in this group. And Roger had really picked up on that—intellectually. But Roger's writing, more importantly, gave me a glimpse of what he had to navigate through—the emotional web of seeing his dad with the policeman, the fight between his parents, all those scary feelings—to even discuss it in a group. I never see the students in the same way after I've read their journals

Classroom Instruction

In addition to individual and group counseling, I also work with students in large classrooms. Recently I spent two weeks in the 8th grade English classes teaching career exploration. We did some values exercises, skill assessment, goal-setting, and lots of discussion. When I began the sessions, I handed out 110 spelling notebooks to the students to keep as journals for our time together. I asked them to record their reactions to classroom activities, their thoughts to questions I asked in class ("Write now for 2 minutes about why you made the choice you did in the dilemma we just role-played"), and personal musings.

I used the journal to ensure that each student in the class connected in some personal way with the topic of discussion. Often in discussion-based classes, the spotlight falls on the verbal, the gutsy, or the smart-aleck kids. In my guidance classes, it's important that each student sift through the issues personally—whether they are willing to participate orally or not. After sitting silently through a 20-minute discussion about decision making, Bobby wrote in his journal:

> I have wanted to get a camera ever since I was in the photography class this spring. Recently, I have found a place to buy good used cameras at reasonable prices. I don't know if I should take money out of my Washington, DC fund to purchase one. I have seen the type of camera that I want to get. It is a Pentax K1000 35mm camera. It would cost about $100 but I am not sure if I should take the money out of my DC fund or if I should wait and save up for it during the summer. Now, I am borrowing an old 35mm camera from my father. I would like to bring the new camera down to Washington DC when I go but I don't want to lose or break it. The only good camera that we have now is an instamatic that my father has. We do have other cameras but they all have minor problems that make taking pictures difficult.

Bobby knew very well that his careful and deliberate approach to buying a camera would not be embraced by his peers, who were agonizing over tapes and skateboard purchases. Consequently, he never shared his entry with others. Nevertheless, it gave me an indication that he was thinking seriously about our discussions. Two days later, his journal offered me another insight into this quiet boy who sat next to the wall:

> I have found that I relate better to animals than people because animals don't tease you.

The journal offers a place for middle school students, desperately seeking and maintaining some sense of image and role, an opportunity to "try on" different attitudes without having to explain or defend them to their peers. To the question "What kinds of decisions do you see yourself making over the next five years?" Vickie, an eighth grader well-known for her mouthy and belligerent remarks, wrote:

> What to do for homework? What to do for the summer? Should I do good in school? Should I have anything to do with politics? Should I be influenced by friends? What about drugs? Alcohol? Sex? What to do about my friends that might push me into something? Should I get my license? Why do I love?

I asked her at one point to write about why she responded so intensely and "fully"—she wrote prolifically during the class sessions:

> Well, you can put more things on paper than what you can say out loud. Even to a friend. I've said more things to a piece of paper than I ever would to my friend.

Through journal writes, I am able to take a peek at each individual student in the large classroom. Classroom writing allows me to identify students for individual counseling, for membership in small groups, or to come to a richer appreciation of each individual in my "audience." In a 5th grade class we were discussing individual differences, and how kids treat other kids who have learning problems. At the end of the class, I asked the students to summarize their feelings about our discussion. Mary wrote:

> We discussed things about people the have problems. Like I have some problems too. I am not that smart. Some kids lafe at me because I do not wot a word is, it hers me a lot some time I go home frustraded and mad because they make fun of me and some time when I am really mad I go up staris and cry say to my silfe wat did it have ta be me some dime.

This girl would not have shared this publicly, but her painful experience taught me a great deal about her. I have written back to her— I too benefit from the privacy of this special way of communicating— and we have become pen-pals.

I pay special attention when students digress from the assigned class topic. In the career exploration class, I asked students to support a decision they made in a classroom activity. Some of them did not write about that, but about something that related to a more central curriculum:

> I talked to my mom about moving out of the house. I kind of decided not to but I really have just put if off for now. It seems that so many ideas are crowding my head and i'm really confused...I have already had enough decisions and crap jammed in my head as if I was 100 years old.

When asked the same thing, another student, whose father had died six months ago, wrote:

> We are moving to Simmons this summer. I am excited about moving and meeting different people but my father is buried here. I waited for spring so I could ride my bike up to the graveyard. I know that if I want to talk to my father I can because he is always listening I like going to the graveyard and talking with him. The decision I'm talking about is when we move and the following winter comes will we come out? And if we do will I come out to see him? because I can't say anything in front of anybody else but I feel closer to my father when I'm there.

Journals are an effective way for me to identify kids who are having serious problems. However, students—particularly adolescents—are not always eager for insight, to say nothing of self-actualization. Sometimes I'm able to learn a great deal about students in spite of themselves.

When I was doing a "decision-making" presentation in the 8th grade, I identified a group of skeptics in the back of the room. The only thing the crew distrusted more than "decision-making" was "this writing stuff." But the writing was private, and that allowed Ben, the head honcho of the group, to seriously respond to a question without losing face. On goals, he wrote:

My biggest goal in life is to try to get a good job with good pay and have some kind of inshorence of some sort. But I have more than one goal—I'd like to have a fun hobby. Something else to make money on. I like to work on watt I like not watt someone tells me to that way I work hardest and do better jobs at it. I wouldn't whont to have some one always telling me watt to do. I wouldn't whant a job with a bose like that.

I wrote the student back in his journal: "You know a lot about what you want: it's as important to know what you DON'T want to help you figure out what you DO want." His classroom behavior didn't change (sorry, no Cinderella stories here), but I wasn't as uncomfortable with it either. A couple days later, after a values clarification exercise, I asked the kids to write about what they believed was most important to them. The same student scrawled in his journal: "I don't know jack about values." That was it.

I caught him after class and we were able to talk for a couple of minutes. This young man had a very strong sense of values—his independence and tenacity, his sense of pride in his work, as long as it's his own. This kid knew lots...but I wouldn't have understood that with confidence without the journal-write.

It would be dishonest of me to present all students as flaming converts to journals. Like all public school teachers, I have met up with the recalcitrant blocker, determined to be impervious to all effects I might wish on him. But, even in its most negative reaction, John's put-down of the class writing assignment betrays its very message:

This dumb junk I wrote was just written so I did not have to stay after school. I don't think differently than I did before. This writing unit has no effect, and it's a bunch of garbage we have to do. Well then again, it might have an effect. This journal-writing has not affected me a lot. The whole idea stinks, because there really isn't no point to these journal writes that we do every day. Its only effect is how to express myself and the truth clearly, just like I've done.

References

Jauncey, P.G. (1976). Client writing as a facilitation of the counseling process. (Doctoral dissertation, New Mexico State University). *Dissertation abstracts international, 38*, 114A. (University Microfilms No.77-14310)

Millard, E.R. (1976). The effects of writing assignments upon rational thinking and level of self-disclosure in group counseling (Doctoral dissertation, Fordham University). *Dissertation abstracts international, 37*, 813A. (University Microfilms NO. 76-17908)

Staton, J. (1980, May). Writing and counseling: Using a dialogue journal. *Language Arts, 57:5.*

32.

The Team Journal

JEAN GRAYBEAL

What is teaching? Aside from the avowed curricular and departmental goals of passing on to students the central concepts and methods of our disciplines, what is it really all about? Why do those of us who choose teaching go on? Is it for the sake of the preservation of the sacred disciplinary tools? Is it to insure the continuity of civilization that we exhaust ourselves trying to communicate with students?

I believe that for many of us teaching isn't primarily about the transfer of knowledge and information in our disciplines, but is more a matter of trying to pass on to students some of the existential and emotional engagement we ourselves have discovered in our studies. We are "in love" with what we do, and we seek ways to help students take pleasure and find meaning in the same activities that we love. As scholars and teachers, we deeply *enjoy* the processes of reading, writing, speaking, and listening—activities that are in themselves both satisfying and frustrating; they keep us in a tenuous balance between knowing and not-knowing, a balance we have learned to tolerate and to cherish.

It is this capacity for ambiguity, this curiosity and desire, this willingness to suffer the tensions of learning and thinking that we most want to hand on to our students. We don't expect all of our students to major in our field; we don't really even imagine that they will remember the vital concepts and methods, much less names and dates, ten years from now. What we really hope for is that they become fuller human beings, capable of rational and creative activity, ready for responsibility, citizenship and productive, satisfying lives. We hope that a thirst for learning and an ability to take pleasure in the life of the mind will be among the lasting results of their university education.

Within this context, the development of linguistic skills becomes a central concern. One method I have developed for helping students to exercise their writing and thinking abilities is the "team journal." I use this device in my introductory Study of Religion course to help introduce students to the basic methods and concepts involved in the academic study of religion. I divide the class into permanent working teams at the beginning of the semester. These teams, composed of five or six students, work together as a unit for some part of almost every class session. I ask them, for example, to brainstorm lists of "big questions," to decide whether a short account of an experience qualifies it as a "mystical" or a "numinous" one, or to figure out together what the ethical implications of a certain view of creation might be.

In addition to the time the teams spend working together in class, each team creates over the course of the semester a team journal. These journals are simply spiral notebooks kept at the reserve desk in the library under the course number and team name. Each team member is required to go to the library at least once a week, before a fixed time, and to write an entry in his or her team's journal. I ask students to aim for two pages, or to spend at least an hour working on this. The assignment is to read what other team members have written on the topic for the week, to respond specifically to what they have written, and to express their own ideas and feelings related to the topic. At the beginning of the semester, I suggest topics that teams might choose to write about; after a few weeks, individual teams are choosing their own topics during class. The only requirement is that they be able to say how the topic is related to "religion." Usually teams generate topics that are connected to issues under discussion in the course, but they are free to pursue what interests them.

Every week at the due time, I go to the library and check out all of the journals. I read or skim through what students have written and comment generally on a separate page about how the team as a whole is doing. I may encourage them to respond more directly to each other, or to choose more controversial topics, or to do more connecting with other subjects. I make note of the names of students who have contributed in that week, and give them credit for that entry. The journals are not graded, but participation in the journal is a requirement of the course. Students who miss more than a couple of entries (leaving room for illness and human error) have their overall grade for the course lowered by as much as one full grade.

People who use other kinds of student journals in their teaching are already aware of their benefits. The general benefits I have observed include an increase in students' appropriation and integration of course material, development of personal interest and investment in the topic, independent wondering and questioning and connecting, and even the improvement of writing skills, especially fluidity and ease of expression.

Team journals also work in many of these same ways, but they have additional dimensions which result from writing for an audience of peers. Team journals make possible an *exchange* of energy and ideas that is virtually impossible in a journal written ostensibly for the student herself or himself, but actually handed in to and evaluated by an instructor. No teacher can respond adequately to all that is happening in those individual journals. For one thing, we don't have the psychic energy to interact intimately with so many students. In addition, we are not really a part of the worlds that students inhabit. Their daily concerns, their ways of expressing themselves, the worries and joys that are particular to their own lives, are often not readily accessible to faculty. faculty.

Yet in a course like religious studies, one of the major goals is to get students to see how universal and existential the questions are to which religions respond. A team journal encourages team members to try to connect concepts and terms discussed in the course to their own experience. For example, they mull and muse over whether they themselves have ever had a "religious experience." To do this, they have to redefine in their own words what such an experience is. The language they use and the freedom they feel writing for each other allows them to explore and express their own existential situations, and then to try to see if any of the things going on in the course are indeed relevant. If and when they discover that there are connections, their motivation and interest increase. They may become inspired by seeing someone else find an application or example they would not have thought of.

In what follows, I have taken one team journal from a recent class and tried to categorize some of the kinds of things that I see going on in some entries.* I have focused on a few of the entries that demonstrate the benefits of an audience of peers engaged in a mutual, playful, yet serious exchange, rather than on the kinds of entries (of which there are also many examples) that one might find in another sort of journal, or in an essay or theme paper.

1. *Dissent.* Students seem to feel more free to express criticism of basic ideas of the course in a team journal than they do in an individual one. Perhaps the knowledge that they only have to write, not be evaluated on what they say, helps to encourage their powers of dissent.

> I don't believe that *most* people really want 'ultimate' answers. I'm beginning to believe that most people, (and this includes most of my associations with 'religious' people all of which practice formalized and accepted or popular forms of religious practice). That most people want anything to stop the process, and often a painfull one, of really looking at things closely.

2. *Deep Confusion.* Deep confusion, as opposed to superficial confusion, is a positive aspect of the learning process. Students are often reluctant to expose the depth of their quandaries, either verbally in class, or in writing for the teacher. They know better than to make themselves that vulnerable, even if they've been told that it's okay. In team journals, deep confusion comes out, stimulates other team members' own questions, and has a chance to ferment.

> I wonder—maybe some people *don't* go to church because they are afraid to look at things too closely. And maybe some people *do* go to church because they are afraid to look at things closely and want security (a "cover-up"). Now I'm getting myself confused! But I agree with you Jeff. That looking at such a touching topic as this *closely* can be painful and pull your roots out just when you thought you were secure.

> We *all* seem to be confused, maybe we should talk about confusion...My confusion—does confusion take place, creep in, surface, whenever change occurs? Is confusion an indication of something? Confusion is like trying to grab ten birds with two hands.

*Privacy and confidentiality are important in developing good team journals. I have changed the names of students in these excerpts and have also obtained their permission to quote from their journal. Sometimes problems arise when outsiders are found to be checking team journals out and reading them. It is a good idea to work with reserve desk personnel to avoid such problems.

Confusion is digging deep for something solid and finding out all you have is a hole...What if we all get T-shirts (I like this idea) and have 'I'm confused' printed on them. Think of all the new friends we'd have.

3. *Self-Awareness* and *Self-Criticism*. When students read other students' writing, they begin to compare their own intellectual processes with those of others. They notice differences and wonder about what they mean.

I've never looked at or interpreted things the way Jeff and Sandra do. I guess I look more at the surface than they do. I am satisfied knowing only the things which I can see, touch, feel and understand. For instance, I have no desire at all to leave my body. I feel that I don't want to leave this reality I am living in. I don't know what I would be looking for, perhaps I am afraid of what I might find. Regardless, the desire is not there so I find it so hard to relate...On the days when I'm well-rested and energetic I find this motivating. On bad days (like today) I feel frustrated.

4. *Safety in Numbers*. Of course, all journals are a great way to get in touch with the deeper self. Free association or other fairly spontaneous writing can acquaint us with aspects of ourselves we normally repress, censor or avoid. Evidently in some teams the knowledge that others will be reading what they write doesn't inhibit students so much as it reassures them that someone will be there when they confront what they really feel.

[After making up her own myth of creation] Gosh, what have I done? I've just written down my greatest fears of the myth of creation. This is not what I actually believe—it's just a story— Thank gosh. What terrible, frightening thoughts—being created by merely a game, being disappointed with the creation and therefore, being thrown away to be all alone, and God actually creating all the terrible things of the earth (although my examples were meant to be humorous). I am now depressed—and have run out of time— see you in class—I'll be happier, I promise.

5. *Affirmation and Reinforcement*. Students really know how to reward each other. Their positive feedback and appreciation is genuine and effective, and the journals often start to become self-motivating projects. Criticism and disagreement are almost always couched in a context of positive comments, unlike many of the criticisms offered by teachers.

I really enjoyed this. It really felt like you were in the present while writing. I got much more of a sense and feeling of this part of your person. As opposed to your first entry. I miss Lou. I miss his brightness (glow), I miss his enthusiasm. Anybody know what's up with him?

6. *Community Building*. All of these exchanges work together to build a group of people who are talking to each other not only in class (which they start doing from the moment they come into the room) but also in writing throughout the week. The groups really do start to

function as "teams." They know each other better, in some ways, than they know their friends and families, simply because they have confronted each other over some very basic issues which are ordinarily not raised in daily discourse. A sense of trust and solidarity builds in some teams, a sense which contributes immensely to the atmosphere and ethos of the class as a whole.

Well, I have to run—I can't wait to talk about all of this in class!

Lou, where were you today in class? Where? Sherry, where were you? Kelly? Sandra? Sean? Jeff? Where were we? Were we unprepared? In outer space? In the park? Out next weekend? ...Dead, I'm sure. Twice kicked, tickled and prickled, de-tongued, gut-soaked,...hairless, hideless lump—it's time to wake up! Do we need to work on our class participation? Jesus, it's 2:15, I'm late for class—

Wouldn't that be fantastic to take a break—a summer—a spring—a fall—a year to walk around, experience *Life*. I haven't done much traveling... It would be fascinating to get about four enthusiastic searching, yearning, awe-struck, lost in wonder people and walk through the U.S. Yessiree!

This journal is always so fascinating. Sherry and I ask questions and Sandra answers them. Jeff goes mad and can't stop. And Lou and Sean throw in their extras. This small notebook is an entire class. I'm learning so much. I'm also becoming more confused. But it all gives me so much to think about!

In this brief description I have tried to give a sense of what goes on in some of the team journals in my classes. The particular journal I picked to excerpt from was unusual in some ways. One of the team members was an artist, and in addition to his verbal entries, he included numerous photographs and collages, which were endlessly intriguing. Some teams and team journals never get off the ground. The chemistry isn't right, the critical mass isn't there, some kind of magic is missing. But in many teams, their collective journals become a favorite part of the course, and some student evaluations identify them as the most valuable experience of the course.

I have found team journals to be a good way to encourage students to engage themselves both with the specific issues of a course in religious studies, and with the larger enterprise of making sense of themselves and their world. The experience of encountering other thinkers, who are also their peers, playfully, respectfully, and deeply all at the same time, in an environment free from judgment and evaluation, with the common purpose of understanding and exploring the world, is deeply affirming. It encourages students to take themselves and each other seriously, and allows them to experience the communal and cooperative character of learning. It gives them a taste of a community of inquiry and helps them to see themselves as worthy contributors to such endeavors.

Team journals are useful not only for students but for teachers as well. The communities created by teams make the classroom atmosphere warm and informal, thus making discussion easy and natural. Reading or skimming team journals gives me a good means of access into students' worlds and helps me know exactly how they are appropriating and understanding what we are doing in class. Using team journals gets students to do a good amount of writing that does not need to be graded or evaluated for form; it is writing that resembles most of the writing they will do throughout the rest of their lives, for the purpose of communicating with peers about issues of mutual concern. Finally, these journals are a source of great pleasure and satisfaction to me as a teacher. When I go in to check them off, I know I will be sitting down to some good reading, reading that energizes and inspires me, because it shows that students are indeed growing and questioning, wondering and searching...participating in that addictive activity I've been hoping they would discover.

33.

Letting Them Write
When They Can't Even Talk?
Writing as Discovery
in the Foreign Language Classroom

KAREN WILEY SANDLER

Teacher: "J'ai vu Dune hier soir. C'etait bizarre. Qu'est-ce que vous en avez pense?"

Students: —silence—

Every foreign language teacher dreads that silence. It's not just the quiet that pervades the room when no one knows the answer or the fidgety hush that tells you no one has done the assignment. Worse than these is the silence that interrupts the free flow of conversation, that tells you your students are decoding again. They are taking apart your French question, separating it into translatable chunks, putting these chunks in English, processing the meaning (if there's any left), and then translating their answer back into the foreign language by the same method. And all the while, conversation is frozen, spontaneity fizzles, and thought is constricted by grammar rules, fear, conservatism, self-consciousness. It's a miserable feeling and it happens too often.

When I tell colleagues that I use writing at every language level to bypass the decoding phase, they look at me strangely. "You let them write when they can't even talk?" is the usual response, followed by "Are you crazy?" Although their concerns are legitimate, the answer is "No, I'm not crazy." There is writing and there is writing. The foreign language class, as many others, can profit from the use of non-graded, creative, exploratory writing exercises to free students from their fears. Rather than an explosive ready to harm them, language becomes a tool, a key to discovery, even a plaything.

I have found that even at the most elementary levels journal writing, free composition, and other exercises that encourage students' uninhibited use of language to explore their thoughts can bring surprising progress in language learning. Too often the foreign language classroom presents students with psychological barriers to communication. Rather than breaking down inhibitions, foreign language teachers often find themselves in the uncomfortable position of having to enforce grammatical or phonetic restrictions to communication before students have even discovered the joy of experimenting with language. Ungraded and self-expressive activities, when used as an alternate mode to everyday drill and conversational practice, offer just the kind of encouragement needed to inspire students to play with language in a non-threatening situation.

Having said all this, I have to add some caveats. (I am truly not crazy.) Second-language learning is, after all, a completely different process from first-language learning, especially at the beginning levels. We do not learn our first language in classrooms, nor do we enforce what we learn at first by writing and reading. In a foreign language elementary class, students compress their linguistic baby steps into a matter of weeks, and then move rapidly towards maturity with varying degrees of success.

In this context, in the intensive atmosphere of the beginning class, ungraded, playful writing serves as an appetizer, not a steady diet. Why? Common sense. Encouraging play, we also encourage mistakes. In second-language learning, the need to correct these mistakes early is far more urgent than in first-language situations where nearly correct models are readily available to the student at all times. However, expressive writing offers two advantages: (1) it develops students' confidence and spirit of adventure and (2) it shows students that there is often more than one correct answer.

The Fine Art of Making Mistakes

One of the most delightful aspects of journals and free-writing assignments in the foreign language classroom is the very element of mistake-making. Making mistakes and benefiting from them is even more vital to the learning of the second tongue than to the development of the mother tongue. Short of sending our students abroad for a few years, there is nothing so productive as teaching them to experiment fearlessly, to develop their abilities to correct their mistakes while learning from them. Under the pressure of timed writing exercises, motivated by the desire to say what they are thinking in their journals, students stretch their linguistic abilities to the limit. At first this means horrendous damage to the structures of the language under study. But little by little, as the teacher corrects by suggesting alternatives instead of by punishing with low grades, students come to depend on the language for expression of their ideas. This ultimately means that a student who is at first unsuccessful in expressing an important thought will have a motive to learn an appropriate way to communicate it. Journals that start out full of anglicisms and unrecognizable forms quickly take on the flavor of the person writing as that person learns from mistakes how to put thoughts into meaningful form. The journal gives reason to the search for meaning.

Elementary Classes

As students first learn something about the new language, they are eager to try it out. They need little encouragement to play, to experiment, to make do. Here is where ungraded writing is ideal—both in and out of class.

Out-of-class Writing

I have asked beginning students to keep "journals" as early as the second or third week. Students must "write" in the language two or three times per week. Since they are so new at manipulating the language, I make suggestions.

1. *Lists.* "Write a list of things you like or dislike. See how long you can make it in a week." Or, "Make an inventory of what you have in your pocket today." Students love the fun of these lists. They become very imaginative and playful with their lists, sometimes mixing fact and fantasy to confuse the teacher:

> Dans ma poche, j'ai un calculateur, deux crayons rouges, trois gommes (je fais des fautes!), quatre photos de Brooke Shields, cinq cigarettes, et six cartes de France.

2. *Categories.* Ask students to write about things that belong to the same classification or have been listed together in the vocabulary in their textbook: "Qu'est-ce que vous mangez pour le petit dejeuner?" "Quels sont les sports que vous preferez?" "Quels animaux aimez-vous?" Gradually expand the assignment to ask for some comment on the lists: "Write about the colors you see." "Write about the courses you study." "Write about the people you work with."

3. *Verb + Attribute Exercises.* Fortunately, the beginning vocabulary in any elementary textbook will give students almost immediate command of simple structures using verbs like "to be," "to have," or "to do" followed by substitutable attributes. A simple manipulation of "I am" and the many adjectives at hand in chapters one or two can be turned into an introspective essay of some length. Try "My professor is" and you will find out more than you sometimes wish:

> Mon professeur est sympa, mais un peu folle. Elle aime les chiens, les photos, et le francais. Elle est energique. Nous aimons le francais. Nous detestons les dictees. Les dictees de mon professeur sont trop difficiles.

4. *Pictures.* At the beginning stage, I ask students to use their journal as a holding tank of sorts, as a repository of as-yet-inexpressible ideas. Nothing seems to give them such a good motive for mastering the language than the existence of this sort of repository. The journal helps them realize that they do have things worth saying, worth thinking about, that while their language skills are still rudimentary, their thoughts are not. With this goal in mind, then, I encourage students to record their thoughts in languages other than French. Pictures, diagrams, doodles. English is forbidden. For instance, "Cut out a picture that says what you would like to say but don't know how yet." After all, a picture is worth a thousand words, even words students don't yet know.

In-class Writing

Aside from the "journal" assignment and simple workbook exercises, I avoid giving students written work to do at home. At home, they become overly concerned about what they don't yet know and they try to say more than their command of the language will yet permit. In the classroom environment, I can control the tension, limit their expectations, and use the students' intensity in constructive ways. The following three activities give plenty of opportunity to practice under my watchful eye and yet encourage imagination and playfulness because they are upgraded.

1. *Timed Free-Write.* In this exercise students must write without stopping to correct or re-read for a fixed (and announced) period of time. I bill this as a game, a challenge, and I assure students frequently that they won't be graded on their grammar, spelling, vocabulary, or misuse of these elements. When a student doesn't know a word, he or she leaves a blank or draws a picture. Any means of communication is allowed except English. I select the topics carefully; at the first stages, there is hardly any sentence structure, just lists. Gradually, they become more complex:

Use your *faire* constructions to tell me what you're doing today.

Aujourd'hui, je fais du francais. Je fais mes devoirs. Il fait beau, mais il fait -'brrrrrr'- et il fait du soleil. Mon professeur fait la dictee et je fais beaucoup de travail. La classe fait bien. Faites-vous du francais aussi? Je prefere faire du tennis ou—'zzzzzz'....

2. *Imaginative Dialogues.* I like to encourage an imaginative rather than a real-life dialogue in the early stages of language acquisition because it sets fewer expectations and nudges the students toward play-fulness. Conversational paradigms are the forms first introduced in language textbooks and the first to be mastered by students. Often I have the students cut out a provocative, humorous, or bizarre picture from a magazine (advertisements provide an unending supply of these) and then compose a dialogue between the principal people in the picture. The zanier the better, as the students soon learn!

3. *Picture-Inspired Group Writing.* The same pictures can be useful in stimulating cooperatively written descriptions and stories. I usually select the most outrageous pictures available and tailor the picture to the grammar or vocabulary we are studying. For instance, after we have learned a number of descriptive adjectives (tall, short, fat, blond), I give the students a series of photos and ask for a timed, free-written description. The "description" can be anything from a list of physical attributes to a more philosophic rendition ("he looks sad") to a fake job wanted ad. After the students have had time to work in groups reading each other's pieces and cutting and pasting, the finished products are then presented out loud to the class.

One essential point: students must be required to use only what they already know. Students are then forced to call upon their reserves instead of reaching for the artificial aid of textbook and dictionary. I have found that the first few times we do this exercise, the results are less than satisfactory. However, if I precede the exercise with a few demonstrations done as a class and if I persist in the activity on a regular basis, students come to enjoy the game. Of course, the exercise is ungraded. I always spend some time asking students to act out the best dialogues; this gives me opportunity to correct errors in context of the dramatic production and not as a written assignment.

Expressive writing works at the beginning levels of foreign language classes to promote playfulness and freedom from constraint. The ungraded and uninhibited nature of the exercises contributes greatly to the students' confidence and enjoyment of language learning and language use. These attitudes in turn ensure success in later stages of foreign language acquisition.

Intermediate Levels

Intermediate level students usually have more linguistic ability than they suspect. It sometimes surprises them to learn that they can manipulate most of the major tenses in order to tell a story; that they know the rudiments of sentence structure; that they can ask and answer essential questions; and that they have a large latent vocabulary just waiting to be used. The best use of writing at this level lies in giving students the opportunity to extend their understanding of what language can do, to suggest to them that their reserve of structures and vocabulary is far more flexible and useful than imagined.

Journals serve an expanded role at the intermediate level. The students can now go beyond simple lists and short comments to telling stories, reporting on dreams, analyzing feelings, and complaining about daily frustrations. I'll accept anything in the journal except a daily log of activities and I assign a grade based on the frequency and length of the entries rather than on their grammatical content. Experience has shown that when students know that their entries will be graded, they revert to using the simplistic constructions already learned in elementary French. They shy away from richer, more descriptive, more flexible expressions in favor of continual baby-talk. By contrast, ungraded journals encourage the experimentation—and failure—that leads to ultimate success. My students frequently remark that what led them to conquer a new structure was their need to find a more nuanced way of expressing themselves. I correct but do not grade individual entries, offer suggestions and encouragement, and let this natural inquisitiveness take its course.

Too often in intermediate language classes, students are given long lists of new vocabulary and then not offered much opportunity to master the use of these words. Nor are they encouraged to master the grammatical concepts by using them in conversational settings. Free-writing exercises offer a non-threatening opportunity for the student to manipulate new phrases, structures, concepts. The writing exercises in my class frequently precede a conversational activity, supporting and preparing the spoken phase of language acquisition.

1. *Pre-Conversational Free-Writes.* For example, if the vocabulary in your text centers on university life, give the students five minutes to write on "the class I hate the most." Or, if you're reviewing a past tense, try "an embarrassing moment." I'm sure many of us have used the question "if I had all the time or money I wanted" when a conditional construction is under study. Remember, the students need to know that you will not be grading them on *what* they write (only *if* they write) and you must make it part of the game to keep writing for the full five minutes. No re-reading, no sitting and digging for a word, certainly no

dictionaries, and no English. Pictures, doodles, sounds are all acceptable, however. This type of exercise followed by a discussion of the topic produces more flow to the conversation. I ask students to write first, then to put the papers away and to summarize to someone else what they said. As a final step, the whole class discusses the topic. The difference in energy, commitment, and willingness to participate is gratifying.

The intermediate step of describing to someone else what you wrote has two advantages. First, it eliminates the deadly problem of students who read what they have written instead of talking about it. Second, it eases the students' tension by giving them a chance to practice with someone of their own choosing before having to say something to the whole group. Not incidentally, it helps build interest in what will ultimately emerge as the class opinion on a subject since I never hide my burning curiosity to know what people are saying or thinking on a topic. My interest helps reinforce the concept that they are actually using language first to explore ideas and then to give shape to them.

2. Imaginative Dialogues. The playfulness of expressive writing can be emphasized at this level, too. Imaginative dialogues work well in the intermediate classroom, using more sophisticated pictures or vocabulary. I will frequently bring in a picture high in emotional impact (a sad, undernourished child looking in the window of a fancy restaurant) or one that is quite silly (the American Tourister ads have been effective). Students write timed pieces, using the pictures as a starting point for their dialogues. Humor and creativity almost always characterize these pieces. My favorite was a conversation between an overweight chef with a thundercloud face and a petite gum-chewing waitress. The students wrote quite a romantic dialogue for them in which the chef turned out to be explaining to his fiancee why he wanted to pursue his Ph.D. in philosophy so that he wouldn't feel inferior to her when she finally became a brain surgeon in a few years.

3. Feelings. The intermediate level is the appropriate time to help students learn to express more complex emotion than "I'm happy" or "I'm angry." One way to get to this goal is to show the class a picture of a great work of art or to play them some music and have them write about their feelings. Another is to have them react to a recent current event high in emotional overtones. For example, a class was asked to write reactions when a woman recanted her claim that she had been raped and requested that the accused man be freed after six years. One student began by talking about the wrong committed by the woman's perjury, but quickly passed to a question of justice in general:

> Je ne peux pas croire que le juge renvoit l'homme en prison. Ou est sa tete? Il semble qu'il y n'a pas de justice. Les innocents sont envoyes en prison et les coupables sont libres. C'est une idee curieuse de la justice!

Of course, the French isn't perfect. But it's good. If I am totally accepting and uncritical as the pieces are shared with the class, students will ask for a correction of their grammar afterwards. I never correct more than necessary for comprehension as we share in class. What works best is to use the insights gained through these free-writing exercises as the base for a more formal writing exercise done at home. I make every effort to keep the exploratory nature of the former separate from the more structured demands of the latter.

Using What They Know

Intermediate classes are particularly frustrating for teachers and students. Students don't even know what they know, nor how much they know, and they're not prone to trying to find out. Writing helps them discover all this. Because the writing exercises I use are timed and ungraded, they challenge students to draw instinctively on reserves they would tend to overlook if they had time and access to a dictionary. I once had a student who needed to define "piscine" and I wouldn't let him use English. I told him he knew enough to tell me in French. He did: "Une piscine, c'est un grand lavabo."

"A swimming pool is a large washbowl" was a perfect definition; everyone understood right away what he meant. Free-writing exercises, like journal writes, bring this sort of self-sufficient creativity to the surface, usually only after students have complained loudly that they can't possibly do what you're asking them to do. They can.

Advanced Levels

At the more advanced levels, language takes on the same exploratory and ordering function it does in our native tongue. Students still do not have the sophistication of structure nor the richness of lexicon that they do in their mother language, but they are developing towards these goals and they are far more confident about their use of the new language.

1. *Free-Writes.* Here, more is possible because of students' confidence and linguistic sophistication. Free-writes can now take on the tenor of discovery drafts. For example, students can make lists of their goals and attitudes prior to a class discussion of career planning or nuclear disarmament or abortion. Later, they can react to the lists they made in a second timed free-write. At this level of complexity, students can see beyond the playful aspects of language use to its deeper psychological function in their lives.

2. *Journals.* This is the quintessential tool in an advanced conversation/composition course, serving much the same purpose as journals do in a mother-tongue writing class. Many students who persevere to this level will complain that what they know how to say is literary or philosophical in nature instead of the everyday and conversational idiom they will need to live comfortably in the foreign setting. Journals help bridge the gap between what the students read or discuss in class and what they actually think about in their out-of-class experience.

Journal writing also helps them confront major problems and deeper anxieties—perhaps for the first time in the foreign tongue. In fact, often they confront issues they avoid discussing in English because they are writing in a second language. They may feel that their perspective is different, a step removed, when they think and write in that second tongue. It's as if they develop different personae as they develop

their thought patterns in a new language; this persona provides objectivity and distance while not cutting them off entirely from their own
feelings about situations. A first-year student commented in her journal
about the difficulty of rooming with someone as competitive as she:

> Il est difficile de decrire en anglais, donc je ne sais pas si je peux
> l'expliquer en francais. Mais je pense que les deux de nous, nous
> avons besoin de sentir que nous sommes le centre de tout.

It was a difficult concept to describe and to face, but her journal gave her
the impetus and perhaps the distance to do it.

3. *Games.* Playfulness remains a key factor in expressive writing at
this level. At the advanced conversation stage, it is sometimes difficult to
get students to use concrete nouns and verbs, to exchange the known
(and insipid) nominal and verbal structures they learned in elementary
class for more demanding constructions that offer more nuanced, more
specific, more varied views of their world. One technique for accomplishing this goal is to provide a collection of physical objects at the
beginning of the class and give students the opportunity to write
whatever comes to their minds as a result of handling the objects,
arranging them, or describing them. Timing the exercise is necessary,
but the time allotted should be somewhat longer than it would be in a
first-language class. It's also helpful to discuss and describe the objects
beforehand so that the basic vocabulary is available to all. (I write the
essential words and phrases on the board.) Students can share what they
have written in small groups and select what they consider to be the best
pieces for discussion by the entire class.

The most annoying trait of students in a foreign language situation
is their refusal to comprehend that their teacher is interested in the
quality of their writing above and beyond the accuracy of their grammar.
Expressive writing assignments can go a long way to dispel the myth
that all a student has to do to get a good grade is to turn in a paper (no
matter how dull or disorganized) that is grammatically accurate. Since
the assignments are not graded *at all,* the teacher is free to develop his or
her students' abilities to express ideas, to experiment, to play, to push
beyond accepted limits. And since the assignments are timed, the student
knows the teacher doesn't expect perfect constructions. He or she may
begin to suspect that there is something beyond grammar towards which
the exercises are geared. Once the student discovers the teacher's commitment to language as a tool for ordering, discovering, playing, and
creating, he or she may be less tied to repeating the ordinary and
unadventurous structures already learned for fear of making a mistake.

Advanced Literature Courses

At the most advanced level, students of a foreign literature can profit
from all the aspects of expressive writing already described. The journal
and the timed writing in class are especially effective for developing
students' ability to speak about the literature with authority. More than
merely an ordering tool, expressive writing at this level functions as an
esthetic stimulus, helping students articulate and discover their feelings

about the works studied. Freed from the constraints (real or imagined) that students expect to govern their more formal writing, literature students engage in expressive exercises with no preconceptions of what the teacher wishes to hear. The sharing of these exercises in small groups or in a collective class situation can provoke discussion and reinforce students' confidence in their own powers of literary criticism.

The blank page confronting a student in a journal-write or a timed, in-class writing exercise serves another purpose. It forces a student who may otherwise remain dependent on other opinions (especially critical opinion expressed in secondary sources) to look at the text being studied in a new light. For just a short time, the student becomes the critic, the only critic; he or she may at first panic but will ultimately become more sensitive to what his or her response to the world of art really is.

What may come as a surprise is the effectiveness of the imaginative dialogue in advanced literature classes. What may seem like a frivolous activity actually succeeds in deepening my students' understanding of what the writer experiences when he or she creates a lasting work of art. Once we have read several texts by an author or have studied various authors writing in a particular style, I ask my students to write an imaginary dialogue among the authors. I try to situate the dialogue outside the normal context for the authors; for example, I ask the students to imagine that the writers meet at a writers' conference and begin to argue about their varying esthetic views. Or, I will situate the conversation outside of the writers' period, placing Renaissance writers in contemporary society, for instance. Although the technique works well even as an exam question, I find that it is most effective in an ungraded situation so that students can give free rein to their imaginations and creative instincts.

Summary

Encouraging journals and expressive writing in the foreign language classroom may at first seem an impossibility. However, journals can be introduced even at the beginning levels and continued, with increasing sophistication and usefulness, through each stage of the language acquisition process. Ungraded writing assignments encourage students to use the new tools they have for immediate communication with the person who best understands them: themselves, and from this point to move towards exploring new feelings and ideas in a new tongue. Expressive writing exercises gradually free students from the constraints of looking for "the right way" to say something and force the more sophisticated language learner to develop critical opinions and sensitivities to literary texts. Although the foreign language teacher can never expect the same depth of focus or nuance as can be found in the first language, he or she can expect the students to develop a fuller sense of adventure with language, a more confident approach to self-expression, and ultimately a willingness to see language as a critical tool to ordering and managing his or her new world, the world of the second culture.

Part IV

Journals and the
Quantitative Disciplines

Journals are useful in science, the social sciences, engineering and mathematics as they are in any discipline where thought and speculation are important. In these disciplines journals are more likely to be called *logs* or *workbooks*—or to be included as part of field or lab notebooks. What they are called, however, doesn't matter so long as they remain places in which writers can (1) discuss as well as collect data, (2) pose and solve problems, and (3) think visually about any and all matters concerned with their course of study. This final section presents samples of journals from a fair number of quantitative disciplines to suggest what might be possible in courses where so-called hard data often dominates.

The first three chapters, 34, 35, 36, focus on journals in physics and chemistry. In "How Writing Helps Physics Students Become Better Problem Solvers" high school teacher Judy Grumbacher includes a variety of actual student samples to make her case that physics logs help students learn physics better. In "Writing in College Physics" Verner Jensen presents journals as places in which to ask students to internalize concepts such as the laws of motion, gravity, and energy. In "Focused Learning in Chemistry Research" George Meese reports the results of a semester-long internship in which a senior chemistry student kept a journal to document her laboratory research.

Chapters 37 and 38 present the use of journals as aids to the study of mathematics at both elementary and college levels. Barbara Schubert's "Mathematics Journals: Fourth Grade" describes the results of a year-long experiment using journals to help students learn fractions, including the students' own assessment of the project. Stephen BeMiller's "The Mathematics Workbook" suggests that informal writing not only helps college students solve math problems but relieves math anxiety as well.

The next set of chapters, 39, 40, and 41, is written by college social scientists. In "Academic Journals and the Sociological Imagination" Henry Allen and Lynn Fauth demonstrate that journals can help students think broadly about sociological issues and make connections to their own lives. In "Journals and Political Science" David Brodsky and Eileen Meagher look at the strengths and weaknesses of using journals, concluding that they work well in some classes but less well in others. In "Journals in Economic Geography" Bradley Baltensperger describes what happened when he used journals as the sole writing assignment in a sophomore geography course.

In the final chapter of this book, "There's a Place for a Log in the Office," Karen Hickman makes a good case that methodical but informal writing is useful for coordinating the work in complex and hectic office settings where secretaries, typists, and receptionists can use them for both speculative and dialogical purposes.

34.

How Writing Helps Physics Students Become Better Problem Solvers

JUDY GRUMBACHER

> We talked about motion today. I've never really thought of such a simple thing before. We are always in motion everyday. I see motion every day. But we never realize it. I know I realize it when I'm in the backseat during a long trip with all the windows rolled up. I look up from a book and everything looks a little distorted. I feel warm and sick. Car or motion sickness is nothing new to this traveller. It's even worse on a boat. You walk one way and the boat is going in the opposite direction. Gag! That's gross. You don't actually get somewhere as fast—or maybe you do. I'd like to learn about all of that.
>
> Sara

That was written by a high school senior during the first week of a PSSC physics class. In the process of writing about what she already knew about motion, Sara made several discoveries important to her learning physics well. She related what we were studying—motion—with things in her own experience—motion sickness and walking on a boat. And she asked herself a question—what happens to an object's speed when it moves in a direction opposite to a boat's—and expressed the desire to find an answer. While writing she also stumbled upon the way in which the direction of motion can change an object's relative velocity.

A short time after Sara wrote that we began to study vectors, quantities which have a size and a direction. I used her question about walking backwards on a boat to introduce vector algebra. Doing that led me to an obvious discovery: students pay attention more when they are learning how to answer their own questions. As we continued to study and write about vectors, Sara observed:

> I like vectors. I actually understand them. I'm learning the same thing in Trig—it's fascinating how it all ties together. It proves how math and science are related. In one way you are solving a math equation and on the other hand you are understanding physics. It's pretty neat.

Sara wrote about her encounters with learning physics in her learning log, something I require all my students to keep. Keeping a log about what they are learning in class is new to most students. Some students, like Sara, quickly discover that writing about physics helps

them learn physics. Other students never make this discovery because
they never really keep logs; they just write down an occasional formula
or laundry list of words that have shown up on the blackboard. Still
others wonder how they are "suppose to write about something [they]
don't understand in the first place."

I don't know what makes some students good log writers and others
non-log writers. At first I thought that the split occurred along grade
lines: good students kept good logs, poor students kept no logs. However, a student in one of my classes for gifted and talented students upset
that theory. Steven refused to keep a log even though he knew it was a
requirement for the course. He wrote:

> I have an extreme aversion to taking notes. I have put myself in the
> position where I feel that anything I should know from class I
> either retain from hearing it in class or figure it out when it is
> necessary. Therefore I do not keep a log.
>
> Steven

Steven, using class discussions the way other students used their
logs, did his thinking aloud. This technique works well when the class
is small and the assignments are teacher-focused. However, Steven did
not do well on independent kinds of activities where log writing was
important for organizing and learning new material. He also showed
some confusion about the difference between notes and log entries.
When I asked students to explain differences they see between notes and
logs, I heard responses like "logs are more organized," "notes are kinda
messy," "logs have more depth," and "in logs the thoughts are your
own." I think most students can tell the difference, but not all students
understand the importance of such distinctions to their learning physics.

Sara took the first step toward becoming a good problem solver in
physics when she began to write about her understanding of the ideas of
physics. After reading several articles (Fuller, 1982 and McDermott, 1984)
about the difficulties beginning physics students have with problem
solving, I became interested in finding out what happens to problem
solving abilities when students write to learn physics. Fuller and
McDermott point to students' lack of conceptual understanding of the
ideas of physics as the major stumbling block in problem solving.
Students who don't understand the physics behind the equations can't
meaningfully use those equations to solve problems. I think writing can
help students gain that insight. Sara's writings show this. Nor is she an
isolated case. You can almost hear Nick and Kate thinking as you read
their log entries.

> First of all, you said that the center of mass was not exactly the
> center of gravity. Why not? I don't understand, please explain.

> O.K., on with it. Center of mass is one of the most practical
> things to know for everyday living. Since we know that the lower the
> C of M is, the steadier an object will be. This makes so much sense.

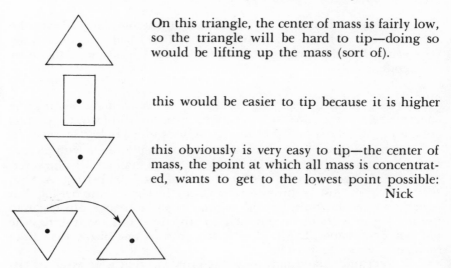

On this triangle, the center of mass is fairly low, so the triangle will be hard to tip—doing so would be lifting up the mass (sort of).

this would be easier to tip because it is higher

this obviously is very easy to tip—the center of mass, the point at which all mass is concentrated, wants to get to the lowest point possible:
Nick

The Greeks had an interesting, although completely fallacious, concept of how objects fall. Their concept, especially that of Aristotle, was formed because of observations. Aristotle, without a doubt, observed that a feather fell to the ground much more slowly than a rock. He came to the conclusion that, the heavier an object, the faster it falls to the ground. This is a very simple but logical conclusion that can only be refuted by very careful observation. I myself, when very young, came to the same conclusion. It seemed obvious to me that the heavier object would fall faster. I guess the Greeks were really the children, while we are now the adults.
Kate

Students like Sara, Nick, and Kate are good problem solvers. Reading their logs and watching them work problems made me wonder about the process they used to solve problems. I wanted to find out what they were doing—besides getting the right answers—that less successful students were not. Through interviews and questionnaires, I found that good problem solvers (1) articulate what is needed to answer a problem, (2) visualize and verbalize the process they use to solve the problem, and (3) check their work by asking "Is this a reasonable answer?"

Successful problem solvers also have one other trait in common: they use their learning logs in substantially different ways from other students. They use their logs to synthesize their new knowledge about physics with their prior knowledge and experiences. In this entry Ben relates what he is learning about the velocity of waves with his experience on the golf team.

Today I noticed something interesting on the golf course. I was standing on the ninth tee watching the people on the first tee. The first guy hit the ball and I was watching it travel through the air and then I heard the club hit the ball. This was the most evident I had ever seen and heard the difference between the speed of sound and the speed of light. The next guy got up to hit the ball and as he swung I looked at my watch, about a second later I heard the familiar WHACK!!! I realized that if I had had a more accurate watch I could have figured out the distance from me to the other golfer.

                                                                    Ben

Writing in their logs gives students practice in manipulating the concepts behind the equations in physics. Students can learn the process good problem solvers follow by practicing the process in logs or journals.

Stephanie, a bright, conscientious student, had trouble with physics in the beginning of the year. Her work improved dramatically, however, when she changed the way in which she kept and used her log. At first, she recalled, she just "copied problems from the board" into her log. But after a first, terrible quiz, her log writings began to change. She began to use her log to write notes to herself, to raise questions about things she did not understand. The following log entry is one of the first times Stephanie wrote to herself:

> I don't understand how to do the problems that were assigned last week. When Mrs. Grumbacher explained it on the board the very first day I thought it was pretty, well, easy enough. When I got home and read the book, it seemed to be contradicting what Mrs. Grumbacher just said. I tried the acceleration problems anyway. I have a lot of questions to ask in class today!

What Am I GIVEN?
What Do I have to FIND?

Remember to ask these things first before solving a problem.
                                                                    Stephanie

From this point on in her log, Stephanie wrote "notes to myself explaining how to do something. Like when you ask us to write a paragraph to a brother or other person explaining how to do the problem." Her log began to include entries like the one on p. 327 where she explained how to answer a question that asked what would happen to an object's acceleration if its mass were doubled and the force acting on it were increased five times.

This is an especially interesting log entry because Stephanie starts out trying to plug numbers into an equation. If she had continued this way, she would have arrived at an incorrect answer. However, as she wrote about the reasoning needed to solve the problem, she corrected her earlier mechanical mistake. By dealing with the conceptual relationship between variables before she worked with numbers, she correctly solved the problem.

Stephanie said that doing this kind of work helped her to discover that the explanations, not just the formulas, were important. On her own she began to keep a log in her math class. Since she began to write to learn in physics, she found that she took better notes in other classes

WORK	THINKING
$5F = 2m(5.20\frac{m}{s^2})$ $5F = 2m(100\frac{m}{s^2})$ $a = 100\frac{m}{s^2}$ $100\frac{m}{s^2} \times \frac{1}{2} =$ $50\frac{m}{s^2}$	First I would ask, "What does the question ask?" It wants me to find the acceleration after the force has increased 5 times & the mass doubles. First I set up the equation algebraically according to Newton's Law of Motion (F=ma) When Force increases acceleration increases. I would multiply F x 5 and 2 x m and 5 x a. $5F = 2m(5.20\frac{m}{s^2})$ 5×20 equals $100 \ m/s^2$ From the same law I know $a \propto \frac{1}{m}$ When one increases the other decreases. If the mass doubles, acceleration decreases by $\frac{1}{2}$.

In math and physics Stephanie concentrated on learning the process of problem solving. "I used to get frustrated when I couldn't remember how or why to do something. Knowing the process eliminates that frustration."

I think Sara, Stephanie, Ben, Kate, and Nick have a lot to say about the way students learn physics. Physics begins to make sense for students as they connect physics concepts with experiences from their lives: walking backwards on a boat, watching a golf ball, recognizing the Aristotelian nature of a childhood belief. When we were studying projectiles, I asked my students to write a problem about some projectile with which they had had firsthand knowledge. I received a variety of responses. Some unexpectedly poignant questions were written by students who had lived in Cambodia and Laos and knew a great deal about falling bombs. Other responses dealt with baseballs, spitballs, parachutes, and rappelling. One student's involved a bird and how not knowing where a projectile would land made her late for school because she had to go home and wash her hair. Students need opportunities to play with the ideas of physics and think about the role physics plays in their lives. My students' examples were not as "neat" as textbook examples. Because they were dealing with real situations, we had to look at the differences between real and idealized projectile motion. Most introductory texts deal only with idealized projectiles, which ignore air resistance, because the consideration of other factors can obscure the theory behind the motion of projectiles and the math is less complex. But my students created problems where air resistance was a significant factor. When students raise such questions, they are prepared and willing to deal with more involved explanations and equations than we require or think they can understand. My students taught me this when I told them that the math needed in some of their questions was more involved than what we had been using and I thought that they'd find it too confusing.

I began my research on what happens when students write in physics class not knowing what I would find. I discovered that:

1. the best problem solvers in physics are students who are able to relate the theories of physics to experiences in their lives;
2. writing helps students find the connections between experience and theory;
3. students will do more work than is required if they are seeking answers to questions they initiate;
4. keeping learning logs on a regular basis encourages students to initiate such questions;
5. students need many opportunities to play with the ideas of physics; they need time to work with a concept in a number of different contexts before rushing on to new information. This means that we may cover fewer topics, but that students will have a better chance of understanding what we cover.

My students use writing and their logs the way real scientists have always used writing and journals: to clarify their thinking, to explore the ideas of science, to search for connections between theory and practice, and to ask questions.

What I've described in this paper didn't happen overnight. The first two years I had students write about physics, the results were not very good. I had read an article about journals across the disciplines and attended an in-service program on writing to learn. It sounded good, and I was willing to try anything which might help my students learn physics better. In the beginning I'm not sure if I could distinguish between notes and logs, or even if I thought much about the difference. I had never kept a learning log and didn't know anyone who had, outside of the examples I'd seen in journals.

Having my students write to learn physics really became productive after I began keeping a learning log about my own learning and teaching, something I learned to do while attending a summer workshop run by the Northern Virginia Writing Project. During that summer conference I also began to write on a regular basis. I now write with my students whenever I ask them to write in class. I've found that this is essential: students need to see their teachers writing. I may not always write on the same topics my students do, but I do spend our writing time writing and thinking about physics teaching.

I'm not a writing teacher. Rather I'm a physics teacher who uses writing to help students think. One of my students told me, "I enjoy finding out what's in my brain, what comes out, because sometimes I don't know what it's doing or thinking." Learning logs help students make those kinds of discoveries.

Notes

The students' names in the article were changed with their permission. Some of the writers selected their own pseudonyms, others had me select a name for them. I am grateful to them for allowing me to quote from their writings and interviews.

The major drafting of this paper was done in a teacher research course offered through George Mason University. Marian Mohr and Marion MacLean, the instructors of the class, provided constant and valuable help over the course of my research. In addition they helped me to understand the need for teachers to become researchers in their classrooms. The members of my reading/writing group, Virgil Davala, Leslie Gray, and Lin McKay, also willingly provided sound advice and support whenever I asked.

References

Fuller, R. (1982, September). Solving physics problems—How do we do it? *Physics Today*, 35:43-7.

McDermott, L. (1984, July). Research on conceptual understanding of mechanics. *Physics Today*, 37:24-32.

35.

Writing in College Physics

VERNER JENSEN

While the process of writing is typically associated with communication and the cultivation of communication skills, the process is also useful for learning and the cultivation of thinking. Physics students can use the writing process to clarify their thinking and understandings about physical phenomena through their written articulation of relationships. Learning physics requires many different mind processes including abstract thinking. Writing can assist the student with this process.

Physics isn't just equations and symbols. These abbreviated statements so frequently associated with the science represent a summary of logical thinking, observations, and experimentation. Reading the statements or reading about them, or even memorizing them, doesn't always mean that students understand them. Knowledge needs to become a permanent and active aspect of the thought and analysis process. Writing about the concept and explaining it to others helps one understand that concept.

One example where writing helps learning would be the knowledge and understanding of the conservation of energy. Students understand this principle primarily through solving problems, but the understanding can be enhanced through a free-writing experience. It should be so actively on the mind that the student almost unconsciously asks the question in the analysis of any problem, "What's happening to the energy in this interaction?"

Academic physicists frequently remark to one another, usually in private, that if you really desire a complete and wide understanding of a particular area of physics (mechanics, electricity and magnetism, quantum mechanics, etc.) then you should ask for an opportunity to teach it. When one expresses and articulates these ideas, one understands them. Writing about physics concepts has a parallel result.

Journal-keeping Procedure

Journal-keeping in physics class can be included as a part of the regular classroom procedure during the usual lecture period without a great modification of one's teaching style. Regularly scheduled journal entries can be made on an assigned topic during a five- to seven-minute writing period in class. The writing period is most frequently conducted at the close of the period but could on occasion be at the beginning or in the middle of the hour. Students are expected to get started during the writing period, but finish later in the library, dormitory room, or wherever they study. They write each entry and date it in the small notebook which serves as the journal. Students are also encouraged to keep a personal section for private reflections, as well as an academic section related to physics, but this is strictly for their own use.

The course in which journals were used was a two-semester standard, non-calculus physics course for students who were mainly majoring in one of the sciences or in industrial technology. Fewer than ten percent of those enrolled were selecting the course to fulfill a general education elective. The students enrolled were principally freshmen and sophomores, with approximately one-third being juniors and seniors. The textbook used for this course was *Physics, A General Introduction,* authored by Alan Van Heuvelen. It should be noted that an audience other than the teacher is suggested for some writing exercises. The free-writing style seems less inhibited, less formal if the student is also imagining that the explanations are being directed to a sympathetic listener. Following is a sample of the journal topics assigned to the class in the fall of 1983; similar topics were given throughout the winter and spring.

9/21 Explain Newton's 3rd Law to your roommate, including examples from the real world.

9/24 Explain to your lab partner what friction is, including why it is sometimes helpful and sometimes a nuisance.

9/26 Describe the concept of momentum to your kid brother.

9/28 Explain why (in the event of a collision) the passenger in a smaller car is more likely to be injured in the interaction with a large car.

10/3 Explain to your mother why water stays in a pail when swung in a vertical circle around your head.

10/8 Explain the differences and similarities between translational and rotational acceleration.

10/12 Describe the relationship between work and energy including the different forms of energy.

10/15 What is your understanding of the Law of Conservation of Energy?

10/17 Describe to your dad the physics related to machines.

10/22 Explain why deserts get hot while islands at the same latitude remain temperate.

10/24 Describe the demonstrations you saw today on systems of heat transfer.

10/26 Explain the several methods of heat transfer and discuss how they apply to the human body.

10/29 Explain to your younger brother why blowing across your soup or a cup of hot chocolate cools it—include at least two reasons.

10/31 Discuss the net effect of leaving the refrigerator door open.

Student Journal Entries

It may be instructive to include some samples of student journal entries exactly as these have been written. Consider the responses to the writing topic "Explain to your roommate the concept of the kinetic thoery of molecules."

> It's time for your weekly physics lesson, Steve, and you'd better pay attention because this one is not easy to understand. I'm going to tell you about the Kinetic Theory of Molecules. In general, it has to do with the speed at which molecules in the air tend to move. This speed or rapid motion is caused by atoms and molecules which collide with themselves and the sides of containers or other things. It's kind of like putting a bunch of people in a room and blindfolding them and telling them to keep walking. If the room were made smaller the people would obviously collide more, as do air molecules under similar circumstances and the result is a greater pressure. Assume we tell the people to walk faster, which simulates the heating up of a confined amount of gas. The result is also an increased number of collisions and again the pressure of the gas is increased.

The student's ability to explain this to "Steve" indicates that he gained a good understanding of the topic. The analogy to people in a room suggested by the student was quite appropriate and was one that he had thought of quite independently: it had not been suggested by either the lecturer or the text author. Another response appears as follows:

> The kinetic theory of molecules is a really neat topic..., and I'm sure you'd like to hear about it! In this theory we see how particles in a box relate to each other. The particles in the box are in constant motion, bouncing off each other and bouncing off the walls of the box. Some move up and down, some left and right, and some forward and backward. One aspect of the theory is that the length of the box sides will affect the time between collisions. Also, the faster the molecules move, the less time there will be between collisions. Kinetic energy, the energy produced as a result of motion, is the result of one-half the mass of the particle times the velocity squared of the particle.
>
> Let's look at the velocity of one particle. It will depend on two factors. First, the larger the box, the faster the particle will move after bouncing around. Second, the smaller the molecule, the faster it will be able to move. An analogy would be a warm room. The larger the room and the heavier the gas, will affect the rate at which the particles hit you—make you warm! As the molecules move faster they travel greater distances...especially if their mass is small.

This student appears to be clarifying understandings as the writing develops. Initially, the writing seems to be very closely related to what may have been read in the text or to remarks and explanations made by the lecturer. But toward the close of the writing, the writer is starting to explore or extrapolate some applications which is an indication that the concept is understood. Another category of response follows:

> Everything that exists is made up of molecules and all these molecules are moving. In a gas state the molecules move very quickly and bounce off each other and the container they are in. Gases consist of atoms and molecules in rapid motion. When the molecules and atoms collide against the walls of the container they are in, this causes the pressure against the walls. As the temperature increases the atoms and molecules become more active causing more pressure to be exerted.

In this case the writer is merely reflecting what was presented in the lecture. The writer may have committed the information to memory, but his writing doesn't indicate that he fully understands the concept. Another response appears below:

> I can't believe all the calculations he did today in physics! Okay, the kinetic theory of molecules: The force that a particle has times the time it takes it to move is equal to twice its mass times velocity, but I'm not supposed to explain it to you in mathematical terms, so: The energy a particle has while it's moving is the same...
>
> Well, I guess I don't really understand—maybe I'd better read about it some more.

In this student's case, it is obvious, especially to the student, that he doesn't yet understand the subject matter and concept; further study is necessary. That, too, is of pedagogical value. The student might otherwise have believed that he actually knew the topic.

Journals were collected three times a semester. They were scanned very briefly by the instructor and read somewhat more thoroughly by a physics major who included an occasional comment and evaluation. At the close of the semester, the journals were reviewed somewhat more carefully by the instructor and a grade assigned. The students were told at the beginning of the semester that they could improve their course grade by as much as one-third of a grade point (e.g., from a C to a C+) with a well-kept journal. This served as a motivation for many. More than 90 percent of the students participated actively. Judgment of the journals was largely related to the *quantity* that was written. Approximately two-thirds of the students were awarded the extra one-third grade point. The important aspect of this writing exercise isn't so much the evaluation, but that an opportunity is provided for the students to do some writing—to do some thinking on paper. It thrusts the student into an active role in the classroom and changes the pace of learning. The majority of the students seemed to welcome this.

Evaluation of the Effectiveness of Free-Writing Exercises

An experiment was conducted to establish the extent of the contribution of free-writing to the learning of physics and to improved writing skills. Two consecutive sections of the non-calculus general physics were taught by the same instructor using identical syllabi, texts, demonstrations, assignments, lecture notes, and tests. One section made instructor-assigned entries in a journal during each of the lecture days. The students wrote during the last five minutes of the 50-minute class period and continued and completed the writing out of class. Some students continued their writing immediately, being seated in a hallway or in adjacent classrooms; others continued at some later time. Students in both sections were asked to write and complete an essay on a physics-related topic during a class period near the beginning of the fall term, at the end of the fall term, and at the end of the spring term. The topics for the hour-long writing exercises, which were submitted at the end of the period, appear below:

Beginning Topic

Aristotle believed that if he dropped both a heavy object and a light one at the same time, the heavy one would fall to the ground faster. Skeptical of this, Galileo decided to see what would happen if he dropped two stones of different weights from the top of a tower.

Let's assume that you, too, want to test Aristotle's hypothesis. Describe the sort of experiment that you would design. How would you go about doing the experiment? Where? With what devices, apparatus, specimens, etc.? Explain why. Be sure to give as full an explanation/account/discussion of your procedure as possible and of the reasons for following them.

Mid-Topic:

A child and her parent, equipped with identical parachutes, jump from an airplane. One of the following will happen: the child will arrive at the ground first, the parent will arrive first, or they will arrive at the same time. Describe the sort of experiment that you would design to determine what will happen. How would you go about doing the experiment? Where? With what devices, measuring apparatus, etc.? Explain why. Be sure to give as full an explanation/account/discussion of your procedures as possible and of the reasons for following them, taking into consideration the basic laws of physics and of fluid dynamics.

End-of-the-Year Topic:

Benjamin Franklin, seeking to formulate a theory of electricity and to understand the nature of lightning, flew a kite in a thunderstorm and miraculously survived the effects of the spark drawn to his finger from the iron key suspended on the linen string. He concluded that there was an excess or deficiency of some kind of "fluid" and he called the excess "positive" and the deficiency "negative."

Design and describe the sort of experiment that you might use to test, prove, or formulate a theory of electricity and to understand the nature of lightning. How would you go about doing the experiment? Where? With what devices, measuring apparatus, etc.? Explain why. Using what you know from your study of physics, give as full an explanation/account/discussion of your procedures as possible.

During the second semester, the roles of the two consecutive classes were reversed; the journal-keeping section became the non-journal-keeping section and vice versa. The standard statistical comparisons were made, using analysis of variance with the resultant findings that there were no statistical differences in physics learning between the two groups at the end of either semester as measured by objective, problems-oriented examinations. Differences in writing skills did occur, however. The essays were read and evaluated by both the physics instructor and an English teacher. The difference noted is perhaps best stated in an observation by the latter: "This class (the journal-keeping class) as a whole wrote more relaxed, less stiff papers the second time than did the other class."

Student Attitudes About the Writing Experience

Perhaps the real key to the effectiveness of this activity is the reaction of the students. A questionnaire was distributed with the instructions that the responses should be candid and should not reveal the identify of the responder. The results appear below:

Only your section of General Physics 1 kept a journal throughout the semester.

	Yes	No	Not sure
How do you feel about keeping the journal. Did it help you to understand physics better?	37	9	20
Do you think keeping the journal helped you to write better?	28	22	16
Do you think keeping the journal was a worthwhile activity?	45	7	14

Make any comment in the space below which can help explain your feelings about keeping the journal.

Some positive responses:

> I enjoyed writing in the journals. They helped me put physics into my own words. It helped to be able to make up examples that were directly relevant to me.

> It made me really think about whatever we learned in class, so I could explain it to someone else.

> I think that writing in the journals may have helped me to better understand physics, because in things I didn't understand, I wrote them out and they became a little clearer. I also think it was good

that you gave topics to write on. In other classes that I kept journals in, we were allowed to write on any topic. Every day it seemed harder to find one, but a given topic made it easier to write freely.

I thought it was an excellent idea. It made me stop and think about physics and other things. Most of the time I am going 100 mph just doing, doing, doing. The journal was a chance to stop and think. I plan on keeping it up.

I did learn how to write more informally than previously and in some circumstances I think it improved my understandings of the concept being written about.

Not everyone agreed.

It took away from class time and study time that could be used otherwise, but it did help writing skills and thought processes.

A journal should be kept in English, not physics, classes where its evaluation and correctness could be analyzed.

Concluding Observations

Journal writing can be integrated easily into a physics class without significant changes of the traditional approach to the teaching of physics. While initial evaluations based on objective testing would seem to indicate that physics learning is not especially enhanced through the free-writing process, it might be discovered that long-term understandings will be better retained. The writing process does appear (not surprisingly) to help students to write more freely and easily. Students seem to respond well and positively to the writing activity. They, too, recognize that writing experiences are necessary for a complete education for today's world.

36.

Focused Learning in Chemistry Research: Suzanne's Journal[1]

GEORGE MEESE

In the spring of 1984, Ms. Suzanne Bauer, a senior in chemistry at Michigan Technological University, asked to do an independent project in humanities. Suzanne had already written a good expressive and topical journal in an earlier humanities course, Ethics & Technology.[2] We wanted to see if similar journal writing would help her to learn both the technical practices and the social implications of her chosen field, chemistry. Accordingly, we agreed that she would devote thirty hours to writing a journal about her job as a chemistry laboratory assistant (three hours each week for the ten-week term). In addition to the journal, Suzanne agreed to meet with me for one-half hour each week, so that we could discuss the previous week's entries and raise pertinent questions.

Her lab job involved assisting Dr. Marshall Logue, Associate Professor of Chemistry and Chemical Engineering, in the synthesis of C-nucleoside analogs (potential chemotherapeutic agents). Suzanne liked the open-ended freedom of a journal format, but she initially decided to focus her writing on topics of special importance to her: 1) her choice of the chemical industry for her career and her plans for graduate school in chemistry; 2) her knowledge of applied chemistry and basic research; 3) the working assumptions that lie behind the procedures she was carrying out in the lab; and 4) her personal values as they either supported or conflicted with professional values and the expectations of her mentors in chemistry (including Dr. Logue, graduate students, acquaintances in the field, and other professors). To simplify this report of her journal work, I have shown how Suzanne found a comfortable "voice," have given samples of her thinking about chemistry, and have analyzed how she negotiated with her mentor and found ways to write about her chemistry in connection with cultural issues.

Promoting Learning Through Journal Writing

Some teachers may consider senior undergraduates, in their final term before graduation, as closed to new paths of inquiry. With plans for careers or graduate school pressing in on them, with the distractions of spring weather, social engagements, graduation itself, and celebration of their accomplishments all competing for attention, what original thinking is possible? I don't mean to imply that journal writing is effective when students are in a period of self-indulgence. Rather, I wish to emphasize that journal writing can be a powerful heuristic for intellectual growth even in the face of tantalizing distractions and at a point in a student's development where there may be considerable resistance to upsetting the student's frame of secure reference and dependable assumptions.

My own agenda for Suzanne's project, then, was to use her randomly produced descriptions of her laboratory procedures, her identification of problems or puzzles about her work, and her expressions of concern, self-doubt, or confusion, as springboards into more thoroughly considered, written contemplations. By requiring her to deliver her journal one day in advance of our weekly meetings, I could prepare to zero in on entries that showed inconsistencies or problems or gaps in understanding, thinking, or imagination. I did not set out to teach any chemistry (clearly outside my training in rhetoric and literature). Rather, I hoped her journal would exercise Suzanne's thinking about a life's work in chemistry. I saw the journal experiment as a way to explore values, the philosophical foundation of her work, and the integration of her ideas about "profession" with the concepts of specialist knowledge, citizenship, and ethics we had taken up in the earlier course. I wanted her journal to become a means for Suzanne to carry out her own professional development with a perspective that embraced humanistic questions as well as technical ones.

Descriptive and Expressive Beginnings

Suzanne's first journal entry began with a straightforward description of her duties and activities in the lab.

This is my first entry so I will describe in general what I did today. First of all, I started out by rotary evaporating fractions #5 and 6 after redissolving the supposed product in CCl_4....

After jumping so precipitously into laboratory procedures, it apparently struck her that I would have some problems as her reader, because she began to interject short explanations that she would not need with a chemist; e.g., "the other solvent is still present in large quantities and wrecks the IR spectrum. *Well it doesn't wreck it, but a poorer quality of spectrum is produced.*"[3] As she found her most comfortable voice, she dropped her clinical tone and adopted a persona that was open, candid, and ready to identify problems:

I let the run become exposed to air for at least an hour and Dr. Logue said that I shouldn't have because organometallics can decompose when exposed to O_2. However, I am almost positive that we did the same thing the first time we did the run, and Dr. Logue set it up that time. This just goes to show that *I don't take careful or detailed enough notes*....I plan to find out exactly what reaction happens if O_2 is involved, but right now I won't know what happened until I analyze the composition through IR....

Quite interestingly, Suzanne's descriptions of lab work almost always led into reflective expressions about her relationship with her mentor, Dr. Logue. I realized that she was looking at him as a role model and testing her behavior and assumptions against his. At first, these entries were strongly self-effacing:

> I guess it comes with experience, but sometimes Dr. Logue says well if we let it [the reaction] go, nothing should happen, like he doesn't know for sure. I don't know if I should just trust his judgment, or if I should try to look everything up or not. *Sometimes I feel so ignorant* when it comes to actual chemistry, and I've spent four years here already. No wonder companies prefer people with experience rather than fresh college graduates....Actually I'm being pretty irresponsible by not finding out specifically what Dr. Logue is doing. I'm not putting myself in a position to take on more responsibility concerning the reaction since I'm not bothering to learn more about it. I guess I should attempt to change my attitude some.

Characteristically, Suzanne used this admission of a problem to focus her next week's work and remove misunderstandings. Her developing identification with her profession continued through the term (see "Relationships with Mentors," below). Later in the quarter she rose above her self-criticism and began to regard herself as a competent assistant with contributions to make to Dr. Logue's research.

Thinking About Chemistry

Suzanne was curious about aspects of the experimental reactions she had to perform. In the many pages devoted to her procedures in the lab, she repeatedly raised questions, nearly always as asides and interjections among the descriptive passages:

a. When I came in the reactions had been left stirring. Well, reaction 1 was no longer stirring. I suspect Dr. Logue turned it off, actually I know he did because he said something to that effect later. Supposedly the reactions stir for about 18 hours, but due to my scheduled lab hours they usually stir longer, like over 24 hours. Dr. Logue says as long as they aren't exposed to the atmosphere it shouldn't hurt them, but I wonder why the directions don't say stir for at least 18 hours, then, instead of "stir for eighteen hours."

b. I don't know why n-butyllithium is necessary unless it does something with the chloride from isobutyryl chloride. I should find this out.

c. Why is the THF necessary for the run then? Why wouldn't it make more sense for the acid chloride and phenylacetylene to be thrown together w/nothing else? Good question.

d. I spilled some of the liquid collected in fraction #7....I wonder if only solvent spilled? I can't imagine how only solvent would have leaked out, though, since the product is dissolved in the solvent....I know how I could find this out, by looking up the melting point of the product.

Having identified these issues in writing, Suzanne was able to use her journal to direct her library research. She wrote in subsequent entries the results of her searches and the answers to her questions:

a. All reactions have an equilibrium situation under certain conditions, where no further reaction takes place no matter how long the reaction is allowed to mix...of cource scientists would want to spend as little time as possible waiting, so that's why a specified time is listed.

b. I've found it I think. This is the reaction desired:

$$PhC\equiv Ch + (CH_3)_2CH \overset{\overset{\textstyle O}{\textstyle \|}}{C}-Cl \rightarrow PhC\equiv C-\overset{\overset{\textstyle O}{\textstyle \|}}{C}-CH\ (CH_3)_2$$

The $CdCl_2$ reacts w/$PhC\equiv CH$ to form $PhC\equiv C-CdCl$, which then forms $PhC\equiv CLi$ and the Lithium comes from n-butyllithium, $Ch_3CH_2CH_2CH_2Li$. This is because Li compounds can react more easily than some halides, and $PhC\equiv C-Cd-Cl$ is a halide. However, it is fairly difficult to get Li onto a C next to a multiple bond, therefore butyllithium is used, not just Li metal. Butyllithium is a common reagent in organometallic reactions.

c. What is the purpose of THF? Well, I know for sure it is the solvent because it is quite in excess compared with everything else.

THF, 6 ml
n-butyllithium, 1.4 ml
PHC≡CH, 0.21 ml
isobutCl, 0.21 ml

Well, most of the books I found said basically the same thing. Ethers are generally unreactive and therefore good solvents. They are immiscible in water and therefore can be used to extract organic compounds. They are also especially good to use in Grignard reactions which are ones involving Mg and a halogen. The above reaction involves Cl, a halogen, and also Li, which acts very similarly to Mg. One book even went so far as to say tetrahydrofuran is the best ether to use for halogen and cationic metal reactions, so that is why THF is used.

d. Before I can look up the melting point, I have to be able to figure out the name of it. I tried every reference book in the library but couldn't find it listed. It's probably too uncommon. This means I'll have to ask Dr. Logue.

Relationships with Mentors

Suzanne knew at the outset that she could freely admit to me her ignorance of any procedures or details of the chemical reactions. She also knew that she could speculate freely:

I really don't know why he [Dr. Logue] wants me to continue performing the same basic reaction over and over. He did initially say that he was working on the synthesis of a few particular cyclic compounds, but one of the intermediates he uses in the process is hard to make, so what I'm doing is to try to find a better way to make this intermediate. However, I don't know anything about the drug compounds Dr. Logue is interested in so actually he might be doing something I wouldn't approve of.[4]

Suzanne's maturity and her experience in chemistry at the time of this journal writing was that of a strong candidate for admission to graduate school. (In fact, she has since been accepted and is doing well.) As a neophyte researcher, she was engaged in *becoming* a member of a learned profession. She not only had to master her chemistry, but also demonstrate the values of the research community which she aspired to join. Asking the type of questions quoted in the previous section is clearly one of the most desirable habits of mind in any scholarly group, and indeed most conventional teaching in the sciences helps students develop technical curiosity. In this regard, Suzanne had already mastered the skills necessary to investigate chemical phenomena. As the quotation here indicates, she was now learning a different but crucial kind of knowledge, namely the motives and standards of her mentors.

In my teaching experience, the beginning of a mentor-student relationship is a rewarding—and risky—moment. Too easy an acceptance of the scholar's presuppositions indicates an uncritical attitude in the student, while too facile a defense of the accepted practices of a profession indicates—at least to the better students—a lack of rigor in the mentor's approach. Both parties approach this stage of their work together with parts of their professional personality exposed. This appeared to be the situation when Suzanne questioned Dr. Logue's work.

I've found that a wide-ranging journal of the type Suzanne wrote helps students and me to negotiate the "mentor period" with clearer understanding and more mutual growth. For example, as Suzanne thought about her work, she naturally called into question both her own and her mentor's motives (e.g., "he might be doing something I wouldn't approve of"). In spite of her otherwise outgoing and self-assured personality, she wasn't ready to voice her concerns directly. She instead used the neutral ground of her journal to raise the issue of the end purpose and context of Dr. Logue's research. Once she raised it she had to follow up with careful homework.[5]

Suzanne first talked with Dr. Logue and got a better overview of his research. She didn't go into the implications, risks, testing procedures, applications, or ethics of the project. The terse journal entries show her findings in her most objective tone:

He is studying carbohydrates and c-nucleoside analogs. He is especially interested in their synthesis. C-nucleoside analogs are potential chemotherapeutic agents, the ones that are known to have either antitumor, antiviral, or antibiotic activity. The carbohydrate studies are important because if they can be synthesized then complex carbohydrates or nucleosides can be made by converting available ones into them rather than using scarce reagents and starting from scratch.

Note that the questions of "should this be done?" or "what happens after the research is finished?" or "in whose interest is this project being done?" are all skirted. Suzanne was only in the middle of her investigation, and she was maintaining her critical distance. In the library, she added more information:

I found four articles of the five Dr. Logue has published. One journal we do not have in the library, but it wasn't his most recent one.

The first article was entitled "Conversion of Pyrimidine Nucleoside 2', 3'-orthoacetates into Pyrimidine 2'-azido-2' -deoxynucleoside" [she then summarizes the contents]...it doesn't say much about their antibiotic value or what specifically is their function. *If I were a scientist reading this article I would want to see what kind of value there is in the compound being synthesized before I got excited about possible ways to make it...*

The second article...relates to what I'm doing for my research [long discussion of similarities and differences in the reactions being investigated]....

[The third and fourth articles are reviewed]

It seems as though these articles are addressing only the syntheses of intermediate compounds. Apparently *if I want to discover the ultimate goal*—what happens once these various nucleosides are made—I'll have to talk again with Dr. Logue. ...It seems all to be for the benefit of mankind—chemotherapy, etc.

The journal work on this issue helped Suzanne prepare to talk knowledgeably with her mentor. Her informed discussion of his research confirmed the context that she had constructed by reading the appropriate literature and assembling her conclusions in her journal entries. Commenting on this part of her writing to me, she acknowledged that it made her meetings with Dr. Logue more focused and productive, and she was glad to see how her lab work fit in to the larger research questions. She also discovered a kind of learning process that was newly challenging:

I consider myself quite motivated, but it's frustrating because I'm not advanced enough to clearly understand journal articles enough to speculate intelligently upon the work presented, so all I can do is to try to build up my reservoir of knowledge gradually and hope to attain that level sometime soon.

This realization brings up one final observation I would like to make about mentors, research, professional literature, and the role of informal writing in the education of young researchers. Mature scholars know well that forthright recognition of one's limits of understanding is a necessary starting point for original inquiry. Undergraduates (and beginning graduate students) may have been told this truism in as many words, but their early studies—mostly prescriptive—often give them the impression that it is unseemly to admit confusion or less-than-comprehensive mastery of the fundamentals of their field. Trying to identify themselves with their mentors, students sometimes interpret formal writings (journal articles, conference proceedings, texts, and the like) as having come easily for the mentor. Students rarely see professional scientific papers as the end products that result only after the tortuous and often messy business of research projects is finished.

Mentors might consider using more broadly defined research journals, with room in them for speculative and reflexive writing, to help students make the transition from naive awe of professional literature to reasoned respect and criticism. That is, the journal can be a sounding board for several emerging professional voices, and mentor and student can discuss the propriety of each voice for the many occasions when scientists exchange information and findings. Before raising expectations to the level of "publishable research reports," mentors might better allow students to exercise themselves in the arts of weighing data, evaluating arguments, and formulating research questions. This is precisely what Suzanne's journal permitted her to do. With relatively minimal investment of her time, Suzanne applied healthy skepticism and curiosity to her lab assistant experience. Since the journal was not expected to be formal, her risks of intellectual embarrassment were low. In this structured but generous environment, she not only began to see herself as a young research chemist, she also raised more than thirty specific inquiries about chemistry. Stated another way, she was able to act like a researcher concerned with about three good questions each week. Most scientists would be pleased to share a lab with an assistant who was so productively focused on ideas.

Chemistry and Culture: Using the Journal for Integrative Learning

The majority of Suzanne's pages in the journal were concerned with chemistry, her labs, and chemical industry applications of university research.[6] Thus I was surprised when she read back over her whole journal and wrote me a summary report that did not reflect the quantitative distribution of her term's writing for me:

I have known for a long time that I'm concerned with the ethics of social behavior in general. Keeping the journal made me more aware of my concern with ethics related to scientific research. My four major concerns are the use of animals for laboratory testing, accuracy of reported data, research influenced by politics, and lastly, to me it makes a difference what the ultimate goal of given research is.

Part of the explanation for her weighting of the journal's topics surely came from our previous work in the course on ethics and technology, and the larger role that we both gave to ethical issues in our weekly half-hour meetings. Another factor seems to have been at work as well: Suzanne's growing awareness of the time she forsees devoting to her career in organic chemistry, and her recognition of social roles that professional chemists are called upon to play in our society. Thus some of her most animated writing is focused on issues that begin in her lab experiences but which have broad implications.

She at one point surmised that any drugs that came out of her lab research would eventually have to be tested before human use. This led to a discussion with me about the kinds of animals that are used in testing, and I took exception to her willingness to use some species but not others. Reacting in her journal, Suzanne tested the proposition that some animals are more appropriate research subjects than others; she listed some thirty-five species, then her honest attitudes toward them, and then tried to find a pattern in her reasoning. She wrote, "I guess what it boils down to is that the animals that I tend to care less about are either not physically attractive or they scare me." This led to further discussion about reasonable grounds for objections to chemical vivisection (such as the sanctity of living things generally).

Regarding accuracy of data recording and reporting, Suzanne made an important discovery. She had made two journal entries on separate occasions, one explaining how she weighed the products of her reactions (on a Mettler balance), and another relating how another lab instructor had said that the Mettler balance was accurate enough to record the weight of a fingerprint on a flask. Reading back over her entries, she realized that using the weights of the flasks that had been inscribed on their sides, rather than weighing every flask for every run of the experiment, would seriously skew her results—the weight of the marker ink itself would change the weight of the flask, as well as any fingerprints or other external contamination. Regular class labs operated at rough enough approximations that these accuracies didn't matter, but her own research involved small quantities. She wrote: "I had an opportunity to find the true weight of one of the flasks I have been using and its value is 47.038 g and the labeled weight was 47.049 g." The result of this concern didn't end at improved data collection procedures alone. Suzanne recognized that telling Dr. Logue about this problem was the same kind of action as telling him about other sources of possible error, i.e., she was acting on professional principle, not an isolated concern about one experiment. She further applied this issue in an extended reflection upon falsification of data for political purposes, reacting to an article she had read about yellow rain in *Chemical & Engineering News.*

Another news item led Suzanne to fuller discussion of the purposes of scientific research and the ways that individual scientists affect their fellow human beings. In her first entry she reacted narrowly:

> There are some kinds of research I do feel are trivial and money-wasting. One project in particular comes to mind. My mom told me of a governmentally-funded research project in which the conclusion was sick people are generally more depressed than healthy people. That is pretty silly and it took quite a bit of money to figure it out scientifically. ...Either the government officials do not use common sense or open their eyes, or such projects are more complex and politically involved than I can imagine.

My response to this entry was simply to write in the journal's margin a quote from Samuel Taylor Coleridge's *Biographia Literaria:* "Until you understand another man's ignorance, consider yourself ignorant of his understanding." When we discussed the week's work in conference, Suzanne wondered at my cryptic note, and I explained that I had tried to make Coleridge's words my motto for the first round of any academic or political debate. She wrote back:

> I don't understand what you are getting at here. Are you saying that I shouldn't judge the research...because there might be more to it that I don't understand? Or are you justifying the research because until there is documented proof upon the relationship, it cannot be completely understood?...
>
> I suppose the study could have originally been to study a variety of things connected to illness and depression, or maybe even something altogether different, but the conclusion was the only concrete piece of evidence they could find. I can tell right now that it is impossible to logically discuss an issue on hearsay; I need to read the article before going any further.

My marginalia this time simply said, "All of this!" It was clear to me that in the very act of Suzanne's writing her answer to me, she had felt the power and wisdom of Coleridge's words. Thus it was with real joy that I read her final summary of our journal experiment and found this:

> The most significant knowledge that I gained from this writing and thinking exercise, the journal, is awareness of the concept behind, "until one understands a man's ignorance..." I cannot get this quote out of my mind. I truly feel enlightened! It makes perfect sense and is a sure deterrent for being a wise-guy in inappropriate situations. I can safely say this lesson in not pre-judging is the most important thing I discovered this term. I hope I'll remember it for the rest of my life. At any rate it should keep my foot out of my mouth a few times.

Suzanne closed on a personal note, befitting our agreement that the journal could follow whatever topic was important, as long as she based her writing on her laboratory work and her interest in chemistry:

> Keeping a journal benefited me in another way—it gave me peace of mind. I am referring to the time where I questioned the value of being an organic chemist when there were horrible problems all around us. You suggested that I decide which roles I have to fill by being alive and then defining what successful fulfillment each of them would entail, and finally comparing my current actions against that model. This really helped me to find peace of mind. The overall idea of not being responsible for everything that goes wrong merely by being human has cheered me up immensely....
> The final thing I learned is that the more I find out about life and myself, the more there is to know. One question has led to another and it never stops. This is fun because it guarantees excitement and surprises—continuously, if one chooses to look for them. I will never be bored!

Applications of Journals in Science

Being a professor of humanities, I don't presume to say that journals are more effective than other techniques for mastering specific knowledge in the sciences. Other chapters of this book address discipline-specific writing and suggest effective journal strategies. My purpose here has been to review a single experiment in journal writing that was attached to a laboratory assistantship in order to allow the student to reflect widely upon her learning. Suzanne's own writing testifies to the relative success of her journal; I'm convinced that her project led to demonstrable learning in social, philosophical, and personal aspects of organic chemistry research.

There has been considerable criticism of undergraduate curricula in recent years, and at the national level, much of this criticism has claimed that "vocational" interests have displaced broader cultural enrichment. Whatever the case may be in general terms, teachers ultimately must attend to the education of individual students, and we are hard pressed to include broad perspectives in every major-field course. Focused journal writing guarantees that teachers will be able to monitor individual students' thinking (as opposed to their memorization) about a subject, and journals are a particularly appropriate forum for students' contemplation of the cultural context in which specialist learning takes place. I have never yet had a discussion of teaching objectives with any colleague in any discipline of science or technology, when we did not agree that students should know their field's assumptions, methods, history, and cultural roles. Adaptations of Suzanne's journal experiment, negotiated between students and teachers to address their specific learning needs, can help us all to meet these objectives and, in the process of writing, to better understand our disciplines and each other.

Notes

[1] I wish to acknowledge Ms. Suzanne Bauer's generosity, both for giving me permission to use her journal and for participating in the journal experiment so willingly. I also thank Dr. Marshall Logue, Associate Professor of Chemistry and Chemical Engineering at Michigan Technological University, for his cooperation and review of this manuscript for accuracy of the chemistry. Dr. Elizabeth A. Flynn helped me clarify several points in draft.

[2] The course (HU252), which Ms. Bauer took during summer quarter, 1983, involved extensive journal writing. Students first responded expressively to case studies of ethical issues involving technology, then wrote more fully developed positions on the topics, often basing the focused section on their technical expertise from their major field. For example, a student might express her personal frustration over media coverage of nuclear waste disposal proposals, then work in her journal toward a resonable public statement of her position, using her advanced knowledge of materials science.

[3] My emphasis. In subsequent quotes from the journal, all emphases have been added.

[4] In this journal, Suzanne routinely considered the ethics of chemical industry projects, extending the work we had begun in the Ethics and Technology course. She later confirms the fact that Dr. Logue's work is not only being conducted carefully, but that it has strong potential for helping people. Her freedom to raise ethical questions as directly as she does in this passage is one of the advantages of the relative informality of journals.

[5]Had Dr. Logue been reading the journal, Suzanne might not have raised her questions so directly in writing either. In my experience, when students are in the process of exploring sensitive questions, they go ahead and express their concerns, and then they are highly motivated to do their homework on the questions before the next journal review or conference. That is, the risks seem to be perceived as less threatening.

[6]Of the 64 pages, 35 are exclusively concerned with lab procedures, data, and research design, 14 about ethical issues, 4 about poor oral presentations by scientists, 6 about science and religion, and 5 are on wholly tangential themes (pyrokinesis, sports and politics, and student facilities on campus).

37.

Mathematics Journals:
Fourth Grade

BARBARA SCHUBERT

"The math journal helped me because what was in my mind I couldn't get on paper but when I started writing about it I knew more about it than I thought I did." Amanda has spoken Truth. A truth that is well known by writers but perhaps less well understood by teachers of mathematics. The truth she spoke came in an evaluation discussion held in a fourth grade classroom in LeClaire, Iowa. For ten weeks the boys and girls in my math class had written an entry each day in their math journals. Each entry was in response to a question I had posed at the beginning of each math class.

The study of fractions is singularly difficult for most ten-year-old students. The text calls for them to be able to distinguish between a region and a set, describe an equivalent fraction, tell what each number in the fraction stands for, be able to distinguish whether multiplication or division should be used to find the fractional part of a number, find the fractional part of a number by dividing by the denominator and multiplying by the numerator, find sale prices using fractions, show how equivalent fractions are made by multiplying, understand the meaning of lowest terms, reduce fractions to lowest terms, understand that a fraction with a very large denominator has very small pieces and use this and its converse to compare fractions and determine their relation to one another, add and subtract fractions with like and unlike denominators, recognize mixed numbers, be able to make a mixed number into an improper fraction and vice versa. The D. C. Heath textbook provides twenty lessons in chapter six to cover this learning sequence. The publishers expect it to be taught in about four weeks.

I use daily sequential and extended math journal writing based on the principles underlying the use of writing to develop author ownership and the understanding that writing about a topic ensures active participation in the learning process. I used math journals for the first time in the 1982-1983 school year. I have used them each year since.

Each day we use a similar format. I write the journal entry question on the chalkboard. I read the question aloud with the class and accept any questions or concerns raised by the children. The next step is to teach the material necessary to answer the question. In order to be most effective and efficient, I write the answer to each question for myself before beginning to teach it. I use language I think my fourth graders will be likely to use. I teach by means of that language, trying to keep the presentation on a single concept and uncluttered by examples which raise questions rather than show solutions. I show examples and label parts of the problems. Then I ask children who are willing to come to the chalkboard and label and explain a similar problem. When most of the children appear to have a fairly clear idea how to begin answering, I ask the children to tell me in writing their answer to the original question. I leave all the examples on the chalkboard to reduce anxiety and to help them write clearly. Then I tell them to put the finished journal entry in the sorter, a metal shelf we use to collect and store papers, and begin the assignment for the next day.

The children write on wide-line loose-leaf notebook paper, as they do in science and social studies. They head the paper "Math Journal." The date is put on the left and the name on the right. It usually takes from five to fifteen minutes for each child to complete the entry. I circulate around the room, encouraging and helping those children who are obviously floundering. I talk with each one who asks, in order to rehearse what might be written, then leave them to work out their individual response to the question. Each night I take the journal entries home and spend thirty minutes to an hour responding to the answers.

Lessons

The following questions and replies from various children's journals give a sample of how the process works. These samples are quoted verbatim from the children's journals.

12/8 Lesson 68

Objective: 1. write a fraction to tell what parts of a region has a certain property.

2. name denominator, numerator.

3. identify equivalent fractions.

Journal Entry: Write what you would say to another fourth grader to describe a fraction.

A fraction is a thing ware you devide parts of the shape. Fore ezaple if you had a squar that had five parts and tow parts were shaded in yow woud pout on your paper 2/5 the 2 meens howmeny parts are shaded that is called the numerator. The 5 stands for how meny parts are sheded in it is caled the denominator. Fractions seem hard but their not after you get the hang of it.

In the margin of that paper I wrote: "This is the best explanation I have ever read written by a fourth grader." Benji is an average student who has some problems in school, and writing to learn proved helpful to him.

Sarah, on the other hand, found this question quite easy. Here is her response:

All you do is to make half of the number. Its like division lets say this is the fraction 1/3 = /9 all you do is this. nine divided by three is 3 so you put a 3 over the 9.

This is how I would explain. If you had a cherry pie that had 10 peices and there were 5 eatin already this is how you would make the fraction. 10 would be the Denominator and 5 would be the numorator. This is your fraction

$\frac{5}{10}$ - numerator

$\overline{10}$ - Denominator

By contrast, when you look at Jesse's entry you can see that he will need a great deal of help:

ther is alot of new strang words to start you will need a lot of help you will think alot.

P.S. they are hard

a fractian has to digets when you do it you have to think if you have one lets say 1/2 and then they give you a /6 how wod you get the other diget 2 a times to get 6 and their wod be 3

To this I responded: "Keep trying to write it. It will help you get the idea clearly in mind."

In Lesson 69 we were trying to establish the difference between a region and a set. Ryan wrote this entry:

A region is if you have a box and it has 4 squares. 2 are colerd in. You would say 2/4 are colored. That is a region. A set is if you have 6 apples. You group them in twos. You step on two. You steped on 2/6 of the apples.

Next day Ryan continued by describing the region:

You have a pizza that has 6 pieces. My brother eats 4. What fraction of the pizza is left to eat.

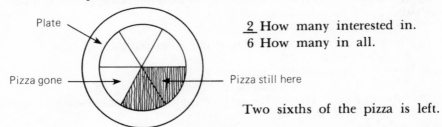

$\underline{2}$ How many interested in.
6 How many in all.

Two sixths of the pizza is left.

My comment, although superfluous, was: "Good! Terrific! Very clear and correct."

Jeff experienced trouble with the concepts for a very long time. His entry for the explanation of region and set follows my assignment:

Journal Entry: When we learn about fractions we use the words "set" and "region." Give an example of a fraction problem using a set. Give another example of a fraction problem using a region.

Jeff's entry:
A region is a regular fraction

And a set is different

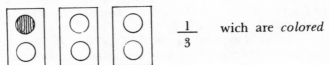

$\frac{1}{3}$ wich are *colored*

A region is like a story
there was 9 bottles of vinilla 2 got
used at a bakery.

$$\frac{2}{9}$$

On Jeff's entry I wrote: "No—not complete" and "No, bottles of vanilla are separate. They are a set. Cake and pie and pizza are regions."

cheese pizza   lemon cake   cherry pie

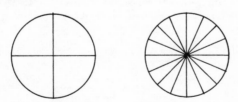

By January 7, we had moved to the concept of lowest terms.
> *Journal Entry:* "When you divide a region into the fewest pieces, you get a fraction in its lowest terms. What does it mean when I say a fraction is in its *lowest terms*?

Amanda's response:
> A fraction is in its lowest terms when, you divide Betty had a pie she said to her mother would you want 1/4 or 1/16 her mother said 1/4 she asked why she said. Take a pie divide it into 4 parts. You get bigger pieces. Now divide it into 16 pieces they are small. You get larger pieces in fewer parts.

Carrie explained her understanding of lowest terms in this way:
> A fraction is in it's lowest terms when you divied two times. And the lowest terms the lesser you will have. You can times two times and get answer and then the answer you got you can divied two time by going backwards and get lowest terms.

I wrote: "You have the right idea!" Although Carrie's response was not textbook clear, she had grasped that multiplying a fraction by a series of numbers resulted in equivalent fractions, and dividing a fraction (or "going backwards") reduced it to the lowest terms.

Comparing fraction size is very difficult for fourth graders. They can see readily which is the larger and smaller fraction when the numerator is one. But when the numerator is more than one the difficulty is increased. Here is an answer from Nikki:

> *Journal Entry:* What must you think about when you are comparing fractions to decide which is larger and which is smaller? I almost can't say it but I'll try. You need to pay close attention to your noumerator and denomonator. That's how you get your answer.

(example)
1/3 > 1/4

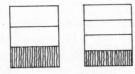

I wrote back the following message: "That works if the numerator is one. What must you watch closely here?"

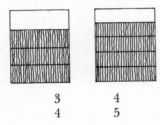

$$\frac{3}{4} \qquad \frac{4}{5}$$

In writing about comparing fractions Benji had very clear ideas and stated them with the exactness of a pro.

> 1/14 You must think about the denomentor or some times the nunater to compair fractions.
> Say yow had 1/4 and 2/8 whtch is biger the one with the smales numbers is biger I yow ask why I will tell yow if yow
> had tow squars this is how you woud compair

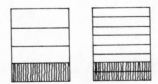

> one forth is biger becuse it has biger pices.

Benji has a problem here. He uses 1/4 > 1/7 in the illustration and does not recognize that 1/4 = 2/8 are equivalent fractions. This does not detract from his understanding of the concept but rather shows two other possibilities. Benji did not have enough experience with fractions to see the equivalent fractions when he was attending to the writing about comparing sizes. Benji has an observable problem writing down his thoughts accurately, possibly a perceptual problem of some kind. The usefulness of the math journal entry from each child each day when working with new or difficult material is that there is an opportunity to catch such potential problems immediately, and I can comment positively on the strength and clarity of the writing even when some aspects of the information miss the mark. Benji has firm grasp on the idea that fractions which have digits close to zero on the numberline have fewer and larger parts than fractions which have munerators and denominators of numbers farther away from zero. This is, after all, a basic underlying concept of fractions that often is missed by students and teacher alike. This is only one observation of how writing to learn is such a powerful heuristic.

One of the most difficult tasks in this fraction unit is to learn how to add and subtract fractions with *un*like denominators. During this time, I ask students to make journal entries according to set objectives:

Lessons 80-83 (spanning 1/20-1/31)

Objective: to add fractions having unlike denominators.

Journal Entry: Adding fractions which do *not* have the same denominators is easy, too. But you must remember the first step. Describe how you add fractions that do *not* have denominators that are alike. Give an example and tell what each number means.

Journal Entry (cont.): When adding fractions with different denominators, you must do three steps and show an example. Label the steps 1, 2, 3.

Journal Entry (cont.): Make a number story problem. Use two fractions that have different denominators. The problem must require addition or unlike fractions. Solve the problem and label the answer.

Journal Entry: Describe what you do when you add fractions with like denominators.

Objective: to subtract fractions having unlike denominators.

Journal Entry: Write a story problem for subtraction with unlike denominators. Show your work. Label the answer. Draw a picture to show your problem and solution.

Objective: to practice adding and subtracting fractions having unlike denominators.

Journal Entry: You go through four steps when you add or subtract fractions that have different denominators. Write out these four steps.

Responding

I use positive comments whenever possible. When the child's answer is wrong, I try to show the author where the answer is off track. I thank the author for the effort, then I write the correct answer on the paper. The next day at the beginning of math class I read aloud the papers that were correct and especially clear. Sometimes I comment orally and sometimes the children comment on the strengths of the answers. I return the papers to the owners, who clip each paper to the previous paper with a brad. The only record I keep is a check mark indicating that I have read and responded to the entry. I do not attempt to value the learning process with a grade.

As I repeat this process, the children begin to penetrate the fraction concepts with their questions. Their use of fraction vocabulary becomes more frequent and reliable. Very shortly, children begin to ask "what if" questions that lead directly into the next session.

Evaluations

During the first year that I used math journals for teaching fractions, I held an evaluation session. I asked the children to think about what we had studied in the fraction unit. At the beginning of the project I had told the children that we would use the journal entries to write about fractions when we completed the chapter. After the post-test had been given, we spent several days together at math time generating completions to the following:

Fractions are used for...
Fractions are used to...
Fractions are helpful when...
Fractions make life easier by...
The most important things about fractions are...

These statements were recorded on large sheets of newsprint and hung on the walls around the room.

The last writing assignment for the students was to finish the following statement: "Before we started the chapter on fractions I didn't know much about fractions. Now I know that...." They were asked to spend as long as necessary completing this statement. These papers were placed in the sorter when finished. At the end of the term I asked the children what was helpful about using journals to learn fractions. Here are some of the comments.

- Drawing them [the fraction problems] makes them a little bit better, because when you're just writing, you pay more attention, usually, to what you're writing than to how you're doing.
- On the pretest, things that I could hardly think of how to do them, are really easy now.
- One thing I like about it is when we had something to write in the journal, I'd write down what I thought about it and then I'd turn it in to you and you'd correct it and I'd look over it and I'd try to get that in my mind and I'd try to figure it out and then whenever I'd run into a problem, that I couldn't figure out, all I'd have to do is go back in my journal.
- Like what she said, on the journal writing, I looked back and I found lots of things that I didn't know and I was looking for one thing and then I found another and then another.
- I got everything out of my head that I was trying to. I showed my parents stuff about it.
- The little notes you write on our math journals help us. If you have a problem and it's urgent that we get it down and we can go back and sometimes you have what we need to know.

- When we did something wrong and you write the notes, you wanted us to go back and find out what we did wrong and understand about it.
- On the pretest, it took me a while to figure out what it meant and how to do it, but on the post test I could just look at it and know it.
- It helped me a lot. I learned a lot. On the pretest I only had 4 right and on the post test I got 24 right and it was a big difference because I learned a lot—from 4 to 24.

We observed other benefits which may have resulted from the use of writing to learn about fractions. First of all, on all the remaining pretests throughout the year, the children were able to solve the word problems for the material they had not yet studied. This may have been because they had constructed and solved so many word problems that the problem itself was no longer intimidating. Perhaps the children had learned to solve word problems more easily because they knew how to construct them.

The children showed a clear facility in using the specialized vocabulary of fractions, and they began to use the appropriate math terms in the next chapter very quickly.

When they began to study multiplication and division, many students made comparisons to the fractions concepts. For instance, they easily grasped the idea of having a partial set as a remainder in division.

The children observed that if they could write about the ideas being presented in the current chapter, they could do better learning them. This was not done because of a lack of time. Their point was well taken, however: what you write about, you understand and remember.

Although pretest and post-test scores are not the only indicators of what children have learned, the scores can be used to point to one aspect of the project's success. During the first year that we used writing to learn about fractions, the pretest scores ranged from 0 percent to 32 percent. When the post-test was scored, 32 percent of the class had scores of 96 percent to 100 percent and 44 percent of the children made scores of 71 percent to 89 percent. Only 24 percent of the children scored below 70 percent.

A year later we looked at the scores of these same children on the pretest for the first fractions chapter taught in grade five. The range of the pretest scores was 0 percent to 96 percent, with three of the children who had used journals to study fractions the previous year scoring 75 percent, 78 percent, and 96 percent. We then compared these pretest scores with the pretest scores of the class which did not use journals in the previous grade and found their pretest scores to range from 3 percent to 58 percent. The average score for the journal users on the successive year's pretest was 32 percent compared to the average pretest score of non-journal users at 24 percent.

When asked, the fifth grade teachers said that the children who used journals to learn fractions in fourth grade seemed less anxious than the other children about the fifth grade chapter on fractions and that they seemed to acquire very quickly the necessary proficiency with the fraction material. This subjective observation was confirmed when we compared the post-test data. On the post-test for the fraction chapter in grade five, previous journal users had a range of 71 percent to 100 percent, with an average score of 94 percent. Non-journal users' scores ranged from 35 percent to 100 percent with an average score of 81 percent.

Observations

Teaching with journals has become a way of life for me: I use it across the currciulum during each day throughout the school year. We begin the first day of each school year with a journal entry. The question is always the same: How do you feel about coming to fourth grade? The children date the first page of their new spiral notebook and begin what will be experience journals used daily to write about what is important in their lives. I also write. At the end of five minutes I ask, "Who would like to read what you have written?" Usually two or three hands are raised. When one reader finishes, I thank him or her; and when all have finished, I tell the children to put their journals away where they can find them easily, because we will write in them every day. So our year begins.

The journal is an integral part of the fabric of instruction and response in our class. The experience journals serve as a place to store observations about family and friends, record discoveries about life, and try out writing topics. But it is much more than that. It becomes a place where I can respond to the clarity of the author's view. My response in the journal is a private dialogue, affirming, encouraging, asking for more information. It is a way for me to keep up with the life of each of these fourth grade children in a sympathetic, understanding way. It is through the experience journal that I begin to build a repository of trust. Each comment is crafted to affirm the author and encourage more writing. By the daily use of the experience journal I am also saying that this activity has a secure place in our day and is so important that we will not let one day pass without writing. Furthermore, by responding frequently in writing to the journal entries, I say to each writer that I value your experiences and your writing about them. The experience journal becomes the foundation for all the other writing the children do in fourth grade.

For the first six weeks of the school year our writing is limited to the experience journal. We write daily at the first time of the day when all the children and I are together for an extended period of time, right after reading class. The children all arrive at school by bus. They have A.M. recess until all buses have arrived. Then I gather my class, take attendance, say the Pledge of Allegiance, and send the fourth graders off to their various reading groups. When the class reassembles, we get out our journals and write. We write for five minutes and read for ten minutes. At first the entries are only one or two lines. They are laboriously written in big manuscript or carefully formed cursive handwriting. When five minutes have passed, I invite the children to read. I ask each person who is going to read aloud to put his or her pencil away and those who are not going to read to put their journals and pencils away. I make a short comment after each reader finishes, thanking the reader for sharing.

On the surface this process appears to be straightforward. But I have observed a number of things happening concurrently. First, the author is practicing self-selection of topic. This will become the basis of author ownership in the writing workshop which will begin after the fall writing sample is taken. Second, the author is becoming accustomed to sitting still and writing for five minutes at a time. The physical conditioning is as important as the mental stimulation. As the year continues, some children write well over a page during a five-minute journal time. Third, the children become aware of writing for a fixed period of time. They learn to write on command, which is important in this setting because in school we don't always have the luxury of choosing when, where, what, why, and how we will write. In addition, the writer learns that even when he or she thought there was nothing to write about, the act of writing helps generate writing and this writing was also acceptable. The oral response to the experience journal is a model for the positive response I'll use during the writing workshop. It is also a model for responding during peer sharing.

During the first six weeks of school I make written responses to journals. I draw five names out of a pitcher each Friday. I take home these five journals and write positive comments in each one. The process continues until I have written in every journal once. After that I respond to each experience journal on request or randomly. It is especially helpful for reluctant writers to receive response; it seems to help them keep up with others who are more observant, fluent, and capable.

As the weeks slip by, we begin to do other kinds of journal writing. For instance, as we work through the first social studies unit I give topics like this one: "Tell what you understand about map scale and how map scale is used to help you understand a map." I collect these writings and use the same positive responding method I have been using in the experience journal. I respond overnight and begin the next day's lesson by reading some especially good entries and returning the entries to the owners. These are saved in the social studies folder.

In science class, we write predictions and observations. Usually I ask the children to tell me in writing what happened in an experiment and what it means. I repeat the responding procedure, and soon the children are writing longer and clearer descriptions of what they saw and did. The groundwork that was laid in the experience journal is transferred to the journal writing in social studies and science.

In early October we begin the writing workshop. I have set the tone for self-selection of topic, authentic author ownership of the writing process, peer response during the drafting phase of the writing process, author control of the writing conference, and the use of positive response during sharing of published work. All this was underlying the seemingly simple write-five-minutes, read-ten-minutes of the experience journal. The writing workshop continues throughout the year. Children write and publish many, many books in which the main idea was first generated and explored in the experience journal. From October to December we continue using experience journals daily and content journal writings as appropriate. We work through the writing process of drafting, responding, revising, responding, content conference, revising, responding, editing, responding and publishing. By December, when we are ready to tackle the traditionally traumatic task of fractions in math, we have the tools and experience to apply to that study.

So the journals have come full circle. From experience journals, through writing workshop, and to writing in the content areas. When I'm using math journals, I don't try to respond to experience journals, nor do I use written response in science, social studies, reading, or writing workshop. I rely on positive oral comments in these areas and allow for peer response where it is helpful and appropriate. Such a trade-off makes using writing to learn a manageable strategy and guarantees that we are writing every day. Writing becomes second nature to the students. We know that anything we can talk about, we can write about. And I believe that anything we can write about we have learned.

It is my task to let each learner discover the writer within. With adults it is harder because years of negative criticism may have buried that writer in us so deeply that we have lost touch with that part of ourselves. We may need an awakening experience to help us emerge as writers. But children are avid storytellers and given time and opportunity to tell their stories, they will. They are eager and humorous and love to be on stage in the spotlight. They love a private note to the teacher and revel in a personal reply. Writing is a way to channel that natural desire to be on center stage, and writing leads to significant learning.

38.

The Mathematics Workbook

STEPHEN BEMILLER

I have taught mathematics for nearly 20 years. During this time my teaching had all the desirable appearances: students rated my courses "excellent" and recommended me to their friends; colleagues complimented me after visiting class or attending one of my colloquia or workshops; and I knew that I was sincerely trying to teach effectively. Still, I was vaguely dissatisfied with my teaching, for I sensed that the accolades correlated with my proficiencies instead of with achievements by my students.

In the midst of this concern, the concepts of "teaching" and "learning" began to separate for me. To nurture this developing awareness, I embarked on studies new to me: learning theories, problem-solving, creativity, human development, interpersonal relations, psychology, and education. I learned much, and what I learned helped. I began to shift my perspectives and classroom activities from me, a professor professing, to students learning. What I still lacked was a uniform methodology that could encompass my new ideas and activities: I found that in the concept of "writing-for-learning."

Learning Mathematics

Learning theory is great; practical processes are better; but both is best. In this sense then, writing-for-learning gave me both. My evidence comes from my students' writing:

At the beginning of the semester, I thought that writing about Math...was a waste of time, but coming to the end of the semester, I feel that I have increased my skill in writing and understanding algebra. By writing about the problem, I was seeing it not only in its present state, but how I got to the goal state. Actually writing about how I got to the goal state helps me see the problem in different ways.

This journal was a pain at times, but the more I wrote and practiced the more I appreciated the opportunity to have a chance to talk about a problem and see how I did it. It helped me to think clearly and it helped me to think clearly in my other classes, not only in Math.[1]

This student, one of the first under my writing-for-learning methods refers to the collection of writings as a journal. At first I did use the collective noun *journal* to encourage a personal approach to learning and knowledge. Many of those early students, however, imposed the same barrier to learning that we can see in this excerpt: the idea of a journal conflicts with their conception of mathematics. Because my objective was not writing *per se* but rather the facilitation of learning, I replaced "journal" with "log" to encourage constant recordings of observations. Better yet, I now use the term *workbook* to emphasize that learning can result only from working—by the students.

For me, writing has become the basis for teaching in all university mathematics courses whether basic skills courses, liberal arts surveys, or upper division courses. Although I focus mostly on the processes engendered by the students' writing, the workbook also permits a product orientation because it develops into a personalized textbook. Like the formal textbooks used in these courses, a workbook contains problem solutions, expositions, examples, remarks, generalizations, exceptions, analyses, etc. Thus, in addition to all the new-fangled learning theories that writing-for-learning employs, it builds also on one of the oldest: to learn, teach. Students, in constructing this personal textbook, are comfortably teaching the concepts to themselves and to any willing friend. While writing, the student is processing concepts, as this next example records:

> This log, or book as I like to think of it as, is a completion of a semester's work in Intermediate Algebra. It is an accumulation of many long hours spent engaging in thinking, writing, reading, and understanding, as well as associating with the algebraic materials.

The workbook is central to my students' learning, but the concept of writing to improve learning is new to most students still. Consequently, I introduce the idea to my students through a progression of writing activities. On the first day, I distribute, discuss and exemplify *Workbook Suggestions*[2] that include these four items:

> *What is a workbook?* A workbook is a place to learn and to practice thinking, problem solving, and writing. In your workbook include your practice work, assigned problems, and personal observations and commentaries on your educational experiences.

> *What to include:* lots of practice work; explorations of possible solution paths to problems; formalizations of assigned problems; writing about problems, activities, concepts, and ideas; self-discussions of the courses' challenges; your feelings, moods, and experiences; arguments with the professor and others; disappointments and confusions; etc.

> *When to write:* Daily! Put at least one hour of concentrated, practice work into your workbook. Also generate extended writings in your workbook at least three times a week. Most importantly, develop the habit of using your notebook even when you are not in an academic environment. Good ideas, solution paths, questions, experiences, etc. don't always wait for convenient times for you to record them.

How to write: You should write in whatever manner you feel like writing. YOUR exploration and personality are most important. The point is to *think* and *learn* visually on paper without worrying about spelling, punctuation, structure, grammar, right answers, or the instructor's expectations. Use your personal voice; language that comes naturally to you and expresses what you want to express. *Write for yourself* (not for the instructor).

Transactional Writing

To explore this workbook concept, James Britton's distinctions among expressive, transactional, and poetic writings are useful.[3] About two-thirds of the writing in a workbook is transactional; that is, writing that informs, instructs, and generally communicates to others. I ask students to do three types of transactional assignments: (1) directed writing during class, (2) conceptual writing outside of class, and (3) mini-reports on assigned problems. The first of these, directed writing during class, are timed, written responses to prompts such as:

List the stages in problem solving that *we use* in solving word problems. As time permits, give sub-stages of each.

You have studied and tested your comprehension of concepts introduced in chapters 1 and 2. Outline your understanding of these concepts.

Explain the relationship between a linear equation and its graph.

Define "slope of a line," and explain why we can talk of *the* slope of a line.

In your own words, express the main idea about equations developed to "represent" straight lines.

Use five minutes to summarize all you know about the multiplication of polynomials.

Illustrate each of our main ideas about factoring.

The second type of transactional writing is done outside of class when the students write in order to develop their understandings of mathematical concepts. At the beginning of a course, I suggest topics for these writings; progressively during the semester I diminish the number of topics I offer; and by the end of the semester, each student generates all the topics for these writings. Here are two examples of this type of transactional writing, the first of which notes applications of a course concept:

Literal equations seem to have a great deal of relevance in a rounded college education. This is my fourth semester here and I have already used a great deal of these equations. In macro-economics, I made usage of the simple interest formula, along w/ the formulas for depreciation, discount rate, proceeds of a discounted note, amount of simple interest loan, exact simple interest,

marked price of an item and of course the demand function. I also
used some of these formulas in statistics, and may have used them
in other classes without even noticing. Anyway, they seem very
practical.

The next example of transactional writing reveals the student working
at self-instruction:

> Friday we went over the concept of coordinates. At first, this was
> confusing to me and I couldn't see a straightforward approach to
> solve the problem posed. But as the concept was explained, I noted
> two important "sub" concepts. The way in which the coordinates
> were ordered and the fact that coordinates are a unitized basis. That
> is for how many elements there needs to be in a basis that is the
> exact number of coordinate values. Also the order in which each
> vector (coordinate) is lain out determine the numerical values.... I
> believe the reason this was so hard to grasp was the fact that for
> many years, I have been conditioned to think in x, y, z terms not y,
> x, ... [student's ellipsis] Coordinates merely show that in fact the
> standard is not the only foolproof method.

The third main type of transactional writing in my classes consists
of mini-reports on designated problems. The mini-report for a problem
must clearly communicate—to the assumedly ill-informed reader—the
problem's solution(s) and related concepts. While writing is central to
this informative report, I also encourage other appropriate forms of
communication, including symbolic languages, graphic representations,
and modeling. Exhibit A is a sample mini-report; there "p.s." means
"present state",[4] or where the problem solver perceives the problem to
begin, and "g.s." means "goal state," or what the solver perceives as
required achievement.

Expressive Writing

About another third of workbook writing is expressive; that is,
writing for oneself as a means of thinking. Expressive writing is usually
informal, personal, self-expressive, talky, tentative, speculative, exploratory, digressive, and searching. (For that matter, some workbook writing
is even poetic in Britton's sense of the term.) The main idea is for the
student writer to engage her/himself in the course's concepts by com-
mitting thought to visible, written form. Thus writing encourages
processing. As one student wrote:

> I was late getting home from class today which was unfortunate. I
> like to come right home and write in my workbook. This way I
> remember what I did in class and am able to reinforce it by
> working through it in my workbook. Actually I can remember
> quite easily what I did today in class. I took a test. I really prepared
> for the exam, yet somehow it doesn't seem like it was worth it. I
> found the exam to be somewhat difficult. I had only little difficulty
> coming up with an answer for 5 of the 6 problems. I still felt it was

problem 19   page 23

Suppose two particles are moving in 3-space according to the following equations:

$$1^{st}\ \text{particle:}\quad x(t) = (-2,-3,0) + t(5,3,1)$$

$$2^{nd}\ \text{particle:}\quad x(t) = (5,-6,8) + t(-1,-3,2)$$

Here, t denotes time and $x(t)$ denotes the position of the particle at time t. Do these particles collide?

gs.   ps

Find if the particles collide.
Find a value for t s.t.
the equation of the first particle
is equal to the equation of the
2nd particle:

ie.
$$(-2,-3,0) + t(5,3,1) = (5,-6,8) + t(-1,-3,2)$$
$$(-2,-3,0) + (5t,3t,t) = (5,-6,8) + (-t,-3t,2t)\quad \substack{\text{distribute } t \\ \text{and perform vector} \\ \text{addition to both side}}$$
$$((-2+5t),(-3+3t),(t)) = (5-t, -6-3t, 8+2t)$$

$$\begin{cases} -2+5t = 5-t \\ -3+3t = -6-3t \\ t = 8+2t \end{cases} \Rightarrow \begin{cases} 6t = 7 \\ 6t = -9 \\ 3t = -8 \end{cases} \Rightarrow \begin{cases} t = 7/6 \\ t = -9/6 \\ t = -8/3 \end{cases}$$

No. | Obviously there is no $t \in \mathbb{R}$ that will satisfy all three of these last equations simultaneously. In other words, let us think of x as the first coordinate, y the second, and z the third s.t. a coordinate described in $\mathbb{R}^3 = (x,y,z)$. Now then, for the particles to meet in the x direction, $t = 7/6$. similarly, in the y direction $t = -9/6$, and finally in the z direction $t = -8/3$. Besides there being different t values for the different directions, it is curious that along the y and z axis t takes on a negative value. It is not a usual way to think of time as moving in a negative direction an hence if the t value was the same for all three and negative we might say the particles have already collided and are moving apart.

Exhibit A

difficult because I *really* had to think about the problem before I did it. I wanted to be able to look at it, and see immediately what had to be done. One of the problems I found extremely difficult. I'll try to rewrite here, but since I didn't come right home, I think I forgot some of the problem. Solve for D, $S = (n/2) [a + (n - 1)d]$ (this is close). Anyway, I had a really difficult time with this problem. I know my answer was $d = aS$, but I'll have to see if I'm right.

Notice how this writing is extending the test as a learning tool: the student is reviewing both the test and his comprehension of the related concepts. Also, the one problem that gave this intermediate algebra student particular difficulty is reconsidered. Even more learning would have occurred, of course, had this student used this opportunity to continue his work on this test problem.

In addition to academically-oriented expressive writings, many writings are even more informal and personal. I encourage these because I believe that the effectiveness of learning depends upon one's entire psychological, physiological, emotional, and social being. Personal writing often clears the mind and emotions of barriers to learning. Here is an example of such writing, produced near the end of the term:

I've sure got a lot to do. It seems as though everyone does. I didn't really procrastinate at all this semester but I've sure got a lot of "finishing up" to do. Two programs, one analysis, two homework assignments, 4 finals, and a partridge in a pear tree.

The teacher who prefers not to have personal entries can modify the workbook suggestions so that students filter out these topics.

Altogether then, the workbook consists of all mini-reports on homework assignments, all transactional and expressive writings both in and out of the classroom, class notes, and practice work. By term's end the student completes the workbook by:

1. finishing the page numbering
2. designing a cover page
3. making a Table of Contents for the ten most significant entries
4. writing an introduction
5. closing with an evaluation of the workbook's contribution to (the writer's) learning.

The table of contents, introduction, and conclusion promote reflection on learning and accomplishment. Typically a table of contents charts a student's growth, an introduction provides a retrospective overview of the course, and the conclusion offers an evaluation. Because conclusions usually focus on the effect of writing on learning, let's look at four excerpts:

Well I take back everything bad that I ever said about keeping a workbook. I even find myself defending the principles behind keeping a workbook. What I like most about my workbook is that it is an excellent source of reference. When I forget a concept I can look it up in my workbook. I usually know exactly where to look, for my workbook is a very personal thing. My workbook also shows my growth and progress in linear algebra. It shows my low points and how I over came them to hit my high points. My workbook shows me how I deal with stress and how I over act to situations. All my homework can be found in one place and in a very neat and efficient order.

It is not only a record but a learning tool in itself. By writing things down, an idea that otherwise might be lost, faded, or confused is permanently etched on something that can easily be indexed.

I think that this was a great and creative way to teach Algebra by having us use a workbook. At first it seemed rather a hard way of teaching & learning from but the more I used it, the better it became....Most classes just give you a problem & have you solve it without showing how you got the answer you did. This way I know where I messed up where I did, not that I just got a wrong answer (and then trying to remember how you did!)

This notebook has taught me the value of a clearly expressed goal state, and how writing things down is an integral part of real learning. This notebook will be added to my library of class notes but unlike the others it will probably get used. It is *my* notebook, not a copy of some instructors notes.

Propositions

Our knowledge of how we learn is, after many years and much study, still fragmentary and rudimentary; we just have not found how-it-works answers about learning. Out of my experiences however, I will risk some soft assertions about the processes whereby writing effects learning—any learning.[5]

First and most obvious, writing gives concrete form to ideas. This concreteness, for example, is the basis for redrafting a paper. When we represent our abstract ideas in visible written form, we can interact with them and consequently visualize more interrelationships and better expositions of those ideas.

Secondly, pursuing an idea through writing requires us to think in a focused way. Writing—whether expressive, transactional, or poetic—requires us to engage our thinking processes and mentally to manipulate ideas, concepts, and symbolic representations.

Third, writing demands an internal monologue on the ideas under consideration. Writing constantly requires new descriptive phrases, connectives from one idea to the next, decisions on inclusions and omissions, rank ordering of competing thoughts, etc. In contrast, "mere" thinking about a mishmash of ideas permits flitting from one to another, abandoning sticky points, avoiding decisions, and surrendering without real discussion. While writing can have these qualities of incompleteness too, visible evidence of failing encourages attention to the task of learning.

Fourth, writing out thoughts allows us to move beyond the more trivial and immediate ideas in order to consider the more complex, novel, and subconscious ones.

Fifth, writing in a workbook throughout a term allows the student to more accurately measure (1) what she knows and doesn't know, (2) how much effort she put into learning, (3) how much she has developed during the course, and (4) where her learning difficulties are. Given this concrete evidence of studying and understanding, the student can't easily misread herself. Furthermore, I, as a final evaluator, have a powerful means of monitoring both academic progress and personal growth throughout the course of study.

Finally, writing is truly individualized instruction. In its expressive forms writing allows every student to explore, discover, connect, translate, and personalize knowledge. Most critically, this processing in the classroom goes on in all students simultaneously. Rather than listening to few students' verbal answers, all students are engaged at once in writing. What more could a teacher want: individualized instruction on the group level.

Notes

[1] It will be clear to readers which set-off selections are written entries taken from my students' workbooks. As with most teachers, I am uneasy about showing my students' work lest I, like Aristotle, be known chiefly through the perceptions of my students. Still, I present these writings unedited because we are interested in students and their writing.

[2] Workbook suggestions are adapted from a handout Toby Fulwiler shared during his workshop on "Writing Across the Disciplines" at CSU Chico, January 1983.

[3] Britton, J., et al. (1975). *The development of writing abilities, 11-18.* London: Macmillan.

[4] Adapted from Rubinstein, M. F. (1975). *Patterns of problem solving.* Englewood Cliffs, NJ: Prentice-Hall.

[5] My knowledge is towards the incomplete end of Edward de Bono's continuum of understanding presented in *Practical thinking: 4 ways to be right, 5 ways to be wrong, 5 ways to understand.* London: Jonathan Cape, 1971. For a high level understanding, consult, for example, Janet Emig's Writing as a mode of learning in *College Composition and Communication,* v.28(1977), pp. 122-128.

39.

Academic Journals and the Sociological Imagination

HENRY ALLEN and LYNN FAUTH

Many undergraduates consider sociology a mysterious enterprise. For students who mistake it for a more sophisticated version of social work, its abstract theories, esoteric terminology, and multiple methodologies seem pedantic, irrelevant, or intimidating. Many students ignore sociology altogether because they feel that they are already experts in it by virtue of having lived as social beings. To counter these naive predilections, we sociologists must communicate to our students the distinctive spirit of the sociological perspective. Because each of us has had different mentors, however, each of us is likely to communicate somewhat differently. Hence, in teaching undergraduates, usually freshmen and sophomores, our primary goal as sociologists should be to encourage students to perceive the spirit as well as to understand the content of sociology—to stimulate them to develop, as far as possible, the capacity to perceive life sociologically—to develop what is called the sociological imagination.

Rationale for Using Journals in Sociology Classes

C. Wright Mills in his classic treatise about the discipline defines the sociological imagination as "a quality of mind" which enables its possessors "to use information and to develop reason in order to achieve lucid summations of what is going on in the world and of what may be happening within themselves" (*The Sociological Imagination* [New York: Oxford, 1959], p. 5). Mills argues that an individual, to cultivate this imagination, must comprehend the history of society, his or her personal biography, and the interrelationship between these and the social structures of society (pp.6-8). In sociological parlance, Mills seeks to develop in students a critical awareness so that they can shift from macrosociological abstractions to microsociological reality, and vice versa, as well as to develop their intellectual capacity to integrate these within the historical and biographical parameters of human life; the sociological imagination enables its possessor to distinguish between private troubles and the transcendent issues facing society (pp. 8-13). For example, students must discriminate between the individualistic causes of poverty and the institutional or structural factors beyond anyone's personal control which promote its continuance in society. Significantly,

Mills recommends that students undertake a writing project, notably a file or journal, to accumulate and record the ideas and materials necessary for developing and sustaining their sociological imaginations (pp. 195-226). Mills' recommendation is remarkably similar in its design to the academic journal used in many classes and discussed in the pages of this book.

Mills' basic ideas about the sociological imagination have not contributed new perspectives about sociology, but they might stimulate the adoption of the academic journal as an indispensible requirement in sociology courses concerned with developing the sociological imagination. Since students often enter sociology classes with a naive disdain for history or without ever having attempted a sociological analysis of their personal lives and experiences, the journal is a powerful tool to help them develop and use writing skills to evaluate their and others' opinions and theories about sociological issues, to define and comprehend the discipline's terminology, and to assess the impact or relevance of sociology upon their lives. Moreoever, periodic assignment of specific entry-generating questions assures that students will grapple with how society's past has influenced its present and how ancient social patterns are likely to affect society's future—for example, in a course on race relations, students might be required to compare and contrast a militant native American's view of patriotism with that of an assimilationist native American; they could be asked to construct plausible arguments derived from their consideration of what they have learned about the historical and contemporary sociological experiences of this ethnic group.

Mills' insights encourage the use of journals to teach sociology in a second way: they emphasize the significance of helping students to distinguish between private social conflicts and major social issues. In the two sociology courses in which the journal has proven especially useful and enlightening, Race and Ethnic Relations and Poverty and Social Class, students repeatedly have experienced difficulty making distinctions between their private social conflicts and the major social issues of society. Scrutinizing journal entries helps teachers monitor their students' progress from viewing poverty and racism as private concerns to seeing them as institutionalized entities; whenever problems are detected, incisive teacher comments or confutative questions can challenge the students to look beyond their often immature intellectual provincialisms. For instance, if a particular student cannot seem to comprehend that poverty is not exclusively the result of individual laziness, he or she might be encouraged to read Michael Harrington's *The Other America* or William Ryan's *Blaming the Victim* and then write a journal entry from the viewpoint of a poor person who daily lives under the desperate social circumstances these authors depict. Usually such an assignment has a sobering and lasting impact upon such a student; it helps, moreover, to begin the process of development within each student, toward that desired sociological imagination.

Requirements

With such objectives in mind, our first explanations of the role of the journal in class stress that students are allowed to exercise maximum creativity in their journals—there are no "right responses" to questions. They are required to write at least two entries of 100 words or more per week of class; these can be about the course (reactions to lectures, textbooks, films, guests, and other materials), personal biographies, or current academic and collegiate issues that relate to the course or even to idiosyncrasies of the instructor's personality. Surprisingly, the majority of students relish the journal experience and continually exceed length expectations for the project. Although journals rarely count for more than 20 percent of their grade, many students routinely complete daily entries of two or more pages, and include poems, magazine and newspaper clippings, pictures, and artistic entries. Indeed, the astuteness and honesty of students who use their sociology journals to examine current events, family problems, campus affairs, and even dating fiascos surpasses all expectations.

Types

To encourage students to develop the sociological imagination, we try to stimulate at least four types of journal entries during the course of the term: first, they should react to teacher statements, to assertions in their textbooks, or to assigned questions. Second, they should mature from reaction to elementary "sociological" analysis in which they attempt to integrate concepts from their texts with instructor lectures, other readings and personal observations. Third, their writing should develop from elementary analyses to reflective entries, in which they ponder the issues they have confronted and attempt to determine the importance or relevance of certain sociological insights. And fourth, they should move to a synthesis in which they become entry-level sociologists, attempting to temper their reactions, develop their elementary analyses and to consider their reflections on the issues using the terms, insights and methodologies acquired from the readings, lectures and oral and written discussions of the issues confronted. Through the journal-writing process we would like them to eliminate their simplistic notions about society and to develop a multi-dimensional perspective of life.

What the journal does so well is make them move from an external, abstract view of sociology—something the sociologist does—to something that is, for the student, a new way of seeing—something that "I can do too." And, the sociological imagination developed through the students' journal writings affords them new ways of looking at themselves and their society and leads them to a new relevance: they are forced to use sociological perspectives to consider, understand and analyze issues and events in light of how social groups influence networks of social interaction.

Examples and Analysis

The earliest type of journal entry most students complete is a reaction; they react to a term, a concept, an instructor's comment, or something they have read in the textbook or other assigned readings. The objective of this assignment is to get the student active and to consider something, be it an issue, or a personal response to the instructor's mannerisms. Students are asked to consider and, we hope, to dispel their preconceived notions in these reactive entries.

In this unsolicited reaction written on the first day of class, the student attempts to come to grips with her notions of poverty, as a big thing beyond her:

> Poverty. The very word gives me a feeling of hopelessness. I'm not sure why. It could be because I'm empathizing with those in poverty, or it could be because the problem is an overwhelming one in my own eyes that seems insurmountable. I tend to think the latter is the case. What can I, one small person, do about poverty? Should I jump into the problem with both feet? Or should I give my emotions a break and visualize poverty as something distant from my own experience and place of habitation?

Like the poor people she will be studying in the Poverty and Social Class course, this student writer has begun to see that poverty is beyond the person, that people might be poor through some overwhelming forces outside of themselves. She takes a private trouble and begins to see it in terms of a societal problem—she's not aware yet that most poverty is institutional, but she senses that it is more than a private matter. Her reaction to the term *poverty* stimulates her intellectual discontent and causes a felt disharmony, both necessary to produce the sociological imagination.

In another unsolicited reaction, this time to an assigned book, Michael Harrington's *The Other America*, a student moves beyond a merely prefunctory reading of the text toward an understanding of the multi-dimensional aspects of poverty:

> Harrington's position on poverty is a wholistic view; showing that poverty is a product of both the individual and structural factors which together contribute to the poors condition. After reading his book I have realized this to be the case. Prior to our class work, while I never believed the poor could actually become wealthy off of welfare, I more/less thought it gave them sufficient funds to get by—if they used their money wisely. Harrington has taught me that providing *some* money is not the answer to *our* dilemma. Rather, welfare, as it exists today, only delays the time to come when we will have to deal with poverty.

Through the expressive writing in her journal entry, this student moves from merely reacting to two abstractions—poverty and welfare—to the observation that the problem, and its assumed cure, are more complex than she had previously thought.

As the student demonstrates in her final sentence, students not only react but they also attempt rudimentary sociological analysis in their journals. After they are given terms and introduced to the theoretical perspectives these terms encompass, students attempt to analyze their own lives and social interrelationships in light of what these perspectives reveal. One student writes:

> From class I've discovered that I tend to have a cultural perspective of poverty. Is that good or bad? I guess I'm guilty of assuming that

adults are less human than children. That's not true! The impoverished are *not* different than the well-off. They have the same
emotions, values and dreams of any human being. None of this
ceases to be at 21. Therefore adults and children both are victims of
poverty.

Still, there is some validity in giving impoverished children
special attention. The accounts of Naye and Willie still stand out
in my mind. I only wonder where they are now. Are they still in
poverty?

I'm struggling to develop a clear, realistic perspective on poverty.
It doesn't work to put a bandaid on a gaping wound.

In this entry, the student discovers she has assumed a cultural
perspective of poverty—that the poor are poor because they come from a
deviant culture which is transmitted across generations. In her primitive
analysis, she is empowered somewhat by her use of insights gained
through sociology—e.g., that the cultural perspective one has when she
views poverty affects her understanding of it. Her struggle to develop a
"clear, realistic perspective on poverty" is a task that will be accomplished as she acquires the sociological terms, insights, and theories to
help her comprehend what she sees and to articulate what she feels.

And once the student is able to comprehend and articulate, she is
well on her way to developing reflective journal entries. In the following
journal entry a student begins to analyze directly a situation in her social
world and reflects on the ramifications of something as seemingly
innocuous as a high school basketball game:

I am appalled...I heard a cheer that is being used by a private
prep school...at this time. It is so racist, I can hardly believe the
students are allowed to use it. It goes as follows:

That's all right, that's okay!
You will work for *us* someday.

They say this cheer when they play city teams. I can't believe that
the administration of this school allows its students to degrade
others in this way. If I were on the receiving end of this cheer, as a
player or a fan, I'd be furious and want to lash out at the users of
the cheer. It would hurt me deeply and then that hurt would turn
to anger.

The cheer *assumes* ranking and position of people from the city
with no thought of city people being above the prep school.

No wonder prejudice is so widespread. Kids think it's fun and
cute to tear peoples' self-esteem apart! What a sick society.

From this unsolicited entry in her journal we can see a student who
uses her sociological imagination to apply sociological perspectives to a
"typical" social situation—a basketball game. Perhaps for the first time
she sees that a game is more than just a recreational event—it's a social
event, fraught with class struggle and class awareness. She is sensitized;
it is as if the scales of ethnocentrism have fallen from her eyes. For the
first time sociological concepts—racism, prejudice, social stratification,
city versus suburban status groups—have personal significance. She has
internalized abstract concepts and now sees the situation from the

viewpoint of an oppressed minority; she sees the situation from outside herself...indeed, she grapples with the dynamics of social life.

The journal entry expresses her consideration and application of textbook concepts to everyday life events. No longer are sociological concepts mere textbook abstractions: they have become experiential realities—each concept adds a further layer of meaning to the event, and her evolving sociological imagination enables her to perceive much more to life than she had before her experience in her Race and Ethnic Relations Class.

In a related entry, this time responding to her instructor's prompting following his reading of the "you will work for us someday" entry, the student reflects further on her intellectual quest to understand race relations. Prompted by the question, "How has my thinking about race and ethnic relations developed during this semester?" she responds:

I came into this class thinking that I knew a little bit about Italians, Native Americans and blacks, and I am going away seeing how very little I really knew.

The doors of knowledge and information have been opened for me, but I long to know so much more. I want to be around more of a mixed ethnic community. I want to learn, experience and suffer, if I have to, in order to understand better.

I struggle with my own prejudices...*deeply*. I will continue to struggle.

I want to have more ethnic experiences! I want to teach others. I want to keep learning, *most of all*....I'm scared!

Here is a student who has a thirst for knowledge. She's gained knowledge that helps her to understand life and she has come to understand how much more she needs to know. What the entry reveals is the type of attitude necessary to prevent ethnocentrism. And significantly, from a sociologist's perspective, she wants to move from a comfortable homogeneous environment to one of more ethnic/racial diversity. For a student in a lower division sociology course in an ethnically homogeneous college, this is a momentous achievement. Likewise, her reflection on her own prejudices indicates a maturing sociological imagination.

In another example of a response to the question, "How has my thinking about race and ethnic relations developed during this semester?" a different student responds on a less personal but more analytical level:

...ethnic groups cannot be compared and put on a level where they are all together. It is not beneficial to group them all together as one, in an attempt to assimilate or understand all of them. Instead each group has their own heritage, background and responses to the dominant group. This is extremely important in trying to learn about other cultures and their ideas...It is not usually recognized that each group can be so different. It is possible to compare them according to their similarities and their differences. By doing this you can really see how extremely special each group becomes. This means that each group should be treated special, and others should be aware of their backgrounds.

In this sample, the student recognizes two central sociological issues: that ethnic groups have fundamentally distinct sociological experiences; and that it is not desirable to give ethnic groups identical treatment. To recognize the fundamental differences between ethnic group experiences is important, sociologically, because it goes against the Horatio Alger myth and refutes the incipient racial ideology students bring with them to class, as exemplified by the statement, "Why can't 'those people' be like us?" Likewise, the student has recognized that it is poor sociology to treat all ethnic groups as if they are the same. Each ethnic group needs to be understood and appreciated from its own perspective and merits, not on how it conforms to the dominant culture. In this example, the journal entry reveals how much sociology the student has learned in one semester, a telling example of the journal's usefulness in developing the sociological imagination and in the teaching of sociological concepts.

In the final example, a student synthesizes her knowledge in order to come to grips with a fundamental irony of the American economic/political system's inability to eradicate poverty.

Poverty is a national problem & thus needs national intervention. That thought/concept sticks in my mind from Monday's discussion. Why doesn't this happen? Because our nation is decentralized politically. Is that frustrating? To me it is! It seems like the potential solution to the problem is dead because the federal government's hands are tied. They can dole out the money, but they have little control over how the money's used. That's the state's responsibility.

Even though the U.S. is decentralized politically, it is centralized economically. That creates a lot of problems, doesn't it? I'm not an economist or political scientist, but if one element of society is structured oppositely of another, a tension is certain to result.

This example demonstrates a student's mind at work, synthesizing what she has learned with what she feels. She tries, in this unsolicited entry, to grasp the complexities of poverty as a social problem and sees that even the nation's social structure inhibits a solution to poverty; these structures operate to make solutions problematic, as her second paragraph suggests. Her entry is illustrative of the essence of the sociological imagination which enables its possessors to discover such problematic ironies in social life.

Applications and Unexpected Outcomes

These journal entries illustrate what is being done to make sociology accessible to disinterested and skeptical undergraduates at a homogeneous upper-middle-class religiously-oriented liberal arts college. Through journals, as Mills encouraged, the sociological imagination is being developed and, in turn, better sociology students result. In fact, in partial response to the successful journal experiences of many students, some take additional sociology courses—some even continue keeping their journals. An additional benefit to the use of journals, one not wholly expected, is that the journal has improved pedagogy in at least three ways.

First, the journal allows teachers to determine overall teaching effectiveness. By canvassing entries, we are able to determine where and how we might clarify or adjust aspects of our lectures or other assignments to facilitate our students' comprehension of course materials. Second, the journal helps us go beyond the usual superficial level of instructor-student communication. All of the entries cited above precipitated teacher comments, questions, and calls for clarifications. Through the journal we get to know our students' personalities, experiences, struggles and accomplishments. Third, as anyone who reads this chapter will attest, the quality of writing in the journals is remarkably good; it is relatively free of the usual grammatical and syntactical errors most teachers lament. Somehow, it seems, when students are left free to develop and consider their own ideas and responses to issues of significance to them, without the spectre of a teacher with a proof-reading agenda in mind hovering over them, grade book and red pencil in hand, students ease up and their writing is coherent, incisive, and relatively error free. And fourth, the quality of classroom discussion, of other writing assignments, particularly essay exam responses and research papers, is improved—no doubt due to the extra amount of writing that is done in the journal.

Journal entries are excellent bases for class discussions because students seem to be more willing to talk about ideas they have written on prior to or during class. Moreover, other writing assignments improve because the journal forces students to write more frequently and extensively than they might otherwise choose to do.

Using journals in sociology classes increases important aspects of the sociologist's teaching of the discipline. Students' sociological imaginations are developed. They learn and apply textbook concepts to real-life situations. And, they take more sociology courses. In addition, not only do students learn more sociology, but their teachers learn more about them and are able to adjust their course presentations to meet student needs.

40.

Journals and Political Science*

DAVID BRODSKY and EILEEN MEAGHER

Initially, I used journals with the hope that I could help students improve their writing skills by giving them numerous opportunities to write in what I saw as a relatively unthreatening context. Students defined when and how they would write and what they would write about. They also knew that I would grade neither the individual entries nor the entire journal. Instead, I would communicate with them through responses to what they had written. The journals had only to meet a few requirements: first, that students make at least three entries a week, showing the date and time of each entry; second, that the entries relate in some way to the subject matter of the course; and finally, that the entries be as long as possible. I made no specific assignments which required students to prepare a written response in their journals. In sum then, I initially treated the journals as an adjunct to, rather than an integral part of, the courses where I required them.

When I asked students in these first classes to tell me what they thought about journals and their effectiveness, I received widely divergent responses. However, all the students, whether they liked the journals or not, agreed on one thing—that the journals seemed like busywork rather than a "serious" part of the course requirements.

Integrating Journals

I altered the fit between journals and other class activities in several ways. First, I assigned a specific share of the overall course grade (initially from 10 to 25 percent and later up to 75 percent) to the journals. Second, I started to use the journals in ways I hoped would either facilitate class discussions, encourage students to keep up with assigned readings, enable students to master the subject matter covered in the course, or lead students to apply what they learned in class to specific situations. Third, I required students to complete specific assignments in addition to allowing them the freedom to include journal entries of their own choosing. And finally, I shifted to a system of frequent (at least biweekly) review and grading in order to encourage students to keep their journals current and to impress upon them the importance I attached to their journals.

*In this collaborative effort, Dr. Meagher, after reading a substantial number of student journals and after several weekly consultations with Dr. Brodsky, developed a chapter outline. Dr. Brodsky used the outline to order and develop his experiences, and Dr. Meagher wrote the section, "Do Journals Improve Writing?"

I used a number of techniques to achieve my purposes, techniques related to the form I wanted the journals to follow, to the types of assignments required of students and to the criteria used in grading the finished product. At the start of each class I distributed a mimeographed handout (See Figure A) which discussed in detail the form I wanted the journals to take, the specific requirements students would have to fulfill and the minimum number of entries required for a given grade. The handout also offered suggestions about when, where and how to write in the journal.

Figure A

GUIDELINES FOR USING JOURNALS*

A. *What is a journal?*
   A place to practice personal writing; a place to work out ideas and concepts discussed in class or in assigned readings; an individual record of your experiences during a class.

B. *What should I write?*
   - personal reactions to class, students, teachers
   - informal jottings, notes, clippings
   - explorations of ideas, theories, concepts, problems, discussion topics
   - reactions to readings, TV, events, people reflecting public policy questions
   - whatever you want to explore or remember
   - specific journal assignments made in class or given as homework
   - an evaluation of each week's classes reviewing what you learned (or did not learn), problem areas, etc.

C. *When should I write?*
   - three to four times a week
   - any time; early in the morning, and late at night
   - when you have problems to solve, decisions to make, confusions to clarify
   - when you need to practice or try something out

D. *How should I write?*
   - however you feel like it
   - don't worry about formal language conventions, including spelling, punctuation and grammar.
   - take risks
   - freely

E. *Specific requirements*
   - Purchase an 8½ × 11" looseleaf notebook.
   - Date each entry (include the time at which you are writing).
   - Write long entries as often as possible to help develop ideas fully.

*The content of this handout borrows heavily from materials distributed at a four-day workshop conducted by Toby Fulwiler at UTC in May 1983.

- Make lots of entries; quantity is the best measure of a good journal.
- Use a pen (pencils smear).
- Index at the end of the term; include page numbers and table of contents for significant entries.
- *Do not* include class notes in your journal; however, you may include your reactions to classes and class discussion.
- Clearly label and number each entry as an in-class assignment, an out of class assignment, or an extra assignment.

F. *Grading*

Your journal grade will be based on two components—one quantitative and one qualitative. The *quantitative* component will be assigned on the following basis:

D All requirements noted in E above
  At least 16 in-class journal assignments
  At least 16 out-of-class journal assignments
  At least 25 entries in addition to specific assignments
C All requirements noted in E above
  At least 20 in-class journal assignments
  At least 20 out-of-class journal assignments
  At least 29 entries in addition to specific assignments
B All requirements noted in E above
  At least 22 in-class journal assignments
  At least 22 out-of-class journal assignments
  At least 34 entries in addition to specific assignments
A All requirements noted in E above
  At least 28 in-class journal assignments
  At least 28 out-of-class journal assignments
  At least 42 entries in addition to specific assignments

A quantitative grade will be assigned each time the journal is collected. These grades will be used to adjust your final quantitative grade. The *qualitative* component will be assigned on the basis of such factors as the quality of each entry, the relationship of the entries to the objectives of this course, and the cognitive and analytical skills reflected. I will then assign a *qualitative* grade for each submission. I will deduct one letter grade for each day your journal is late.

In-Class Journal Assignments. The mix of journal assignments required during any given course pursued specific objectives including "encouraging" students to keep up with their reading assignments, improving the quality of class discussions, promoting the mastery of course content and providing opportunities to "use" the knowledge gained in some practical application. In-class journal assignments made at the start of class served to orient the students to the subject matter I would cover during the class or to monitor whether or not they had completed the assigned readings. If I had doubts about whether or not the students had kept abreast of the readings, I would collect the day's entries, review them, assign a grade and return them at the next class meeting. In-class assignments made at the end of the period afforded students an opportunity to reformulate in their own words one or more aspects of the material covered during the class or to apply these materials to a specific problem. For example, following a lecture focusing on the importance of problem definitions in formulating public policies, I might give students a set of facts concerning pay inequities among various classes of faculty at a university and ask them to prepare a brief problem statement. The class would then have an opportunity to discuss the various problem statements developed and to consider the policies which might flow from each statement. The assignments at the end of class also served as a place where students could lay the groundwork for another assignment or for the next class.

Out-of-Class Journal Assignments. Out-of-class journal assignments supplemented those given in class and pointed toward several objectives. First, many of these assignments asked students to list or discuss the key points raised in one or more of the assigned readings. Consequently, they put a great deal of pressure on students to keep current, and they also contributed to more informed student participation when the class discussed new materials. Second, the out-of-class assignments frequently required students to apply concepts or techniques presented in class or in the assigned readings. Thus, an assignment following a class discussion of various criteria used in evaluating public policies directed students to identify the values implicit in proposals to allow physicians, with the patient's informed consent, to forego "heroic measures" to sustain life. And finally, the out-of-class journal assignments provided opportunities for students to evaluate the work of political scientists. For example, students in research methods class had to assess the fit between the conceptual and operational definitions used in an article focusing on ethos theory and voting behavior in local referenda.

Extra Entries. The third type of journal assignment, extra entries, depended on student initiative. Although I required students to complete at least three of these extra entries each week, I imposed only two restrictions on their form or content: that the content of the entry fit the subject matter of the course and that the student provide a written statement which showed this connection. The search for these extra entries led students to such sources as national newspapers and news magazines, professional journals and texts used in other classes, and included such topics as the questions used in a *CBS News-New York Times* poll, reactions to a television show on child abuse, or reliability and validity. In all cases, the extra entries provided me with an opportunity to assess student progress, to identify problem areas and to offer suggestions or encouragement.

Class Evaluations. I also required students to provide a written evaluation of each week's classes. The instructions asked students to avoid recitation of what had transpired in class and instead asked them to focus on what they had learned, what materials they felt unsure about and what areas they would like me to repeat or supplement. The evaluations also included reactions to specific topics raised in class including such things as the widely disparate spending on health care in the Western industrial democracies and the apparent lack of correlation between the amount of money spent and the quality of health as measured by such indicators as life expectancy and infant mortality.

Grading. I used three criteria in assigning grades to the student journals. First, any journal which failed to meet the format requirements set forth in the syllabus automatically received a failing grade. Second, each letter grade required a minimum number of in-class, out-of-class and extra entries, a *quantiative grade.* And finally, each journal received a *qualitative grade* based on my assessment of the effort put forth by the students and their mastery of the course content. Thus, a student with a quality grade of *A* might only receive a journal grade of *B* if his or her journal failed to meet the minimum quantitative requirements for an *A*.

When I first started using journals, I chose to graft them onto the existing course requirements rather than to revise these requirements to incorporate the journals. As I became more comfortable with journals and as I acquired the benefit of student evaluations and my own experience, I began to build journals into the basic structure of the courses where I wanted to use them. More importantly, I began to assign a greater share of the overall course grade to the journals.

Do Journals Improve Writing?

The use of the journal improves student writing if the instructor has made clear to himself and to the class the objectives of the course, if assignments are carefully and sequentially planned, and if the instructor monitors journal use.

Getting at Meaning

Expressive writing or exploratory writing dominates the journals. Expressive writing helps students to get at meaning, to raise questions, and to clarify their own thinking. In responding to a poll on the gender gap in *USA Today*, one student clarified the issues for herself in the following manner. (This and all subsequent quotations from student journals are copied verbatim.):

> This looks like a pretty extensive survey. The article doesn't say how many women Wirthlin [the pollster] interviewed, but it says he broke them down into 42 categories. That's a lot of categories. I suppose they were based mainly on demographic factors but their had to be more than just that to get 42. At least, that's what I would think. Did he put them in categories before he interviewed them or was that the breakdown of his analysis—as he was analyzing the collected data of the whole? Wirthlin says he found 22 reasons why Reagan does less well with women than with men. Wouldn't he have to interview some men too before he could draw that conclusion? Does this have something to do with validity?

Here we see a student initially impressed by the survey but needing to ask a question or two about the pollster's methods. Having done that, she proceeds to discover a basic flaw in the polling technique and subsequently questions quite properly the validity of Wirthlin's findings.

Revealing the Student's Voice

The journals of these students make for interesting reading because the expressive writing releases the students' own voices. In the effort to analyze concepts, to explore subjects, to articulate problems, the students are using their own language. As a result, one hears the voice of each student as he or she reacts to readings and offers opinions. The writing is lively; gone is the stiff writing that is an attempted facsimile of textbook language. As students move through the journal, they develop language fluency and their voice becomes clearer and unencumbered with jargon. The journals are, in fact, remarkably free of jargon. The students are so involved with the material that they make it their own and test it by applying it to hypothetical or real events and situations.

Audience Awareness

Through the journal, students revealed their awareness of an audience or of readers in several ways: they wrote explanatory notes in the margin to make a pronoun reference clear; they indulged in metadiscourse at the beginning of entries in order to explain to themselves and to the reader what it is they were about; and very often they consciously addressed the instructor by asking questions, by making witty remarks, and by writing so passionately about a particular social issue that they invited an automatic response. One student was so inflamed by a piece of research on birth control pills that her journal entry took the form of an outraged letter to her instructor. She questioned the morality of the methods used by the researchers and declared:

> They were not doing research—they were tampering with people's lives...the decision to bring a new life into this world is probably the most important decision that a human being has to make. As such, it should be made solely by the individual—not by a bunch of mad scientists.

She was face to face with the grey areas of ethical research for the first time. Subsequently her journal entries tended to focus on the ethics of respective methodologies.

The journals gave evidence of minds alertly at work, analyzing, sorting, evaluating, and creating—until toward the end of the journals it was clear that the students were saturated with political-science thinking. Many of them testified in their final entries that the world would never seem the same to them again. The following comment is typical of the assessments made of the journal: "I've learned that in 22 years I had never really sat down and determined what my own personal opinions are on public issues...."

Sentence Structures

Complex Syntax. Because the students were asked to perform four different intellectual acts with each task—define, report, analyze, and interpret—they necessarily found themselves using complex sentence patterns. For some students, this was more difficult at first and became less difficult as the semester wore on. One student admitted early on: "I don't feel like I know enough about it. I'm not even sure just yet what to look for. I guess you know by now that I have to ease into these things slowly. I must be a late bloomer." Her first attempts at complex thinking resulted in sentence patterns and syntax that were somewhat garbled. For example, she wrote:

> If you asked demographic questions at the beginning, as opposed to the end, it will probably turn the respondent off because they feel you are just being nosy. Especially with questions on age and income.

Yet only a month later, she wrote the following paragraph:

> The biggest problem is the fact that people not interviewed cannot be depended upon to return the cards, and those who do return them are not representative of the sample. Therefore, it is impossible to accurately detect falsified interviews.

Transitions. The more students used expressive writing to solve problems and to establish relationships between ideas, the more adept they became at using appropriate transitions. Expressive writing helped them to see the precise nature of the connections between ideas, and the nature of the assignment—define, report, analyze, evaluate—nicely determined the internal order and flow of answers. Where students neglected to follow the four steps above, there usually resulted an overly long and circuitous paragraph with a hodgepodge of assertions and little internal logic. When students were truly engaged in making sense out of a survey or report, their ideas were stated early, were backed up with examples, and were related to one another. But when the assignment was to summarize a chapter, many students took the easy way out by using the author's language. Consequently there were no transitions or they were forced and unnatural. Student writing was at its clearest and best when the assignment forced students to analyze rather than to recapitulate.

Minimizing the Passive Voice. One of the most obvious characteristics of expressive writing in the journals was the clear statement of subjects and the corollary—minimum use of the passive voice. In fact, one has to search hard to find instances of the passive form of verbs. Perhaps because political science by its very nature is about forming opinions, there is a built-in tendency to name subjects clearly and to express ideas without equivocation. When students are grappling sincerely to get at meaning, there is little room for the passive.

Because students were told that mechanical problems such as spelling and punctuation and grammar problems such as subject-verb agreement and the like would not hurt their journal grades, they seemed to write much more freely and fluently. One student stated succinctly—though passively—her understanding of the journal:

> Since the purpose of the journal was to encourage personal observation, thought, and correspondence with the professor, the entries were written in an informal "thinking on paper" style with frequent dialogue type statements and little consideration of correct spelling or grammatical rules.

This particular student engaged herself so much with the material, that her grammar infractions were few and superficial.

A couple of students didn't take the journal seriously and as a result their work showed a minimum of thought, considerable strained syntax, and a host of mechanical errors. The obvious lesson here is that if students are going to enter into the journal process, they must be motivated to learn and to think, and to grapple with issues until they make sense. If students don't accept that challenge, learning will not take place and of course writing will not improve.

Do Journals Facilitate Learning?

Application

Journals contribute to student performance in a number of ways. First, journal assignments often provide students with opportunities to apply the lessons learned in class to actual situations. For example, students in a research methods class had to read and react to an article which discussed problems with the federal government's efforts to measure the levels of criminal activity. According to one student:

> Data gathering, in this case, shows obvious inconsistencies in methods of gathering info. Because the police department's records are "in house" types of data gathering, some loss of objectivity can occur if one's job is on the line. I think this report proves that data gathering techniques almost always aren't as objective as they appear, which may alter the way the info is interpreted.

Analysis and Understanding

Journals often provide students with a place where they can develop their analytical capabilities and their understanding of key concepts. In classes which include an examination of public policies and the policy making process, students often have trouble understanding policy making as a process involving a number of decisions over a period of time and a series of stages from problems to definition to implementation. The following journal entry shows how a student in a senior level class on American public policy used his journal to work through the policy as process model:

> Policy can't *really* be defined as such until the *implementation* stage—the bridge between what the government says it's going to do and what it actually does. You can't, for instance, really call the "separate but equal" segregation stance in this country after *Plessy v. Ferguson policy* because the "equal" part of the deal was never implemented.

Although students may grasp such concepts as political feasibility or political culture, they often have problems applying these constructs to actual situations. Journals afford them the opportunity to do so. For example, a political science major in a comparative public policy class made the following assessment of the chances of the United States opting for a nationalized health care system:

I feel that it would be almost totally impossible for the United States to convert to a nationalized health care system. First, the people would reject it prior to even hearing any of the details or anything it seeks to accomplish. Most people are against strong government control. Yet it would bring down medical cost substantially and reduce the amount of competition among doctors.

Questions

Students frequently use journals to ask questions that any number of factors may prevent them from asking in class. Following a discussion of various flat tax proposals a student used his journal to ask:

My question is, wouldn't a flat tax *inevitably* end up becoming as complex as the one we have now as this marginal utility difference would have to take into account differences between, say, two corporations which make the same income but have quite different numbers of employees?

This question prompted a written response in his journal and some additional discussion of the problems likely to confront those pursuing tax simplification.

Self-Teaching

Journals also make it possible for students to teach themselves. The following journal entry from a student taking a research methods class shows how she used her journal to make a connection between her own experiences as an interviewer working for a survey reseach firm and the ethical questions surrounding deception in research:

I am not sure if I feel it (deception) is appropriate but I do feel that it is necessary at times to obtain a "true" survey. I do feel that if the deception is carried too far it will affect the validity of the survey. It can also be harmful to the participants. Blind deception of the actual surveyor is often, if not usually, necessary to keep it from being biased by his judgement. For example, when I have surveyed in the past for a particular study, I was not told for whom the survey was being conducted (even though it is often easy to determine who) to avoid my view from jading how the questions should be answered.

Self-teaching also takes place when students begin to make connections between the concepts advanced by different authors or when the need to write an extra journal entry forces them to consider a topic or issue new to them. The following entry illustrates this form of self-teaching:

Fuchs and Mcrae and Wilde seem to agree pretty much on the basic elements of the market system (supply and demand and their scarcity). Whereas Fuchs looks at the market system from an individualist viewpoint (*scarcity* forces individuals to make choices), Mcrae and Wilde look at it from a *system* approach (*efficiency* defined as the proximity the gov't gets in allocating resources—to satisfying consumers' and producers' preferences).

Reactions

The opportunity to react without fear or censure appears to facilitate learning by helping students to sort out their thoughts and feelings. Reactions to material covered during class range from those of an "aha" or "light bulb turning on" sort to those expressing relief that class discussions clarified some point which previously had eluded them. The following sample illustrates reactions to class discussions:

> It hadn't really occurred to me, but your assertion that *doctors* were major beneficiaries of Medicare was pretty well on the mark. I don't think it's any small coincidence that medical costs skyrocketed since 1965 in part because of federal outlays.

Dialogue

Students frequently use their journals as an alternative medium for communicating with the instructor, a link which often bridges the social distance between student and faculty. In either case, however, they allow students the opportunity to tell their instructor what's on their minds:

> I enjoyed Tuesday's class, but I think I'm still suffering nervous trauma from the "prisoner's dilemma" you gave us. I guess most of us displayed rational behavior in thinking mostly from our perspective (and self-interests), but your mathematical model of the alternative perspective (the "us" situation) was enlightening.

How Do Students See Journals?

A number of students use the journal as a device to enable them to get organized and to actually do the work required in a class, a viewpoint reflected in the following entry:

> ...I have stayed interested more consistently, caught up all the time—it's unreal! It would worry me if I did this all the time. There is such a stabilizing effect w/a class like this. I am not accustomed to being organized. A super learning experience.

Many students see journal writing as an opportunity to develop their ideas and to sharpen their abilities to think critically. A non-major taking a senior level public policy course for graduate credit put it this way:

> In writing my own journal I can see a shifting and then a development of ideas. As you move through the journal, it appears that there is some vacillating on issues. However, this was rather my groping with a number of grey issues, and out of my groping I have clarified my position on several particular issues. Additionally, I feel competent to analyze other emerging political issues.

A senior political science major, who wrote that he came to a health care policy class with a great deal of skepticism about the required journal, concluded his evaluation of the journal with the following statement:

> The journal was excellent. It made me look outside the textbook for information concerning our class, and situations we deal with.

I learned a lot from the journal by reading the articles and then responding to them using the concepts discussed in class.

Not surprisingly, the freedom to select the extra entries required to fulfill the journal requirements in each course also contributes to the students' view of the journal as an aid to acquiring information beyond the confines of the class. In the words of a junior political science major:

The supplemental journal entries were fun because I got the chance to choose my topics. I took things which interest and concern me, wrote about them, and applied them to the new things I learned in class.

In addition to the benefits already discussed, students feel that journals help them in several other ways. First, some students believe that journals help them improve their writing skills, a belief which coincides nicely with one of the main purposes for using journals in the first place. The evaluation offered by a student in a public policy class directly makes the connection between the writing required for journals and improvement in his own writing:

All the writing that was required for the journal was extremely helpful for me...Always before when I had to write something I would agonize for as long as I could before I sat down to the drudgery of writing. But when I *had* to write every day, I had to resign myself to the fact that my thoughts had to go down in paper and ink whether I liked it or not. I'm not saying my writing was excellent or even close to it but I was able to get my point across in a generally acceptable way from day to day...I know the experience has made me a better, more relaxed writer.

Second, other students see journals contributing to the quality of class discussions either by requiring students to keep up with the assigned readings or by providing the stimulus for questions or comments in class. As one student put it:

Its biggest benefit was as a base for class discussion. It allowed me to keep topics discovered the night before fresh in my mind.

Third, students use journals as an aid in studying for upcoming examinations, generally in the form of possible essay and objective questions accompanied by answers. As one student who used this approach observed after taking a test:

Friday's test was much as expected. I was well prepared for the questions that were asked, and found the multiple guess questions particularly easy.

Fourth, because journals represent an alternative way in which students can communicate with their instructor, students lacking the confidence to speak up in class view them as an alternative way to show the instructor what they know. One such student articulated her perception of this benefit in the following words:

For me, the journal is excellent. I do not relate well when I have to speak in class, so the journal is a place I can write what I think without having to open up publicly.

And finally, journals offer students a permanent record of their experiences. In the words of one student:

Much to my surprise, I have learned from past journals that they have a continuing value. I've looked back at collections of the last few years and, even though I didn't write about how I felt, these things were revealed anyway. A particularly good entry says much about my mental state on the day in question, just as a terrible one suggests too little sleep or too much of something else.

How Do Journals Help the Instructor?

To this point I hope I have made clear my belief that journals can and do help students in many ways. However, I don't believe that journals benefit only students. To the contrary, my experiences suggest that the use of journals in political science classes also provides a number of advantages to the instructor. For one thing, the decision to use journals places instructors in a position where they must explicitly confront the objectives they hope to achieve and the content they want their students to master. Journals can also furnish instructors with timely and regular feedback on their performance in class. Finally, the strategic use of journals can help the instructor because journals build student commitment and enthusiasm, as the following journal entry attests:

I have such a good feeling about this class that for the *first* time the grade is secondary because I know what *I* got out of the class, feel I certainly got my money's worth.

Since I began requiring journals in my political science courses, I have read well over five hundred journals written by freshmen and seniors, by majors and non-majors, by committed students and by students who couldn't care less about political science. My experiences have taught me several lessons: First, for journals to really work as tools to strengthen student writing or student learning, they require a significant commitment from the instructor who chooses to use them. Second, in the absense of this commitment, both the instructor and his or her students will find journals a painful and time-consuming exercise in futility. Third, if the instructor makes the necessary commitment at the front end, he or she will find that journals make a substantial contribution to the educational process, especially to one's own sense of efficacy and to students' sense of accomplishment. And finally, journals can work in any political science class, regardless of the subject matter, as long as the instructor makes the necessary commitment of time and energy.

Having said this, I will continue to use journals in many, but not all of my classes. As a general rule, I have decided not to use them in any of my introductory classes simply because the large number of students involved makes it extremely difficult for me to devote the necessary time without neglecting my own research and public service interests or my students. However, in other classes, especially senior level seminars and almost any class taught during our shortened (five to seven weeks) summer sessions, I cannot imagine doing without journals and their positive contributions to my teaching.

41.

Journals in Economic Geography

BRADLEY H. BALTENSPERGER

In my sophomore-level economic geography course I have always emphasized the numerous theories and models of economic behavior in a spatial context, typically including applications to the "real world." I stressed concepts to be understood, rather than facts to be memorized. Even so, students seemed to focus on facts instead of concepts and on the apparently technical nature of the course instead of the applicability of various models to an understanding of human activity. My standard lecture-exam teaching method seemed to carry a message about the course material and the discipline that was not what I wished to convey.

Many students preferred to act as passive receptors of information, on the assumption that enlightenment flows from a font of knowledge into waiting vessels. Attempts to stimulate discussion of course material or even to solicit ideas or hypotheses from the class were stifled by the blank stares of those who couldn't imagine that anything a student says could possibly be as valuable as pronouncements issued from behind a lectern. Each question has one answer, they believed, and each problem has a solution. The lecture presentation followed by exam regurgitation strengthened that belief, even in a class of twenty students where discussion was encouraged.

I have two major objectives in this course. I want to expose students to the geographic perspective—to teach them to observe locational patterns and to ask questions about those patterns. I also want them to grasp the basic locational theories in order to answer their own questions about geographic patterns. To accomplish these ends, I introduced journals.

In order to prevent students from ascribing too much importance to factual knowledge at the expense of comprehension of concepts, I decided to give no examinations and to base grades on journals alone, with performance determined principally by frequency of entries, volume of writing, and apparent effort and thought expended. Journals were supplemented by assignments and an evaluation of class participation. I announced that grades would be either A, B, or F, on the assumption that any student who became involved in the course and in writing a journal would learn enough to justify at least a B. An F was reserved for those who might seek to earn credit by taking unfair advantage of a pedagogical experiment without participating fully and without gaining any of the geographical insights which I believed would accrue from this process.

The ten-week term included lecture, class discussion, and small group projects. Journal entries included topics assigned for in-class and out-of-class writing, summaries of lectures and text material, student-generated reflections, and short entries designed to stimulate class discussion.

Discussing

This latter form was especially rewarding. Too often, I think, the lack of response to questions in class is due to either student hesitancy to commit errors in front of peers, an unwillingness to spend a short time in reflection for fear of being called on in the middle of that speculation, or the assumption that someone will answer the question and thereby take everyone else off the hook.

In this class a question was initially answered in journals rather than orally. After an appropriate length of time, ranging from one to ten minutes, depending on the topic, I asked the question again, drawing oral responses from journal entries. The answers frequently led to vigorous discussions that, under my traditional approach, were rare, indeed. Students had the time to think, could devise answers confidently, and were able to defer to their more extroverted colleagues.

One such assignment was to compare the maps of wheat and tomato distribution found in the text and to explain what factors were most responsible for the differences observed. This assignment, given in the second week of the course, introduced students to map analysis and geographical ways of asking questions. In spite of the urban background of most of the students, they first described the different patterns and then proceeded to seek explanations. Paul wrote, "It...appears tomatoes are produced in urbanised areas such as California and Michigan. Wheat appears to be produced out on the plains...where there are a lot less cities." He then sought an explanation in terms of transportation and distance, "Tomatoes, which perish quickly, should be very near to markets where they can be sold or processed quickly." Another student speculated, "There is...the possibility that the price of land will have an effect on whether or not wheat will be produced. This can be noted by considering North Dakota where land is cheap and the production of wheat is high." These conjectures about locational forces, specifically distance, commodity characteristics, and land value, set the stage for my presentation of several models of the location of agricultural activities.

Later in the term a similar assignment was given regarding the factors involved in the location of manufacturing enterprises. Simply introducing industrial location theory without student speculation would have been confusing at best and counterproductive at worst. The journal entry I assigned was to consider what factors influenced the location of farm machinery manufacturing, a topic with which none of the students was familiar. The responses focused on the role of the market as a locational force, and on the importance of labor cost, skills, and availability in secondary economic activities. Several entries stressed the need for "access to a fairly good transportation system." Again, many of the essential components of an economic geographic model were identified in journal entries and subsequent class discussion before being formally introduced.

Standing Back

Near the end of the course, the class played a game simulating land use. During the game the action is intense, with competing teams purchasing land, locating industries, stores, and residences, negotiating loans, and approving community expenditures. Students must become familiar with numerous data tables relating to transportation costs, payroll, income, expenses and taxes. Typically, they become so involved in the activity and the details of accounting that the lessons of the game fade into the background. Journals provided the opportunity to stand back and analyze the spatial processes occurring in the game.

Some students used their entries to plan game strategy. Others analyzed their problems and compared them to the successes of other teams. Many began to see the role of tax rates in stimulating economic development, the advantages and disadvantages of community debt, and the importance of technological changes in transportation as they relate to spatial patterns of economic activities in urban areas. Most significantly, students saw how the models they had been considering all term were replicated in "their" community by their own actions. The abstractions they had been examining now acquired some grounding in reality.

Students evaluated the course quite favorably. They especially appreciated the greater opportunity to pursue their own interests, greater flexibility in studying by not cramming for exams, and the informal nature of the course. Several liked the way journals were used to stimulate discussion: "It's an involvement class. The whole class has to take an active role." Others noted that their interest in the course was enhanced by the journal. Said one, "In our journals we were able to raise questions and try to reason why things occurred as they did, but in class we were able to openly discuss topics and state our viewpoint. I think this was really valuable because, at least for me, it stimulated interest in the class."

None of this should suggest that all students found the journal system easy. Dave wrote, "Sometimes I will just get a blank and can't think of anything [to write], but usually another idea will come to me. If I hadn't been writing them down, they would probably have been lost for good." Another observed, "It's important that you write your journal within one or two days of the class" if the journal is to have value.

Only one student indicated a preference for exams, rather than journals, even though the amount of effort required was almost certainly greater under this system. The absence of exams helped most of the students enjoy the course. In response to the question, "What did you like best about this class?" on the course evaluation form, one student wrote, "No tests! Took the pressure off of memorizing certain things and made it easier to open up on views." But did they learn as much as if they had been tested regularly? In his review of the course, Bruce wrote, "To me, the journal was more useful than any test I could have taken. I have been able to review class sessions, text material and material related to the class in depth and I can honestly say that the material I have learned will stick with me a lot longer than had I crammed for the test(s) the night before."

Charles noted, "I have found that I am really putting some serious thought into the subject matter. When I sit down to write I will thoroughly consider everything that was discussed in class and then go on to other thoughts that are stimulated by our discussions." A third student responded on the class evaluation, "Journals helped me to learn in a new way, by forcing me to look hard and deep at a situation and also by encouraging looking [beyond] material covered in class."

I made a crude attempt to analyze whether students had actually learned as much in this experimental system as they had under the lecture-exam method. I extracted a number of questions from exams given in previous years and presented them to this class. In spite of my having changed texts, presented material differently, made no attempt to correlate exam questions perfectly with the course material, and given no advance notice of this mock exam, these students seemed to perform as well on both factual and conceptual items as students who had been evaluated solely on the basis of exams.

In terms of my objectives for the course—exposure to the geographic perspective and asking and answering locational questions—I have no doubt that students who participated in this experiment benefited tremendously. They seemed better able to focus on the concepts presented. By actively articulating their understandings on paper, often several times, and then presenting their insights to the class, their comprehension was considerably more sophisticated than under the lecture-exam method, and they were more likely to retain that understanding well beyond the end of the term.

This journal-discussion method resulted in students who were more likely to have read the text and produced substantial improvement in the quality of class discussion. Instead of trying to induce the class to provide answers or ideas, I found myself standing back and listening to student contributions and occasionally trying to get discussion back to the subject at hand. As the term progressed, the amount of self-generated writing increased. Most students found they could go into greater detail on a given subject and pursue implications which were especially interesting to them.

From my own standpoint, the journal method had considerable appeal. Students were enthusiastic about their learning experience. According to Jeff, "This class is fun." And Bruce summarized the feelings of many when he wrote, "It was one of the most...enjoyable, educational classes I had here." Because of these and similar responses, I repeated the process in the spring of 1985 with equally rewarding results and will continue to organize this course in a similar fashion.

42.

There's a Place for a Log in the Office

KAREN M. HICKMAN

The expression "hit the deck running" seemed best to describe my return to the office last August after a three-week institute in London, a five-week summer institute in the office, and two weeks visiting out West with the in-laws and outlaws. I was settling in after vacation, and it meant dealing with a rapid office pace and my reflecting on how best to manage an office where its Director, Don Gallehr, continually takes on new work while monitoring older programs and tasks as well. "Hit the deck running" was an understatement. It translated to "survival means you need a new game plan!" The busiest year yet was beginning at the Northern Virginia Writing Project, George Mason University.

The Project had grown since my accepting the job of administrative secretary in August of 1982. It had grown from offering four in-service education courses to eleven a semester, from 117 Teacher/Consultants to 200, from a few activities to over a dozen full-fledged programs: programs concerned with research, evaluation, publications, parents, business and professional writing, to name but a few. Growth reflected the constant communications between Directors, Associate and Assistant Directors, the Teacher/Consultants and the public. Phone messages doubled and tripled; the messages on those little pink slips during an average month could paper the office walls.

I started the Office Journal Log as an experiment that hot August afternoon by writing:

8/20

...This is our office log—designed to maintain the continuity NVWP needs—designed to enable all of us to work together and keep the office pace moving—designed to save your sanity too! Log: important calls, actions, and questions.

This is an experiment; the purpose is to help everyone, but don't feel you are a slave to the looseleaf—get the job done!

I was determined to maintain communication and continuity. My two assistants worked less than half-time each and their hours rarely overlapped. I needed their help to complete ongoing tasks. The office log offered me the unique opportunity to reach both Stacy and Sherri with the same messages, requests, instructions, and information while simultaneously gaining daily feedback about what shape various assignments were taking. For example:

8/24

We will need 20 packets made up by 9/8 too. So between 695 courses and Progoff next week will be busy for everyone. Use institute key for packets.

Monday a.m.: mailing to all t/cs. Please leave one set of envelopes for all t/cs ready to go on my desk.

For Friday also: I want a mailing station created in the conference room on the supply shelf #1 with envelopes labeled & ready to go for NWP, NVWP, newsletter, Progoff, etc. Thanks.

The mimeo machine has been fixed. Packets for 695 courses—next priority.

More importantly, the Office Log was an experiment that worked. The three of us are journal writers, either keeping personal journals at home or classroom logs for our college courses. The goal was to establish effective communication which in turn kept the work flowing among the three of us. Yet, as a place to put thoughts about our daily activities, the log grew into so much more.

9/17

Today, I did the following:

1. "Created" an "original" of the NVWP (yellow) flyer. It's at quick copy being xeroxed (330 copies). File Original in the VWP file. Thanks. (This was later comment on the log entry of 9/17 written by Karen in a different color ink.) Probably will be ready this afternoon. (also other things there too)
2. Proofread the t/c mailing list—there are about 4 or 5 corrections. THANKS.
3. Called Helene to invite her to my school tomorrow. She'll be in at noon to work for us then we'll both be going to class together. Just the good old days of high school.
4. Called Kevin. He misses me, but—too bad bucko! School first! Good for you, Stacy!
5. Don's a promoter, Karen's a controller, and I'm a supporter. Sounds accurate to me.

Sherri, what are you? Can we ever cross quadrants? Maybe we should take the professional identity test again next year. Worked on t/c mailing list; I am to publish come Monday—no one is allowed to move or change their name until then!

Confirmed t/c meeting for Sat. In 2602 Robinson for continuity program.

Sent out 14 teacher/theorist letters for Don; they'll just love finding out their theory paper is due in December.

Set up British Institute mailing to close out funds, (solicit papers).

Sent notices to Eileen Rice/Mike Hoover re: parent program.

Sent Dietz, Anderson, Greer notice to submit grades by Dec. 18; copy memo from Continuing Education.

Sent Humberston maps to forward to presenters.

Typed mail for Don to Murray/Medway re: presenting in the spring.

Ordered copies for 696—also known as break the xerox budget—but it all balances out someday—received invitation from Anne MC. To come to lunch. I told her when I can see the wood on my desktop, I'd be over—maybe Christmas.

Gotta run and pick up the band members, etc.

or

Thoughts ending when Tuesday ended:
  695 instructors to be hired.
  Continuity calendar from Culley.
  Mailing list updated with school changes.
  Presentation description forms/file in master book.
  695 handout material for initial class ready.

That particular "hit the deck running" day in August gave rise to a variety of requests and activities that were to be handled between the multiple interruptions. The log became a sanity saver. Interruptions may have been legitimate needs for others, yet not the best time for my taking action. I thus logged calls and important transactions, including travel arrangements, fare quotes, messages from deans and Teacher/Consultant requests. My "deal with soon" list found a home in the log. Nestled among the looseleaf pages were ideas as well; its format grew from the blank pages.

Yet deciding what to log has to no hard and fast rules. It's a value judgment on the part of each one of us. Often, we consider what others might ask about specific events. We anticipate needs, but by not being held to rules and regulations for creating the log's scope, style, or format, the three of us have developed a valuable ongoing dialogue.

  There are over 118 sites to the National Writing Project. Please check your NWP xerox labels over and find out why the stack is so short. If you do it, you'll learn about them. If I do it, it will keep you ignorant. Thanks.

The log itself is a binder filled with looseleaf dated daily and sometimes starred [*] to alert co-workers to re-read if further action is needed. Sometimes using different pen colors serves to highlight noteworthy specifics. Sometimes inserting different colored sheets of paper helps focus on certain events. Yet the log is more than a collection of one-time notations to be inadvertently scanned in another year. For notations receive responses from each of us as well as marginal commentary which may reflect humor, advice, questions that occur while working or acknowledgements, and thank you's! It is the human side to the log that underscores its importance for all of us.

12/10

Exams, semester project, studying, agony—is there a cave nearby where I can hibernate until next week is over?

Ah! To contemplate truth and beauty, once again—I got an extension on a paper once based on that excuse. It didn't help—the paper still needed doing afterwards.

Should people call to say they are coming to Airlie Conference or Christmas party: check the list (green sheets). Thanks.

Stacy—remember when Don had you go through all the English/ Education 695 course files to verify courses—and six days later you came up for air—where is the verified list? Does it still need to be typed?

Sent out letters to Werner, Mohr and Glaze per Don's request.

Filed 2½ lbs. of stuff! It has to be measured in pounds these days.

Consequently, the log is a professional work with personal notes. It gives direction while noting accomplishments. Through the log, we all gain perspective. The following notations help illustrate this point:

2/12

Once again, I am freaking out—I have so much to do outside of work and I'm constantly calculating how to get it all done. Any suggestions? Anyway, I put the envelopes that have labels on them in zip code order and only managed to get a few more labels on envelopes. I left a message for Sue K. to call us about Bernie's message. Also, Dotty F. called and said that she got a letter from the finance office stating she owes the $300. Karen, can you please call them and find out what the problem is? Dotty would like you to call her at school and leave a message for her. I'll be in at 2:30 tomorrow.

My margin responses to Sherri's notations included:

Pace yourself—no freaking out—make lists! I took care of Dotty's problem and left a message at her school. If Sue K. calls, ask her what day is best in the spring to have a 695 class at her school.

As log entries indicate, our dialogues are ongoing.

I picked up where Sherri left off on the address list and finished it— double checking the labels that were left over. Karen has the labels that do not correspond with an address on the list and she'll check them out with Chris. At this point, the addresses with the dashes need to be typed. I'm off to class (actually, I'll be hiding in the conference room, doing homework—don't tell Don).

- mailed off info. to Mark Gulesian.
- Stacy, a thousand thanks for finishing the address list! *You're welcome!*
- started typing labels and cutting them on envelopes—marked the place to begin tomorrow,
- One aside comment: Karen, I made myself a list this weekend and I'm getting schoolwork done. I definitely feel better!

You can be an inspiration for me—once I come to grips with there's no getting ahead then I can deal with the schoolwork. Pace yourself—I used to say and try to do—now it's "don't trip while running in place"—we no longer have irons in the fire, now we're jugglers with balls in the air!

Go network list—go! Thanks for a job well done! That mailing is always a monster!

While it helps keep tabs on activities in progress, the log also enables us to focus attention on what has happened during the day by listing not only what we accomplished, but also what thoughts occurred during this time as well. Uniquely, this is by no means idle thinking, but the type of thinking that benefits the Project. We discover in our dialogue better ways to accomplish tasks. We also pick up on the need for preparation for future tasks with deadlines suitably noted as we write about what we are thinking. The office log becomes an action-oriented calendar where preliminary planning can be routinely managed. Thoughts shared about coping with various events help contribute to a better and more efficient system. It seems that when more people brainstorm on a problem, a variety of creative solutions emerge. Since we tackle ideas in an ongoing dialogue, everyone seems to benefit.

Because my assistants participate in job-sharing, leaving instructions is made easier by a log. A noteworthy example is during times when the log enables me to leave messages for callers as well as notations as to what calls to expect.

1/4

If Thaiss, Arbogast, McKay or Duffey calls, ask them if they are interested in teaching a 695 course in the spring; starts week of Jan.21/lv. msg. with Don.

If Nancy Hoagland calls, tell her the C.U. meeting on the 10th of Jan. starts at 3 pm.

The next insert page has a list of t/cs who may call in to say yes or no to giving their presentations. Letter is FYI; just take a message of yes or no and give to Don.

As the notations indicate, I am able to state what answers to relay to callers without going into detail. Most times, callers will completely understand the message that Stacy or Sherri relays, yet a lengthy background explanation didn't have to be given to either assistant. The log conveys important tasks to co-workers and focuses on the priority of the day. We all know where tasks stand and what has to be done.

The log is a visual feast, for we all have a tendency to respond to logged material both honestly and freely. The mental graffiti put to paper adds humor to our day, heightens interest in our work, and awakens in all of us a real sense of what the human side of the office is. It was nearly three months before Stacy and Sherri met other than in their log encounters. Reading marginal notes reveals frustrations, common sense advice, humor, and responses appreciated by all. For example:

9/27

Thanks for packet work (NVWP) copies, Stacy. Next project is the zip code order for Matrix of the t/cs, friends, liaisons, distant cousins, bargain hunters and curious citizens, etc. that seem to be collecting for bulk mailings!

1/4

- sent off Airlie III schedule to Dave, Peg, and Marian.
- sent off letter to Bernie & 695 Coordinators.
- I'm up to April 1984 on newsletter project—I'll probably finish

tomorrow. What will be the next step? Typing it out in alphabetical order by name?

- Stacy, I was touched that you felt you had learned something about me from the journal (hope it was good stuff!)

Sherri, yes, it's all good. We don't work together (at the same time) as I am sure you have noticed (!) by now, so I'm glad I have some type of mechanism in which to learn about you....

Responding to co-workers personalized a job that could be otherwise deemed humdrum. The log becomes the human side in what could be labeled a collection of mindless tasks, for stapling articles and sorting envelopes into zip code order may actually lead to commentary of significant value that would have remained as mindless as the lackluster task. Reading notes within the log, like the writing, clarifies thinking. Beginning anywhere leads to growth, and whether it be in knowledge or spirit, it can be significant.

The log was the tonic I needed during the rapid pace last August. I went from a steno pad of cryptic notes that only I might be able to decipher to a journal log that communicated ideas and facts. As ideas occurred, they found a place to be kept to be considered later. Like planting seeds, some ideas germinated. Initiating new procedures sometimes came from seeing the direction we were taking through the log. Perhaps some notations may be of historical import to NVWP, but more significantly, the log is a lifeline for all of us within the office. It keeps us all in touch. It nurtures us.

I know there's a group of readers saying, "Lady, if you had my job, you wouldn't have time to write about it!" I know because I do have a job like yours, and I would have said the same thing last summer. But I know too that having the opportunity to communicate to others through the log is an invaluable management tool for me. The efforts of an administrative secretary are said to reflect clarity, responsiveness, accuracy and persistence—the log mirrors those skills.

Moreover, the log serves to build group rapport. It demonstrates how humanizing the office leads to efficiency. For me, the routine goes more smoothly when I feel I have some control in a situation. The log fosters this sense of control. For control aptly describes my nature in dealing with the myriad of background details for everything from workshops to institutes to dinner parties to travel plans to you name it. Control is fostered through those moments I put my thinking on paper. I share my noted actions and the responses of others. In those moments, writing can be significant. I always have an easily accessible answer in the log that I am continually creating. My brain is no longer on information overload and unable to fix priorities. I have control in that writing in the log sustains our thinking. What began as the skeleton of data and information placed in one location has led to a unique book of knowledge—a flesh and bones, mind and body of personalized, shared information offering insight for all. While journals and logs are promoting writing and learning in school, they represent a highly useful management tool for professionals as well.

Contributing Authors

Henry L. Allen is an assistant Professor of Sociology at Bethel College, St. Paul, Minnesota. He received his bachelors degree from Wheaton College in Illinois and his Masters from the University of Chicago. Currently, he is a Ph.D. Candidate at the University of Chicago. Allen's research interests include the American academic profession and the sociology of science.

Jane Ambrose has been teaching music at the University of Vermont for twenty years. As well, she performs widely on both baroque and modern flutes. Her current research is on music by women. A graduate of Skidmore College, she earned an M.A. at UVM and has done additional graduate work at Harvard and Michigan.

Nancie Atwell, formerly an eighth grade teacher at Boothbay [Maine] Elementary School, is currently director of Writing to Learn, a project of the Bread Loaf School of English. She is also a consultant to Bread Loaf and to schools throughout the U.S. and Canada. She is co-editor with Tom Newkirk of *Understanding Writing* and is author of *In the Middle*, as well as many articles and book chapters about writing and reading.

Bradley H. Baltensperger is Associate Professor of Geography at Michigan Technological University. He received his Ph.D. from Clark University in 1974. He is the author of a number of articles on the geography of the Great Plains and recently published *Nebraska: A Geography.*

Pat Belanoff is Associate Director of the Writing Program at the State University of New York, Stony Brook. Previous to that she was Assistant Director of The Expository Writing Program at New York University. She is co-author (with Betsy Rorschach and Mia Rakijas) of *The Right Handbook* and is currently working with Peter Elbow on a textbook, *A Community of Writers*. In addition she has given papers and published articles on the evaluation of writing and the image of women in Old English poetry.

Stephen G. BeMiller received an A.B. in Humanities and B.S. in Mathematics from Michigan State before moving to the University of California, Davis, where he received an M.A. in Applied Mathematics and a Ph.D. in Mathematics. He teaches courses in mathematics, business, history, and humanities at California State University, Chico.

Ann E. Berthoff is Professor of English at the University of Massachusetts, Boston. She is the author of *Forming/Thinking/Writing: The*

Composing Imagination, The Making of Meaning: Metaphors, Models, and Maxims for Writing Teachers, and *Reclaiming the Imagination,* a collection of essays by philosophers, artists, scientists and others which offers philosophical perspectives for writers and teachers of writing.

David Brodsky has been a faculty member at the University of Tennessee at Chattanooga since 1971. He served as Head of the Political Science Department from 1976 to 1981. Prior to completing graduate school he worked in a number of private organizations and public agencies. These experiences and subsequent ones in the classroom convinced him that the ability to write contributes to learning and to success in professional work.

Christopher C. Burnham has been the Director of Freshman Writing, Co-Director of the New Mexico State Writing Project at New Mexico State University since 1981. He teaches courses in writing, linguistics, rhetorical theory, and literature. He has published articles in *Research in Composition and Rhetoric: A Bibliographic Sourcebook,* the *Journal of Basic Writing,* and the *Journal of Advanced Composition.*

Jennifer Clarke is a doctoral candidate at the State University of New York at Stony Brook, where she teaches composition and literature. Work on her dissertation takes up much of the rest of her time.

Pat D'Arcy is the English Adviser for the county of Wiltshire (UK) and the co-director of the Wiltshire "Write to Learn" project. She has been chairperson of NATE and worked for two Schools Council Projects: *Reading for Meaning* and *Writing Across the Curriculum 11-16.*

Virgil Davala teaches English at Thomas Jefferson High School for Science and Technology, Fairfax County, Virginia. She formerly taught intermediate students at Longfellow and Frost, also in Fairfax County, and is a Teacher Consultant with the Northern Virginia Writing Project.

James S. Davis is a Language Arts Consultant for the Grant Wood Area Education Agency, Cedar Rapids, Iowa, where he also directs the Iowa Writing Project. Formerly a junior/senior high school English teacher in Missouri, he is active in the National Council of Teachers of English, especially the Conference on English Education.

Mary Jane Dickerson has been teaching writing and literature courses at the University of Vermont since 1966. She has led workshops for university and high school faculty on teaching writing in all disciplines. With historian Henry Steffens she has published *Writer's Guide: History,* which emphasizes ways of writing to learn history.

Peter Elbow directs the Writing Program at SUNY, Stony Brook. He has taught at M.I.T., Franconia College, and Evergreen State College. He is author of *Oppositions in Chaucer, Writing Without Teachers, Writing with Power,* and *Embracing Contraries in Learning and Teaching.* His essay "The Shifting Relationship Between Speech and Writing" won the Braddock Award as the best 1985 article in *CCC.* He is on the Executive Council and Delegate Assembly of the Modern Language Association.

Lynn Fauth is Professor of English at Bethel College in St. Paul, Minnesota. He received his Ph.D. from Indiana University. Research interests include writing across the curriculum, general education, and faculty development programs. Fauth directed Bethel College's Writing to Learn/Writing Across the Curriculum Faculty Development Program.

Laura Fulwiler is an English teacher turned college counselor turned middle school counselor. With a B.A. in English and Masters in Counseling from the University of Wisconsin, she is presently a doctoral student in Education at the University of Vermont.

Megan Fulwiler is currently a junior at Essex Junction High School in Vermont. She's busy dancing, laughing and looking at colleges. Right now, she's into U2, The Smiths and The English Beat (but not physics or trigonometry).

Toby Fulwiler directs the writing program at the University of Vermont, where he also teaches classes in composition and American literature. His recent publications include *Teaching with Writing* and *Writing Across the Disciplines: Theory into Practice.* (He is not, as Don Murray charges, the head of a dynasty of writers, but he is pleased that those close to him write well.)

Leon Gatlin received his Ph.D. from the University of Iowa and is now Associate Professor of English and Co-Director of the Writing Project at UNCC. Teaching interests include Victorian literature, writing, and classroom research. He has published articles on Hardy's poetry and teaching writing.

Jean Graybeal has taught in the Department of Religious Studies at California State University, Chico since 1985. Before moving to California, she taught at LeMoyne College in Syracuse, NY. She earned a Ph.D. in religion at Syracuse University.

Judy Grumbacher teaches physics at Falls Church High School in Fairfax County, Virginia. She is teacher/consultant with the Northern Virginia Writing Project, a Physics Teacher Resource Agent for the American Association of Physics Teachers, and a fellow of the Woodrow Wilson Summer Institute on High School Physics.

Fred Hallberg is an Associate Professor of Philosophy and Humanities at the University of Northern Iowa. He came to UNI in 1967 after receiving his B.A., M.A., and Ph.D. in Philosophy at the University of Minnesota. In addition, he completed an M.S. in counseling psychology in Gestalt psychotherapy with the staff of the PMC Institute of Oak Brook, IL.

Karen Hickman has been the Administrative Assistant for the Northern Virginia Writing Project since 1982. Prior to that she taught and worked in various educational programs in the Monterey, CA area. She is currently completing a Masters Degree in Library Science from Catholic University of America.

Verner Jensen is Professor of Physics at the University of Northern Iowa, where he has been teaching for 30 years. His undergraduate degree is from the University of Nebraska, his graduate degree from Iowa State University. He has interests in solid state physics, acoustics, physics demonstrations, and general education.

Otis Terry Kent teaches Philosophy at Indiana Central University. He received his Ph.D. at the University of Iowa. He has been a visiting philosopher at Michigan Tech, Rose-Hulman Institute of Technology, and Indiana University, Indianapolis.

Catherine Larsen has taught music methods and supervised field experience programs for DePaul University and Loyola University, and served as Education Director for the Old Town School of Folk Music in Chicago. She received an M.A. in Education from Seattle Pacific University, and is currently Supervising Teacher of Music at Price Laboratory School, University of Northern Iowa.

Gary Lindberg was Professor of English at the University of New Hampshire, where he directed the Freshman Writing Program from 1981 until his death in February 1986. Before coming to UNH he taught at the University of Virginia and Rhode Island College. Professor Lindberg was the author of two books: *Edith Wharton and the Novel of Manners* and *The Confidence Man in American Literature.*

Sharyn Lowenstein is Director of the Alternative Freshman Year at the University of New Hampshire at Manchester. Previously she taught at the University of Massachusetts, College of Public and Community Service. She is an Associate of the Language and Thinking Institute at Bard College. Her dissertation is on the relationship between the journal keeper and the journal.

Patricia McGonegal began her career in New Jersey and now teaches fifth grade in Richmond, VT. She has taught for several of the last 21 years, taking a large portion of time out to mother her four sons. Her other interests include running, drawing, tennis, and time by the ocean.

Eileen Meagher, Professor of English at the University of Tennessee at Chattanooga, has been Director of Composition and Director of Writing Across the Curriculum there since 1980. She inaugurated a writing-across-the-curriculum program with a substantial grant from NEH. She has conducted writing seminars for faculty at a number of universities, colleges, and high schools.

Peter Medway has been a Senior Research Fellow at the University of Leeds since 1985. He has taught in high schools in various parts of England and has lectured widely on education on both sides of the Atlantic. He is author of *Finding a Language* and numerous articles, and co-author with Mike Torbe of *The Climate for Learning.*

George Meese teaches technical communication, literature, applied ethics, and rhetoric at Michigan Technological University, where he conducts research in visual media and rhetorical analysis of scientific and engineering discourse. Since receiving his Ph.D. from the University of Chicago, he has taught at Chicago State and the University of Virginia. He has published articles in *Business and Professional Ethics, Kentucky English Bulletin,* and *Technical Communication.*

Margaret Merrion is the associate dean in the College of Fine Arts at Ball State University. Prior to that she taught in the Department of Education at the University of Northern Iowa.

Bernadette Mulholland teaches history at Lake Braddock Secondary School in Burke, Virginia. She is active as a workshop leader, writer, and consultant for the Northern Virginia Writing Project.

Ruth G. Nathan is Adjunct Assistant Professor of Psychology and Co-Director of The Reading Research Team, Oakland University, Rochester, MI. She is also director of The Elementary Process-Writing Project for two school districts: Birmingham Public Schools, Birmingham, MI, and Walled Lake Consolidated Schools, Walled Lake, MI. Ruth earned her Ph.D. at Oakland University, Reading Department. She is co-author of *The Beginnings of Writing.* Her research interests are writing and reading acquisition. (Claudia Rose, whose journal Ruth shares with us, is now a third grader at Burton Elementary School in Berkley, MI.)

Stephen North is an assistant professor of English at SUNY Albany, where he also directs the Writing Center. For more of his work on journal writing see "Journal Writing Across the Curriculum: A Reconsideration" in *Freshman English News,* Fall 1985; and on the case studies described here, see "Writing and Learning Philosophy: Three Case Studies" in *Research in the Teaching of English,* May 1986. Steve is also author of *The Making of Knowledge in Composition.*

Bill Reif is an elementary teacher in Cedar Rapids Community School District, Cedar Rapids, IA. Now in his thirteenth year of teaching, all with 5th and 6th grade students, he is a graduate of Winona State College in Minnesota.

Karen Wiley Sandler is Assistant Dean of the College at Gettysburg College. After receiving her Ph.D. in Romance Languages (University of Pennsylvania, 1972), she taught all levels of French language and literature at The University of Vermont until 1985. She has written *Tour de Grammaire: A Study Guide for French Grammar* (with Susan Whitebook) and articles on Renaissance French literature and teaching techniques.

Barbara Schubert has taught fourth grade at Cody Elementary School, LeClaire, IA, since 1970. She participated in the 1980 State of Iowa Writing Project and now serves as an instructor. She received an NCTE Research Grant in 1984 to study the development of clarity in children's writing. She is a Ph.D. candidate at The University of Iowa.

Henry Steffens has been a faculty member of the University of Vermont since 1969. He received his M.A. and Ph.D. degrees from Cornell University. His teaching interests include the history of science, European cultural history, and the philsophy of history. He has published *Science, Technology and Culture* with H.N. Muller, *The Development of Newtonian Optics in England, James Prescott Joule and the Concept of Energy,* and *The History of Science in Western Civilization* with L.P. Williams. He recently completed *The Writer's Guide: History* with M.J. Dickerson.

Jana Staton is currently conducting research on the use of dialogue journals in counseling and family communication with Fairfax County Schools. She is editor of *Dialogue,* published by the Center for Applied Linguistics, Washington, DC, and trains experienced teachers in oral and written language development through George Mason University.

Peter Stillman combines three careers: he has been an English teacher at every level from seventh grade through college; has been an editor and editorial director for educational publishers; and is a published writer of poetry, articles, juvenile and adult trade books, and texts, the most recent, *Writing Your Way.* Stillman is affiliated with Boynton/Cook Publishers.

Geoffrey Summerfield's recent books include *Welcome,* selected poems; *Fantasy and Reason,* a prelude to Wordsworth's *Prelude;* and, with Judith Summerfield, *Frames of Mind* and *Texts and Contexts.* He is currently writing a book on the semiotics of deviancy in literature, and teaching at New York University.

Judith Fishman Summerfield currently teaches at Queens College, CUNY, and is assistant chair for composition in the Department of English. Her publications include *The Random House Guide to Writing* (with Sandra Schor); *Responding to Prose* and, with Geoffrey Summerfield, *Frames of Mind* and *Texts and Contexts.* She is currently at work on a text: *Reversals: From Exposition to Narrative.*

Richard Sweterlitsch is an assistant professor of English and director of English Graduate Studies at the University of Vermont. He received his doctorate in 1976 from the Folklore Institute, Indiana University. He has published articles and reviews regarding folklore in *Proverbium, Journal of American Folklore,* and various regional journals.

Phyllis Tashlik has taught at all levels of the academic terrain, from junior and senior high to college. She has been published in numerous professional journals and has written columns on education for *Newsday,* a Long Island newspaper. Currently, she teaches at Manhattan East, a public alternative junior high school in New York City.

Christopher J. Thaiss is Director of the Plan for Alternative General Education at George Mason University. Active in the development of school and college writing-across-the-curriculum programs since 1978, he also coordinates a national network of these programs. Since 1978 he has been associate director of the Northern Virginia Writing Project. Thaiss's publications include *Speaking and Writing: Classroom Strategies and the New Research* (co-edited with Charles Suhor), *Writing to Learn: Essays and Reflection on Writing Across the Curriculum,* and *Language Across the Curriculum in the Elementary Grades.*